Published by Manchester University Press
Altrincham Street, Manchester M1 7JA

www.manchesteruniversitypress.co.uk

British Library Cataloguing-in-Publication Data
A catalogue record for this book is available from the British Library

ISBN 978 1 5261 5275 6 hardback

First published 2021

Typeset
by New Best-set Typesetters Ltd

Armed non-state actors and the politics of recognition

Edited by Anna Geis, Maéva Clément and Hanna Pfeifer

MANCHESTER UNIVERSITY PRESS

New Approaches to Conflict Analysis

Series editors: Peter Lawler (School of Social Sciences, University of Manchester – United Kingdom) and Emmanuel-Pierre Guittet (Centre for Conflict, Liberty and Security, CCLS, Paris - France)

Until recently, the study of conflict and conflict resolution remained comparatively immune to broad developments in social and political theory. When the changing nature and locus of large-scale conflict in the post-Cold War era is also taken into account, the case for a reconsideration of the fundamentals of conflict analysis and conflict resolution becomes all the more stark.

New Approaches to Conflict Analysis promotes the development of new theoretical insights and their application to concrete cases of large-scale conflict, broadly defined. The series intends not to ignore established approaches to conflict analysis and conflict resolution, but to contribute to the reconstruction of the field through a dialogue between orthodoxy and its contemporary critics. Equally, the series reflects the contemporary porosity of intellectual borderlines rather than simply perpetuating rigid boundaries around the study of conflict and peace. *New Approaches to Conflict Analysis* seeks to uphold the normative commitment of the field's founders yet also recognises that the moral impulse to research is properly part of its subject matter. To these ends, the series is comprised of the highest quality work of scholars drawn from throughout the international academic community, and from a wide range of disciplines within the social sciences.

PUBLISHED

Christine Agius
Neutrality, sovereignty and identity: the social construction of Swedish neutrality

Tim Aistrope
Conspiracy theory and American foreign policy: American foreign policy and the politics of legitimacy

Eşref Aksu
The United Nations, intra-state peacekeeping and normative change

Michelle Bentley
Syria and the chemical weapons taboo: Exploiting the forbidden

M. Anne Brown
Human rights and the borders of suffering: the promotion of human rights in international politics

Anthony Burke and Matt McDonald (eds)
Critical security in the Asia-Pacific

Ilan Danjoux
Political cartoons and the Israeli-Palestinian conflict

Lorraine Elliott and Graeme Cheeseman (eds)
Forces for good: cosmopolitan militaries in the twenty-first century

Clara Eroukhmanoff
The securitisation of Islam: Covert racism and affect in the United States post-9/11

Greg Fry and Tarcisius Kabutaulaka (eds)
Intervention and state-building in the Pacific: the legitimacy of 'cooperative intervention'

Naomi Head
Justifying violence: communicative ethics and the use of force in Kosovo

Charlotte Heath-Kelly
Death and security: memory and mortality at the bombsite

Richard Jackson
Writing the war on terrorism: language, politics and counter-terrorism

Tami Amanda Jacoby and Brent Sasley (eds)
Redefining security in the Middle East

Matt Killingsworth, Matthew Sussex and Jan Pakulski (eds)
Violence and the state

Jan Koehler and Christoph Zürcher (eds)
Potentials of disorder

Matthias Leese and Stef Wittendorp (eds)
Security/Mobility: politics and movement

David Bruce MacDonald
Balkan holocausts? Serbian and Croatian victim-centred propaganda and the war in Yugoslavia

Adrian Millar
Socio-ideological fantasy and the Northern Ireland conflict: the other side

Jennifer Milliken
The social construction of the Korean War

Ami Pedahzur
The Israeli response to Jewish extremism and violence: defending democracy

Johanna Söderström
Living politics after war: Ex-combatants and veterans coming home

Maria Stern
Naming insecurity – constructing identity: 'Mayan-women' in Guatemala on the eve of 'peace'

Virginia Tilley
The one state solution: a breakthrough for peace in the Israeli–Palestinian deadlock

Armed non-state actors and the politics of recognition

Manchester University Press

Contents

Figures

Tables

Contributors

Dr Jan Boesten is Fritz-Thyssen-Stiftung Research Fellow at the CONPEACE Programme of the Changing Character of War Centre, Department of Politics and International Relations, Nuffield College, University of Oxford. He is also Postdoctoral Fellow at the Institute of Latin American Studies at the Freie Universität Berlin. His work has appeared in *Latin American Research Review* and *Colombia Internacional*.

Dr Chien-peng Chung is Professor of Politics in the Department of Political Science at Lingnan University, Hong Kong. He received his PhD in political science from the University of Southern California and also holds a master's degree in economics from the University of Toronto.

Dr Maéva Clément is a senior lecturer in International Relations and Peace and Conflict Studies at the Institute of Social Sciences, University of Osnabrück. She received her PhD in political science from Goethe University Frankfurt. Her research interests include international politics, interdisciplinary emotion research, (armed) non-state actors in world politics, and political violence and terrorism research.

Dr Véronique Dudouet is Senior Advisor at the Berghof Foundation in Berlin, where she coordinates collaborative research on resistance and liberation movements, civil resistance, negotiations and mediation in asymmetric conflicts, and inclusive post-war governance. She also gives policy advice and capacity-building support to conflict and peacebuilding actors. She has published three books and numerous articles on conflict transformation and non-violent resistance, and holds a PhD in conflict resolution from the University of Bradford.

Dr Anna Geis is Professor of International Security and Conflict Studies at Helmut Schmidt University/University of the Federal Armed Forces Hamburg. In 2018 and 2019, she was a visiting researcher at the Vrije Universiteit Amsterdam and the Centre for International and Defence Policy at Queen's University in Kingston, Ontario. Her research interests include theories of peace and war, security governance, conflict transformation, transitional justice and international political theory (democracy, legitimacy, recognition).

Dr Carolin Görzig leads the independent research group 'How "Terrorists" Learn' at the Max Planck Institute for Social Anthropology in Halle (Saale). She and her team have conducted field research in Palestine, Turkey, Kyrgyzstan, Niger, Egypt, Spain, Great Britain and Northern Ireland with the aim of generating insights on learning processes of terrorist groups.

Dr Christoph Günther is the Principal Investigator of the junior research group 'Jihadism on the Internet: Images and Videos, their Dissemination and Appropriation' in the Department of Anthropology and African Studies at the University of Mainz. Christoph's research interests include religio-political movements in the modern Middle East, visual cultures and iconography, and the sociology of religion.

Dr Stephan Hensell is Senior Researcher at the Research Centre for International Relations, European Politics and Political Theory at the University of Bremen and a visiting researcher at the Institut d'Études Européennes, Université libre de Bruxelles. He holds a PhD from Humboldt University Berlin and has held positions as a researcher and lecturer at the Institute for Peace Research and Security Policy and at the Institute of Political Science at the University of Hamburg.

Dr Annette Idler is Director of Studies of the Changing Character of War Centre, Pembroke College; and Senior Research Fellow at the Department of Politics and International Relations, University of Oxford. She is also Visiting Scholar at Harvard University's Weatherhead Center for International Affairs. Her work has appeared as a monograph with Oxford University Press and in journals such as *World Politics* and *Journal of Global Security Studies*.

Dr Tom Kaden is a sociologist of religion working in the Department of Cultural Sciences at the University of Bayreuth. Previously, he worked as a research associate at York University (Toronto) in the 'Science and Religion: Exploring the Spectrum' project. His research interests include fundamentalism, the relationship between science and religion, and creationism.

Dr Michael Nwankpa is Founding Director/Director of Research at the Centre for African Conflict and Development. He holds a PhD in sociology from the University of Roehampton, London. His main research area is the nexus between conflict and development, including the concept of a human rights-based approach to development, as well as counterinsurgency and counterterrorism.

Dr Hanna Pfeifer is Professor of Political Science, with a Special Focus on Radicalisation and Violence Research, at the Peace Research Institute Frankfurt (PRIF) and Goethe University Frankfurt. She is also the head of the terrorism research group at PRIF. Her research focuses on the Middle East and North Africa, in particular Islamist and jihadist actors, state and non-state violence, and global and regional politics of order.

Dr Jamie Pring is a visiting post-doctoral researcher at the Center for Transnational Relations, Foreign and Security Policy at the Otto Suhr Institute for Political Science at Freie Universität Berlin. Supported by the Swiss National Science Foundation, she is conducting a comparative study of regional conflict prevention institutions in the Global South. Her PhD at the University of Basel examines the promotion of inclusivity in the mediation process led by the Intergovernmental Authority on Development in South Sudan from 2013 to 2015.

Dr Klaus Schlichte is Professor of International Relations and Politics in the World Society at the Research Centre for International Relations, European Politics and Political Theory at the University of Bremen. His main research fields are the sociology of war and states, and the historical sociology of international relations. He has conducted field research in Mali, Senegal, Uganda, France and Serbia.

Dr Mitja Sienknecht is a post-doctoral researcher at the University of Münster and a guest researcher at the Berlin Social Science Center. She received her PhD from the European University Viadrina, where she also had a position as a post-doctoral fellow at the Center B/ORDERS IN MOTION. Her research fields include Peace and Conflict Studies, world society theory, and global responsibility relations between global and regional institutions.

Arrliya Sugal is an MA candidate in Peace and Conflict Studies in a joint award degree with the University of Kent and Philipps University Marburg. Her research focuses on interdisciplinary approaches to conflict analysis and peacebuilding processes in the Horn of Africa region. It specifically emphasises the role of diaspora involvement in conflict resolution processes. She has a background in political science, sustainability sciences and global migration studies.

Dr Harmonie Toros is a reader in International Conflict Analysis at the University of Kent. She investigates conflict resolution and transformation approaches to terrorism and advises governments and intergovernmental organisations on the potential for negotiations with non-state armed groups. She has increasingly adopted an autoethnographic approach to research as she focuses on the experience of researching war and political violence.

Dr Harold Trinkunas is a senior research scholar and Deputy Director at the Center for International Security and Cooperation at Stanford University. His recent research focuses on the role of armed non-state actors in local governance in territories where the state is weak or absent.

Acknowledgements

As theorists of recognition have argued so convincingly, experiencing recognition is a vital human need. It is a great delight for us as editors of a volume on recognition practices to acknowledge the fantastic support and collaboration of many people and institutions that rendered the conception and production of this book such a pleasure.

The motivation to produce a volume on the (non-)recognition of armed non-state actors (ANSAs) was inspired by the observation that recognition-related studies have been growing in International Relations since the early 2000s but that they predominantly deal with inter-state relations. An edited volume focusing systematically on ANSAs and the role of mis-recognition of such actors in violent conflicts has been missing in this burgeoning field at the intersection of International Political Theory, International Relations, and Peace and Conflict Studies.

The volume draws on an international workshop which was held at Helmut Schmidt University/University of the Federal Armed Forces in Hamburg, Germany in June 2018. We are especially grateful to the German Foundation for Peace Research for funding the event, and to Lennard Eccarius, Jennifer Franke, Susanne Latzel and Jonas Nawrath for supporting us in preparing and implementing the workshop.

The fantastic discussions with the participants – experts on armed non-state actors and/or peace processes and conflict transformation in specific regions of the world – motivated us to create this volume. For all contributors, it was an innovative endeavour to apply a recognition perspective to their case studies and empirical data, and discuss the merits of this concept. We wish to thank all the participants for their continuous commitment throughout this project and the great collaborative spirit that made this book possible. Special thanks goes to Véronique Dudouet who held a public key note speech in Hamburg, providing us with many thought-provoking insights on the highly political and changing nature of the 'labelling' of ANSAs. We are also very grateful to Harold Trinkunas, who accepted our invitation to write a concluding chapter which, despite a tight deadline, provides a very insightful reflection on the book, its merits and future trajectories for research. We also thank Christopher Daase whose role as a critical discussant and observer during the workshop allowed us to detect broader patterns across our case studies. Finally, we received very constructive comments and encouragement from the reviewers – thanks to them, the book has grown further!

We are very grateful to the editorial staff at Manchester University Press, especially Jonathan de Peyer and Robert Byron, for their excellent support.

Finally, we thank our student research assistants Friederike Uhl, Pascal du Hamél, Lena Wiggers and Nils Worbes for helping us in the final – and thus most critical – production phase of the volume.

Anna Geis, Hamburg
Maéva Clément, Osnabrück
Hanna Pfeifer, Frankfurt am Main

Abbreviations

AMISOM	African Union Mission in Somalia
ANC	African National Congress
ANSA	armed non-state actor
AQ	al-Qaeda
ARCSS	Agreement on the Resolution of the Conflict in South Sudan
aS	al-Shabaab
AU	African Union
AUC	Autodefensas Unidas de Colombia (United Self-Defence Forces of Colombia)
BACRIM	Bandas Criminales (Criminal Bands)
CONVIVIR	Servicios Especiales de Vigilancia y Seguridad Privada (Special Vigilance and Private Security Services)
CPA	Comprehensive Peace Agreement
CPC	Communist Party of China
CPP	Communist Party of the Philippines
CVE	countering violent extremism
DDR	demobilisation, disarmament and reintegration
DRC	Democratic Republic of the Congo
ELN	Ejército de Liberación Nacional (National Liberation Army)
EPLF	Eritrean People's Liberation Front
ETA	Euskadi Ta Askatasuna (Basque Country and Freedom)
ETIM	East Turkestan Islamic Movement
ETLO	East Turkestan Liberation Organisation
FARC	Fuerzas Armadas Revolucionarias de Colombia (Revolutionary Armed Forces of Colombia)
FGS	Federal Government of Somalia
FLN	Front de Libération Nationale (National Liberation Front)

FRELIMO	Frente de Libertação de Moçambique (Mozambique Liberation Front)
FRETILIN	Frente Revolucionária de Timor-Leste Independente (Revolutionary Front for an Independent East Timor)
GoS	Government of Sudan
GRSS	Government of the Republic of South Sudan
ICRC	International Committee of the Red Cross
IDF	Israeli Defence Forces
IGAD	Intergovernmental Authority on Development
IHL	international humanitarian law
IO	international organisation
IPOB	Indigenous People of Biafra
IR	International Relations
IRA	Irish Republican Army
IRGC	Islamic Revolutionary Guard Corps
IS	Islamic State
ISI	Islamic State in Iraq
ISIL	Islamic State in Iraq and the Levant
ISIS	Islamic State of Iraq and Syria
ISWAP	Islamic State in West African Province
KCD-E	Kongreya Civakên Demokratîk a Kurdîstanîyên Ewrupa (European Kurdish Democratic Societies Congress)
KLA	Kosovo Liberation Army
KNK	Kongreya Neteweyî ya Kurdistanê (Kurdistan National Congress)
LTTE	Liberation Tigers of Tamil Eelam
MENA	Middle East and North Africa
MEND	Movement for the Emancipation of Niger Delta
MOSOP	Movement for the Survival of the Ogoni People
MPLA	Movimento Popular de Libertação de Angola (People's Movement for the Liberation of Angola)
NGO	non-governmental organisation
NPFL	National Patriotic Front of Liberia
NSAG	non-state armed group
OAG	Other Armed Group
OAU	Organisation of African Unity
PACE	Parliamentary Assembly of the Council of Europe
PAIGC	Partido Africano para a Independência da Guiné e Cabo Verde (African Party for the Independence of Guinea and Cape Verde)
PIRA	Provisional Irish Republican Army
PKK	Partiya Karkerên Kurdistanê (Kurdistan Workers' Party)

PLO	Palestine Liberation Organisation
PRC	People's Republic of China
PYD	Partiya Yekîtiya Demokrat (Democratic Union Party)
RENAMO	Resistência Nacional Moçambicana (Mozambican National Resistance)
QF	Quds Force
RAF	Red Army Faction
SPLA	Sudan People's Liberation Army
SPLM	Sudan People's Liberation Movement
SPLM-IO	Sudan People's Liberation Movement-in-Opposition
SSDF	South Sudan Defence Forces
STL	Special Tribunal for Lebanon
SWAPO	South West African People's Organisation
UNIFIL	United Nations Interim Force in Lebanon
UNITA	União Nacional para a Independência Total de Angola (National Union for the Total Independence of Angola)
UNSC	United Nations Security Council
UNSG	United Nations Secretary-General
VEO	violent extremist organisation
YPG	Yekîneyên Parastina Gel (People's Protection Units)
ZAPU	Zimbabwe African People's Union

I

Recognition of armed non-state actors: concepts, theory, history

1

Recognising armed non-state actors: risks and opportunities for conflict transformation

Maéva Clément, Anna Geis and Hanna Pfeifer

Introduction

Internal wars are the prevalent contemporary type of violent conflict (Sarkees and Wayman 2010). Many violent conflicts involve armed non-state actors (ANSAs) such as insurgents, rebels, guerrillas, warlords, militias, paramilitaries and private security companies. In addition, the so-called 'global war on terrorism' indicates that transnational terrorist networks are considered to be one of the major security threats today. Whatever label is used for a certain armed actor by a government, official authorities are usually hesitant to enter into informal talks and negotiations with ANSAs, especially with those they have labelled 'terrorists' (Podder 2013: 16). However, in many violent conflicts, such (often secret) 'talks' are initiated at some point (Görzig 2010; Toros 2012). Some of the groups involved may have gained such relevance in the course of a protracted armed conflict that governments face increasing pressure to negotiate with them; some ANSAs may have suffered military losses and seek such talks out of weakness; and sometimes third parties intervene and exert pressure on both state and non-state conflict parties to start negotiations.

The recent – very fragile – peace agreement between the US and the Taliban, signed on 29 February 2020 in Doha, Qatar, is a striking example of how engagement with a violent actor can change over the years. The Taliban regime was overthrown in 2001 by the US-led military intervention after being blamed for providing a safe haven for al-Qaeda, which was accused of having committed the terrorist attacks of 11 September 2001. While many actors have rejected negotiations with the Taliban despite the protracted violent conflict in Afghanistan, a reconsideration has come about since 2018. Several attempts to initiate talks failed, for example after the opening of a Taliban office in Doha in 2013 (Bell 2014: 264). The start of the US–Taliban peace talks in 2018 – excluding the Afghan government from the negotiation table, as the Taliban refused to negotiate with what it regards as a 'puppet regime' – was a major step. While the negotiations were being conducted, the Taliban continued to use violence, mainly against Afghan forces and government officials, but also resulting in civilian casualties. As this book is being written, the controversial peace pact is being met by resistance from the Afghan government and has also failed to stop the Taliban's violence (Allen 2020).

Talking and negotiating usually imply gradual steps of recognising the counterpart. Engaging with ANSAs is thus considered risky by governments (Miller 2011; Toros 2012). In successful cases, armed non-state actors can be transformed into non-violent political parties and their legitimate goals can be incorporated into state policy. In unsuccessful cases, armed non-state actors might escalate their violent struggle, which often results in governments being perceived as weak. With regard to international humanitarian law and humanitarian issues in general, any kind of engagement with ANSAs is often difficult to avoid, leading to similar concerns of (in-)directly recognising or legitimating armed groups through engagement (Barbelet 2008; Herr 2015; Jo and Thomson 2014; MacLeod et al. 2016).

When dealing with armed non-state actors, the complex role of recognition merits far greater attention than it has received so far from researchers in the field of Peace and Conflict Studies. Only few researchers have dealt with the issue of the (non-)recognition of ANSAs and sought to analyse the kinds of consequences recognition has on conflict dynamics (Aggestam 2015; Bell 2014; Biene and Daase 2015; Herr 2015). This is surprising, given that 'recognition' is a crucial concept in Social Science and Philosophy which has recently gained more attention in the discipline of International Relations (IR) (Hayden and Schick 2016: 1–2). Experiencing recognition in private and public life is considered a vital human need (Taylor 1994: 26). Misrecognition, which individuals or collective actors experience as humiliation, disrespect or false representations of their identity, is seen as a major cause of political resistance and as a significant factor in the escalation of potentially violent conflicts.

Scholars have thus argued that recognition can have positive consequences on conflict dynamics in inter-state conflicts and in domestic conflicts, in which minority groups struggle for the recognition of their rights and identities.[1] The present volume seeks to address the research gap in the scholarship on armed non-state actors and to advance both recognition research and Peace and Conflict Studies by analysing which impacts – positive or negative – practices of (non-, mis-)recognition have on conflict dynamics in the short and long term. The application of analytical-conceptual tools from recognition research informs the theoretical frameworks of the case studies of the book, which cover (i) a broad range of ANSAs from different *regions*, as well as *transnationally* operating actors; and (ii) a broad range of *political objectives* for which ANSAs claim to fight, including ethno-political, politico-religious and 'revolutionary' ones. The introductory chapter first outlines different concepts of (mis-)recognition that have been developed in Political Theory and IR and discusses their merits and challenges for studying armed non-state actors. In the subsequent section, the focus is shifted to the armed non-state actors themselves, stressing different types and characteristics of ANSAs, and problematising the complex interplay of seeking and granting recognition in asymmetric violent conflicts, that is, conflicts in which actors of different status (state, non-state) are involved as conflict parties. The final section discusses the (ambivalent) short-term and long-term effects of recognition in processes of conflict transformation.

Recognition concepts in Political Theory and International Relations

'Recognition' is a prominent concept in several disciplines such as Social Philosophy, Psychology, Sociology and International Law, with the latter focusing on law-based acts of formal recognition of states. Political 'struggles for recognition' (Honneth 1995) have also received growing attention from empirical Political Science, as well as Peace and Conflict Studies.[2] The most intensive debates on social recognition started in social philosophy and Political Theory in the late 1980s and 1990s. The increase in different forms of 'identity politics' and struggles for recognition by minorities and social movements in liberal societies at that time stimulated attempts at theorising these phenomena (Fraser 2000; Fraser and Honneth 2003; Taylor 1994).

'Recognition' is a fuzzy term that is used quite differently by authors and speakers. Three interrelated usages can be distinguished (Ikäheimo and Laitinen 2011: 8–11). First, the term can be used as a synonym for '*identification*'; secondly, it is roughly synonymous with '*acknowledgement*'; this implies recognition having '*evaluative or normative entities or facts* as its objects, so that we can acknowledge something as valuable, as valid, as giving reasons, and so forth' (Ikäheimo and Laitinen 2011: 8). The third use of the term is most prominent in Hegel-inspired accounts of recognition and refers to interpersonal recognition, as exemplified by the works of Axel Honneth (Schmitz 2019). Recognition of a specific identity, of rights and/or of a certain status has been regarded as one of the goals of (new) social movements organised around class, gender, sexuality, ethnicity, religion or language. Drawing partly on Hegelian theoretical ideas (Markell 2003), and partly on empirical studies from evolutionary psychology, recognition theorists conceive of recognition by other individuals or by society as a vital human need. It is only when an individual is accepted as having certain qualities that (s)he will be able to develop self-esteem as well as an 'intact' personal identity (Taylor 1994: 26–37).

With regard to society, recognition operates as a mechanism that constitutes a normative status (of equals) and allots rights and duties within a society (Fraser 2000; Honneth 1995). The desire for recognition is not only inherent in individuals but also in social groups. For instance, as Alexander Wendt argued: 'What groups want is for Others to recognize them, not necessarily to recognize Others. Nor does it mean that groups are forever unchanging. Group identity is a process not a thing, and its transformation into larger collective identities is precisely what begins to happen through mutual recognition' (Wendt 2003: 516).

According to recognition theorists, acts of mis-recognition constitute acts of injustice in so far as they violate personal integrity and impede people from becoming full members of a social collective. Experiences of mis-recognition can provoke strong responses, including violent resistance, on the part of affected individuals or social groups (Heins 2010: 150). Despite its relative importance, mis-recognition has attracted less conceptual debate than recognition (Martineau et al. 2012: 3). Axel Honneth identified 'the core of all experiences of injustice in the withdrawal of social recognition, in the phenomena of humiliation and disrespect' (Fraser and Honneth 2003: 134). Nancy Fraser developed an alternative approach to identity-based forms of mis-recognition by conceiving of recognition as a question of social status:

> Misrecognition, accordingly, does not mean the depreciation and deformation of group identity, but social subordination – in the sense of being prevented from participating as a peer in social life. To redress this injustice still requires a politics of recognition, but in the 'status model' this is no longer reduced to a question of identity: rather, it means a politics aimed at overcoming subordination by establishing the misrecognized party as a full member of society, capable of participating on a par with the rest. (Fraser 2000: 113)

With regard to the study of ANSAs in violent conflicts, Heins aptly points out that one should keep in mind a blind spot of Hegel-inspired accounts of recognition: disrespected and marginalised groups might not necessarily struggle for inclusion into the community from which they were excluded.

He stresses: 'They might as well struggle for inclusion into an altogether different community *yet to be created*' (Heins 2016: 79).

In contrast to conceiving of recognition as a single act (Agné 2013: 100–102) or as a thing which one 'has' more or less of, we regard recognition as a process, as a social interaction 'that can go well or poorly in various ways' (Markell 2003: 18). Similarly, we think of struggles for recognition as an 'ongoing activity rather than as a project with a fixed goal' (Markell 2003: 16; Tully 2000: 477). Recognition in real-world politics can thus be based on single formal or symbolic acts of recognition (such as being officially invited to peace negotiations or being awarded the Nobel Peace Prize) but it can also unfold as a gradual process and, as such, can also be 'stopped' or (gradually) 'reversed'. Recognition and non-recognition, that is, the deliberate withholding or denial of recognition, occur in complex and entangled forms. They constitute two poles on a continuum of policies and outcomes, ranging from highly formalised to very informal modes of recognition. This notion of gradual recognition implies that recognition is not only granted or withheld among actors of equal legal/social status, but also within asymmetric power relations (Daase et al. 2015; Wendt 2003: 511–514). With regard to ANSAs, one can distinguish between several types of act: formal acts (e.g. putting an actor on or removing it from 'terror lists', letting a group run in elections, etc.); symbolic acts (e.g. invitation to a negotiation, hand-shaking, etc.); discursive/speech acts (e.g. changing the discourse on an actor, changing conflict narratives); and material acts of recognition (e.g. redistribution of resources).

Since recognition is closely linked to the formation of individual or group identities, the concept has in particular attracted the attention of social constructivist scholarship (e.g. Ringmar 2002; Wendt 2003). One of the main questions in recognition-related IR studies is whether and how the mis-recognition of *states* promotes violent conflict and, vice versa, whether and how recognition fosters peaceful relations. To what extent such insights can also be applied to armed non-state actors is a question that has not been addressed in the scholarship so far. The authors of the present volume thus explore new ground in their case studies. It is a certain challenge to apply recognition concepts from Political Theory to ANSAs in violent conflicts: many armed groups seek to attain political goals and might be willing to refrain from using violence once they have reached these goals – which implies a change of their identity over time (Herr 2015: 92). Thus, in the long term, an armed non-state actor may transform into a political party, be part of the government or become a state-builder (Huang 2016: 91; Podder 2013; Schlichte 2009: 178–202). Hence, in contrast to the more stable collective identities of states, the group identity of an ANSA can change far more quickly, also due to changes in leadership, decreasing or increasing support of followers, or failures and successes in violent conflicts. They can re-group, re-name and develop new narratives and agendas. As several chapters in this volume show, identities are shaped and changed by the very (non-, mis-)recognition experiences with 'significant others' over time (see Dudouet; Görzig; Hensell and Schlichte; Pfeifer; Sienknecht in this volume).

It follows that more empirical research is required to analyse the types of political claim or identity trait for which a specific ANSA seeks recognition. It is a plausible assumption that ANSAs with political goals (especially those holding some territorial control) do seek recognition from significant others in order to enforce their agendas – since recognition can increase their legitimacy and help to mobilise material and symbolic support from local and regional actors or the transnational community, resulting in gains of status and reputation (Duyvesteyn 2017: 675; Herr 2015: 84, 95). As Thomas Lindemann (2012: 221) points out, 'the quest for recognition is often quite strategic and reputation is a resource in the struggle for power'. Some armed groups might also be willing to comply with specific norms of international humanitarian law in order to gain recognition, and the political and material benefits that come with it (Herr 2015: 235–240; Pfeifer in this volume). Insights like these underline that struggles for recognition are not only about identity questions – as social constructivist research in IR often seems to suggest – but also imply material gains and strategic rivalry considerations for social groups. In a similar vein to state-centred IR research on recognition, studies on ANSAs should not be limited to 'culturalist' interpretations only (Geis et al. 2015: 5–6).

Given that the application of social recognition concepts in conflict transformation studies is still a research gap, we suggest that concepts which allow for capturing gradual processes and 'shades' or gradations of recognition can be especially useful (Geis et al. 2015: 15–18). A well-known conceptual approach is the distinction between 'thin' and 'thick' forms of recognition, as briefly introduced by Wendt (2003: 511–512) and further developed by Lindemann (2010), Pierre Allan and Alexis Keller (2012) and Lisa Strömbom (2014). 'Thin' recognition between conflicting parties refers to recognition of each other 'as agents, as autonomous "entities" [that have] the right to exist and continu[e] to exist as an autonomous agent' (Allan and Keller 2012: 76). 'Thick' recognition requires much more than accepting the other as an autonomous agent and negotiating partner; it means that 'each party needs to understand the Other in terms of essential elements composing its identity' (Allan and Keller 2012: 77). The quest for a stable and just peace, it is argued, requires 'thick' recognition among the conflicting parties, including an understanding of *one's own identity*. It is evident that this is a demanding challenge for most parties involved in violent conflicts and requires the long-term transformation of narratives, rules and institutions by the actors involved (more in the final section).

Recognition of political actors often occurs in gradual steps and is not necessarily an intended result but an eventual outcome of negotiations. In order to grasp such different degrees of 'recognition *as*', Janusz Biene and Christopher Daase (2015: 223–225) suggest the identification of several 'recognition events'. They assume that armed non-state actors can seek recognition strategically. The gradual granting of recognition could influence their strategic options: the first step is 'thin' recognition as a party to the conflict. This is relevant since states often try to deny the existence of a conflict to delegitimise armed non-state actors. The next step is acceptance as a participant in *informal* talks, indicating their relevance in the present and the future for successful conflict management. The third step is the invitation to participate in *formal* talks. This move signals that the state government acknowledges the possibility that an ANSA might have legitimate claims to bring to the table (Biene and Daase, 2015: 224). A final degree of recognition is realised if a non-state actor is recognised as a political authority, as a legitimate representative of a collective with the capacity to enforce binding decisions.

Analysing the (non-/mis-)recognition of armed non-state actors and its impact on conflict transformation can also provide insights into related research fields, for instance into the 'politics of legitimacy' of armed groups (Duyvesteyn 2017; Schlichte and Schneckener 2015) or 'rebel governance/diplomacy' (Arjona et al. 2015; Huang 2016; Mampilly 2011). Such studies examine the agency, the diplomatic and 'lobbying' efforts, and strategic calculations of rebel groups vis-à-vis different domestic and external actors. The case studies of this book do not refer to the concept of 'rebel diplomacy', given that this volume probes a different conceptual perspective. However, the chapter on the Kurdish PKK (Sienknecht in this volume) clearly identifies such elements of 'officialisation' (Hensell and Schlichte in this volume) – for example the professionalisation and institutionalisation of political representation of the PKK in European countries, especially in Brussels and Strasbourg.

'Recognition' and empirical-analytical concepts of 'legitimacy' are very closely linked (Hensell and Schlichte in this volume; Herr 2015: 98–100), insofar as legitimacy depends on the social recognition of the legitimacy *claims* of actors:

> Political actors are constantly seeking legitimacy for themselves or their preferred institutions and in doing so they engage in practices of legitimation. Because

> legitimation is a normative process, it is characterized by actors seeking to justify their identities, interests, practices, or institutional designs. ... An actor making [such] a legitimacy claim does not mean, however, that she commands legitimacy – only when such claims are *recognized* as *rightful* within the political realm in which the actor seeks to act ... would this be the case. (Reus-Smit 2007: 159–160; emphasis added)

Some authors seem to conceive of recognition as a kind of precondition for achieving legitimacy: 'Armed opposition groups may want to achieve recognition as a viable political entity, which is a necessary step towards achieving legitimacy' (Jo and Thomson 2014: 326). A similar point was made in the context of states' recognition of states (Mastanduno et al. 1989: 464): for new states 'external validation involves first and foremost the quest for diplomatic recognition. Gaining the recognition of the international community appears to be an exceptionally powerful means for a nascent state to establish legitimacy in the eyes of its domestic population.'

However, in our view there is empirically no clear-cut causal relationship between legitimacy and recognition in the context of studying ANSAs. A specific armed non-state actor might gain legitimacy by being recognised by a state government – but it might also lose legitimacy in the eyes of some constituencies in society that perceive this government to be particularly corrupt. It is also conceivable that an actor is (normatively) legitimate and finds a high degree of acceptance (empirical legitimacy) among some people, but is not recognised by 'significant' interaction partners – that is, it is legitimate both normatively and empirically, but not recognised as and for what it seeks to be recognised. Conversely, significant others may grant recognition to an actor without him/her being legitimate – neither normatively nor empirically. To conclude this section: the extent to which an ANSA enjoys legitimacy and/or recognition is an empirical question, which is dependent on the respective legitimacy- and recognition-granting of 'others' and their 'significant' relationship to the ANSA.

The complex interplay between recognition-seekers and recognition-granters

Social actors always want to be recognised as and/or for something by other (groups of) actors. Aside from multiple practices of recognition, mis-recognition and non-recognition, diverse actors are involved in such dynamics. The chapters in this volume focus on armed non-state actors as recognition-seekers. As for the actors that grant recognition, the contributions to this volume show that there is a great variety of states, international and regional organisations, as well as non-state actors from which ANSAs may seek recognition. Moreover, several actors may become involved in recognition dynamics as a third party, both as promoters or spoilers of the process. What is often neglected in the recognition-related literature in International Relations, International Law, and Peace and Conflict Studies is the role of domestic populations as potential recognition-granters – not only in democratic governance contexts but also in areas of contested or fragile statehood. Recognition practices are often considered as some kind of '(semi-)official' interactions between organised actors, such as social groups, states and organisations. In our view, this is an unwarranted narrowing-down of recognition practices in politics. Armed groups in particular have also to rely on the support of parts of the population. Seeking recognition by local communities, by regional or nation-wide audiences is an important element of recognition-seeking behaviour of ANSAs. Gaining or losing recognition by 'ordinary citizens' can have a significant impact on the chances of survival, (domestic and international) legitimacy, reputation and transformation of an armed group. Several chapters in this volume indicate how important populations as 'significant others' are, for example in Colombia, Northern Ireland and Lebanon (Boesten and Idler; Görzig; Pfeifer in this volume).

Academic accounts of ANSAs and recognition dynamics

The umbrella term 'armed non-state actors' unites quite diverse types of actor. A basic distinction can be made between ANSAs that have a political agenda and those whose activities are motivated economically (Ezrow 2017: 85–86; Schneckener 2006: 30), even though this is not always a clear-cut opposition. This volume analyses ANSAs with a political agenda, since they can be expected to make more pronounced recognition claims. ANSAs can be defined as 'distinctive organizations that are (i) willing and capable to use violence for pursuing their objectives and (ii) not integrated into formalized state institutions …, [and that] (iii) possess a certain degree of autonomy with regard to politics, military operations, resources, and infrastructure' (Hofmann and Schneckener 2011: 604). It is sometimes difficult to distinguish between states and non-state actors, since ANSAs usually have a much more problematic relation with the state than other non-state actors, such as non-governmental organisations (NGOs) or companies (Barbelet 2008: 54–55). Many of them not only try to escape the state's control but also actively seek to overthrow it (Aydınlı 2016: 3–5). Yet, other ANSAs are – more or less deeply – intertwined with state structures. This is certainly true for those ANSAs that are both a violent actor and a political party (Pfeifer in this volume), as well as those which receive funding from their own or an external state. Moreover, ANSAs that are capable of gaining and maintaining territory, as well as exerting effective control over it, can establish structures similar to a state (Boesten and Idler; Kaden and Günther in this volume). Some ANSAs even coordinate their activities and engage in a form of 'complementary governance' (Idler and Forest 2015) among themselves and with the state. Thus, relations between ANSAs and states are multifaceted and often ambivalent. They impact a state's willingness to recognise ANSAs and for what it would grant recognition.

There are many academic efforts to develop typologies of politically motivated ANSAs. Their agendas may be socio-economic, nationalist or ethnic, religious or sectarian, or a combination of all of them (Zohar 2016). Other scholars distinguish groups according to their specific political goals, which range from setting up a state and providing state-like functions, to influencing global, regional or local policy, to transforming governance and obtaining political power and control, to challenging local or global value systems (Ezrow 2017: 85–117). Our case studies cover a broad spectrum of political motivations and goals which ANSAs can have. Actors striving for statehood, independence or secession should be expected to be denied recognition, given that they threaten the integrity of a given state, sometimes even the state system as such, for example in the case of ISIS (Kaden and Günther in this volume). But the chapters in this volume show that states do not always react to such movements in the same way, sometimes not even within one country: state reactions may range from the (partial) recognition of claims by one ANSA to harsh security measures against another (Nwankpa in this volume). Yet another strategy of how to deal with such ANSAs is to actively recognise them for something they do not themselves identify with and claims they do not bring forward. Such acts of mis-recognition are often accompanied by the non-recognition of the claims actually made by an ANSA, and sometimes by violent state practices (Chung; Nwankpa in this volume). Interestingly, if ANSAs are not successful in gaining recognition by states, they may turn to other actors instead, for example other states or international organisations, as was the case with the PKK seeking recognition from the EU (Sienknecht in this volume).

Besides goals and motives, most typologies distinguish between strategies and tactics employed by different groups (Ezrow 2017; Schneckener 2006; Zohar 2016). ANSAs may strive for change or the preservation of the status quo. Depending on their goals, they may or may not have territorial aspirations. To pursue their goals, ANSAs employ different methods of warfare, including conventional fighting, terrorism and guerrilla tactics. Moreover, ANSAs can be classified according to their internal organisation, and in particular with regard to the characteristics of a group's leadership and its (local) supporters, as well as the relationship between them (Staniland 2014). Some ANSAs have a strong leadership with hierarchical command structures and a high level of compliance and discipline by supporters on the ground (integrated groups). On the other side of the spectrum, ANSAs may be very fragmented, with both a weak leadership core and low levels of control over local adherents. Depending on how it is organised and what its respective goals are, an ANSA may limit itself to local activities or engage on a transnational level. Thus, ANSAs also differ with regard to their degree of transnationality (Zohar 2016). Indeed, the transnational ties of an ANSA may play an important role for recognition dynamics. For instance, in the cases of Hezbollah and al-Shabaab, one important strategy of the respective state and the international community is the claim that these actors are exogenous to Lebanese society and politics or, respectively, the conflict in Somalia (Pfeifer; Toros and Sugal in this volume). This specific version of mis-recognition may be met by a similar claim on the part of the respective ANSA vis-à-vis the state, as is the case with al-Shabaab and the Somali government. The reciprocal allegations of being 'foreign' or 'controlled from outside' equal a mutual denial of the other actor's legitimacy as part of the conflict – and of its solution (Toros and Sugal in this volume).

Finally, ANSAs vary with regard to the scope of representation they can claim and perform. Representation consists of two (sometimes conflicting) potentials: assuring 'regeneration' of the armed group and managing 'overstretch' (Aydınlı 2016: 11–15). An ANSA needs to be able to both keep old members and attract new ones. It can achieve this, first, through creating a compelling identity, in particular by defining the goals and scope of its agenda. Secondly, an ANSA needs to gain legitimacy among actual and potential members, that is, credibly demonstrate that it is capable of satisfying their needs and pursue common goals successfully. Thirdly, an ANSA needs to find ways of generating loyalty among its members. Besides common experiences and rituals, as well as everyday practices, ideology plays an important part here. On the other hand, ANSAs also need to make sure that their regeneration efforts do not lead to an overstretch of their agenda and/or organisation. For the larger a group gets, the harder it is to implement agendas and maintain control. Moreover, if an agenda becomes too encompassing, it becomes more difficult to achieve success.

The question of representation points to an important dimension of recognition processes: ANSAs usually seek recognition by several actors, and often for different identities and grievances. One addressee of recognition claims is the members and supporters of an ANSA, but also the broader community and local population in its areas of activity. This need for recognition becomes particularly pronounced in cases where an ANSA transitions towards a new role in a conflict and embraces a new identity – in such cases, it may lose parts of its supporters while gaining recognition from the state and other conflict parties (Görzig in this volume). It is at this point that other actors may become involved in recognition dynamics: competing ANSAs and other conflict parties. In this regard, recognition processes may sometimes have ambivalent effects for conflict transformation. An instructive case is the recognition process of the Colombian FARC, which went hand in hand with a disarmament and demobilisation process. The FARC had enjoyed some degree of acceptance in many rural areas of Colombia where it had the *de facto* monopoly of violence. The local population had recognised it as a political authority which set the rules. With the withdrawal of the FARC from these areas and the simultaneous failure of the Colombian state to fill this gap, the fear of new violence among the remaining armed conflict parties arises. Recognition alone – and in particular the recognition of *one* actor in a multi-party conflict by one actor, that is, the state – is not sufficient for successful conflict transformation (Boesten and Idler in this volume).

Conversely, however, the attempt to simultaneously grant recognition to several conflict parties in conflict transformation efforts, for example by including them in mediation processes, may be equally problematic. Inclusion into a peace process may be perceived as a form of mis-recognition if, for instance, another actor is included according to the same standards and thus grouped together with an actor who perceives him- or herself as radically different. Inclusion is thus essentially different from recognition because it may precisely misconstruct an actor's identity (Pring in this volume). Finally, some ANSAs do not seek recognition from states or international organisations at all – on the contrary, it may be part of their agenda to remain in the role of a villain and an outsider to the state system, as is for example the case for ISIS (Kaden and Günther; Dudouet in this volume).

ANSAs' recognition claims

These complex actor constellations demonstrate that recognition dynamics are always context-bound and sometimes ambiguous, and that they unfold at multiple levels. ANSAs may address their recognition claims to various actors. Generally speaking, such claims are demands for recognition addressed to a politically significant other; they are not fixed in time and may change in the process of (non-/mis-)recognition.[3] More specifically, these demands can take two forms. First, ANSAs may seek recognition *as a certain kind of actor*, or for a certain quality they claim to possess, such as being a politically autonomous actor (solely) representing a given community, mattering as a conflict party or having more legitimacy than other ANSAs. Secondly, ANSAs may seek recognition *for their own political grievances*, or those of the community they claim to represent. For instance, ANSAs may claim that a certain social or ethnic group is not sufficiently represented in the political process or suffers from economic marginalisation, that a religious community is discriminated against, that certain values are not respected adequately, and so on. Of course, such claims may not always mirror the grievances as perceived by the community for which an ANSA professes to speak. Moreover, if the addressed actors actually grant recognition for some grievances, this does not mean that they simultaneously recognise the respective ANSA. For instance, an ANSA may seek recognition as an ethnic minority in order to be granted certain rights, but the state may seek to cure these identity claims by socio-economic policies (Chung in this volume). It is, of course, possible that an ANSA's leadership or follower base misreads such a partial, grievance-related recognition as being recognised as an armed group as well. Given that 'recognition' is a very complex and often not formally validated social phenomenon, certain mismatches between what a recognition-granter is exactly recognising in the other, and what the recognition-seeker perceives on his/her part can be quite common.

Interestingly, some ANSAs explicitly emphasise whom they do not seek recognition from, for example 'the West', the international community (Dudouet; Kaden and Günther in this volume). This is usually the case when the agenda of an ANSA concerns the state system or global normative order as a whole. Yet, this does not mean that these ANSAs do not seek recognition at all: rather, they turn to other addressees, for example certain parts of the population, transnational communities, and so on. Sometimes, ANSAs are recognised for a quality or grievance for which they did not make any demands. In such cases, these acts are perceived as forms of mis-recognition (Chung; Pring in this volume). Finally, actors who are addressed by an ANSA's claim may choose not to grant the actor or its cause any recognition. Whenever there is some form of engagement with an ANSA that goes beyond fighting it, however, we hold that there is some degree of recognition involved. This leads to the question of what options and strategies are actually available for actors, and particularly states, in dealing with ANSAs.

In this context, the political use of certain concepts for ANSAs is even more important than the academic efforts to categorise them and develop typologies as sketched above (Barbelet 2008: 43–57). For a volume on recognition, it can even be counterproductive to start from a fixed typology for case selection: the political practice of *labelling* ANSAs is deeply intertwined with processes of (mis-/non-)recognition. Practices of naming and labelling are what constitutes ANSAs as an 'other' in the first place. Thus, it is precisely the framing of an ANSA which is contested, negotiated or imposed in recognition processes. For example, if a government or the European Union 'lists' an armed group as a 'terrorist organisation', this will have an impact not only on the identity of the ANSA but also on the possibility for negotiations or engagement with the group so labelled (Dudouet; Pfeifer; Sienknecht in this volume). At the same time, however, practices of *renaming* also enable recasting an ANSA's identity, thereby opening up a space for the recognition of these actors or their claims and, potentially, for conflict transformation.

The effects of recognition on the transformation of asymmetric conflicts

Researchers have discussed a variety of approaches on how to deal with ANSAs, addressing different levels of action (individual, group, societal and international) and considering strategies as disparate as repression and dialogue. Both democratic and autocratic states, however, often employ hard measures, such as counterinsurgency, counterterrorism or warfare (Cronin and Ludes 2004). Formal or informal talks are often perceived as detrimental (Steinhoff 2009: 301). Many states adhere to a no-negotiation policy (at least publicly) and sometimes prohibit engagement by law (Dudouet 2010; Pecastaing 2011: 171). Arguments against engagement include the unreliability of outcomes (Zartman and Faure 2011: 5), the possibility of failed attempts provoking further escalation of violence (Steinhoff 2009: 302), and the fear of losing political credibility (Pecastaing 2011: 188) or of raising non-state actors' legal and/or social status (Miller 2011). However, repressive measures often result in the radicalisation of non-state actors' agendas and/or the escalation of violent means. As such, the need to engage politically with ANSAs is increasingly acknowledged in research, with all the political, legal and ethical dilemmas that come with it.[4]

Acts and processes of recognition in asymmetric conflicts

At a basic level, acknowledging that there *is* a conflict is not enough; the state actor needs to recognise the opposing non-state actor as a party to the conflict (Biene and Daase 2015). Although recognition can be started by a single act (e.g. an official speech), it is understood as a process, which takes time and commitment to take root. As outlined above, there are different ways and forms to grant recognition, such as thin and thick acts of recognition. While thin acts are necessary to 'move conflict in a more peaceful direction' by opening minimal space for dialogue (Strömbom 2014: 171), they are not enough for transforming a conflict from antagonism to agonism. Conversely, thick acts of recognition are very difficult to attain and require much iteration in order to transform conflict relations over time.

The recognition of an ANSA as a legitimate conflict party constitutes a case of thin recognition. It is easier to reach thin acts of recognition than thick acts in asymmetric conflicts characterised by a particularly unequal distribution of political power, military resources and legal status. Crucial to this end is the conflict parties' recognition of their mutual interdependence, which might be possible in situations where neither conflict party has the capacity 'to force the other side to yield to their demands' and where their effective power is thus 'essentially equivalent' (Levinger 2013: 48). Thick acts of recognition are very demanding and usually embedded in long-term reconciliation processes in post-conflict societies. Strömbom (2014: 170) stresses that identity is at the core of acts of recognition aiming to 'transform destructive relations into ones that allow for differences and promote shared responsibility for injustices in the past'. Indeed, moving towards understanding, accepting and respecting the other's subjectivity and difference not only modifies the interaction between conflict parties, but also slowly changes each party's identity and, ultimately, each party's perception of the relationship. Such changes within the conflict structure usually take a long time.

Although the case studies in this volume do not study post-conflict reconciliation processes but analyse prior stages of violent conflicts, we briefly outline what thick acts of recognition might look like in a conflict transformative perspective. While this is no exhaustive catalogue, thick acts generally play a role in the following processes: the recognition of social dignity, the recognition of mutual responsibility for the past, and the recognition of the former opposing party as an inherent part of one's social tissue. A typical example for the first process – the recognition of the opposing party's social dignity (Poder 2019: 76) – would be the recognition of an indigenous people's rights in a multi-ethnic society. Especially in contexts where the humiliation of a social collective dug deep into fundamental rights – what Poder (2019) calls 'dignity humiliation' –, redressing former acts of mis-/non-recognition is very important (Haldemann 2008). For instance, it may require showing respect for the leaders of former enemy group(s) as symbolic carriers of the social dignity of a collective.

The second process – the recognition of a mutual responsibility for the past – is aimed at the co-existence of different macro- and micro-histories. It can consist in fostering truth inquiries, the emergence of inclusive histories, multi-voiced historical reappraisal, and so on, all processes which have been documented for instance in Northern Ireland (Dybris McQuaid 2019). According to Strömbom, a particularly fruitful way to do so is to weave thick recognition into narratives about past experiences of a conflict;

narratives of war would thereby be 'reversed' by 'narratives of recognition' (2014: 176–177). The third process – the recognition of the former enemy group (and, beyond that, community) as an inherent part of the larger social tissue – aims to move beyond mere co-existence. Increasingly shared by members of a society (not just elites), such a conviction over time generates forms of reconciliation and fosters regaining trust in community relationships.

Specific obstacles to the initiation and continuation of recognition processes

Beside the obstacles traditionally encountered in mediation efforts and peace processes, the politics of recognition-claiming and recognition-granting entails specific challenges. Broadly, these can be subsumed under two categories: (i) the transnational prevalence of a specific regime of recognition; and (ii) the differentiated perception of acts of recognition within a given conflict. Both potentially impact the initiation and/or the continuation of a given process of recognition.

Regarding (i), ANSAs' claims to recognition have a higher likelihood of being heard and considered as legitimate in specific international normative contexts. The 'global time' plays an important contextual role (Hensell and Schlichte in this volume). 'Recognition regimes' (Ringmar 2015) have changed since the end of the Second World War. An example of a favourable regime for recognition-claiming was the global time of decolonisation in the 1960s and 1970s: ANSAs were granted recognition comparatively more easily for their participation in liberation struggles. The current recognition regime, on the other hand, is characterised by the disqualification of ANSAs' political agendas based on the actions that they use. Under this regime, recognition claims are suppressed under the counterterrorism norm (see Dudouet in this volume). Not only is it harder for recent ANSAs to be cast as anything other than terrorist organisations, but older ANSAs are also reconsidered and mis-recognised under this norm (e.g. the FARC in Colombia after 9/11). The current 'recognition regime' thus contains higher normative barriers for recognition-claiming and, consequently, for recognition-granting than before. Further, this regime affects disproportionally those ANSAs who (claim to) represent Muslim communities (Clément 2014; Kaden and Günther; Nwankpa; Pfeifer in this volume). For example, ANSAs claiming to represent the Uyghurs have been negatively impacted by ISIS's repeated declarations in which the organisation stated that it had supporters as far as China (Chung in this volume). In short, since the early 2000s, the counterterrorism norm has enabled state actors to increasingly ignore and largely disqualify ANSAs' recognition claims.[5]

Practices of mis-recognition tend to have long-lasting impacts. Casting an ANSA as a terrorist organisation, for instance, confers a label that is particularly 'sticky', even when the ANSA is not listed as a 'terrorist organisation' or perceived as such by most states (Dudouet; Sienknecht in this volume). Sticky labelling impacts the way in which the majority population, as well as third parties, perceive an ANSA's struggle and its responsibility in the conflict. Further, it constrains the scope of future responses that the state will be willing to take. States that have cast an ANSA as a terrorist organisation tend to reject dialogue and favour repression over de-escalation (Toros 2008).

Regarding the second category, when a state starts engaging in acts of recognition, such acts might not be acknowledged as such, especially in the conflict situations mentioned above. Indeed, attempts at initiating a recognition process might not be perceived as acts of recognition by the recognition-seeking ANSA, or might be misperceived as ungenuine acts of recognition. Where non-perception or misperception bars the way to the parties' reciprocal recognition, mediators might be able to help conflict parties 'recognise recognition'. Arguably, this may be more difficult in intractable conflicts, which display a 'boiling emotional core ... replete with humiliation, frustration, rage, threat, and resentment between groups and deep feelings of pride, esteem, dignity, and identification within groups' (Coleman 2014: 720).

Yet, micro-sociological research shows that emotional phenomena such as trust, hope, loyalty and forgiveness are fostered in peacebuilding activities, which enable cooperative interaction among participants and empower them over the long run (Bramsen and Poder 2018). This opens possibilities for attributing more value to recognition efforts over time. In the short term, however, recognition efforts may destabilise the fragile social tissue further. In conflict-torn societies, in which parts of the population have become used to governance by armed groups, changes to the status quo can raise new fears among local communities (Boesten and Idler in this volume).

The impacts of recognition acts and processes

We argue that there is no clear-cut causal relationship between entering a process of recognition and transforming conflict dynamics. The politics of recognition between state and non-state actors may move the conflict towards non-violent resolution (conflict transformation), may result in almost unaltered interactions between the opposing parties (conflict continuation), or may backfire and make interactions deteriorate (conflict escalation). In the following, we discuss some of the more damaging unintended consequences of recognition acts and processes.

First, the costs of granting recognition to an ANSA may be too high in regard to human life, human rights and liberal values. For example, recognising al-Shabaab as a potential partner in negotiation with the Somali government and, eventually, a legitimate political actor may have dire long-term consequences for the Somali population, especially considering al-Shabaab's positions on human rights issues (Toros and Sugal in this volume). The recognition of an ANSA may also have very negative short-term impacts on the population. For instance, the recognition of the FARC in Colombia resulted in the worsening of the local population's well-being in areas formerly under FARC control, as these were suddenly exposed to other armed non-state actors profiting from the temporary power vacuum (Boesten and Idler in this volume). Similarly, in Nigeria the government's 'pay-outs' to former Niger Delta militants to maintain the peace under the amnesty contract is seen as largely disregarding the plight of the civilian victims (Nwankpa in this volume).

Secondly, the recognition of an ANSA may strongly affect other non-state actors which are occupying the same political space, especially competing ANSAs which do not gain (the same) recognition. The recognition of some conflict parties but not others may alleviate tensions in the short term (e.g. with the largest ANSA) but risk aggravating them in the long term (e.g. with smaller ANSAs). In the case of South Sudan, the SPLM – the larger opposition actor – was eventually invited to the negotiation table, while all other ANSAs which had opposed the regime were treated as one group with one voice. While such a practice was expedient, and a peace process was signed, mis-recognising the other ANSAs as one group negated their differences (and different needs), which ultimately led to a new armed conflict (Pring in this volume). Fuelled in part by the values the mediator held as key to a successful process, this transformation failure can be imputed to the unbalanced redistribution of recognition. Hence, the paradox is that by recognising *one* conflict party, others are (even more) excluded or reified. This bears potential for direct conflict escalation or a future relapse into armed conflict, in a slightly modified configuration of conflict parties.

In addition, the recognition of an ANSA indirectly impacts the non-state actors which use *non-violent* means. Such actors may disappear after the normalisation of a former ANSA. They may also be actively suppressed by state authorities that are unwilling to make more concessions in the future and prefer to pre-emptively crush any other form of contestation. The state repression of the IPOB movement in southeastern Nigeria, paralleling the recognition efforts towards Boko Haram, illustrates this (Nwankpa in this volume). In short, the costs of recognising an ANSA are often borne by non-state actors who do not resort to violence.

Thirdly, the recognition of an ANSA by various types of third party, while it is not (yet) recognised by the state actor to the conflict, can aggravate the conflict situation. In theory, the recognition of an ANSA's legitimacy (claims and representation) by another state, a community of states or a mediating party would provide it with some measure of protection and force the state party to peace talks. In practice, though, ANSAs' recognition by third parties is often used by the state actor to delegitimise the ANSA, casting it as a foreign element, an import from malevolent foreign powers or alien ideologies (Chung; Pfeifer; Toros and Sugal in this volume). The unintended consequences range from conflict continuation to conflict escalation.

Studying recognition in violent conflicts

In social science research, recognition is often seen as a means to de-escalate conflicts and promote peaceful behaviour. As we have argued so far, it would be illusory to expect recognition to act as a panacea for transforming armed conflicts. In certain contexts, recognition may backfire and produce counterproductive precedents and new modes of exclusion in intra-state and transnational politics. More empirical research is needed to analyse the complex and sometimes unexpected consequences of the (non-/mis-) recognition of ANSAs in violent conflicts. The present volume contributes to this research gap by including a diverse range of case studies discussing asymmetric conflict dynamics under the prism of recognition. Further, it features case studies from various world regions: some are 'classic' cases, others have rarely been dealt with in the extant literature. Table 1.1 presents the case studies along four key analytical categories. It captures succinctly the form of (mis-/non-)recognition studied, the main political agenda pursued by each ANSA (i.e. the recognition-seekers), their respective addressee(s) (i.e. the potential recognition-granter[s]) and the phase of conflict at stake in each chapter.

The case-study chapters illustrate various socio-political configurations in different conflict stages. They pinpoint the forms social recognition may take in asymmetric conflicts and discuss the short- and long-term risks and opportunities which arise when local, state and/or transnational actors recognise armed non-state actors, mis-recognise them or deny them recognition altogether.

In addition to the introductory and concluding chapter, the nine case studies are contextualised by two further chapters that address more encompassing aspects on a macro level of international 'labelling' trends and recognition regimes. The next chapter (Hensell and Schlichte) is devoted

Table 1.1 Case-study chapters by analytical category

No.	Chapter	Recognition concept(s) used	Recognition-seekers' political agenda	Addressees	Conflict phase analysed
3	Nigeria/Boko Haram; Niger delta; IPOB; Fulani militia **Nwankpa**	Mis-recognition, non-recognition	Heterogeneous; differ according to the four ANSAs (religious-political agenda; economic rights; greater political inclusion and autonomy)	Nigerian state	During the armed conflict
4	Somalia/al-Shabaab **Toros and Sugal**	Mis-recognition	Religious-political agenda	Somali population; other states	During the armed conflict
5	Syria and Iraq/IS **Kaden and Günther**	Recognition order	Religious-political agenda	Sunni *ummah*; Sunni tribes in Syria fighting Assad's regime	During the armed conflict
6	Turkey/PKK **Sienknecht**	Recognition, non-recognition; mis-recognition	Independence; later: cultural and political rights	States; international organisations	Various conflict phases; currently stalemate
7	China/Uyghurs **Chung**	Mis-recognition	Cultural rights; political autonomy and independence	Chinese state	Stalemate/repression by the state
8	Lebanon/Hezbollah **Pfeifer**	Mis-recognition	Recognition for its defence of Lebanese society and state; recognition as important transnational actor in the region	Lebanese publics; transnational Shiite community and regional actors; Western states	Stalemate/post-Lebanese civil war; Syrian war; 'war on terror'
9	Ireland/PIRA **Görzig**	Recognition	Religious-political agenda; independence	PIRA followers; other ANSAs	Entering peace negotiation
10	South Sudan/SPLM-IO **Pring**	Mis-recognition	Political inclusion	IGAD; mediating parties	Peace mediation process
11	Colombia/FARC **Boesten and Idler**	Recognition	Political inclusion in local institutions	Local civilian population	Peace process post-accord

Source: the authors.

to a historical overview of recognition regimes since the Second World War and their diverging impacts on the chances of success of ANSAs' recognition claims. The case studies are then structured in three parts corresponding to different conflict phases: Recognition during armed conflicts (part II), Recognition in conflict stalemates (part III), and Recognition in mediation and peace processes (part IV). The volume ends with a chapter discussing the consequences of labelling practices on conflict transformation, from the vantage point of practitioners' engagement with conflict parties, and a chapter offering concluding remarks on the politics of recognition of armed non-state actors.

We are completing this introductory chapter with some reflections on methodological issues. How can we recognise recognition? Studies in International Relations and International Law that deal with recognition practices rarely offer details on how they identify phenomena of (non-/mis-)recognition. In International Law, it is usually the study of formal acts, such as formal declarations between officials, sustaining diplomatic relations or the act of awarding membership to international organisations. The International Relations scholarship on recognition among states tends to focus on speech acts among officials and their emotional impact, such as anger at perceived humiliation or the display of empathy for the predicament of another state (e.g. Lindemann 2010: 87–133; Wolf 2011: 126–132). Drawing on methods developed in research on emotions would be a fruitful way to study the collective experiences of mis- and non-recognition (Clément and Sangar 2018).

To study (changing) identities, discursive approaches, including storytelling and narrative analysis, are a useful way of identifying recognition processes, as Erik Ringmar (2012: 6) has argued (see also Görzig in this volume):

> In the end, identities are created through an interplay of these two alternative perspectives. We start by telling stories about ourselves, which we go on to test on people around us. We let other people know who we believe we are, and they let us know whether or not our account is reasonable. In this way, our stories about ourselves are, or are not, recognized. Stories are told about states in much the same fashion. A community of storytellers could be referred to as a 'nation'.

Process-tracing can be a useful tool to analyse 'recognition events', that is, the gradual steps towards recognition (Biene and Daase 2015). Studying recognition practices related to ANSAs seems more difficult than studying state-centred recognition-seeking and -granting, given that armed groups partly act as clandestine organisations and have different ways of engaging and communicating with the outside, and that interactions between state officials and ANSAs often do not take place in public during violent conflicts.

In this regard, the authors of this volume draw on written (and audio-visual) material produced by ANSAs themselves, as well as fieldwork, using interviews with experts from different areas, including members of ANSAs and/or local communities.

Towards a more competitive recognition regime in global times of 'great power competition'?

As a number of chapters in this volume suggest, recognition practices are at least partly influenced by overarching regional or global norm contexts. The strong impact of the 'global war on terror' narrative, emerging after the terrorist attacks of '9/11', on the recognition and labelling practices of many ANSAs around the world since the early 2000s has been noted in many contributions. While some of the ANSAs have their roots in the Cold War period, others experienced their highest relevance during the heyday of the liberal international order in the 1990s and the first decade of the millennium. The extremely complex conflict constellations in the Syrian violent conflict(s) of the 2010s underline that the number of ANSAs can grow rapidly within a short period of time, and they can rename themselves and realign quickly, but also that great powers seek to instrumentalise certain ANSAs within the increasingly competitive global politics environment. As Harold Trinkunas argues in the final chapter to this volume, global recognition regimes might enter into yet another 'stage' by the global politics of great power competition among the US, China and Russia.

'Timing' is an important element of recognition practices also in another respect: it is far from clear when the right 'timing' for the recognition of an ANSA might be. Given that policy-makers can use recognition strategically, the issue of timing is crucial but can also backfire in a violent conflict. Future research should address the timing issue more systematically and also explore the political and legal restraints that an actor, such as a national government willing to recognise an armed group, is facing on the domestic and the international level.

In addition, in the digitised era of 'hybrid' warfare enhanced strategic disinformation and the emergence of transnational and global audiences can also impact recognition practices of ANSAs. 'Recognition' in violent conflicts is not just a social interaction process among two or more actors – it is witnessed by domestic, regional and international audiences. 'How these audiences might react and interact is likely beyond the analytical capacity of most policy-makers or state bureaucracies, which will in turn place a premium on the ability for states to adapt and react quickly to the effects of recognition on peace processes' (Trinkunas in this volume: 268). While the volume is not able to address such future changes, we hope to demonstrate with the book that studying recognition practices in asymmetric violent conflicts can provide an important analytical lens for understanding conflict dynamics more deeply – without assuming that recognition always has beneficial effects for conflict transformation.

Notes

1 See, for example, Daase et al. (2015), Fraser and Honneth (2003), Geis (2018), Lindemann and Ringmar (2012) and Wolf (2011).

2 A detailed state of the art on recognition research in International Relations, Peace and Conflict Studies and International Political Theory is beyond the scope of this introduction; see for this Geis et al. (2015) and Geis (2018).

3 Non-state actors do not seek recognition from *everybody*. They also struggle over the question of 'which particular individuals, groups or institutions are worthy sources of recognition. ... Freeing oneself from the very need for recognition from particular quarters is an essential part of liberation' (Heins 2016: 80).

4 See, for example, Byman (2006), Dudouet (2010), Görzig (2010), MacLeod et al. (2016), Podder (2013), Toros (2008, 2012), Zartman (2009).

5 While this is not a completely new phenomenon, as the Liberation Tigers of Tamil in Sri Lanka and the PKK in Turkey were already labelled as terrorist organisations in the 1980s and 1990s, this practice reached a transnational scope with the 'war on terror' script.

References

Aggestam, K. (2015), 'Peace mediation and the minefield of international recognition games', *International Negotiation* 20:3, 494–514.

Agné, H. (2013), 'The politics of international recognition: symposium introduction', *International Theory* 5:1, 94–107.

Allan, P. and A. Keller (2012), 'Is a just peace possible without thin and thick recognition?', in T. Lindemann and E. Ringmar (eds), *International Politics of Recognition* (Boulder: Paradigm Publishers), pp. 71–84.

Allen, J. R. (2020), 'The US–Taliban peace deal: a road to nowhere', available online: www.brookings.edu/blog/order-from-chaos/2020/03/05/the-us-taliban-peace-deal-a-road-to-nowhere/ (5 March); last retrieved 7 April 2020.

Arjona, A., N. Kasfir and Z. Mampilly (eds) (2015), *Rebel Governance in Civil War* (Cambridge: Cambridge University Press).

Aydınlı, E. (2016), *Violent Non-state Actors: From Anarchists to Jihadists* (Abingdon and New York, NY: Routledge).

Barbelet, B. (2008), *Engaging with Armed Non-State Actors on Humanitarian Issues* (York: York University Dissertation).
Bell, A. (2014), 'The roadblock of contested recognition: identity-based justice claims as an obstacle to peace negotiations in Afghanistan', *International Negotiation* 19:3, 518–542.
Biene, J. and C. Daase (2015), 'Gradual recognition: curbing non-state violence in asymmetric conflict', in C. Daase, C. Fehl, A. Geis and G. Kolliarakis (eds), *Recognition in International Relations* (Basingstoke: Palgrave Macmillan), pp. 220–236.
Bramsen, I. and P. Poder (2018), 'Emotional dynamics in conflict and conflict transformation', in *Berghof Handbook for Conflict Transformation (Online Edition)*, available online: www.berghof-foundation.org/fileadmin/redaktion/Publications/Handbook/Articles/bramsen_poder_handbook.pdf; last retrieved 8 April 2020.
Byman, D. (2006), 'The decision to begin talks with terrorists: lessons for policymakers', *Studies in Conflict & Terrorism* 29:5, 403–414.
Clément, M. (2014), 'Al-Muhajiroun in the United Kingdom: the role of international non-recognition in heightened radicalization dynamics', *Global Discourse* 4:4, 428–443.
Clément, M. and E. Sangar (eds) (2018), *Researching Emotions in International Relations: Methodological Perspectives on the Emotional Turn* (London and New York, NY: Palgrave Macmillan).
Coleman, P. (2014), 'Intractable conflict', in P. Coleman, M. Deutsch and E. Marcus (eds), *The Handbook of Conflict Resolution* (3rd edition, San Francisco, CA: Jossey Bass), pp. 708–744.
Cronin, A. K. and J. M. Ludes (2004), *Attacking Terrorism: Elements of a Grand Strategy* (Washington, DC: Georgetown University Press).
Daase, C., C. Fehl, A. Geis and G. Kolliarakis (eds) (2015), *Recognition in International Relations: Rethinking a Political Concept in a Global Context* (Houndmills: Palgrave Macmillan).
Dudouet, V. (2010), *Mediating Peace with Proscribed Armed Groups: Special Report 239* (Washington, DC: United States Institute of Peace).
Duyvesteyn, I. (2017), 'Rebels and legitimacy: an introduction', *Small Wars & Insurgencies* 28:4–5, 669–685.
Dybris McQuaid, S. (2019), 'Nothing is agreed until everything is agreed: institutionalizing radical disagreement and dealing with the past in Northern Ireland', in I. Bramsen, P. Poder and O. Wæver (eds), *Resolving International Conflict: Dynamics of Escalation, Continuation and Transformation* (London and New York, NY: Routledge).
Ezrow, N. (2017), *Global Politics and Violent Non-State Actors* (London: Sage).
Fraser, N. (2000), 'Rethinking recognition', *New Left Review*, 3: May/June, 107–120.
Fraser, N. and A. Honneth (2003), *Redistribution or Recognition? A Political-Philosophical Exchange* (London: Verso).
Geis, A. (2018), 'The ethics of recognition in International Political Theory', in C. Brown and R. Eckersley (eds), *The Oxford Handbook of International Political Theory* (Oxford: Oxford University Press), pp. 612–625.
Geis, A., C. Fehl, C. Daase and G. Kolliarakis (2015), 'Ambiguous consequences: rethinking recognition in International Relations', in C. Daase, C. Fehl, A. Geis and G. Kolliarakis (eds), *Recognition in International Relations: Rethinking a Political Concept in a Global Context* (Houndmills: Palgrave Macmillan), pp. 3–26.

Görzig, C. (2010), *Talking to Terrorists: Concessions and the Renunciation of Violence* (Abingdon: Routledge).
Haldemann, F. (2008), 'Another kind of justice: transitional justice as recognition', *Cornell International Law Journal* 41:3, 675–737.
Hayden, P. and K. Schick (2016), 'Recognition and the international: meanings, limits, manifestations', in P. Hayden and K. Schick (eds), *Recognition and Global Politics: Critical Encounters between State and World* (Manchester: Manchester University Press), pp. 1–22.
Heins, V. (2010), 'Of persons and peoples: internationalizing the critical theory of recognition', *Contemporary Political Theory*, 9:2, 149–170.
Heins, V. (2016), 'Recognition, multiculturalism and the allure of separatism', in P. Hayden and K. Schick (eds), *Recognition and Global Politics: Critical Encounters between State and World* (Manchester: Manchester University Press), pp. 69–84.
Herr, S. (2015), *Nichtstaatliche Gewaltakteure und das Humanitäre Völkerrecht* (Baden-Baden: Nomos).
Hofmann, C. and U. Schneckener (2011), 'Engaging non-state armed actors in state- and peace-building: options and strategies', *International Review of the Red Cross*, 93:883, 603–621.
Honneth, A. (1995), *The Struggle for Recognition: The Moral Grammar of Social Conflicts* (Cambridge: Polity).
Huang, R. (2016), 'Rebel diplomacy in civil war', *International Security* 40:4, 89–126.
Idler, A. and J. J. F. Forest (2015), 'Behavioral patterns among (violent) non-state actors: a study of complementary governance', *Stability: International Journal of Security & Development* 4:1, 1–19.
Ikäheimo, H. and A. Laitinen (2011), 'Recognition and social ontology', in H. Ikäheimo and A. Laitinen (eds), *Recognition and Social Ontology* (Leiden/Boston, MA: Brill), pp. 1–12.
Jo, H. and C. Thomson (2014), 'Legitimacy and compliance with international law: access to detainees in civil conflicts, 1991–2006', *British Journal of Political Science* 44:2, 323–355.
Levinger, M. (2013), *Conflict Analysis: Understanding Causes, Unlocking Solutions* (Washington, DC: United States Institute of Peace).
Lindemann, T. (2010), *Causes of War: The Struggle for Recognition* (Colchester: ECPR Press).
Lindemann, T. (2012), 'Concluding remarks on the empirical study of international recognition', in T. Lindemann and E. Ringmar (eds), *The International Politics of Recognition* (Boulder, CO: Paradigm Publishers), pp. 209–225.
Lindemann, T. and E. Ringmar (eds) (2012), *The International Politics of Recognition* (Boulder, CO: Paradigm Publishers).
MacLeod, A., C. Hofmann, B. Saul, J. Webb and C. L. Hogg (2016), *Humanitarian Engagement with Non-State Armed Groups* (London: Chatham House).
Mampilly, Z. (2011), *Rebel Rulers: Insurgent Governance and Civilian Life during War* (Ithaca, NY: Cornell University Press).
Markell, P. (2003), *Bound by Recognition* (Princeton, NJ: Princeton University Press).
Martineau, W., N. Meer and S. Thompson (2012), 'Theory and practice in the politics of recognition and misrecognition', *Res Publica* 18:1, 1–9.
Mastanduno, M., D. Lake and G. J. Ikenberry (1989), 'Toward a realist theory of state action', *International Studies Quarterly* 33:4, 457–474.
Miller, C. (2011), 'Is it possible and preferable to negotiate with terrorists?', *Defence Studies* 11:1, 145–185.

Pecastaing, C. (2011), 'Facing terrorism: engagement and de-escalation', in W. I. Zartman and G. O. Faure (eds), *Engaging with Extremists: Trade-Offs, Timing, and Diplomacy* (Washington, DC: United States Institute of Peace), pp. 57–80.

Podder, S. (2013), 'Non-state armed groups and stability: reconsidering legitimacy and inclusion', *Contemporary Security Policy* 34:1, 16–39.

Poder, P. (2019), 'Humiliation dynamics in conflicts in our globalized world', in I. Bramsen, P. Poder and O. Wæver (eds), *Resolving International Conflict: Dynamics of Escalation, Continuation and Transformation* (London/New York, NY: Routledge), pp. 72–86.

Reus-Smit, C. (2007), 'International crises of legitimacy', *International Politics* 44:2–3, 157–174.

Ringmar, E. (2002), 'The recognition game: Soviet Russia against the West', *Cooperation & Conflict* 37:2, 115–136.

Ringmar, E. (2012), 'Introduction', in T. Lindemann and E. Ringmar (eds), *The International Politics of Recognition* (Boulder, CO: Paradigm), pp. 3–24.

Ringmar, E. (2015), 'China's place in four recognition regimes', in C. Daase, C. Fehl, A. Geis and G. Kolliarakis (eds), *Recognition in International Relations: Rethinking a Political Concept in a Global Context* (Houndmills: Palgrave Macmillan), pp. 49–67.

Sarkees, M. R. and F. Wayman (2010), *Resort to War: 1816–2007* (Washington, DC: CQ Press).

Schlichte, K. (2009), *In the Shadow of Violence: The Politics of Armed Groups* (Frankfurt a.M.: Campus).

Schlichte, K. and U. Schneckener (2015), 'Armed groups and the politics of legitimacy', *Civil Wars* 17:4, 409–424.

Schmitz, V. (ed.) (2019), *Axel Honneth and the Critical Theory of Recognition* (Houndmills: Palgrave Macmillan).

Schneckener, U. (2006), 'Fragile statehood, armed non-state actors and security governance', in A. Bryden and M. Caparini (eds), *Private Actors and Security Governance* (Geneva: Geneva Centre for the Democratic Control of Armed Forces), pp. 23–40.

Staniland, P. (2014), *Networks of Rebellion: Explaining Insurgent Cohesion and Collapse* (Ithaca, NY: Cornell University Press).

Steinhoff, D. (2009), 'Talking to the enemy: state legitimacy concerns with engaging non-state armed groups', *Texas International Law Journal* 45, 297–322.

Strömbom, L. (2014), 'Thick recognition: advancing theory on identity change in intractable conflicts', *European Journal of International Relations* 20:1, 168–191.

Taylor, C. (1994), 'The politics of recognition', in A. Gutmann (ed.), *Multiculturalism: Examining the Politics of Recognition* (Princeton, NJ: Princeton University Press), pp. 25–74.

Toros, H. (2008), '"We don't negotiate with terrorists!" Legitimacy and complexity in terrorist conflicts', *Security Dialogue* 39:4, 407–426.

Toros, H. (2012), *Terrorism, Talking and Transformation: A Critical Approach* (Abingdon: Routledge).

Tully, J. (2000), 'Struggles over recognition and distribution', *Constellations* 7:4, 469–482.

Wendt, A. (2003), 'Why a world state is inevitable: teleology and the logic of anarchy', *European Journal of International Relations* 9:4, 491–542.

Wolf, R. (2011), 'Respect and disrespect in international politics: the significance of status recognition', *International Theory* 3:1, 105–142.

Zartman, I. W. (2009), *Negotiating with Terrorists: A Mediator's Guide*, Policy Brief (Laxenburg: IIASA).

Zartman, I. W. and G. O. Faure (2011), 'Introduction: why engage, and why not?', in I. W. Zartman and G. O. Faure (eds), *Engaging With Extremists: Trade-Offs, Timing, and Diplomacy* (Washington, DC: United States Institute of Peace), pp. 1–19.

Zohar, E. (2016), 'A new typology of contemporary armed non-state-actors: interpreting the diversity', *Studies in Conflict & Terrorism* 39:5, 423–450.

2

The historical mapping of armed groups' recognition

Stephan Hensell and Klaus Schlichte

Introduction

The history of non-state armed groups since the end of the Second World War demonstrates that these groups often follow a particular trajectory in international politics. While initially being denounced as 'criminals', 'bandits' or 'terrorists', they later often become recognised as regular political actors. The most obvious cases are the post-war trajectories of many rebel groups, namely their transformation into political parties, governments and state elites that are recognised by other government-like actors. How armed groups become legitimate actors in world politics has not yet been systematically analysed. In this chapter we will not attempt to suggest a fully fledged answer to this question, but we want to explore some possibilities for developing an answer. We argue that the ultimate legitimation of such actors – their recognition as official actors by other governments – largely depends on historical timing in three subsequent historical contexts.

In order to show this, we suggest two analytical perspectives: seeking and granting recognition. The first relates to the 'politics of legitimacy' of armed groups (Geis et al. 2012; Schlichte and Schneckener 2015). Armed groups, like political actors in general, seek to justify their policies. Be it the overthrow of an authoritarian regime, the secession of a territory or a quest for power-sharing: armed groups justify the use of violence by referring to identities, institutions, interests and political aims. In doing so they make legitimacy claims and engage in strategies of self-legitimation or in the politics of legitimacy.

The other perspective is the politics of recognition of the 'international community' (Daase et al. 2015). States and international organisations are the major actors in the global state system which are able to confirm and validate legitimacy claims of armed groups through acts of recognition. The international recognition of armed groups is in part a reaction to the demands of these groups, but in part also motivated by a host of other reasons, which sometimes seem to defy any logic. Our core argument is that the politics of legitimacy and international recognition of armed groups is subject to historical change, depending on the international contexts of these policies (Hensell and Schlichte 2017: 219–226). Armed groups, one could argue, need the right 'world historical timing' in order to be successful in achieving recognition. With this argument we intend to stress the historicity of international politics of which armed groups are part. We assert that their politics are indicative of deeper historical structures and changes in international politics (Schlichte and Stetter forthcoming).

Our starting point for the discussion is a distinction between recognition and legitimacy. While we discuss legitimacy along Weberian understandings, our theoretical approach to recognition is based on Hegel's dialectic of the lord and the slave (*Herr und Knecht*), the 'Urtext' of the discussion on recognition in social theory (see next section). Via the œuvre of Frantz Fanon it has interestingly also found its way into the reflection of political violence during the period of decolonisation. It occurs thus in the midst of our subject matter. By stressing the interactive and dynamic dimension of both, legitimacy and recognition, we will therefore include practices of governments and armed groups in our empirical analysis. We also suggest an analytical approach to the politics of legitimacy that differentiates between ideational, communicative and diplomatic legitimation strategies of armed groups.

In order to understand the politics of legitimacy and recognition, we argue, global historical contexts have to be taken into account. The techniques and formal steps of recognition might not have changed fundamentally in the period since 1945, but the political messages, the discourses and the concatenations of armed groups have. We distinguish between three main historical contexts or global times that matter for the chances of recognition and ultimately of the legitimisation of armed groups to become formally accepted actors in international politics. In the phase of decolonisation, armed groups could easily claim to be the true representatives of their people's aspirations for independence, and violence as such was not deemed as illegitimate. The international context was favourable for the recognition of armed groups. In the Cold War, recognition of armed groups was bifurcated depending on the East–West divide and the side with which armed groups aligned themselves. In our times, in the era of humanitarianism and multilateral intervention, a third logic seems to prevail. The use of violence by armed groups for political purposes is increasingly delegitimised and the politics of recognition becomes more and more uncertain itself and difficult to calculate for armed groups. In this tentative interpretation we put the dialectics of legitimising and delegitimising effects of violence (Schlichte 2009) at the centre of reflection.

In terms of methods and sources, our analysis is based on long-standing research efforts in Germany on war and armed conflict since 1945. By drawing on a war definition and data-set that does not use quantitative thresholds, we include in our analysis only such armed actors that appear in this data-set as actors of war between 1945 and 2015.[1] Apart from our own case-related fieldwork in Sub-Saharan Africa and Southeastern Europe as well as secondary literature, it is this material that our theses are based upon.

Recognition and the politics of legitimacy of armed groups

As a key category of Political Science, *legitimacy* is an essentially contested concept. We use the term not as a normative concept with the aim to develop criteria of legitimate authority, but in the Weberian tradition as a descriptive category about empirically observable subjective beliefs in the validity of an order. An empirical understanding considers the legitimacy claims of ruling actors and the related positive or negative judgements of their followers itself as observable social facts (Beetham 2013: 6). The 'belief in legitimacy' (*Legitimitätsglaube*) (Weber [1921/1922] 1972: 16) means the shared belief in the rightfulness or moral validity of a political organisation and its activities by a considerable fraction of the governed. In the most general terms, legitimacy is about making claims and the conditions under which such claims are accepted.

The term *recognition* needs to be differentiated from legitimacy. One root of the idea of recognition goes back to the philosopher of German idealism, G. W. F. Hegel, who made the question of recognition part of his dialectical theory of self-consciousness in his *Phenomenology of the Spirit* ([1807] 1970). It has become, since then, a foundational term in social and political theory, as recognition is understood as an act and as an outcome, as an institutionalised result of conflict. In Hegel, recognition is the outcome of fight about life and death that leads to subordination in which both parties recognise each other as mutually recognising subjects (Hegel [1807] 1970: 147). The fight between slave and lord has thus a positive result – legal relations become possible. Despite an enduring power asymmetry, both parties can enter legal relations (cf. Hegel [1807] 1970: 145–155). The core of recognition in this Hegelian argument is in our view that one actor can no longer ignore the existence of the opposing other.

This dialectical model for the transformation of self-consciousness into intersubjective self-consciousness became a model for Marx's theory of class conflict. It was also a theoretical inspiration for one of the main thinkers of 'non-state armed actors', namely of Frantz Fanon in his theory on decolonisation. Fanon, in explaining colonial subordination, also puts recognition at the centre of his theory: in opposition to the Hegelian original story, colonial subordination, in particular in former slave-holding colonial settings like Fanon's home island Martinique, shows a different outcome. While Hegel's version ends with mutual recognition, colonial subordination does not: 'here the master gives a damn about the consciousness of the slave. He does not want his recognition, but only his labour force' (Fanon [1965] 1967: 85, fn. 8). And while in Hegel, the subdued slave concentrates on his work in order to find his satisfaction and later his liberation, the slave wants, if we follow Fanon, to be like his master. The colonial subject does not concentrate on the object of his work but on the master. The colonial subject, according to Fanon, is therefore less self-reliant than Hegel's slave.

Fanon drew radical conclusions from these insights: the French colonial policy of 'assimilation' is dismissed by him (Fanon [1965] 1967). Granted freedom is worthless in comparison to freedom achieved by fighting. In his later work, *The Wretched of the Earth* (orig. 1961), Fanon pleas therefore for a violent fight against colonialism as it is only through the experience of power that the inferiority complex of the colonised can be overcome ([1961] 2001: 37).[2] This position resonates with the attention that violent uprisings in comparison to peaceful protest have achieved in the emerging global public sphere:[3] it is still an open question how far the international system offers a particular premium on political violence (Koloma Beck and Werron 2013). It could also be argued that the world is becoming less violent and accordingly the use of violence within and between states less legitimate. This is plausible not only regarding the decline in the number of major wars but also with respect to the stabilisation of states in regions which used to be hotspots of violence, such as Latin America, Southern Africa and Southeast Asia. Given these tendencies, the use of violence is particularly successful as it increases the chances that the existence of an armed group and its agenda is becoming part of international political communication. Armed groups in many cases are the prime movers to actually set conflicts on the political agenda and force others to act.

Legitimacy and recognition are foundational concepts of political theory. They are also critical for explaining the politics and trajectories of armed groups within the global state system. Like other actors of international politics, we argue, armed groups seek recognition and ultimately legitimacy in the eyes of other state actors. In doing so they are pursuing a broad range of practices and repertoires of self-legitimation which are aiming at generating the legitimacy of the groups themselves or of their political orders (Barker 2001; Hensell and Schlichte 2017; Schlichte 2009: 107–113). The conscious and active striving of violent actors to generate legitimacy is what we call the 'politics of legitimacy' of armed groups (Geis et al. 2012; Schlichte and Schneckener 2015).[4]

A huge amount of the politics of armed groups consists of legitimacy politics within the group and vis-à-vis its immediate social surroundings. Legitimacy is first and foremost a necessary condition for the functioning of the group itself, for its coherence and its coordinated action. A second layer of legitimacy politics is oriented towards the social surroundings of the group, in particular towards its targeted constituency (Malthaner 2011; Schlichte 2009). In the following, however, we will focus only on a third layer of that politics, namely its international dimension.

We differentiate between three strategies of these internationally oriented legitimacy politics. The first is *ideation*. Armed groups possess, construct and develop legitimating ideas in order to justify the use of violence. The reproduction of these ideas and their translation into political programmes builds equally on local beliefs and myths and on global political models such as Marxism, Maoism, nationalism and varieties of political Islam. Such ideational constructions should not be seen as mere fabrications, as simulated guises. Despite all minor tactics, political aims of armed groups, at least among leaders and staff, are rather expressions of true political beliefs.

The second strategy is the *extraversion*. Armed groups need to address international audiences and actors in order to mobilise support for their cause. This includes not only states and international or regional organisations but also transnational supporting milieus and the media or, more generally, the emerging global public. In many cases, armed groups employ forms of strategic communication and framing that include the production of particular narratives and meanings about the conflict, the threats and the enemy (Koloma Beck and Werron 2013).

The third strategy is *diplomacy*. Armed groups often rely on diplomatic practices such as opening offices and representations abroad, establishing organisations responsible for foreign affairs or sending envoys on political missions abroad (Huang 2016; see Sienknecht, in this volume). Diplomacy is what states do. By employing such diplomatic practices armed groups show that they are capable of governing and are often indeed a government in the waiting.

If armed groups are successful with these strategies, the overall result can be what Bourdieu terms 'officialisation' (Bourdieu 1990: 108–109). This means that other governments, and consequently international organisations as well, would recognise an armed group as a subject of international politics, as a potentially legal actor along the norms of international law, and as a potential – or factual – incumbent of governmental power. On a continuum from 'thin' to 'thick' recognition (see the introductory chapter in this volume), there are, of course, many steps or forms of recognition that range far below the level of officialisation. Picking up again the dialectics of Hegel and Fanon presented above, we would suggest starting with seemingly banal, often overlooked practices. When government forces take measures against violent opposition, and be it in repressive forms, then this can be seen as an act of proto-recognition as an enemy is addressed and action deemed necessary. A change in governmental discourse, usually starting by talking about 'bandits' or 'terrorists', is a next step in proto-recognition as it acknowledges that an armed group exists as a party to the conflict. In cases in which armed groups are militarily successful, at least to the degree that they can maintain control over territory, sooner or later second- or first-track diplomacy will set in.

Engaging in the politics of legitimacy, armed groups are in the great majority of cases the first movers. The resulting recognition game, however, is always interactive and involves a host of other actors. First of all, the media play a crucial role. Reporting about armed non-state actors is in many cases the first step in acknowledging the very existence of an armed group as a party to the conflict. Secondly, there are the transnational supporting milieus such as diaspora networks, activist groups or advocacy networks which provide resources and act as political mobilisers. Finally, there are major actors of international politics: states and international or regional organisations which are able to grant or withhold recognition. Not all state-like actors, however, have the same weight and power in the prestige hierarchy of global politics. It matters who recognises. As we will show in the next section, the interaction of these players is highly varied and depends on the world historical context.

Three global times: mapping historical contexts

Our starting point is that the temporal ordering of events or processes matters (Pierson 2004). Explaining the (non-)recognition of armed groups needs to account for the role of conjunctures, sequences and timing in global politics. The politics of legitimacy and recognition can be differentiated with a view to the 'world time' or 'world historical context' within which it unfolds.[5] We distinguish three historical contexts within which the politics of legitimacy and recognition of armed groups is embedded: the age of decolonisation, the Cold War, and the age of humanitarianism and multilateral intervention. Each of these contexts is characterised by specific conjunctures and global events, such as the defeat of the French colonial army in Dien Bien Phu in 1954, the student protests in 1968, the fall of the iron curtain in 1989, or 9/11. We find it plausible to assume that such events may play a triggering role for the decision to pick up arms and for the mobilisation of sympathisers. They are indicators of politicisation across boundaries that has become overlooked in the research on civil wars, bizarrely even in the discipline of International Relations, due to the prevalence of ahistorical approaches. The shift towards fine-tuned studies of micro dynamics of wars (e.g. Kalyvas 2006) has certainly contributed to losing sight of the international embeddedness of political violence.

We consider the politics of legitimacy and recognition both as expression and as indicators of different forms of politicisation in the international system. As a preliminary step, we differentiate between three different such stages which empirically, of course, overlap. We will specify the particular politicisations, discourses and patterns of recognition in short summaries. In a conclusion we then present a few hypotheses on what this tells us about international politics.

The age of decolonisation: unambiguity

The age of decolonisation from the 1940s until the end of the 1960s was marked by the dissolution of colonial empires and the creation of various new states in Africa, Asia and the Middle East, which emerged from the remnants of imperial rule. While decolonisation was overall a rather peaceful process, conflicts between colonial powers and indigenous populations escalated into wars of independence in Indonesia, Indochina, Algeria, Guinea-Bissau and Mozambique. Armed groups or liberation movements that took up arms to fight against the colonisers often quickly achieved international recognition. For instance, during the war of decolonisation in Algeria the Front de Libération Nationale (FLN) declared Algeria as independent in 1958 four years before the end of the war, and several Arab states as well as states from the Non-Aligned Movement immediately recognised the FLN government formally as representative of the Algerian people (Connelly 2002).

Especially with the delegitimising violence that characterised decolonisation wars in Malaysia, Vietnam and Algeria, with India and Pakistan gaining independence in 1948 and with the Chinese revolution in 1949, a considerable part of the world was politically not only outspokenly anti-colonial, but also ready to recognise armed movements fighting against colonial powers, reluctant to withdraw. The Soviet Union had always denounced colonial possessions as Western imperialism and perceived the oppressed colonial people as natural allies of the first proletarian state (Kanet 1975). The United States equally supported the 'new nations' in the wake of Wilsonian ideas of self-determination and decolonisation policy under Roosevelt with its aim of exporting US ideas of political and economic liberty (Ryan and Pungong 2000).

International and soon regional organisations passed declarations against colonial possessions, and in some cases, like the Organisation of African Unity (OAU), support for violent decolonisation movements was even institutionalised. When it was founded in 1963 by thirty African states, the OAU was dedicated to the eradication of all forms of colonialism and white minority rule that existed in Africa. To that end, the OAU supported various independence movements active at that time. The so-called 'Liberation Committee' of the OAU was tasked to mobilise international solidarity for the liberation struggle as well as assisting armed groups financially and materially. Moreover, the OAU recognised various armed groups as the sole representation of oppressed people, such as the African National Congress (ANC), the South West African People's Organisation (SWAPO), the Zimbabwe African People's Union (ZAPU), the Frente de Libertçãao de Moçambique (Mozambique Liberation Front; FRELIMO), the Movimento Popular de Libertacao de Angola (People's Movement for the Liberation of Angola, MPLA) and the Partido de Africano da Independencia da Guine e Cabo Verde (African Party for the Independence of Guinea and Cape Verde, PAIGC). The OAU formally recognised all these groups, sometimes even before they made substantial military progress or effectively controlled territory. The OAU also campaigned for the recognition of these groups internationally, which eventually led the UN to accord representatives of the ANC and SWAPO observer status in the UN General Assembly (Reno 2011: 25, 80).

In retrospect, the amount of international support for organised non-state violence is remarkable. It indicates, as we argue, a different global historical time in which a fundamental line of conflict existed between remnants of imperial logics of actions and a progressing standard of 'national self-determination' (Fisch 2010). Imperial claims were rapidly losing legitimacy – visible even in the attempts of France and Britain themselves to reframe their empires as 'Communauté' or 'Commonwealth'. The political concept of the nation-state became the model after which the post-colonial world should be structured. Impediments to recognition, we would assume, were rather created along the lines of political camps of Cold War dichotomies. In the context of decolonisation, the use of violence for political ends as such was not deemed illegitimate. For colonial powers the only way to legitimise excessive repression of anti-colonial movements was to reframe these conflicts as embodiments of another conflict, namely as part of the fight against the advance of communism. Along the lines of Hegel and Fanon, the violent actions of decolonisation movements were indeed aimed at recognition of the existence of colonial subjects that would no longer be ignored. In comparison to our two later historical times, the chances not only of attaining recognition but also of becoming legitimate actors in newly independent states were high.

The age of the Cold War: bifurcated legitimacy

The era of decolonisation overlapped considerably of course with the Cold War. In the Cold War, non-state violence was interpreted less as violence against foreign rule as used to be the case in the age of decolonisation, and rather as an expression of the conflict between the superpowers. Civil wars in Africa, Latin America and Asia were seen as 'proxy wars', and actors in these regions were seen as fifth columns of the Soviet Union, the People's Republic of China or the United States. As much as this was untrue – all these conflicts originated from local cleavages (Jung et al. 2003) – this politicisation did not spare the actors themselves. Entire regional war complexes, such as in Southern Africa or Southeast Asia as well as civil wars in Latin America and elsewhere, were coded along the lines of the East–West divide. The United States, the Soviet Union but also the People's Republic of China became sponsors of liberation and resistance movements in Africa, Asia and Latin America and supported them with military training, financial resources and weapons (Westad 2007).[6] Maoism and Marxism became ideational and organisational templates for the legitimacy politics of armed groups, while universities in Paris, London, Moscow and Dar-es-Salaam developed into transnational hubs and nodal points for rebel leaders and would-be revolutionaries, and for the circulation of ideas, strategies and techniques (Cook 2014; Gupta 2015).

It would be erroneous, however, to reduce these dynamics to relations between governments in East and West on the one hand and armed groups on the other. The dynamics of legitimacy and recognition were embedded into transnational networks of political mobilisation and of stable political milieus. While the Left in the West saw the future of social revolution in the agrarian periphery of the Third World and declared solidarity with various liberation movements, armed groups built their ideologies on anti-imperialist and social revolutionary traditions of the Left after 1917 (Hobsbawm 1994: 436–460).[7] Progressive Scandinavian governments played a particularly interesting role here, as they were the first to recognise armed groups as legitimate actors in world politics that were still seen as enemies by other Western governments. SWAPO in Namibia, FRELIMO in Mozambique and the Frente Revolucionária de Timor-Leste Independente (Revolutionary Front for an Independent East Timor, FRETELIN) in Indonesia were cases in point.

The Cold War opened opportunities but also set restrictions for armed groups. It could escalate, prolong or internationalise conflicts but it could also shorten wars or help find ways for conflict resolution. This is the foil against which the politics of (external) legitimacy and of recognition must be read in that period. Many armed groups oriented themselves either to the East or the West and so became part of the global constellation of the

Cold War. Groups with leftist beliefs usually gravitated towards the Soviet camp. This applies not only to all social revolutionary guerrilla movements in Latin America but also to various other groups, such as the ANC in South Africa, the Sudan People's Liberation Army (SPLA), the Kurdistan Workers' Party (PKK) or the New People's Army in the Philippines. Others had revisionist or outright conservative orientations that were more compatible with US support, as it applies to the Resistência Nacional Moçambicana (Mozambican National Resistance, RENAMO), the União Nacional para a Independência Total de Angola (National Union for the Total Independence of Angola, UNITA), the mujahideen in Afghanistan or the Contras in Nicaragua (Westad 2007). These groups often triggered massive retaliation by state forces, which can be seen as signs of thin recognition as existing opponents. The fact that they were also openly sponsored by the superpowers can be equally interpreted as basic recognition as a party to the conflict. According to the global political division, this resulted in a kind of binary logic. Recognition was divided, but actors could still calculate who would recognise their claims, depending on the side of the Cold War with which they aligned themselves. Only in a few exceptional cases, the National Resistance Movement in Uganda being one of them, could armed groups stay away from this bifurcated alignment and gain international recognition by becoming *de facto* rulers.

The Cold War is also characterised by the delegitimisation of the violence of the opponent. Legitimacy in the international system was divided, and we assume a normative effect of the discourses of both camps that constantly hinted to the immoderate violence of the respective opponent. The general delegitimisation of violence for political purposes that marks our present was in a way prepared during the late phases of the Cold War, with the emerging human rights discourses paving the way for humanitarianism as the sole remaining source of legitimate violence after 1990 (Barnett 2011; Fassin 2010; Hehir 2010).

The age of humanitarianism and multilateral intervention: incalculability

Despite widespread public imaginings, the end of the Cold War cannot be pinpointed to a particular event. It was itself an ambiguous process that stretched from Tito's death and the *Solidarność* movement in 1980 to the dissolution of the Soviet Union in 1993. With the ambiguity and uncertainty that emerged in that period, the politics of recognition became more and more uncertain itself. This can be exemplified by the contrasting fate of two leaders: while Uganda's current president, Yoweri Museveni, could transform himself from a guerrilla leader to a legitimate head of state in

January 1986 without any international objection, Charles Taylor, leader of the National Patriotic Front of Liberia (NPFL), starting a similar war at Christmas Eve 1989, quickly met with resistance from other governments in West Africa, supported by the West. Even though he was militarily successful in the end and was elected president in post-war elections that were widely considered free and fair, this did not spare him a trial in The Hague in which he was sentenced to fifty years in prison for war crimes and crimes against humanity.

In several other cases strategies of external legitimation of armed groups failed right from the start. When the Soviet Union collapsed, several former socialist and now independent republics were quickly confronted with separatist movements, which also demanded independence and their own state. This included the republics of South-Ossetia and Abkhazia (Georgia), Nagorno-Karabakh (Azerbaijan), Transnistria (Moldavia) and later also the two People's Republics of Donetsk and Luhansk (Ukraine). None of these *de facto* states is fully recognised or at least recognised by a significant majority of states even though they have their own administrations and some of them even print their own money and organise multi-party elections (King 2001; Smolnik 2016).

While Eurasia has become part of a new informal empire, where Russian dominance was for a while accepted and later informally countered, yet without Western military engagement in violent conflicts, Sub-Saharan Africa and the Balkans became the laboratory for new forms of multilateral intervention with a politics of recognition by great powers that seemingly defies any logic. Generally, it seems, international actors are today less likely to recognise armed groups while at the same time insisting that rebels must abide by basic human rights standards. Only massive human rights violations by state forces are able to trigger a quick recognition, often with massive support from what calls itself 'the international community' (Hehir 2010). Kosovo was a paradigmatic case in that regard. The Kosovo Liberation Army (KLA) was especially successful with its legitimacy politics in internationalising the conflict and portraying itself as the defender of Albanian civilians against massive human rights violations by the Serbian state. Its strategy of victimisation not only led to the recognition of the KLA as an official representative of the Kosovo-Albanians but also triggered an international military intervention that has been the main goal of the Albanian guerrilla (Perritt Jr. 2008: 130–151; Phillips 2012). Another case in that regard has been the conflict in Libya, which has been widely seen as putting the so-called 'Responsibility to Protect' into practice. When the Libyan government headed by Qaddafi initiated a violent crackdown on a popular uprising including the use of tanks and troops against civilians in the besieged cities of Benghazi and Misrata, the international reaction followed immediately. While the UN Security Council passed two resolutions and authorised the use of force for the purpose of human protection, France recognised the 'National Transitional Council' that was founded by the rebels only five days after its creation as the legitimate Libyan government. Several other European states followed this move within the next months.

To attain formal recognition was also possible in some cases, as for the Eritrean People's Liberation Front (EPLF) in 1993 (Reno 2011: 18–19) and for the SPLA in South Sudan (see Pring in this volume), where armed groups established new states with the approval of all affected parties including the states of Ethiopia and Sudan. In other cases, the undecidedness of the situation led to long stalemates, as the fate of the Polisario in Western Sahara or the rebels in Darfur demonstrate.

In this last historical phase '*la Raison humanitaire*' (Fassin 2010) prevails, at least in the official sphere. The coding in Western media mostly follows listings of the EU or the United States government about 'terrorist groups' against which 'civilians' need to be secured. Non-state violence has become increasingly delegitimised, with only few exceptions, as the KLA in Kosovo or the Northern Alliance in Afghanistan. Groups that had been listed as 'terrorists' like Hizbollah in Lebanon, the Liberation Tigers of Tamil Eelam (LTTE) in Sri Lanka, the PKK in Turkey (see Sienknecht in this volume), Hamas in Gaza or al-Shabaab in Somalia remained excluded from gaining legitimate status, even if they are nationally legitimate actors or control large territories in state-like manners.

The communicative effects of exerted and experienced violence (Koloma Beck and Werron 2013) have become incalculable, for all parties involved. The 'shadow of violence' (Schlichte 2009) had existed before. But how it is cast now is seemingly determined by uncontrollable effects in a much more internationalised environment with much closer media coverage and advanced public relations. The legitimising and delegitimising effects of exerted physical violence that is first and foremost felt within armed groups and their immediate social surroundings (Schlichte 2009: ch. 3), have thus become incalculable in the global political arena, too.

Conclusion

In this chapter, we could only sketch some broader lines for the purpose of critical discussion. We distinguished three global periods of the politics of recognition: unambiguity in the era of decolonisation, bifurcation during the Cold War and incalculability in the post-Cold War era. This is, of course, a suggestion open to revision based on further research. It is an open question whether 9/11 and the so-called 'age of terrorism' have given way to a fourth global historical time (Toros 2017) in which armed groups are increasingly denunciated as 'terrorist' and, thus, delegitimised.

Secondly, the role of regional politics needs further discussion. There are many smaller regional and sub-regional correspondences, linkages and practices of recognition, along the lines the international system was politically coded, in a communicative relation with domestic lines of conflict. The politics of recognition cannot thus be reduced to the interaction of great powers and armed groups, as there is an endless set of conditions on regional and local levels that shapes the course of external legitimacy and recognition as well. The fact that funding from other governments is still the most often reported source of income for non-state actors is an indication of the role of material resources in recognition acts (Schlichte 2009: 116). Regional power rivalries and hostile relations between neighbouring governments, for example, often lead to contradictory patterns of support and recognition of armed groups, reminiscent of Cold War constellations, but on a smaller scale. These constellations have their historical roots, too, but their perception was often overruled by power competition between governments with regional aspirations. As during the Cold War, in such multiple layers conflict settlement is much harder to reach.

With our short preliminary interpretation, we claim that we can show that the politics of armed groups is indicative of structures and changes in international politics. The politics of legitimacy, we would argue, is not only attached to major international conflicts but is at the same time also an expression of these conflicts. It is, thus, an indicator of politicisation in the international system. We see two main determinants of the effects of interaction between armed groups and other governments, leading to recognition or not. First, it is important for armed groups to inscribe themselves into the cleavages of the international system. In the phase of decolonisation armed groups could easily position themselves along the fundamental line of conflict between colonialism and independence that characterised the international system from the 1940s until the 1960s. The same is true for the Cold War, which allowed armed groups to find a position along the bipolar divide of the international system between the superpowers. In the current phase of humanitarianism, however, this is apparently more difficult. Yet, we do not believe that the politics of legitimacy is just the result of dominating instrumental action and economic interests on the side of today's rebels. Armed groups continue to be more often than not true believers in their political projects (Bakonyi et al. 2006; Schlichte 2009). At least we have no reason to assume that they are less sincere than any other political actor. As stated above, armed groups' politics of legitimisation and of recognition are both a starting condition and an outcome of their insertion into the political world.

Secondly, the international recognition of armed groups by great powers is in part a reaction to the demands of these groups, but in part also motivated by a host of other factors, which sometimes seem to defy any logic. This is especially true for the current historical phase of humanitarianism. Governments' actions seem to follow a mix of previous intervention experiences, colonial legacies, media attention and perceived interests that are difficult to calculate for all actors. The new multilateralism that has emerged after the Cold War grants recognition selectively, but in unforeseeable and erratic ways, as the fates of armed groups in Syria and Libya show. For all actors it is an open question what really counts for international recognition: nationalism and politicised Islam as the dominant ideologies might bring sympathies here and there, but not from the club of great powers that controls the symbolic capital of the United Nation's Security Council. In some cases, as with General Haftar in Libya, leading Western powers are divided over the issue of who should be recognised as a legitimate actor and who should just receive 'thin recognition' (see Clément, Geis and Pfeifer in this volume). The disconcertion that has emerged in the global order does not, however, just affect the politics of armed non-state actors. It should also be a reminder that the historical constitution of the international system is not reducible to neo-realist billiard ball constellations. Instead, it is itself a social production of political attitudes, institutional arrangements and – not least – the historicity of societies. Both observations lead to the plea to overcome the ahistorical formalism of International Relations if we want to understand the politics of recognition and legitimacy.

Notes

1 We rely specifically on data-sets of the 'Arbeitsgemeinschaft Kriegsursachenforschung' (AKUF) at the University of Hamburg and the Micropolitics of Armed Groups Database. The latter is a data-set of eighty armed groups and encompasses biographies of leaders and staff, the practices exerted by groups and their trajectories. See for our earlier works Jung et al. (2003); Bakonyi et al. (2006); Schlichte (2009); Schlichte and Schneckener (2015); Hensell and Gerdes (2017); and Hensell and Schlichte (2017).

2 It is quite compelling to see that this theoretical debate about recognition is not decoupled from real politics. A direct relation is Fanon's work as the ambassador of the not yet independent Algeria to Ghana in the late 1950s. Ghana under Kwame Nkrumah had become an early hub for liberation movements across the continent, still gathering under umbrella ideas like Pan-Africanism. A longer line is to be seen in the reception of Fanon's ideas – and in the similar vein of Maoism – in political contexts and armed conflicts on all continents. Global historical timing is not just a question of armed actors; it is one of theories, too.

3 While the 'public' in international politics for several centuries has been equated with the inter-state sphere, the state system since the 1980s has become embedded in an increasingly transnationalised arena of discourse, contestation and social interaction, which involves private as well as public, state and non-state actors (Ruggie 2004). However, early instances and organisational features of an emerging global public stretch back to the nineteenth century (Jung 2011 and, more generally, Bayart 2004).
4 That does not imply a statement about the interests and motives of the actors. We assume that the politics of legitimacy follows various political purposes.
5 On the role of world historical timing for the explanation of institutional change see Skocpol (1979: 42, 173) and Migdal (1988: 271–272).
6 It would be historically much more correct to think of the Cold War as a tripolar structure since the competition between the Soviet Union and the People's Republic of China made itself felt in many armed conflicts; see for example Legum (1975).
7 This also included the circulation of Frantz Fanon's book *The Wretched of the Earth*', which was extremely influential among intellectual activists and revolutionaries on various continents (Hobsbawm 1994: 443).

References

Bakonyi, J., S. Hensell and J. Siegelberg (eds) (2006), *Gewaltordnungen bewaffneter Gruppen: Ökonomie und Herrschaft nichtstaatlicher Akteure in den Kriegen der Gegenwart* (Baden-Baden: Nomos).
Barker, R. (2001), *Legitimating Identities: The Self-Presentation of Rulers and Subjects* (Cambridge: Cambridge University Press).
Barnett, M. (2011), *Empire of Humanity: A History of Humanitarianism* (Ithaca, NY: Cornell University Press).
Bayart, J.-F. (2004), *La Gouvernement du monde: une critique politique de la globalisation* (Paris: Fayard).
Beetham, D. (2013), *The Legitimation of Power* (Houndmills: Palgrave Macmillan).
Bourdieu, P. (1990), *The Logic of Practice* (Stanford, CA: Stanford University Press).
Connelly, M. (2002), *A Diplomatic Revolution: Algeria's Fight for Independence and the Origins of the Post-Cold War Era* (Oxford: Oxford University Press).
Cook, A. (ed.) (2014), *Mao's Little Red Book: A Global History* (Cambridge, MA: Cambridge University Press).
Daase, C., C. Fehl, A. Geis and G. Kolliarakis (eds) (2015), *Recognition in International Relations: Rethinking a Political Concept in a Global Context* (Houndsmills: Palgrave Macmillan).
Fanon, F. [1961] (2001), *The Wretched of the Earth* (London: Penguin Books).
Fanon, F. [1965] (1967), *Black Skin, White Masks* (New York, NY: Grove Press).
Fassin, D. (2010), *La Raison humanitaire: une histoire morale du temps présent* (Paris: Seuil).
Fisch, J. (2010), *Das Selbstbestimmungsrecht der Völker: Die Domestizierung einer Illusion* (München: Beck).
Geis, A., F. Nullmeier and C. Daase (eds) (2012), *Aufstieg der Legitimitätspolitik: Rechtfertigung und Kritik politisch-ökonomischer Ordnungen* (Baden-Baden: Nomos).

Gupta, S. D. (2015), 'Marxism, modernity, and revolution: the Asian experience', in A. Flüchter and J. Schöttli (eds), *The Dynamics of Transculturality: Concepts and Institutions in Motion* (Cham: Springer), pp. 27–38.
Hegel, G. W. F. [1807] (1970), *Phänomenologie des Geistes* (Frankfurt am Main: Suhrkamp).
Hehir, A. (2010), *Humanitarian Intervention: An Introduction* (Houndmills: Palgrave Macmillan).
Hensell, S. and F. Gerdes (2017), 'Exit from war: the transformation of rebels into post-war power elites', *Security Dialogue* 48:2, 168–184.
Hensell, S. and K. Schlichte (2017), 'Gewalt und Legitimität: Die internationale Politik bewaffneter Gruppen', in H.-G. Ehrhart (ed.), *Kriege im 21. Jahrhundert: Konzepte, Akteure, Herausforderungen* (Baden-Baden: Nomos), pp. 213–228.
Hobsbawm, E. (1994), *Age of Extremes: The Short Twentieth Century 1914–1991* (London: Abacus).
Huang, R. (2016), 'Rebel diplomacy in civil war', *International Security* 40:4, 89–126.
Jung, D. (2011), *Orientalists, Islamists and the Global Public Sphere: A Genealogy of the Modern Essentialist Image of Islam* (Sheffield: Equinox).
Jung, D., K. Schlichte and J. Siegelberg (2003), *Kriege in der Weltgesellschaft: Strukturgeschichtliche Erklärung kriegerischer Gewalt (1945–2000)* (Opladen: VS Verlag für Sozialwissenschaften).
Kalyvas, S. (2006), *The Logic of Violence in Civil War* (Cambridge: Cambridge University Press).
Kanet, R. (ed.) (1975), *The Soviet Union and the Developing Nations* (Baltimore, MD: Johns Hopkins University Press).
King, C. (2001), 'The benefits of ethnic war: understanding Eurasia's unrecognized states', *World Politics* 53:4, 524–552.
Koloma Beck, T. and T. Werron (2013), 'Gewaltwettbewerbe: "Gewalt" in globalen Konkurrenzen um Aufmerksamkeit und Legitimität', in Stephan Stetter (ed.), *Ordnung und Wandel in der Weltpolitik: Konturen einer Soziologie der Internationalen Beziehungen* (Baden-Baden: Nomos), pp. 239–267.
Legum, C. (1975), 'The Soviet Union, China and the West in Southern Africa', *Foreign Affairs* 54, 745–762.
Malthaner, S. (2011), *Mobilizing the Faithful: Militant Islamist Groups and their Constituencies* (Frankfurt am Main: Campus).
Migdal, J. (1988), *Strong Societies, Weak States: State–Society Relations and State Capabilities in the Third World* (Princeton, NJ: Princeton University Press).
Perritt, H. Jr. (2008), *Kosovo Liberation Army: The Inside Story of an Insurgency* (Urbana, IL: University of Illinois Press).
Phillips, D. (2012), *Liberating Kosovo: Coercive Diplomacy and U.S. Intervention* (Cambridge and Boston, MA: MIT Press).
Pierson, P. (2004), *Politics in Time: History, Institutions and Social Analysis* (Princeton, NJ: Princeton University Press).
Reno, W. (2011), *Warfare in Independent Africa* (Cambridge: Cambridge University Press).
Ruggie, J. G. (2004), 'Reconstituting the global public domain: issues, actors, and practices', *European Journal of International Relations* 10:4, 499–531.
Ryan, D. and V. Pungong (eds) (2000), *The United States and Decolonization: Power and Freedom* (Houndmills: Macmillan).
Schlichte, K. (2009), *In the Shadow of Violence: The Politics of Armed Groups* (Frankfurt am Main: Campus).

Schlichte, K. and U. Schneckener (2015), 'Armed groups and the politics of legitimacy', *Civil Wars* 17:4, 409–424.
Schlichte, K. and S. Stetter (eds) (forthcoming), *The Presence of the Past: Imprints of Colonialism and Empires in Global Politics*.
Skocpol, T. (1979), *States and Revolutions: A Comparative Analysis of France, Russia, and China* (Cambridge: Cambridge University Press).
Smolnik, F. (2016), *Secessionist Rule: Protracted Conflict and Configurations of Non-state Authority* (Frankfurt am Main: Campus).
Toros, H. (2017), '"9/11 is alive and well" or how critical terrorism studies has sustained the 9/11 narrative', *Critical Studies on Terrorism* 10:2, 203–219.
Weber, M. [1921/1922] (1972), *Wirtschaft und Gesellschaft: Grundriss der verstehenden Soziologie* (Tübingen: Mohr).
Westad, O. A. (2007), *The Global Cold War: Third World Interventions and the Making of Our Times* (Cambridge: Cambridge University Press).

II

Recognition during armed conflicts

3

Labelling conflict groups in Nigeria: a comparative study of Boko Haram, Niger Delta, IPOB and Fulani militia

Michael Nwankpa

Introduction

Nigeria's diverse ethno-religious composition and its political structure produce a site for constant contest and struggle for power, recognition, and territorial and resource control. The Nigerian state often looks like a battlefield involving inter-religious tension and conflicts between Christians and Muslims and inter-ethnic clashes such as Tiv versus Jukun, Ijaw versus Itsekiri and Ife versus Modakeke, to name but a few. However, the Nigerian state remains a common enemy, although it has managed to prevent the coalition of the oppressed. This is possible because of the fractured nature of the highly centralised Nigerian state. Nigeria's natural resources, resource control and wealth distribution are concentrated in the hands of a small political elite which exerts control over the central government. In a zero-sum game, where power and unlimited access to the 'national cake' are tied to the control of the central government, elites from the multiple ethnic groups engage regularly in rivalry and competition. Hence, while the Nigerian political class appears fractured by ethnic, religious and political (party) alliances, it is united in its pursuit of control over the central government. This creates a deep distrust between the elites and the people, leading to the emergence of armed violent groups such as the Niger Delta militants and Boko Haram insurgents.

The Nigerian political elites have applied, predominantly, violence and, in some instances, affirmative action including consociational measures, amnesty, redistribution of wealth, dialogue and negotiation in crushing or pacifying groups that have arisen to challenge its legitimacy and monopoly of the use of violence. One practice that has been used is 'labelling', as a form of mis-recognition. Labelling in Nigeria is not politically neutral, as each label attracts certain kinds of response. This chapter compares four distinct conflict groups in Nigeria – Boko Haram, the Niger Delta militants, Indigenous People of Biafra (IPOB) and the Fulani militia – considering the underlying political and economic motivation and the implications of the labels. It begins by providing a brief note on the methodology. This is followed by describing the recognition claims and needs of the selected conflict groups. The subsequent sections provide analysis of the mis-recognition process, the implication of mis-recognition/labelling, and the Nigerian state's approach to conflict resolution and its ramifications.

Methodology

This chapter relies on a qualitative research method in the empirical analysis of multiple case studies. The choice of multiple case studies allows for comparison and contrast, in this study between four Nigerian conflict groups. This essentially provides opportunity for drawing generalisations and/or specificities regarding armed non-state actors (ANSAs) in Nigeria. The chapter draws on fieldwork research conducted in Nigeria between 2013 and 2016. In terms of analysis, the study applies interpretive judgement, using four recognition metrics: (1) the type of recognition struggle (type of ANSA); (2) population support; (3) forms of (mis-/non-) recognition (humiliation, disrespect, false representations of individual or collective identity, labelling/ the deliberate withholding or denial of recognition); and (4) recognition-granters (including formal and informal, state and non-state actors) (see Clément et al. in this volume).

Recognition needs and recognition claims of selected conflict groups

Boko Haram

Boko Haram is a Salafi-jihadi insurgent group that is driven by a radical religious ideology. It is an Islamic purist movement that seeks to overthrow the Nigerian secular state and instate a strict Sharia system of governance. It operates mainly in the northeast of Nigeria, across the northwest and middle belt states, and across the Lake Chad Basin countries including the Republics of Niger, Chad and Cameroon. Boko Haram is splintered into several factions, but the two most popular are Ansaru (also known as Jamaʿatu Anṣar il-Muslimana fi Bilad, meaning: 'Vanguards for the Protection of Muslims in Black Africa'), established in 2012, and the Islamic State in West African Province (ISWAP) (since August 2016).

Boko Haram's core motivation has always been to establish a Shariah state – an ambitious project that is not novel in that region, starting from the successful jihad of Ibn Sheikh Dan Fodio (1804–1808).[1] Boko Haram follows in the tradition of puritan religious organisations in northern Nigeria that have risen to challenge the existing traditional religious authority, often with the aim of correcting what the challengers perceive to be a deviation from the pristine ideal of worship based solely on the Qur'an, Hadith and Sunnah of the Holy Prophet Muhammad. Boko Haram emerged officially in 2002 but there is evidence to suggest it actually started in the mid-1990s as a splinter group from the Izala (formally Jama'at Izalat al-Bid'a Wa Iqamat as Sunna, Society of Removal of Innovation and Re-establishment of the Sunna) – a major reformist but liberal Islamic group that emerged in the 1970s to challenge the dominant Sufi brotherhood for their perceived *bid'a* (innovation). Boko Haram started as a social movement, denounced polytheism and claimed that the political and religious elites in Nigeria, especially northern Nigeria, were morally bankrupt and religiously corrupt (Kassim and Nwankpa 2018). Although it sought an Islamic state, this goal was only aspirational and less grandiose than its pursuit since 2009, and more so, in 2014 when it followed in the footsteps of ISIS to gain territorial control. Boko Haram sought initially to escape the control of the Nigerian secular state and the 'corrupt' leadership of conservative Islamic authority (the leadership of the Sokoto Caliphate) in northern Nigeria, rather than confront the 'corrupt' state. As such, Boko Haram seeks to establish its unique religious identity outside the conventional religious model. Thus, Boko Haram seeks to be recognised as the authentic source of religious (Islamic) ideals in Nigeria (see Nwankpa 2015). By extension, it will gain political power as religion and politics are intertwined in Islam. It started first using *da'wah* (preaching) and social welfare schemes to gain converts, but now uses coercion and violence.

Boko Haram's actions at these early stages seem to be within the purview of the Constitution that guarantees citizens religious freedom. The failure of the Nigerian security agencies to recognise and respect this right may have provoked and escalated Boko Haram's descent into violence and terrorism.

Niger Delta

The Niger Delta is home to Nigeria's oil wealth as well as several militant groups that have been carrying out insurgent activities since 2004. Some of the prominent militant groups in the Niger Delta include the Niger Delta People's Volunteer Force, Niger Delta Vigilante, Niger Delta Liberation Front and Niger Delta Avengers (this latter established in March 2016). The militant groups coordinate their activities under an umbrella organisation known as the Movement for the Emancipation of Niger Delta (MEND).

MEND represents the insurgent face of militancy and conflict in the region. The Niger Delta insurgents operate mainly in the south–south states of Nigeria, especially Rivers, Delta and Bayelsa states and across the Gulf Coast of Guinea.

The Niger Delta militants' activities are predicated on injustices and demands expressed in important political documents such as the *Ogoni Bill of Rights* (1995) and the *Kaiama Declaration* (1998).The militant groups are united around common themes that are more economically driven, including self-determination, resource control (mainly oil), economic autonomy, equitable resource distribution, political inclusion, and environmental protection from the pollution and degradation caused by the activities (including oil spillage) of multinational oil companies operating in the region. The insurgents' modes of attack include piracy, kidnapping and hostage-taking, ambush, oil theft/bunkering, oil pipeline vandalisation, and bombing of oil facilities and infrastructure. There is little evidence of deliberate attacks on the public – including civilians and their property – unlike Boko Haram. The targets of attacks include oil executives and workers – foreign and local alike – cargo and passenger vessels around the Gulf Coast, oil installations and infrastructure, and the Nigerian joint task force – a coalition of special forces comprising the Nigerian army, navy, air force and other security agencies. There may be up to 50,000 members or more, of which the majority are from the Ijaw ethnic group, the fourth largest ethnic group in Nigeria.

The Niger Delta struggle revolves around two objectives. First, there is a claim directed at the federal government to recognise the region's ownership and control of its resources. In this sense, the Niger Delta people, rather than the Nigerian federal government, should be the custodian of the resources. The second objective seeks development of the region, environmental protection, political inclusion and higher revenue redistribution that recognises the region's central role as the economic powerhouse of the country (80 per cent of Nigeria's revenue is based on oil).

IPOB

IPOB is one of several secessionist groups that have emerged in the southeast region of Nigeria since the end of the bitter civil war (1967–1970) between Nigeria and its breakaway state Biafra, under the leadership of Nnamdi Kanu. It is largely made up of Igbo youths. Like its predecessor (or parallel group), the Movement for the Actualisation of the Sovereign State of Biafra, IPOB is a separatist group fighting for the resurgence of the defunct Biafra Republic. IPOB believes the Igbos are 'under occupation, servitude and modern day slavery under the Hausa-Fulani controlled Nigerian establishment'.[2] IPOB is therefore motivated by a perceived sense of injustice and marginalisation of the Igbo ethnic group in Nigeria's socio-economic and political space. It seeks to exercise its right to be recognised as an independent state by pursuing self-determination and right to statehood.

IPOB's activities, which are mostly non-violent, include marches, civil disobedience (by abstaining from elections and voting), media propaganda (especially through its online radio network, Radio Biafra, and social media), establishment of diplomatic missions in different countries, and demand for a referendum to decide the Igbo's independence from the Nigerian state. IPOB enjoys mass support, particularly among the majority of Igbo youths, both home and abroad, but has less appeal and support among the Igbo political and religious elites (particularly the Ohaneze,[3] an umbrella organisation that was established to promote and protect the interests of the Igbo ethnic group).

Fulani militia

The Fulani militia is made up largely of semi-nomads – a family of pastoralist ethnic groups with a significant number (up to 15 million people) living in Nigeria's middle belt states. The Fula/Fulani people are mostly Muslims. Since 2000, there have been several vicious and brutal clashes between Fulani herdsmen and farmers, mostly northerners of other ethnicities. The clashes have often been over economic resources such as grazing areas, farmlands and water, with the farmers accusing the herdsmen of damaging their crops and the herders accusing the local farmers of stealing their cattle. The conflicts have been exacerbated by growing climate change leading to desertification and the drying up of Lake Chad (an important source of water and resources to the region), which has seen the herders travelling southwards in search of pasture and water for their cattle.

The context remains the same, but the dynamics of the conflict have increased as the economic motivation has become mixed with political and religious dimensions. The Miyetti Allah Cattle Breeders Association of Nigeria – an umbrella advocacy group (with powerful patrons including top government and religious leaders including the Sultan of Sokoto, the spiritual head of Muslims in Nigeria) that oversees the welfare of the herdsmen – has been accused of supporting violence and terrorism. However, it maintains that, at best, the herdsmen are victims and are only reacting to attacks by bandits, and, at worst, the perpetrators are not its members but infiltrators from outside the country. Nevertheless, the Fulani militia has become more lethal in its attacks, often accused of using sophisticated weapons and engaging in criminal and terrorist activities. The group was considered one of the top five most lethal terrorist groups in 2015 (Global Terrorism Index, 2015).

(Mis-)Recognition processes of Boko Haram, Niger Delta, IPOB and Fulani militia

This section focuses on the recognition processes of the four selected groups. Table 3.1 shows their motivation or recognition struggle, the level of popular support, the forms of recognition received and the identity of the recognition-granter.

Boko Haram

2009 marked a watershed in the trajectory of Jama'at Ahl as-Sunnah li-l-Da'wah wa-l-Jihad ('Group of the People of Sunnah for Preaching and Jihad'), commonly known as Boko Haram. In the summer of that year, the Nigerian military clashed with Boko Haram in a gun battle that lasted for three days, leading to the death of up to 800 Boko Haram members, the destruction of Boko Haram's mosque-cum-centre, and the arrest and extra-judicial killing of its founder, Mohammed Yusuf while under police custody.

The murder of Yusuf is widely accepted as the turning point for Boko Haram and marked its transformation to full-blown insurgency (see Johnson 2011; Walker 2012). Up until this time, Boko Haram had been perceived as any other reformist social movement or group but with criminal intentions (to Nigeria's security forces). It emerged in 2010 under a much more ruthless leader, Abubakar Shekau, Yusuf's former deputy. Boko Haram tendered a set of demands that included justice for the unlawful killing of its leader (through prosecution of those responsible), release of its detained members and their family members, and to be left alone to practise its own religion.

In order to discredit the valid claims of Boko Haram and emphasise the group's clandestine nature, Nigeria's former president Goodluck Jonathan famously said in 2013: 'You cannot declare amnesty for ghosts. Boko Haram operates like ghosts.' The Nigerian government typically shunned dialogue and negotiation and responded with force, by setting up a joint task force. Jonathan's administration established a State of Emergency in three core northeast states – Borno, Adamawa and Yobe (1 May 2013–20 November 2014) – during which the military perpetrated its worst human rights violations, including collective punishment on the northeast youth for their perceived support of Boko Haram (Amnesty International, 2014).

In 2013, Nigeria proscribed Boko Haram under its 2011 anti-terror Act and established a regional counterterrorism multinational joint task force comprising armies of Nigeria, Niger, Chad, Cameroon and Republic of Benin. The United States and the United Kingdom blacklisted Boko Haram in the same year. Other countries such as Australia and the European Union proscribed Boko Haram in 2014 following the group's kidnap of 276 boarding

Table 3.1 Recognition matrix for Boko Haram, Niger Delta, IPOB and Fulani militia

Metrics	Boko Haram	Niger Delta	IPOB	Fulani militia
Type of recognition struggle	• Fundamentalist, Islamist	• Redistribution / resource control	• Secessionist / self-determination / separatist	• Redistribution / resource (land) control
Population support	• High mass support (2002–2012) • Low/tacit/coerced support (2012–to date)	• High mass support 1995–2009 • Significant (but not very high) support from 2009 onwards	• Mixed population support, but significant level of support from the youth	• Strong support among ethnic group (Hausa/Fulani, Miyetti Allah Cattle Breeders Association of Nigeria)
Forms of (mis-/non-) recognition	• Criminal group • Terrorist organisation • Excessive military response (joint task force, multinational joint task force) • Dialogue and negotiation • (ISIS) franchise	• Development commissions (redistribution through derivation principle) • Militants • Force (joint task force) • Creation of Ministry of Niger Delta • Amnesty	• Military occupation • Proscription as a terrorist organisation • Unlawful arrests and detentions	• Silence (tacit support from the federal government) • Anti-grazing laws by some state governments (Benue and Ekiti state) • Reprisal attacks
Identity of recognition-granter	• Nigerian government • Traditional and religious leaders • Islamic scholars • ISIS • Al-Qaeda	• Nigerian government • Multinational oil companies • International community	• Nigerian government • Igbo traditional rulers (Ohanezes)	• Nigerian government (federal and state) • Farmers

Source: the author.

school girls in the Chibok local government area in Borno state. However, since 2014 Nigeria has applied other non-violent approaches, including use of counter-narrative, deradicalisation programmes, economic revitalisation strategies (such as the Presidential Initiative for the Northeast, Victim Support Fund and Safe School Fund) and negotiation (as seen in the successful release of many of the kidnapped Chibok girls and all but five of the kidnapped Dapchi girls).[4]

In 2015, Abubakar Shekau pledged allegiance to Abu Bakr al-Baghdadi, the then leader of ISIS (killed by the United States Special Force in 2019). Boko Haram became recognised as an ISIS franchise and rebranded as the Islamic State in West African Province. However, in 2016 ISIS deposed Abubakar Shekau as leader of ISWAP, causing it to splinter into two groups: the Shekau-led Boko Haram and al-Barnawi-led ISWAP.

It is also noteworthy that the northern religious and political elites have maintained a somewhat ambivalent attitude towards Boko Haram. On the one hand, in the pre-insurgent period (2006–2009), and especially at the early period of the insurgency (2009–2012), the northern Islamic scholars challenged Boko Haram's Islamic perversion and even assisted the authorities in their counterinsurgent operations (Kassim and Nwankpa 2018). This attracted a heavy backlash, as Boko Haram assassinated scores of Muslim clerics around this time. The northern conservative Muslim authority, the leadership of the defunct Sokoto Caliphate and the northern elites canvassed for amnesty for Boko Haram in 2013 and promoted the narrative that Boko Haram was a political creation of the southern-led presidency to undermine the geo-political interest of the north. This tacit recognition of Boko Haram as a legitimate struggle underscores the belief of Christians in Nigeria that Boko Haram conceals or at best parallels an underlying broad political agenda of the north to Islamise Nigeria in a bid to maintain its hegemonic control over other ethnic and religious groups.

Niger Delta

In the case of the Niger Delta, unlike Boko Haram, a development intervention pre-dates the military response and continues to be the main approach. The Niger Delta has long been recognised as a peculiar area needing special development intervention.[5] Despite the differences, both conflicts have attracted disproportionate use of military force by the Nigerian state. For the oil-related Niger Delta conflict, there is 'no simple or linear evolution in the pattern and dynamics' (Joab-Peterside et al. 2012: 6). However, the prevalent approach remains development strategies. It is therefore not surprising that over the years successive Nigerian governments have set up several development boards (such as the Niger Delta Development Board, 1963) and Presidential Commissions including the Oil and Mineral Producing Area Development Commission (1992), Niger Delta Development Commission (2000) and the Ministry of Niger Delta Affairs (2007), to address the peculiar development challenges faced by that region. The consequence of such development strategy was the constitutional establishment of the Derivation Principle that makes special monthly allocations to oil-producing states in the Niger Delta – since 1999 standing at 13 per cent of oil revenues (Udoh 2019: 81).

The government's soft approach towards the Niger Delta took a violent turn in the 1990s. The military regime of General Sani Abacha (1993–1998) responded harshly to the non-violent campaign by the Movement for the Survival of the Ogoni People (MOSOP) against environmental degradation of Niger Delta land and waters by multinational oil companies operating in the region and to criticism of the government's poor regulation of the operations of the oil companies. The campaign was led by Ken Saro-Wiwa and other leaders from Ogoni ethnic minority groups through MOSOP in 1995. The Niger Delta struggle (through MOSOP at this time) received international support from international non-governmental organisations such as the Unrepresented Nations and People Organisation, Greenpeace International and Amnesty International. However, Ken Saro-Wiwa and the eight Ogoni leaders were executed in 1995 after a farcical trial conducted by the brutal regime of General Abacha. MOSOP and other groups and movements (including the press and other instruments of democracy such as the Constitution) across the country protesting the repressive regime of General Abacha were banned.

MOSOP's influence was undercut by the death of its leader, but another group, the Ijaw Youth Council, comprising mainly the Ijaw ethnic minority group, picked up the struggle. Like MOSOP, the activities of the Ijaw Youth Council were largely peaceful and non-violent. Nonetheless, the government responded militarily. For instance, in 2001 President Obasanjo ordered the military invasion of Odi, a small town in Bayelsa state, leading to the massacre of up to 2000 civilians, including women and children, and destruction of properties. Although the Niger Delta struggle remained largely non-violent until 2003, the militant groups embraced violence from 2004 until 2009, when the administration of President Umaru Musa Yar'Adua offered amnesty in 2009 to roughly 30,000 Niger Delta militants who surrendered their weapons in return for a monthly stipend from the government and educational training.

The amnesty programme significantly reduced violence in the region until the end of 2015 when the programme was coming to its end. President Buhari's new administration threatened not to extend the amnesty programme funding, leading to the resumption of oil installation attacks and emergence of new groups such as the Niger Delta Avengers. However, the government quickly opened a dialogue with the militants to prevent a full-scale recommencement of insurgency. Nonetheless, the joint task force remains a visible presence in the region and often clashes with insurgent groups and activities that have been degraded to mere criminality.

IPOB

IPOB seems to provide the lowest security threat but nonetheless has attracted a heavy-handed response from the Nigerian government. Some of the government's security responses include using tear gas and live ammunition on unarmed IPOB protesters and rioters; unlawful arrest and detention of IPOB members, including its leader, Nnamdi Kanu; military occupation of Biafran states ('Operation Python'); an unsuccessful attempt to shut down Radio Biafra, which is sited in the United Kingdom; and the proscription of the group as a terrorist group. The heavy-handed approach by the administration of President Buhari, a Fulani, provides incentive for IPOB to evoke the Biafran legacy and cast its unfair treatment as Hausa/Fulani bias against the Igbos.

The ugly memory of the Nigerian–Biafran civil war (including the death of millions of Igbo people) and the perception of persistent unjust treatment of the Igbos continue to haunt the present and hurt relations between the ethnicities in Nigeria. The present administration's response to IPOB departs hugely from that of General Gowon's post-civil war government. The federal forces' victory after three years of bitter civil war with Biafran separatists in 1970 was followed by the establishment of the demobilisation, disarmament and reintegration (DDR) programme constructed as the 3Rs: 'reconciliation', 'rehabilitation' and 'reconstruction'.

Nigeria's post-civil war peace policy is considered successful by some observers because of its perceived non-discriminatory and targeted response to the structural conditions that caused the civil war (Paden 2005; Stremlau 1977). Aided by the oil revenue windfall of the 1970s, the government was able to conduct targeted and deliberate economic reconstruction, across the whole country (not just in the Biafran states) taking cognisance of the ethnic fissures and special social cleavages. The federal military government's approach is a deliberate response to the perceived source of the civil war, a political past characterised by 'believed oppositions, of dissent and distrust' (Kirk-Greene 1971: 109; see also Jega 2000).

The post-civil war policies were also not without criticism. For example, the Indigenisation Decree of 1972 strategically disempowered and marginalised the Biafrans (largely Igbos), as the lack of recognition for their currency excluded them from the Nigerian economy, hence giving other ethnic groups unfair advantage. Ojeleye (2010) therefore argues that 'the DDR exercise, though presented under the guise of justice and fairness, had inbuilt in it seeds that prevented the establishment of a harmonious inter-group relations in the country' (Ojeleye 2010: 163; see also Ibrahim 2000). IPOB is therefore a consequence of the failure of Nigeria to establish a national identity that integrates all of the nation's diversities. Although it is non-violent and bottom of the scale among the four selected case studies (in the use of violence against the state), it has attracted the negative label of terrorism, while the Fulani militia has avoided any labelling, despite its egregious attacks on civilian lives and properties.

Fulani militia

In the case of the Fulani militia, the Nigerian government, especially under the administration of President Buhari, a Fulani man, has been deemed complicit for its reluctance to condemn the group and even proscribe it, despite the viciousness of its widespread attacks and public outcry. Fulani militia was considered the fourth largest terror group in the world in 2014 (Global Terrorism Index 2015). Yet, the government's response ranges from silence to denial. The clashes between the Fulani herdsmen and the farmers in Nigeria are long-standing, yet delineating the Fulani militia remains a difficult task. As suggested by Matfess (2018: 1), 'Fulani militias are not a centralised armed group operating under a specific agenda'. In essence, the Fulani militia's violence, unlike Boko Haram, Niger Delta and IPOB's, is not directed towards the Nigerian state. This argument is legitimate considering for instance the fact that the inter-communal rivalry and clashes between the Niger Delta ethnicities of Ijaw and Itsekiri, and between rival militant groups, did not weaken the Niger Delta struggle. The plethora of competing Niger Delta militant groups united under MEND to challenge the Nigerian state.

Yet, one cannot disregard the influence of the patrons of the Miyetti Allah. The Fulani militia/herders have powerful northern elites as patrons. The herdsmen work for these patrons, who own large stocks of the cattle. One can therefore understand the pacifist approach by the Buhari administration and of the northern oligarch. However, the government's attitude towards the Fulani militia may shift as it becomes increasingly difficult to defend a group that is employing sophisticated weaponry in its widespread and growing systematic acts of terror against civilian targets. The Fulani militia may be finally channelling its violence against the state. It has spread beyond its middle belt theatre of operation to virtually every state in Nigeria, sparking fear and accusations of a northern ploy to Islamise Nigeria and extend hegemonic control. This has caused reprisal attacks. Contrary to the federal government's weak response, some affected state governments such as Ekiti and Benue have passed Anti-Grazing laws that seek to curb the activities of the herdsmen.

Impact of labelling conflict groups in Nigeria

By labelling the groups as criminals, militants, insurgents and terrorists, the Nigerian state justifies the use of varying force and violence, depending on the label. Violence is the preferred approach used by the state to counter perceived and real threats presented by the criminalised or proscribed group. All of the selected groups, with the exception of the Fulani herdsmen (who have avoided any official label, despite massive evidence of gruesome and terrorist attacks), have attracted some form of violent response from the state – further fuelling distrust among the ethnic groups. A militarised (hard) approach to conflict resolution has a strong potential to escalate conflict and this is true in the Nigerian cases.

Although there are similarities in the consequences engendered by the overly military response to the conflict groups, there are noticeable differences that manifest in the patterns and dynamics of the responses, including the state and insurgent responses. In the Niger Delta, more military responses against the Ijaw group from 1998 to 2003 only led to the proliferation of militant groups in the region and produced hardened and resilient insurgents. Hence, from 2004 until 2009, when the government offered amnesty to militants who surrendered their arms, the Nigerian state endured a systematic attack on its major source of revenue – oil. While political dialogue, activism and non-violent peaceful demonstrations had been applied by the Niger Delta movements from 1998–2003), from 2004 to 2009, the struggle turned violent. This coincided with the emergence of armed groups such as MEND. Evidently, the military response to the Niger Delta crisis has produced very little impact in hurting the capacity and capabilities of the Niger Delta militants.

Unlike the Niger Delta, the military approach towards Boko Haram has produced some positive results. The joint task force, established in 2011, recorded a relative success in curbing Boko Haram's ambitious spread outside its northeast hotspot zone between 2011 and 2013. During this period, Boko Haram attacked targets outside its northeast epicentre including Abuja, the federal capital territory, northwestern states such as Kaduna, Kano and Sokoto, and north central states such as Kogi and Plateau. Likewise, since proscribing Boko Haram as a terrorist group, the multinational joint task force has played a vital role in defeating Boko Haram's more ambitious agenda: territorial control. However, between 2014 and 2015, Boko Haram had a brief success in seizing and controlling a substantial land mass in northeastern Nigeria.

Boko Haram's trajectory towards terrorist strategies since 2012, including near daily attacks on civilians and public places, largely justifies the Nigerian government's prohibition and the legitimate use of force against members of the group. In this sense, the military response to terrorism remains important. Yet, its effectiveness seems to be guaranteed within the framework of multilateral or inter-agency cooperation, as evidenced by the brief counterterrorism victory that Nigeria enjoyed over Boko Haram under the multinational joint task force. A militarised approach, especially one pursued unilaterally, presents a huge risk of escalating and protracting violent conflict (Crenshaw 2002; Kiras 2007; Schmid 2005a). States fighting terrorism are required to 'maintain the moral high-ground in the struggle with terrorists by defending and strengthening the rule of law, good governance, democracy and social justice' (Schmid 2005b: 144). There seems to be a higher chance of achieving this in a multilateral or inter-agency counterterrorism alliance than a unilateral arrangement. This perhaps partly explains why the military failed in countering the Niger Delta insurgency.

In the first instance, the military response to the largely non-violent Niger Delta struggle was inappropriate. The military, in this instance, was used as an instrument of the state and as a force of occupation with a self-serving interest: to protect the profitable venture controlled by the state in alliance with the multinational oil companies. The heavy-handed approach used by the military and the militarisation of the Niger Delta region were encouraged by the state and the oil companies. In essence, the political economy is a higher priority in the Niger Delta than the Boko Haram conflict.

In the Boko Haram conflict, the Nigerian military gained an unlikely partnership with the civilian joint task force, a coalition of northeast Nigerian youths that had self-organised to combat the twin attacks from Boko Haram and the hostile Nigerian military. The joint effort by the Nigerian military and the (unfortunately) militarised local youths has yielded huge counterterrorism gain, but this partnership must be seen as one of convenience and necessity, as the local youths and the military united against a common enemy – Boko Haram.

The alliance between the military and the civilian joint task force creates a problem of its own, as the latter is highly militarised. There is genuine concern that the civilian joint task force could become a future security threat, especially in the absence of good governance and socio-economic opportunities, and having exercised power (in the absence of traditional power structures -that have been involuntarily sacked by the Boko Haram conflict). It is unclear what alternative source of power and livelihood the government will offer members of the civilian joint task force when the military campaign against Boko Haram is no longer necessary. The vigilante group may be motivated by the material gains made by Boko Haram through violent struggle, and come to believe that only through violent engagement with the Nigerian state can it gain a better deal (not forgetting the collective measurements carried out against the youth by the Nigerian military). Perhaps the Nigerian government will offer the civilian joint task force a similar amnesty deal to that given to the leaders of Niger Delta. Arjona and Kalyvas (2009) find grievance to be constant for both rebel groups and counterinsurgent groups, but significantly find counterinsurgent groups to be more attracted to greed – both material and non-material inducement. Interestingly, as part of the amnesty deal the leaders of the Niger Delta militant groups received big money contracts that included securing oil infrastructure in exchange for preventing insurgency in the region. In essence, both material and non-material rewards may be useful incentives for checking the threat that the civilian joint task force presents as the insurgency winds down.

However, violence has not disappeared in the Niger Delta. Although the scale of violence is often under-reported, there has been a resurgence, particularly in 2015, with the fear that the Buhari administration might follow through with its threat not to renew the amnesty contract that came to an end that year. In this sense, although the Niger Delta amnesty has been lauded as one of the most successful non-military approaches to the Niger Delta insurgency and has been cited as a model and inspiration for a proposed Boko Haram amnesty (see Onuoha 2012; Yusuf 2013), it is little more than a pay-out to militants, and hence a reward to insurgency and disregard of the plight of the victims (Nwankpa 2014; Sampson 2013). In the end, the leaders of the camp enriched themselves by appropriating the amnesty contract money for the whole group. This led to a second agitation (which was successful) and an unsuccessful third-phase bid which continues to resurface, as evidenced by the rise of militancy and militant groups in the Niger Delta. Amnesty appears to be politicised (Nwankpa 2014). It sends important messages to other conflict groups that violence, and violence alone, can force the Nigerian government to the negotiating table, as indicated by the recent negotiations between the Nigerian government and Boko Haram. Additionally, the failure to address the underlying development issues continues to provide the incentive for the rise of insurgency in the region.

To a large extent, the offer of amnesty to the Niger Delta militants brought about relative peace. However, the Nigerian government, particularly under the administration of President Goodluck Jonathan, failed to tempt Boko Haram with an amnesty offer. Arguably, the extreme positions taken by both conflict actors stalled any chance of compromise. For the Nigerian government, Boko Haram is a terrorist group and cannot be negotiated with. More so, President Jonathan's administration was confounded by the clandestine nature of the group and lack of a unified body (like MEND, in the case of Niger Delta) with which to create a dialogue. For Boko Haram, its unreasonable objective of instating Sharia in Nigeria's secular state makes the Niger Delta-styled amnesty undesirable. Conceivably, it is more rewarding to ask if the absence of a unified front rather than difficult, incoherent and impossible demands presents a more plausible explanation for why a Boko Haram amnesty failed to find traction. This is more tenable for a clandestine group such as Boko Haram. Even for an economically driven insurgent group such as Niger Delta, the amnesty has generated no little criticism. However, Boko Haram's release of some of the kidnapped Chibok girls shows that dialogue and negotiating with 'terrorists' can have rewards (Nwankpa 2017). Undoubtedly, it does send a signal to other conflict groups that violence pays, but it creates room for negotiating and navigating the end of the insurgency.

However, the proscription of IPOB as a terrorist group and the palpable silence and indifference of the Buhari-led administration over the rampant killings committed by Fulani militants across the country reveal a profound political economy. In the case of the Fulani herdsmen, the absence of a strong response from the federal government to the blatant attacks on civilians is in sharp contradistinction to its typical response to the other conflicts and to less provocative disturbances. The fact that President Buhari belongs to the Fulani ethnic group and the long-held belief that the northern political elites (primarily of the Hausa/Fulani ethnic group) hold a hegemonic claim and right of political authority over the other ethnicities work to sustain the presumption of biased response to several conflict situations in Nigeria. The Buhari administration has been accused by governors of the most affected states (such as Benue and Ekiti) and other prominent people in Nigeria, such as former general Theophilus Danjuma, of deliberately shirking from its primary responsibility of protecting the lives of every Nigerian citizen. The Nigerian military has been accused of supporting the government's selective response to conflict.

The government has refused to label the Fulani militants as terrorists or even insurgents, despite the group's brazen catastrophic attacks on civilians. Yet, it wasted no time in proscribing IPOB. The government's inaction towards the criminal activities of Fulani militants has emboldened the group, as signified by its near daily attacks and spread across all geo-political zones. In the case of IPOB, the Nigerian government's proscription delegitimises the group, including its legitimate claims of political and economic marginalisation and exclusion of the Igbos. The action also legalises the excessive use of force denoted by 'Operation Python', the military's operational name for the occupation of several southeast states.

Operation Python saw the military invasion of the southeast states and a heavy clampdown on the peaceful gathering and activism of IPOB, leading also to the sudden disappearance of IPOB's leader. Under the military occupation in the southeast and in the absence of its leader, IPOB lost the strong momentum it had gained, symbolised by the mixed response to the 30 May 2018 sit-at-home order to citizens of the southeast in honour of the fallen heroes of the Biafran civil war. Since Nnamdi Kanu resurfaced in Tel Aviv, Israel, IPOB's struggle has gained fresh momentum, following Kanu's outlandish claim that President Buhari died while receiving treatment in London and that the person parading as the president of Nigeria is a clone or Buhari's body double, a Jubril from Sudan. IPOB has also issued instructions to its members to boycott the 2019 general election. The use of force towards IPOB has not been effective so far. Rather, it presents the risk of escalation and pushing it to embrace violence. To date, IPOB has maintained a non-violent but very effective strategy in its struggle for self-determination.

The Nigerian state's approach to conflict resolution and its ramifications

The Nigerian state typically relies on violence and aggression as a counter-force and response to conflicts and security threats in the country. It is not surprising that Nigeria experienced one of the deadliest civil wars of the twentieth century – the Nigerian–Biafra civil war (1967–1970). Nigeria also has a long history of repressive military regimes that has created a psyche and cycle of violence demonstrated by its elites and civil society alike (Akinrinade 2006). Moreover, the Nigerian political class may have inherited an absolutist state structure from the colonial government and has since perfected the craft of violence through the politicisation of ethnic and other primordial identities to the detriment of development (Ake 1996; Falola 2009). Hence, the nature of the Nigerian state tends towards the production of tension and conflict between state and society (Omeje 2007).

Despite the predominant hardliner approach, there is evidence of affirmative actions taken by the Nigerian political class to minimise the tension and problems caused by ethnic, religious and political conflicts that have doggedly defined the Nigerian landscape. In Nigeria, as in many other African pluralist and even non-African pluralist states, the elites from the different ethnic groups have adopted the principle of consociationalism – that is, the use of constitutions and constitutional/institutional arrangements as a political technology that accommodates the rights and concerns of the various ethnic compositions with the view of eliminating ethnic domination and determining patterns of authority (Jinadu 1985; Kuperman 2015; Lijphart 1969; Suberu and Diamond 2002).

Consociationalism involves the use of affirmative actions to achieve a balance of power among different groups in a plural society. Usually, these take any of these forms: 'grand coalition', 'mutual veto', 'proportionality' and 'segmental autonomy' (Lijphart 1969). In Nigeria, the political elites have applied the quota system and proportional representation as consociational measures that guarantee appointment for certain numbers of an ethnic group. As Fraser (1995) rightly notes, affirmative strategies produce a high potential for recognition backlash. In Nigeria, while there has been useful progress, this conflict-regulating mechanism has also yielded negative tendencies such that consociation becomes a conflict-generating tool as well. Some of the limitations of consociation in Nigeria include a do-or-die (zero-sum game) attitude to politics largely owing to the highly centralised nature of the Nigerian state and a flagrant disregard of the rule of law by political opponents that seek the total annihilation of one another.

The politics of identity, largely primordial identities of ethnicity and religion, has remained defiant against consociation efforts (including the principle of 'federal character' that aims at ethnic balance in federal appointments) by Nigerian political elites. There is a self-absorbing and damaging consciousness of identities that yield a strong predilection towards centrifugal rather than centripetal ideals such that ethnicity, religion and regionalism form the tool for mobilising, organising and contesting access to state power (Ekeh 1975; Jega 2000; Oshita 2007; Ukiwo 2003).

The affirmative actions taken towards the conflict groups in Nigeria may have failed to produce an enduring solution because they are mis-recognised as 'compensatory measures', rather than recognised as rights. For example, Abubakar Shekau rejected amnesty for the group as proposed by the Goodluck administration. According to Shekau, 'surprisingly, the Nigerian government is talking about granting us amnesty, what wrong have we done? On the contrary, it is we that should grant you [a] pardon.'[6] One of my interviewees, the leader of the Partnership against Violent Extremism, a coalition of civil society organisations, posits that the 'amnesty programme defeated its aims, led to the army [and] the consolidation of arms'.[7] The underlying development issues are still unaddressed and leave room for future conflict, as evidenced by the rise of new militant groups such as the Niger Delta Avengers in 2016. Another possible reason is the fact that development itself is a façade exploited by the political elites as a means of reproducing political control (Ake 1996) and accumulating wealth (Omeje 2007; Ukiwo 2003).

For instance, the Niger Delta amnesty and the negotiation between the Nigerian government and Boko Haram for the release of over a hundred kidnapped Chibok girls in 2017 exemplify the kind of affirmative measures that yield only short-term gain. It was evident that the Chibok girls represented a bargaining tool for Boko Haram (Nwankpa 2017). The Nigerian government had to negotiate as its military, despite reconnaissance and military assistance from several world powers, failed to rescue the girls. However, Boko Haram gained more and yielded less in the negotiation with the Nigerian government, despite having suffered significant loss at the hands of the Nigerian military with the regional coalition force. Boko Haram received a substantial amount of money plus release of some of its detained senior commandants. Besides securing the release of some of the Chibok girls, the Nigerian government gained little in the negotiation. The government failed to force Boko Haram to abandon its ambition and acts of terrorism. The government should have compelled Boko Haram to pursue any legitimate claims within established political structures. Therefore, it is not surprising that Boko Haram, despite its internal division and in-fighting, has increased its attacks in the region.

Conclusion

The Nigerian case studies present unique dynamism but underlying each of the selected conflict groups is the Nigerian state penchant for violence. The use of militarised force for quelling civil disturbances is a common thread that joins together Boko Haram, Niger Delta, IPOB, and all other conflict groups and situations in Nigeria. Although violence is deeply embedded into the state's security response strategy, the use of violence is often supported, in most cases, through a deliberate demonisation or criminalisation of a group's struggle. In some rare cases and instances such as with Boko Haram, the prohibition of the group and use of special force are justified. Yet, one can arguably posit that the Nigerian state's initial mis-recognition of Boko Haram's religious claim and, particularly, its use of excessive force may have pushed Boko Haram into terrorism. Even if Boko Haram had, from the start, the grand ambition to pursue jihad and overthrow the Nigerian secular state, a better approach from the Nigerian state could have de-escalated the tension. The same is true for the Niger Delta case and instructional in the direction that IPOB will take in the future.

Interestingly, the non-violent or affirmative responses such as the Niger Delta amnesty and negotiations with Boko Haram also portend serious consequences, as seen by the continued militant and terrorist activities of these groups. Just as the militarised approach escalated the conflict and transformed them into insurgent and terrorist organisations, the non-kinetic approaches continue to inspire and hold the potential to inspire greed and the emergence of violent groups. In the absence of transformative strategies which will ultimately involve addressing the structural conditions and root causes (including political exclusion, economic marginalisation, religious freedom, social mobility and good governance), conflict groups will only multiply and increase in intensity. One can identify a common strand in the Boko Haram, Niger Delta, IPOB and even Fulani herders' conflict – a struggle for resources that involves scarcity and distribution. While this is prominent in the Niger Delta and even Fulani militia cases, it is less so with Boko Haram. Its extremist religious motivation undercuts its struggle for resources.

Perhaps there is a strong motivation for the Nigerian state not to remove the structural conditions and to favour the use of force. Mis-recognition of a group's struggle and/or mislabelling it delegitimises the 'genuine' claims of the group and serves to justify the use of excessive force (with no accountability from the state). Also, the variance in the recognition of the different conflict groups by the Nigerian political class may be calculated to pit them against one another and prevent them from forming a coalition of the oppressed. In this way, the struggles cannot be organised as a class conflict but divided along different identities, mainly ethnicity and religion.

Notes

1 'Northern Nigeria is characterised by a long history of religious contestations between different Islamic sects whereby, once in a while, starting from the nineteenth century Jihad of Dan Fodio, you get a leader or group of people who rise up in the effort to purify Islam, to reject impurities in Islam, to expand its scope and take it to those areas where it does not exist', interview respondent: Baba Ahmed (member of the 2013 Presidential Committee on the Northeast), 13 January 2014. Boko Haram follows this tradition.

2 See 'About us', IPOB, available online: www.ipob.org/p/blog-page_18.html; last retrieved 19 February 2020.

3 The Ohaneze is the elite Igbo socio-cultural ethnic organisation that negotiates and promotes the Igbo's geo-political interests and oversees their affairs. It is similar to other regionalist groups such as Afenifere (for the Yoruba ethnic group) and Arewa Consultative Forum (for the Hausa-Fulani).

4 On 14 April 2014, Boko Haram successfully kidnapped around 276 boarding school girls in the Chibok area of Borno state. After two years in captivity, Boko Haram released a set of 21 girls (August 2016) and another 82 (October 2016), following negotiation with the Nigerian government. On 19 February 2018, ISWAP, a Boko Haram faction, kidnapped 110 girls from a Government Girls' Science ND Technical College in Dapchi, Yobe state. ISWAP released all but five of the Dapchi girls.

5 The pre-Independence Report prepared by Sir Henry Willink, Her Majesty's representative in Nigeria, identified the Niger Delta region as a 'Special Area' requiring special development intervention (Willink 1958).

6 Audio statement made by Shekau, April 2013.

7 Jaye Gaskia, 15 March 2016.

References

Ake, C. (1996), *Is Africa Democratising?* (Lagos: Malthouse Press).

Akinrinade, S. (2006), 'An army of ex-presidents: transitions, the military and democratic consolidation in Nigeria', in H. Melber and R. Southall (eds), *Legacies of Power: Leadership Change and Former Presidents in African Politics* (Uppsala: Nordic Africa Institute), pp. 281–307.

Amnesty International (2014), *More than 1,500 Killed in Armed Conflict in North-eastern Nigeria in Early 2014* (London: Amnesty International).

Arjona, A. and S. N. Kalyvas (2009), 'Rebelling against rebellion: comparing insurgent and counterinsurgent recruitment', Paper presented at *Human Security and Ethnicity Workshop: Mobilisation for Political Violence. What Do We Know?*, Centre for Research on Inequality 4, 436–55.

Crenshaw, M. (2002), 'The psychology of terrorism: an agenda for the 21st century', *Political Psychology* 21:2, 405–420.

Ekeh, P. P. (1975), 'Colonialism and the two publics in Africa: a theoretical statement', *Comparative Studies in Society and History* 17:1, 91–112.

Falola, T. (2009), *Colonialism and Violence in Nigeria* (Bloomington, IN and Indianapolis, IN: Indiana University Press).

Fraser, N. (1995), 'From redistribution to recognition? Dilemmas of justice in a "post-socialist" age', *New Left Review* 212, 68–93.

Global Terrorism Index (2015), 'Measuring and understanding the impact of terrorism', Institute for Economics and Peace, available online: http://economicsandpeace.org/wp-content/uploads/2015/11/Global-Terrorism-Index-2015.pdf; last retrieved 19 February 2020.

Ibrahim, J. (2000), 'The transformation of ethno-regional identities in Nigeria', in A. Jega (ed.), *Identity Transformation and Identity Politics under Structural Adjustment in Nigeria* (Uppsala: Nordic Africa Institute), pp. 41–61.

Jega, A. (2000), 'General introduction: identity transformation and the politics of identity under crisis and adjustment', in A. Jega (ed.), *Identity Transformation and Identity Politics under Structural Adjustment in Nigeria* (Uppsala: Nordic Africa Institute), pp. 11–23.

Jinadu, L. A. (1985), 'Federalism, the consociational state, and ethnic conflict in Nigeria', *Publius: The Journal of Federalism* 15:2, 71–100.

Joab-Peterside, S., D. Porter and M. Watts (2012), 'Rethinking conflict in the Niger Delta: understanding conflict dynamics, justice and security', *Niger Delta – Economies of Violence Working Papers* 26, 1–33.

Johnson, T. (2011), *Backgrounder: Boko Haram* (Washington, DC: Council on Foreign Relations).

Kassim, A. and M. Nwankpa (eds) (2018), *The Boko Haram Reader: From Nigerian Preachers to the Islamic State* (Oxford: Oxford University Press).

Kiras, James D. (2007) 'Irregular warfare: terrorism and insurgency', *Understanding Modern Warfare* 224, 186–207.

Kirk-Greene, A. H. M. (1971), *Crisis and Conflict in Nigeria: A Documentary Sourcebook 1966–1969* (Oxford: Oxford University Press).

Kuperman, A. J. (ed.) (2015), *Constitutions and Conflict Management in Africa: Preventing Civil War through Institutional Design* (Philadelphia, PA: University of Pennsylvania Press).

Lijphart, A. (1969), 'Consociational democracy', *World Politics* 21:2, 207–225.

Matfess, H. (2018), 'Fulani militias in Nigeria: declining violence not a sign of lasting peace', available online: https://reliefweb.int/report/nigeria/fulani-militias-nigeria-declining-violence-not-sign-lasting-peace (5 October); last retrieved 19 February 2020.

Nwankpa, M. (2014), 'The politics of amnesty in Nigeria: a comparative analysis of the Boko Haram and Niger Delta insurgencies', *Journal of Terrorism Research* 5:1, 67–77.

Nwankpa M. (2015), 'Boko Haram: whose Islamic State?', available online: www.bakerinstitute.org/research/boko-haram-whose-islamic-state (5 January); last retrieved 19 February 2020.

Nwankpa, M. (2017), 'Dialoguing and negotiating with terrorists: any prospect for Boko Haram?', *Behavioral Sciences of Terrorism and Political Aggression* 9:2, 106–124.

Ojeleye, O. (2010), *The Politics of Post-war Demobilisation and Reintegration in Nigeria* (Farnham: Ashgate Publishing Company).

Omeje, K. (2007), *State–Society Relations in Nigeria: Democratic Consolidation, Conflicts and Reforms* (London: Adonis & Abbey Publishers).

Onuoha, F. C. (2012), 'The audacity of the Boko Haram: background, analysis and emerging trend', *Security Journal*, 25:2, 134–151.

Oshita, O. O. (2007), *Conflict Management in Nigeria: Issues and Challenges* (London: Adonis & Abbey Publishers).

Paden, J. N. (2005), *Muslim Civic Cultures and Conflict Resolution: The Challenge of Democratic Federalism in Nigeria* (Washington, DC: Brookings Institution Press).

Sampson, I. T. (2013), 'The dilemmas of counter-Boko Haramism: debating state responses to Boko Haram terrorism in northern Nigeria', *Security Journal* 29:2, 122–146.

Schmid, A. P. (2005a), 'Root causes of terrorism: some conceptual notes, a set of indicators, and a model', *Democracy and Security* 1:2, 127–136.

Schmid, A. P. (2005b), 'Terrorism as psychological warfare', *Democracy and Security* 1:2, 137–146.

Stremlau, J. J. (1977), *The International Politics of the Nigerian Civil War, 1967–1970* (Princeton, NJ: Princeton University Press).

Suberu, R. and L. Diamond (2002), 'Institutional design, ethnic conflict management and democracy in Nigeria', in A. Reynolds (ed.), *The Architecture of Democracy: Constitutional Design, Conflict Management and Democracy* (Oxford: Oxford University Press), pp. 400–428.

Udo, E. (2019), 'Revenue allocation in Nigeria: implications for sustainable national development', *International Journal of Operational Research in Management* 5:1, 73–87.

Ukiwo, U. (2003), 'Politics, ethno-religious conflicts and democratic consolidation in Nigeria', *Journal of Modern African Studies* 41:1, 115–138.

Walker, A. (2012), 'What is Boko Haram?', *United States Institute of Peace Special Report* 308, 1–16.

Willink, H. (1958), *Report of the Commission Appointed to Enquire into the Fears of Minorities and the Means of Allaying Them* (London: HMSO).

Yusuf, H. O. (2013), 'Harvest of violence: the neglect of basic rights and the Boko Haram insurgency in Nigeria', *Critical Studies on Terrorism* 6:3, 371–391.

4

'Al-Shabaab is part of us': endogeneity and exogeneity in the struggle for recognition in Somalia

Harmonie Toros and Arrliya Sugal

A Somali peace practitioner stood up and in a soft-spoken manner said: 'When you say, "destroy al-Shabaab", you are speaking about destroying us. Al-Shabaab is part of Somali society. If you destroy al-Shabaab, you destroy us.' The large room in Mogadishu gathering senior Somali federal government officials, UN officials, senior diplomats, civil society practitioners, and academics working on Somalia, fell silent.

Introduction

This chapter examines the role of endogeneity and exogeneity in considerations of recognition of armed groups and the impact these can have on conflict transformation. It argues that the academic literature so far has focused – rightly – on recognition of a group's legitimacy and legality. Scholars have however largely overlooked the question of whether a group is recognised as being endogenous or exogenous to a conflict. This chapter examines how the question of being 'of us' or 'not of us' impacts on a group's recognition as part of the resolution of a conflict and worthy of inclusion in the process (Bartelson 2013). It will argue that there is no fixed place/idea (the nation-state, the community, the region) which an actor is recognised as being endogenous or exogenous to, but rather that this place/idea changes depending on the broader socio-political context as well as the discursive context of the iteration. As such, the chapter examines how endogeneity and exogeneity are used to recognise and mis-recognise actors – both state and non-state – and how this can affect the prospect and progress of conflict transformation.

The case of Somalia, and particularly of the conflict opposing the Federal Government of Somalia (FGS) and the non-state armed group (NSAG) al-Shabaab (aS), offers a complex but revealing case of why the endogenous/exogenous criterion needs to be considered as part of the recognition question. As will be discussed here, the question of whether actors are endogenous is not only applied to aS, with direct implications for whether aS is recognised as legitimate and how it is responded to. Indeed, in Somalia this question also applies to the federal state, which is regularly rejected as exogenous – in this case a puppet of foreign powers – by aS and other actors. We argue that in Somalia, both the state and the principal NSAG are recognition-seekers (and to a certain extent recognition-granters). As such, Somalia represents a revealing case study of how the question of endogeneity needs to be included as one of the elements constituting recognition in conflict situations. By analysing formal and informal statements by senior FGS and aS figures, we examine how discursive constructions of endogeneity and exogeneity are used in the conflict opposing, on the one side, the nascent Somali federal state backed by some foreign powers (the United States and the United Kingdom among others) and formal institutions of the international community (i.e. the United Nations and the African Union), and, on the other, al-Shabaab, backed by an overt and covert transnational network of foreign actors, including al-Qaeda.

The chapter is based on a minimal foundationalist approach that understands the discursive and the material as co-constitutive of social reality (Toros and Gunning 2009). As such, the material impacts on discursive constructions and discursive struggles impact on the material. We argue that groups have to greater and lesser degrees links with the foreign actors (whether states or non-state groups) *and* that such links are used to discursively construct an endogenous or exogenous identity, which in turn will be used in attempts to recognise and mis-recognise. Both the material and the discursive factors will also affect whether and how the actors can engage and be engaged with in conflict transformation initiatives.

The chapter is divided into three parts. In the first section, we begin by arguing that the question of endogeneity/exogeneity in recognition has been largely overlooked. We then discuss how we understand the endogenous–exogenous spectrum, why it is relevant to the recognition of state and non-state armed groups, and how it differs but can be linked to self/other binaries. The second part of the chapter will examine how the endogeneity/exogeneity question is particularly relevant in the Somali case, showing how the question impacts on the recognition of the actors. The final section offers tentative reflections on whether and how recognising FGS and aS as endogenous or exogenous can impact on the prospects of conflict transformation in Somalia.

The multiple facets of recognition

Recognition is increasingly seen as a central element of conflict transformation processes in conflicts opposing states and non-state armed actors. Not a simple equation (i.e. recognition = conflict transformation), scholars have increasingly argued that recognition cannot be seen as a 'panacea' to such conflicts (Geis et al. 2015: 18). Indeed, drawing from the work of Jens Bartelson (2013) and Anna Geis, Caroline Fehl, Chistopher Daase and Georgios Kolliarakis (2015) among others, this chapter understands the study of recognition as the examination of a *complex web of interrelations between often numerous groups vying for political, legal and moral recognition within communities, within nation-states and internationally*. It accepts as a basic premise that 'individuals and collective actors seek recognition of certain qualities, positive characteristics, competencies, achievements, or of their status within a specific group, a society, a political system, or the international political realm' (Geis et al. 2015: 3). This search for recognition and its successes and failures need to be understood as a '*gradual* process' rather than a clear binary (Geis et al. 2015: 16).

With regard to non-state actors specifically, investigations into recognition have focused particularly on the impact of recognition of such groups as 'legitimate' political actors (i.e. representative of a salient section of the population and/or of legitimate grievances) on the potential for conflict transformation (including Biene and Daase 2015; Toros 2008, 2012). What has been largely overlooked, we argue here, is the question of whether political actors, in this case violent political actors (both state and non-state), are recognised as being endogenous to a social context or exogenous to it. Before we engage with what we mean by endogenous and exogenous and why this is an important facet of recognition, it is important to lay out some of the key work and understandings of recognition on which this chapter is based. Conceptually, we will draw from the distinction made by the editors of this volume between 'thin' and 'thick' recognition, and that of Bartelson between political, legal and moral recognition. Methodologically, we will discuss the methodological challenge posed by investigating recognition by discussing Bartelson's focus on discursive practices of recognition and the path this offers for empirical work such as that put forward in our case study of Somalia.

As discussed in the volume's introductory chapter drawing on the work of Allan and Keller, the distinction between thin and thick recognition is an important one when examining the role of recognition in the transformation of conflicts involving armed non-state actors (Allan and Keller 2006). Here we differ slightly from the understanding put forward in the introduction to argue that 'thin' recognition means acknowledging the role of a party *in the conflict*, while 'thick' recognition goes beyond this to recognise a party's role *in the resolution/transformation of the conflict*. Our aim is to examine how recognition as endogenous/exogenous relates to the thin/thick distinction.

Although primarily focusing on the recognition of state actors in the international system (as much literature on recognition does), Bartelson (2013) usefully distinguishes between political, legal and moral recognition. 'Political recognition concerns what counts as a relevant actor' (Bartelson 2013: 111); '[l]egal recognition concerns on what grounds a state should be admitted as a member of the international society of states' (Bartelson 2013: 114); and 'moral recognition takes us beyond the mere recognition of rights' into the recognition of 'equal moral worth' (Bartelson 2013: 118). Bartelson offers an interesting account of the relationships between these forms of recognition, such as how moral recognition can be sometimes offered in lieu of legal recognition, or how political recognition often needs to precede moral recognition.

Bartelson (2013: 110) also offers an interesting path to operationalise an investigation into recognition by arguing that practices of recognition 'consist of *speech acts*, or otherwise symbolic acts that communicate the acknowledgement of the ontological, legal and moral status of certain objects and subjects'. As such this chapter will examine the discursive practices of various actors involved in the Somali conflict, in particular in the conflict opposing aS to federal and international forces, and how actors seek recognition as endogenous or exogenous in these practices.

Endogenous/exogenous actors

The key argument of this chapter is that discussions of recognition have so far overlooked the question of whether actors are recognised as being endogenous or exogenous to a social context, in particular to conflictual social contexts. Arguably, endogeneity and exogeneity are implicit in many discussions of recognition. Recognising actors as part of a conflict (see introductory chapter) as included in thin recognition, often means recognising their endogeneity to the conflict. Similarly, Bartelson defines political recognition as 'what counts as a relevant actor' (2013: 111). Being recognised as endogenous to a conflict makes one a relevant actor – although there are also cases in which exogenous actors are recognised as relevant. We argue however that neither of these forms of recognition fully captures the relevance and nature of the endogeneity/exogeneity spectrum. Indeed, as noted, exogenous actors can also be relevant to a conflict – and thus have political recognition – but their recognition as an 'exogenous' player will impact their status and how they are interacted with. Also, endogenous actors can be seen as internal to a conflict but not be recognised as being politically salient.

How are endogeneity and exogeneity understood here? If an actor is viewed as endogenous, it is viewed as 'one of us', a member of the broader community, issued from the social fabric of the community. An exogenous actor is on the contrary viewed as 'not one of us', coming from the outside, and either trying to impose itself onto the community or being imposed onto it. We argue that the endogenous/exogenous distinction is both a question of epistemic recognition – is the group internal or not internal? (Bartelson 2013: 108) – and one of political/moral recognition, primarily leading to questions of whether the group can legitimately claim to have a say/role in a conflict and furthermore its resolution/transformation. Actors can self-identify as well as label others as endogenous/exogenous. We argue that states and NSAGs will tend to seek recognition as endogenous to the referent community they claim to represent, while mis-recognising their opponent as exogenous to that community. As will be examined below, however, this simple binary is rarely visible in complex social realities and needs to be carefully problematised.

A first important question is: what are actors endogenous and exogenous to? Indeed, the referent community that is seen as containing the actor should not be understood as a fixed entity. Opposing actors may make competing claims to endogeneity in a conflict scenario but the referent communities to which they claim to belong may not be exactly the same. Claiming to be 'European' or 'of the European Union' are not the same, nor, as we shall see in our case study, is claiming to be part of the state of the current Federal Republic of Somalia or 'Greater Somalia', the latter a state aspired to by some Somali communities that includes parts of Kenya, Ethiopia and Djibouti. Actors may also claim endogeneity to several referent communities at once – such as being relevant to a specific state but also to the larger Muslim community (generally referred to as the '*ummah*').

Furthermore, although it could be understood as related to the self/other binary that has preoccupied much thinking in political theory and International Relations, it cannot be subsumed under this binary either. Endogeneity and exogeneity are not simply other terms for Carl Schmitt's friend/enemy distinction and indeed should be understood as more literal terms. From endogeneity/exogeneity – being recognised as from within a community or external to it – one can then build discourses of self/other, friend/enemy. We argue that endogeneity/exogeneity is a first step in what can move towards a 'thick' recognition or moral recognition of another as equal in worth, such as can be seen in the self/other or friend/enemy binaries.

How do endogeneity and exogeneity fit into Bartelson's three forms of recognition? Endogeneity as argued above cannot be subsumed to the 'relevancy' criteria of political recognition as exogenous actors may be understood and indeed *recognised* as relevant. Furthermore, endogenous actors may be recognised as being part of a conflict but of little political relevance to it. Exogeneity, on the other hand, can be used to undermine political recognition. Actors are presented as external impositions or imposters pretending to be 'one of us' in order to disqualify them as politically relevant. The relationship between political recognition and the endogenous/exogenous spectrum is thus a complex but salient one.

The relationship with legal recognition may at first appear to be less salient. Legal recognition by the state of non-state armed groups and by non-state armed groups of the state arguably depends far more on whether the actor is seen as engaging in legal practices (non-violent when it comes to non-state armed actors; and only legally sanctioned violence when it comes to state actors) than whether it is endogenous/exogenous. However, NSAGs can be decriminalised or taken off the list of illegal organisations and recognised as legal political actors, and this is often seen as a step in peace processes (see the work of Haspeslagh (2015) and Dudouet (2011)). Furthermore, since the 'global war on terror' and in particular the UN sanctions regime regarding al-Qaeda, ISIS and affiliated parties, links to exogenous actors by non-state armed actors will have an impact on the legal recognition of an armed group. Indeed, links between national NSAGs and transnational ones may be highlighted with the specific aim of denying legal recognition to the former. Of course, as noted above, groups may be both endogenous to a community and conflict while at the same time maintaining strong links to exogenous/foreign actors. Indeed, actors always have multiple identities, likely some endogenous and some exogenous.

The final category of moral recognition is also impacted by endogeneity but again there is no simple equation. An exogenous actor may be recognised (albeit rarely) as of 'equal moral worth' but external, not 'one of us'. An endogenous actor may be recognised as 'one of us' but not of equal moral worth. However, it is argued here that exogeneity can strengthen misrecognition – they are not 'one of us' and thus not as worthy as us – while when endogeneity is added to moral recognition, one can achieve a high status, as the party is recognised as from within the community *and* of equal moral worth. This points to the fact that political recognition may indeed have to precede moral recognition and that endogeneity may facilitate the passage from political to moral, that is, (1) You are relevant; (2) You are one of us; (3) You are equally worthy. Although such a move along a continuum of recognition is not automatic (and likely not linear), it may indeed be seen as an ideal to be sought in conflict transformation processes.

The aim of this section was to argue that endogeneity and exogeneity need to be understood as separate facets of recognition and to examine how they are linked to – but cannot to be subsumed into – distinctions such as thin/thick or political/legal/moral recognition. Whether a party is understood as endogenous or exogenous can have considerable implications on its political, legal and moral recognition, and knowledge of this can be used to impact on an actor's capacity to operate in a political context, how other actors interact with it (e.g. feeling lesser or greater authorisation in the use of violence against it) and in an actor's right to be at a negotiating table. Thus, the endogenous/exogenous spectrum has to be understood as a facet of recognition alongside respect, esteem or status, and honour. Indeed, it plays a role in the *ordering* function of recognition (Bartelson 2013: 114). Endogeneity/exogeneity is used by parties to make claims to certain positions in the hierarchy of actors of a conflict system as recognition-seekers and to accept or refute others' claims to certain positions in the hierarchy as recognition-granters.

Methodology

The chapter will carry out a discourse analysis of official and informal statements from key FGS figures (president) and statements by aS figures or in media outputs publicly associated with the armed group. Drawing on the work of Iver Neumann (2008) on discourse analysis, our empirical investigation sets out to uncover the discursive contestations over who and which institutions are endogenous to Somalia and indeed 'Somali'. As argued by Neumann (2008: 62):

> Because a discourse maintains a degree of regularity in social relations, it produces preconditions for action. It constrains how the stuff that the world consists of is ordered, and so how people categorise and think about the world. It constrains what is thought of at all, what is thought of as possible, and what is thought of as the 'natural thing' to do in a given situation.

We intend to investigate whether both the FGS and aS seek to constrain how their audiences (within and outside Somalia) categorise and think about the world *also* through their representations of what and who is Somali – that is, whether they use endogeneity to seek recognition for themselves and exogeneity to mis-recognise their opponent. We are open to the likely possibility that endogeneity and exogeneity are not absolutes and that the parties may mix the two in representations of themselves and their opponent.

By following Neumann, we delimit our data to official statements and twitter feeds of FGS president Mohamed Abdullahi Mohamed (known as Mohamed 'Farmaajo') and the official feed of the presidency Villa Somalia on the FGS side, and posts on Somalimemo, a website closely affiliated to aS and widely held to put forward its views. The choice of using Twitter accounts is based on accessibility but also on the consideration that Twitter is a key locus for Somali discursive contestations, due to the decades-long conflict that has hindered more traditional forms of media and the considerable cellphone coverage available in Somalia.[1] To delimit the data for manageability we will cover Farmaajo's presidency from February 2017 to December 2019, although we will refer back to some of the statements made during the presidential campaign that led to his election.

We examine statements that seek to establish endogeneity and exogeneity, examining discourses of who/what is represented as Somali and non-Somali. We search for what Neumann (2008: 67) calls 'canonical texts or monuments', that is, texts that 'have a broad reception and are often cited'. These help to identify the main positions. The next step is to identify variations and evolutions of these main positions. In our case, it is particularly interesting to identify similarities and differences between understandings of who/what is Somali in FGS and aS statements. Indeed, we find that the two sides use similar representations and understanding of how endogeneity/exogeneity are identified but use such representations to delegitimise the other. Finally, we examine what functions the main representations and the conflict between these representations serve to the FGS and aS leadership. This is crucial to examine the impact of the endogenous/exogenous element of recognition on the potential for conflict transformation in Somalia.

It is also important to state what our research does not examine. We do not examine the reception by audiences of representations put forward by the FGS and aS leadership. As such, less attention is given to the recognition-granting than to the recognition-seeking. This is no doubt an important element if one wants to understand how the discursive contestations unfold in Somalia, but is beyond the scope of our analysis that seeks to examine whether endogeneity and exogeneity are elements of the recognition equation. A further project will be able to examine the effects of this discursive contestation.

Somalia: recognition and endogeneity

To understand what and who is considered Somali is an essential component for gaining insight into the intricate relationships and dynamics of al-Shabaab, the Federal Government of Somalia and the people of Somalia. This, however, is far from a simple endeavour, as understanding what constitutes *the Somali* is reflective of both the intrinsic struggle of Somalis to define themselves and of the confusion of the international world to decipher what is 'Somalia'.

Brian Hesse (2010: 247) describes Somalia as a myth that is both a 'false belief' and 'an idealised conception'. It is therefore essential to place our discussion and analysis of endogenous/exogenous discourses within a deeper understanding of the politics of Somali identity.

Indeed, the discussion of Somali identity constitutes a well-used trope in politics in and outside the country. The idea of genuine and inherently Somali characteristics in terms of ethnicity, culture, language, dance, music and religion forms one of the bases of the political and social sphere of Somalia and thus the project of Somalia as a nation. However, as Ashley Lyn Greene (2011: 34) highlights, there is an ongoing academic debate on whether one should understand Somali identity as 'originating from shared cultural traits and traditions that precede colonial divisions' or as politicised identity that is fragile and contingent to its colonial history. For example, renowned Somalia anthropologist I. M. Lewis (1983: 9) sees Somali nationalism as embedded in a coherent reading of Somali identity and belonging (socially, culturally and territorially) that pre-dates the materialist and liberation-seeking influences of colonialism. In this context, authenticity inherently becomes the backdrop in front of which belonging and inclusion are measured.

This notion however is challenged by scholars who localise Somali nationalism in a rejection of colonialism (Kusow 2004; Mahaddala 2004). Here, Somali identity is to be understood as heterogeneous and loosely connected but brought together as an answer to colonial injustice. Emerging from this, the idea of '*Soomaalinimo*' – the political term used to describe the unity of a common Somali people that share cultural characteristics despite colonially imposed lines – has developed to be understood as a blanket term that challenges various forms of social and political injustice seen as holding back a transcendent Somali communality. This ambiguity over *Soomaalinimo* acts as a spectre that haunts Somali identity as well as notions of belonging. This narrative of an original greater community – a figure that in the case of aS is also appropriated by the idea of a transcendent Muslim *ummah* – remains key to Somali politics despite being challenged continuously by the deeply fractionalised realities of clan politics and fighting.[2]

The question of discursive inclusion or exclusion needs to be understood in this context, and embedded in a distinctive social geography that adapts and shifts the face of *Soomaalinimo* according to the perceived threat. The narratives of endogenous/exogenous are reflective of dominant, contingent and conditional readings of belonging, entitlements and interpretation of what is inherently and genuinely Somali. As such, the question of endogeneity/exogeneity has long been a locus of power struggle that is central to Somali politics and is deeply engrained in the question of Somali identity. Indeed, where Somalia starts and ends and who can call themselves Somali remain contested. What we aim to highlight in the analysis below is that these contestations are inextricably linked to questions of recognition.

Following Neumann's approach to discourse analysis, we began by trying to identify canonical texts or monuments in the data. Generally scarce in the texts we examined, we did find use of traditional Somali proverbs and speech forms (poetry and rhyme), in particular in aS-affiliated media. This is clearly designed to place statements within an easily identified lineage of Somali culture and fits within broader patterns of radical Islamist groups using poetry in their propaganda (see the work of Kendall 2016). We also found key recurring tropes that were used again primarily by aS-affiliated media but also by FGS to support their statements on endogeneity and exogeneity. Unsurprisingly, these were largely linked to Somalia's colonial history and subsequent history of multiple foreign interventions, including foreign military occupation. Indeed, aS-affiliated Somalimemo repeatedly states that the country is 'divided and controlled by colonisers, apart from al-Shabaab controlled areas' and labels FGS leaders as 'colonialist sympathisers'.[3] President Farmaajo is specifically named as 'a servant to the colonialists who invaded the country and wasted the blood of the citizens to take over the country and turn the rest of them into cannon fodder'.[4] The colonial trope, as we shall see below, is key in aS's discursive campaign to mis-recognise the FGS as not part of the solution to the conflict in Somalia (refusing thick recognition) and to mis-recognise the FGS in terms of moral recognition.

Overall, we find that endogeneity and exogeneity play a key role in both parties' recognition of themselves and mis-recognition of their opponent. As such, the first conclusion we reach is that an analysis of recognition in Somalia and specifically in the conflict opposing the state and armed group al-Shabaab needs to examine strategies of recognition and mis-recognition from both sides. The second, as will be analysed below, is that endogeneity and exogeneity play key roles in these strategies also for both parties. To begin with the FGS discourses, we find that they clearly aim to stress the FGS's endogeneity to Somalia. Farmaajo for example urges 'the Somali people to stand by *their* government'[5] and following attacks speaks of the need 'to heal *us* from *our* wounds'.[6] Such statements link endogeneity directly to thick recognition, presenting the state as a key player in the resolution of conflict and violence in Somalia. 'Our troops are heros that can stand up to terrorist groups', Farmaajo said in June 2017. 'We will meet the need to protect the country and the people.'[7] Farmaajo and the presidency also link endogeneity to moral recognition – that is, recognition of equal moral worth – with the people of Somalia. 'The people and the army should unite'[8] against aS, Farmaajo said in February 2018, and in December 2019 he repeated that 'we need to unite and build a front against the terrorists'.[9] At times, Farmaajo and the presidency also seek legal recognition as the formal internationally recognised institutions of the state. In a March 2019 tweet, Villa Somalia stressed that 'security is the responsibility of the military and security agencies' and in July 2019 that the 'president has instructed federal agencies'.[10] This is likely aimed to contrast with the illegal nature of aS's security structures that are largely seen as effective but do not have legal status.

Importantly, FGS statements seeking thick and moral recognition as key actors to the resolution of the conflict and of moral worth to the Somali people are most often accompanied by statements of mis-recognition of aS. Indeed, although the state recognises the non-state armed group as part of and relevant to the conflict – thus awarding both a thin recognition and a political recognition – they mis-recognise aS in terms of thick and moral recognition. Importantly for our argument, it uses exogeneity as a means to make this move of mis-recognition. Responding to a February 2017 attack, Farmaajo speaks of 'al-Shabaab's barbarism'[11] – barbarism being something that comes from the outside, that is, the barbarians. Even more clearly, in a December 2019 speech carried on twitter, Farmaajo said:

> Somalia, our people and its development cannot be stopped. AS is a terrorist group that works for an international network of terrorist groups and they have been sent to the people of Somalia to shed their blood, to make a genocide of the people of Somalia and to inhibit the development of the country. AS never builds but only destroys. They don't build schools, they don't build hospitals, they don't build education institutions. They don't support the advancement of the Somali public and they don't support the progess of the Somali youth. What they support, and for which they were contracted is to stand against the progress of the Somali people, to fight the Somali public, the Somali youth and the future of this country. … The most recent events have shown that we are in a state of war.[12]

Here Farmaajo clearly links thick and moral mis-recognition to the exogeneity of aS. The armed group is mis-recognised as 'sent to the people of Somalia', '*our* people', by an '*international* network' and '*we* are in a state of war' against them. Interestingly, at times the FGS messages use the colonial trope against aS. For example, in July 2018 Farmaago tweeted that 'al Shabaab and Daesh use the colonial method of dividing our people', adding that 'we have to set ourselves free from these groups'.[13]

This connection can be further noted in the principal attempt made by Farmaajo towards conflict resolution/transformation with aS shortly after his election. Indeed, Farmaajo offered aS fighters amnesty if they laid down their arms in March 2017 using the following terms:

> Those who have been misguided and that are our children, we are telling them to come back to us. You have been pressured to do what you have done. Come back to your mothers, come back to your friends.[14]

Thus, when offering moral recognition (you are our children) and thick recognition (come back to be part of the future with us), Farmaajo stresses the endogeneity of aS fighters.

Adding complexity to this, it is worth noting that the presidential statements on rare occasions use exogeneity – in particular the FGS's international and regional links – to seek thick recognition as key actors in Somalia's future. In April 2019, Villa Somalia boasted that the FGS had 'international support and support from the people. Al Shabaab cannot stand one day and it is a fact: they cannot face the Armed Forces for one hour.'[15] Other statements from the presidency also stressed the FGS's links with regional powers such as Ethiopia. Thus, endogeneity and exogeneity do not have simple binary functions in terms of moves of recognition and mis-recognition. Nevertheless, the data shows that the endogeneity and exogeneity play key roles in moves to seek recognition by the FGS and to mis-recognise aS, and that indeed the president and his office clearly linked their attempts to seek thick and moral recognition through endogeneity to mis-recognising aS also as exogenous and 'un-Somali'.

Statements made on aS-affiliated Somalimemo adopt largely the same main discursive positions as the FGS statements although we found some important variations. Statements associated with the armed group seek recognition using endogeneity as an element; however, they primarily focus on mis-recognising the FGS by denouncing it as exogenous to Somalia and Somalis. Indeed, while the FGS made a balanced number of statements seeking recognition and mis-recognising aS and often linked the two, aS statements mis-recognising FGS as exogenous were more than twice the number of those seeking recognition as endogenous.[16] In their first statement of 2017, aS stated clearly their view of the FGS: 'Somalia is in a state of colonisation and foreign governments have set up their own administrations in the capital Mogadishu.'[17] During the presidential campaign of 2017, they insisted that candidates were 'warlords responsible for the massacre of the people of Somalia, brought in by foreign troops'.[18] Once elected, the armed group often specifically linked President Farmaajo to the United States, where he lived for many years and of which he was a citizen, until he gave up his citizenship in August 2019. This link is made with the clear intention to mis-recognise him as exogenous: 'Farmaajo is indeed a patriot, he is not a Somali patriot, but an American patriot and his *Americanness* is bigger than the suffering of the Somali people.'[19] This mis-recognition went beyond Farmaajo to encompass other government leaders: 'The leadership of the federal government is overseen by foreign-born men, such as the Speaker of Parliament, the Presidency, the Council of Ministers and the local authorities, and it appears that the country is under the control of foreigners who have been disciplined abroad.'[20]

As noted above, the aS-affiliated statements also repeatedly used the colonial trope, accusing the FGS and Farmaajo of supporting the occupation of Somalia by foreign forces. For example, when in March 2017 Farmaajo made a speech inviting al-Shabaab fighters to lay down arms while at the same time threatening them with defeat with the help of the African Union Mission in Somalia (AMISOM), Somalimemo judged that he was ‘legitimizing the invasion’ by the ‘colonialists’. In a poem published on Somalimemo in May 2017, it accused the president of being ‘bought’ by ‘colonising neighbours and those who are international’.[21] In a variation however from the FGS discourse, unsurprisingly aS-linked narratives stress the government's exogeneity not only to Somalia and being Somali but also to Islam and being Muslim. ‘We are telling the heathens that carry Farmaajo's flag that you will follow in the footsteps of those before you’, the group announced in February 2017.[22] In a few exceptional cases, a racial element is also introduced where Farmaajo and the FGS more broadly are mis-recognised as allied to or ‘stooges’ of the ‘white forces’.[23] Thus, the community to which an actor is mis-recognised as exogenous to can change *and* be multiple.

These discourses are again aimed at mis-recognising the FGS and Farmaajo in particular as exogenous to the future of Somalia (thick recognition) and as not of equal worth (moral recognition) to Somalia, to the Muslim world and, to a lesser extent, to Africa through racial mis-recognition. In a strong example of similarities of main positions used against one another by state and non-state armed actors, aS extensively used the colonial trope also used by FGS discourses but added the religious element and on rare occasions a racial element. Less focused on seeking recognition from the broader public than the FGS and Farmaajo discourses present, aS-affiliated media nonetheless use endogeneity to make claims for thick and moral recognition and exogeneity to mis-recognise their opponent also in terms of thick and moral recognition.

Conclusion

Endogeneity and exogeneity should thus be understood as elements of recognition which play a particular role in the thick recognition and moral recognition of parties – state and non-state – in conflicts. Again, the attribution of endogeneity does not necessarily equate with thick or moral recognition and exogeneity with mis-recognition, but they are often used discursively to seek recognition and mis-recognition along these lines. As can be seen with the study of Somalia's discursive battle between the federal state leaders and non-state armed group al-Shabaab, endogeneity cannot be assumed of any side – the state is just as, if not more, adamant in its attempts to be seen as endogenous as is aS. Interestingly, thin recognition and political recognition were less linked to endogeneity/exogeneity as both sides recognise the other as part of the conflict (thin recognition) and as salient (political recognition), while at the same time using accusations of exogeneity to mis-recognise their opponent as not part of the resolution (thick recognition) and not of equal moral worth (moral recognition).

What does this mean for the prospects of conflict transformation? As can be noted by the only peace overture during the period examined (2017–2019), endogeneity was a key element in Farmaajo's offering of amnesty to aS fighters who agreed to lay down their arms. They were invited to 'come back' into Somali society and into building the future of Somalia as '*our* children' – thus of equal moral worth and part of the solution to the problem. This was quickly rejected by aS leaders, who chose to focus on Farmaajo's accompanying threat to use foreign forces (of AMISOM) to defeat aS to underline his alliance with 'colonising foreign' troops. Exogeneity was thus used to reject the offer.

Thus, thick recognition or being recognised as part of the resolution to or transformation of a conflict is clearly essential to conflict resolution/transformation. This can be seen as coming after thin and political recognition – being seen as at least part of and salient to the conflict.[24] Importantly, it does not necessarily imply moral recognition, as a party can be recognised as necessarily part of the resolution/transformation of a conflict but still be considered of inferior moral worth. Moral recognition may be necessary however to *achieve* conflict transformation rather than simply start a process. One can thus see – from the discussion of endogeneity/exogeneity and from the analysis of the Somali case – that political recognition is likely to come before moral recognition and, unsurprisingly, thin before thick. We can also argue that thick recognition is likely to be crucial for a conflict transformation process to begin – such as the start of talks, formal or informal – while moral recognition may be something that emerges during and from such a process.

Much more research into the role of recognition in conflict transformation is needed, whether or not that involves NSAGs. The principal argument made here is that such research should take into account the question of endogeneity/exogeneity particularly when conflicts involve these latter groups. Since such groups are usually illegal and with no formal connection to a clearly identified constituency, attributing exogeneity is an obvious strategy to mis-recognise them. This, we argue, needs to be studied. However, the role of endogenetiy/exogeneity is not only present in the recognition of NSAGs, as our study of the Somali case shows. There, aS also used exogeneity to mis-recognise state authorities in a discursive battle of recognition in which exogeneity and endogeneity continue to play central roles. The prospects of conflict resolution/transformation in Somalia are thus likely linked to the willingness of all parties to see their opponents as endogenous to Somalia and thus necessarily part of the resolution of ongoing fighting there. Whether such a thick recognition is followed by moral recognition is a complex issue that has broad implications in terms of justice, truth and reconciliation – no doubt the subject of future research.

Notes

1 Roland Marchal (2009: 382) warns against over-reliance on online sources with regard to aS, arguing that 'caution is required' because of the 'discrepancies between rhetoric and behaviour' of aS. We certainly support this position. In this chapter, however, we are interested in the discursive positions of aS rather than in whether such positions reflect a material reality on the ground.

2 It is interesting to note that describing aS's role in this conflict already requires making a choice of whether or not it is primarily an endogenous group to Somalia. In a recent publication on Somalia (Toros and Harley 2018), one of this chapter's authors stated that aS emerged from the Islamic Courts Union, a cooperation of armed actors that controlled large parts of south-central Somalia from 1999 until they were ousted by Ethiopian-backed troops in 2006. Some members of the Islamic Courts Union joined the new transitional government, while others formed al-Shabaab that has operated in large sections of south-central Somalia since, although the amount of territory it has under its control has changed substantially since 2010. By writing such a phrase, the author implicitly present aS as an endogenous group, part of a large fractious puzzle that is Somalia's political and security environment today. Other academics and think-tanks describe aS quite differently – essentially making a statement on its exogeneity. Conservative think-tank The Long War (2018) describes the group as follows: 'Over the past week, al Qaeda's East African wing, Shabaab, targeted two markets in southern Somalia with deadly explosions.' For the author Caleb Weiss, aS is attacking Somalia but there is nothing in the description that describes it as Somali. In fact, it is the 'East African wing of al Qaeda', a transnational actor seen as fighting a 'global Jihad' rather than engaged in national or local conflicts. Thus, recognition of endogeneity/exogeneity leaves no space for neutrality and one's position can be very easily denoted discursively.

3 https://somalimemo.net/articles/6468/Maxamed-Sheekh-Axmed-Farmaajo-wadani-waa-yahay-laakiin-waa-waddani-maraykan-ah-Dhageyso; last retrieved 3 April 2020.

4 https://somalimemo.net/articles/7573/Farmaajo-dhiigga-Soomaaliduu-Cadaawaha-ugu-dhawaanayaa-W-Q-Cabdullaahi-Soomaali; last retrieved 3 April 2020.

5 https://twitter.com/M_Farmaajo/status/849924487210467330; last retrieved 3 April 2020.

6 https://twitter.com/M_Farmaajo/status/1051240280756801536; last retrieved 3 April 2020.

7 https://twitter.com/M_Farmaajo/status/872092112208220160; last retrieved 3 April 2020.
8 https://twitter.com/M_Farmaajo/status/833306649901281281; last retrieved 3 April 2020.
9 https://twitter.com/M_Farmaajo/status/1079042754871726085; last retrieved 3 April 2020.
10 https://twitter.com/TheVillaSomalia/status/1109449796010553345 and https://twitter.com/TheVillaSomalia/status/1109449796010553345; last retrieved 3 April 2020.
11 https://twitter.com/M_Farmaajo/status/833306649901281281; last retrieved 3 April 2020.
12 https://twitter.com/M_Farmaajo/status/1210951650225115136; last retrieved 3 April 2020.
13 https://twitter.com/M_Farmaajo/status/1013431029233790976; last retrieved 3 April 2020.
14 https://somalimemo.net/articles/6571/Farmaajo-Al-Shabaab-hal-lug-ayay-ku-taagan-yihiin-lugtaasna-waa-u-bixineynaa; last retrieved 3 April 2020.
15 https://twitter.com/TheVillaSomalia/status/1116347437185159168; last retrieved 3 April 2020.
16 Uncovering the reasons behind this variation would require interviews with FGS and aS leaders that could not be undertaken for this chapter, but we can suggest possible explanations. One could argue that aS is either less worried about being understood as endogenous – it does after all stress several affiliations beyond being Somali, and particularly including its membership in the broader Muslim *ummah* – or that its endogeneity is less called into question than that of the FGS by the broader population and thus it has less need to assert it.
17 https://somalimemo.net/articles/6395/Cameey-Muqdisho-Waxaa-Ka-Dhisan-Laba-Dowladood-oo-Kala-Madax-Banaan; last retrieved 3 April 2020.
18 https://somalimemo.net/articles/6404/Dagaal-Oogayaal-Gacmahoodu-Dhiig-Ka-Daayo-Oo-u-taagan-Xilka-Madaxweyne-Ee-Dowladda-Federaalka; last retrieved 3 April 2020.
19 https://somalimemo.net/articles/6468/Maxamed-Sheekh-Axmed-Farmaajo-wadani-waa-yahay-laakiin-waa-waddani-maraykan-ah-Dhageyso; last retrieved 3 April 2020.
20 https://somalimemo.net/articles/6766/Guddoomiyaha-Gobolka-Banaadir-iyo-Taliska-Nabad-Sugidda-oo-Madax-looga-Dhigay-Siyaasiyiin-Qurba-Joog-Ah; last retrieved 3 April 2020.
21 https://somalimemo.net/articles/6981/Farmaajo-Waa-Maqaar-saar-marin-habaabin-ah-W-Q-C-llaahi-Somaali; last retrieved 3 April 2020.
22 https://somalimemo.net/articles/6555/Sheykh-Cali-Dheere-Xasan-Keena-Ama-Farmaajo-Keena-Dagaalku-Wuu-Soconayaa-Kalimad-Cusub-DHAGEYSO; last retrieved 3 April 2020.
23 https://somalimemo.net/articles/6475/Faah-Faahin-19-Askari-oo-Lagu-Dilay-Dagaallo-Ka-Dhacay-Sh-Hoose-iyo-Al-Shabaab-oo-Masuuliyadda-Sheegatay; last retrieved 3 April 2020.

24 There are conflicts in which parties are not even awarded thin and/or political recognition. This can be seen when states refuse even to acknowledge the existence of armed groups.

References

Allan, P. and A. Keller (2006), 'The concept of a just peace, or achieving peace through recognition, renouncement, and rule', in A. Keller and P. Allan (eds), *What is a Just Peace?* (Oxford: Oxford University Press), pp. 195–215.
Bartelson, J. (2013), 'Three concepts of recognition', *International Theory* 5:1, 107–129.
Biene, J. and C. Daase (2015), 'Gradual recognition: curbing non-state violence in asymmetric conflicts', in A. Geis, C. Fehl, C. Daase and G. Kolliarakis (eds), *Recognition in International Relations: Rethinking a Political Concept in a Global Context* (Basingstoke: Palgrave Macmillan), pp. 220–236.
Dudouet, V. (2011), 'Anti-terrorism legislation: impediments to conflict transformation', *Berghof Policy Brief* 2, available online: http://edoc.vifapol.de/opus/volltexte/2013/4695/pdf/PolicyBrief02.pdf, last retrieved 4 March 2020.
Geis, A., C. Fehl, C. Daase and G. Kolliarakis (2015), 'Gradual processes, ambiguous consequences: rethinking recognition in international relations', in A. Geis, C. Fehl, C. Daase and G. Kolliarakis (eds), *Recognition in International Relations: Rethinking a Political Concept in a Global Context* (Basingstoke: Palgrave), pp. 3–26.
Greene, A. L. (2011), 'Re-thinking Somali national identity: nationalism, state formation and peacebuilding in Somalia', in J. P. Lederach (ed.), *Somalia: Creating Space for Fresh Approaches to Peacebuilding* (Uppsala: Life & Peace Institute), pp. 33–42.
Haspeslagh, S. (2013), '"Listing terrorists": the impact of proscription on third-Party efforts to engage Aamed groups in peace processes. A practitioner's perspective', *Critical Studies on Terrorism* 6:1, 189–208.
Hesse, B. J. (2010), 'Introduction: the myth of "Somalia"', *Journal of Contemporary African Studies* 28:3, 247–259.
Kendall, E. (2016), 'Jihadist propaganda and its exploration of the Arab poetic tradition', in E. Kendall and A. Khan (eds), *Reclaiming Islamic Tradition* (Edinburgh: Edinburgh University Press), pp. 223–246.
Kusow, A. M. (2004), 'Contested narratives and the crisis of the nation-state in Somalia: a prolegomenon', in A. M. Kusow (ed.), *Putting the Cart Before the Horse: Contested Nationalism and the Crisis of the Nation-State in Somalia* (Trenton: The Red Sea Press), pp. 1–14.
Lewis, I. M. (1983), *Nationalism and Self-Determination in the Horn of Africa* (London: Ithaca Press).
Mahaddala, H. (2004), 'Pithless nationalism: the Somali case', in A. M. Kusow (ed.), *Putting the Cart Before the Horse: Contested Nationalism and the Crisis of the Nation-State in Somalia* (Trenton: The Red Sea Press), pp. 59–74.
Marchal, R. (2009), 'A tentative assessment of the Somali Harakat Al-Shabaab', *Journal of Eastern African Studies* 3:3, 381–404.

Neumann, I. (2008), 'Discourse analysis', in A. Klotz and D. Prakash (eds), *Qualitative Methods in International Relations: A Pluralist Guide* (Basingstoke: Palgrave Macmillan), pp. 61–77.
Toros, H. (2008), '"We don't negotiate with terrorists!" Legitimacy and complexity in terrorist conflicts', *Security Dialogue* 39:4, 407–426.
Toros, H. (2012), *Terrorism, Talking and Transformation: A Critical Approach* (Abingdon: Routledge).
Toros, H. and J. Gunning (2009), 'Exploring a critical theory approach to terrorism studies', in R. S. Jackson, M. Breen and J. Gunning (eds), *Critical Terrorism Studies: A New Research Agenda* (Abingdon: Routledge), pp. 87–108.
Toros, H. and S. Harley (2018), 'Negotiations with al-Shabaab: lessons learned and future prospects', in M. Keating and M. Waldman (eds), *War and Peace in Somalia: National Grievances, Local Conflict and Al-Shabaab* (New York, NY: Hurst), pp. 401–411.
Weiss, C. (2018), 'Somali markets targeted in Shabaab explosions', available online: www.longwarjournal.org/archives/2018/05/somali-markets-targeted-in-shabaab-explosions.php?utm_source=feedburner&utm_medium=email&utm_campaign=Feed:+LongWarJournalSiteWide+(FDD%27s+Long+War+Journal+Update) (12 May); last retrieved 18 December 2020.

5

Shifting recognition orders: the case of the Islamic State

Tom Kaden and Christoph Günther

Introduction

When looking at the role recognition plays in political contexts, the Islamic State presents a particularly complex and multifaceted case, reflecting the complexities of recognition relationships and their political consequences overall. Approaching our subject from a recognition theory perspective, we identify two main difficulties. First, the status that relevant actors ascribe to the Islamic State (and its predecessor organisations, which we include unless otherwise noted) is multifaceted and, at times, contradictory. This is even more the case for the status the group ascribes to itself. There is significant change over time regarding what the Islamic State is and wants to be recognised for; a regional protecting power; a quasi-state entity; a transnational Caliphate. Secondly, these changes in status, both ascribed and self-ascribed, entail changes regarding the traits for which the group seeks recognition. While violence plays an important role both in other actors denouncing the group and in the group's own claims to legitimacy, this is by no means the only element in the complex set of recognition-relevant properties. Any thorough analysis of what we term the 'recognition orders' (see below) to which the Islamic State is party must also take account of the group's claims to uphold public order, to represent a divine regime, to act as a religious-political force of unification, as a potent military force and as a liberator from common enemies (for a detailed analysis of the Islamic State's sources of authority see Günther and Kaden 2016).

Throughout its history, the Islamic State has claimed recognition for its mission, accomplishments and status from among Sunni Muslims in general, potential supporters of its cause in particular, and a range of Salafi-jihadi ideologues and other Salafi-jihadi militant groups. Since these claims have frequently been linked with threats of violence against those who deny the group recognition, it might be argued that recognition can, indeed, foster peaceful relations (see Geis 2018: 614). However, there is a distinct 'dark side' to this situation (Biene 2013; see Hofmann and Görzig 2015). Since the Islamic State derives its claims to legitimacy in large part from its ability to exert violence, any act of recognition runs the danger of fostering this behaviour.

The purpose of this chapter is to analyse the ways in which the Islamic State generates and upholds its message through what we term *recognition orders*, that is, complex sets of recognition by various actors for various traits and reasons, as well as complex sets of claims for recognition towards various actors as to what is to be recognised about the Islamic State in which way. This means that, to us, any act of recognition, non- or mis-recognition is part of a social relationship between those granting (or denying) and those the act is directed towards. Consequently, recognition and its others (non- and mis-recognition) are constituted reciprocally.

As Geis (2018: 612) summarises in a recent review on the scholarship, recognition is 'a relational concept because (mutual) recognition is regarded as a prerequisite for successful identity formation and beneficial social action'. Accordingly, mis-recognition, 'which individuals or collective actors experience as humiliation, disrespect, or false representations of their identity, is seen as a major cause of political resistance, and as significant in the escalation of potentially violent conflicts' (Geis 2018: 612).

In this chapter, we will show that this view is particularly useful when it comes to the Islamic State. Our considerations are based on an examination of twenty-three authoritative statements as well as a few texts and videos wherein the Islamic State's ideologues emphasised particular sets of traits for which the group aspired to be recognised as well as sets of actors from which the group sought recognition. These sets of traits and their variation correspond to the series of organisational stages the Islamic State underwent before and after its proclamation as the Caliphate in 2014. Correspondingly, the way in which the group has been perceived has also shifted, though the gap between the group's own claims and what it has been recognised for has never closed.

In what follows, we will describe the sets of traits identified by the Islamic State's ideologues in official statements during four organisational stages since 2003, namely a small-scale rebel group (A) until 2006; the gradual turn into a proto-state between 2006 and 2014 (B), until it reached the height of its power as a self-proclaimed Caliphate until 2016 (C). After 2016 and until the present time (February 2019), the group can be characterised as a rebel group (D). Against this backdrop, we identify recognition orders established by the Islamic State's ideologues, that is, the entirety of social, political and military actions produced by and productive of the specific traits for which the Islamic State's ideologues sought recognition at a certain point in time. Reconstructing the self-image that the Islamic State's ideologues sought to present, we also draw attention to the potential audiences they addressed to gain recognition as a meaningful actor in and beyond a violent conflict in Iraq and Syria.

Analysing recognition orders: conceptual considerations

As we will show in the sections below, the history of the Islamic State and its predecessor organisations reveals them to be highly volatile in terms of the content and scope of the recognition they demand. In order to capture this volatility, we divide our analysis of recognition claims and acts into a number of specific questions. In this, we follow authors who have introduced further differentiations within the general category of recognition. Most notably, we are indebted to Biene and Daase's (2015) introduction of the notion of 'recognition as', by which they differentiate between different grades of recognition of an actor as a party to a conflict, as a participant in informal talks, as a participant in formal talks, or as the (sole) representative of a people or group. In the context of our topic, we feel it necessary to further broaden the range of possible acts of and claims to recognition-as-something by treating it as a generally open category to be filled by the various empirical claims of the actors involved.

Our second inspiration stems from Hofmann and Görzig's (2015) analysis of the 'dark side of recognition', where the authors differentiate between active (granting) and passive (receiving) recognition. Recognition, in Hofmann and Görzig's analysis, turns dark when the conditions for a group to receive the recognition it wants preclude it from getting it. Their example deals with Palestine, where the cooperation between Fatah and Hamas would be a precondition for its ability to recognise Israel (this is Palestine's active recognition), but at the same time would preclude Israel from recognising Palestine (this is Palestine's passive recognition). Since in this case active and passive recognition are mutually exclusive, the recognition order precludes a resolution of the underlying conflict. For our purposes, we add to this concept another differentiation within the category of passive recognition, namely between the recognition sought by and the recognition granted to an actor. Between these two elements of passive recognition, paradoxical effects resembling Hofmann and Görzig's dark side of recognition can also occur.

Equipped with these conceptual tools, we propose two different sets of analytical questions, the answers to which reveal the complex recognition regime of which the Islamic State is part. The first set queries the actor(s) granting or denying recognition:

- For what traits is an actor recognised?
- As what kind of actor are they recognised?
- By whom/in what capacity is the act of recognition performed?
- If applicable, to what point in time or period is the act of recognition referring?

In all cases where we speak of actor(s) granting or denying recognition, we also include the possibility of conscious or unwitting non- or mis-recognition by the actor(s). In our perspective, recognition exists where the way in which an actor answers the above set of questions is met by another set of answers given by the addressee of the actor's recognition. The condition of a recognition relation existing as such is an overlap between the answers the granting actor gives to the above set of questions, and the answers the object of recognition gives to the following second set of questions, which mirror the first.

- For what traits does an actor want or not want to be recognised?
- As what kind of an entity does an actor want or not want to be recognised?
- By whom? Not by whom?
- Referring to what point or period in time?

We call an *order of recognition* the entirety of social actions that serve primarily or partly as answers to these two sets of questions by actors involved (or desired to be involved) in a process of recognition. By matching the answers to these two analytical sets, it is possible to identify to what extent and in what regard a recognition relationship exists. Likewise, an identification of the roots and scope of mis- or non-recognition is possible by analysing a mismatch between the answers given to the two sets. Finally, our concept also allows for the possibility of recognition, non-recognition and mis-recognition existing simultaneously with regard to different aspects of the recognition regime.

We feel that one advantage of this approach is that it renders it possible to treat the definition of recognition in any particular case as an empirical question, based on how the actors involved in creating and maintaining recognition orders determine the directions and goals of their recognition efforts at any given point in time.[1] At the same time, our concept makes clear that any act of recognition, in order to be characterised as such at all, needs to be viewed as a social relationship based, in Weber's classic formula, on any action 'tak[ing] account of that of the others and is oriented in these terms' (Weber 1978: 26). In what follows, we will sketch elements of the order of recognition of which the Islamic State and its predecessor organisations were part. Based on a broad range of authoritative statements by the Islamic State's ideologues, we aim to show that the recognition order changed as a result of the organisation's development, and underwent, largely simultaneously, profound changes in terms of the group's self-image and self-positioning, its geographical scope and the degree of differentiation between its addressees, as well as the traits claimed and those from which the group sought to distinguish itself.

The development of the Islamic State's status and recognition order

Looking at the Islamic State and its predecessors from a historical perspective, four phases of organisational evolution can be discerned. Between 2003 and 2006, the group that was to become the Islamic State can best be described as a small-scale rebel group (A). Between 2006 and 2014, it gradually turned into a proto-state (B), until it reached the height of its power as a self-proclaimed Caliphate until 2016 (C). After 2016 and until the present time (February 2019), the group can be characterised as a rebel group (D).[2] The organisational evolution of the group in part went hand in hand with shifts and adaptations in its ideology which are related to the persons involved and to factors within and outside the group influencing its ideology and action.

Each organisational stage entailed changes in the way in which the ideologues of the Islamic State and its predecessors demanded and received recognition by other actors and themselves granted recognition to others. To depict those characteristics, we have selected twenty-three recorded speeches as well as a few texts and videos in Arabic from the above-mentioned phases of the development of the Islamic State. They were created by core actors within the group, that is, its 'official spokesperson' (*al-mutaḥaddith al-rasmī*), its military leader, leading clerics or the 'commander of the faithful' (*amīr al-muʾminīn*). Each of these statements offers a general description of the respective current state of affairs within the group and delineates its motives and goals. Using a hermeneutical approach, we have reconstructed the Islamic State's order of recognition as it presents itself in these statements, and correlate this with secondary sources on the general development of the group.

Our approach, however, is limited in that we do not attempt to map out the entirety of contemporary and historic references and sources of legitimacy the Islamic State and its predecessor organisations feed into the respective recognition regimes. Still, we acknowledge that the construction of a plausible historicising narrative of salvation is eminent in the Islamic State's legitimation and delegitimation strategies. We also deliberately reduce the polysemy of certain social categories and functions, while knowing that for groups like the Islamic State, whose ideology is dominated by religious frameworks, any political, social and economic collective it relates to is primarily significant in religious terms. The context is of great importance in this regard. For instance, a reference to 'Democrats' in *Hādha wa'd Allāh* (*This is the Promise of God*; see below) must be understood as a religious reference, because the intra-textual context designates them as the ones who deviate from divine ordinances, hence creating the 'wrong *ummah*'. In some cases, the same actor appears multiple times in different contexts and with different designations. For example, in several speeches of the Islamic State's leadership the Muslim community, the *ummah*, is on the one hand designated as a religious actor while on the other it is framed as a political actor, too (see for example al-'Adnānī 2014b; al-Baghdādī 2014b; al-Zarqāwī 2004b).

Phase (A): small-scale rebel group (2003–2006)

Looking at how our first set of analytical questions can be answered with regard to the first phase of the group's history, we find the following characteristics. The group, back then first operating under the label of al-Tawhīd wa 'l-Jihād and since October 2004 formally affiliated with the al-Qaeda network and calling itself Tanẓīm Qā'idat al-Jihād fi-Bilād al-Rāfidayn, was predominantly recognised by those actors opposing its ideology and cause. The traits deemed significant were those that designated it as a violent actor in contradistinction both to the official political structure and competing jihadi groups. Its members were labelled as 'merciless sectarian' slaughterers (Burns 2006; Whitaker et al. 2006) and 'insidious' (Warrick 2015: 220). Predominant characterisations of the group and its leaders were their rejection of secularisation and democracy; moreover, their interpretation of Islamic sources was criticised as faulty (see Günther 2014: 170–173). Overall, the group was recognised as a terrorist group by critics, but also as a force strengthening the resistance against Iraq's occupation by some others.

The main reference groups performing the acts of recognition by attributing the group the above-mentioned traits and characterising it in the ways mentioned were, first of all, the US-led multinational forces and their provisional government structures in Iraq as well as the Iraqi governmental authorities under the lead of Iyad Allawi, Ibrahim al-Ja'fari and Nuri al-Maliki and their executive apparatus. Seeking to stabilise the country in the wake of a growing resistance involving groups from various religious, social and political backgrounds, US authorities singled out the group's leader as 'high value target number one' (Hashim 2006: 142) and some of the power-holders declared '"Jordanian terrorist" Abū Muṣ'ab al-Zarqāwī as the mastermind behind the Iraqi insurgency' (Ritter 2005), thereby fuelling the mythical charging of a person whose actual executive power within the resistance is still being debated. Despite severe criticism of his military methods and rigid interpretation of Islam's holy scripture from several Sunni groups and individuals who were sympathetic to or actively supporting the resistance, al-Zarqāwī had been successful in merging a plethora of foreign volunteers with local forces and Sunni resistance groups (Fisher and Wong 2004). He thus forged alliances that granted his group a sustainable local basis and support from the population that recognised his group among others as legitimate fighters against multinational occupation (United States Institute of Peace 2005: 12–14).

With regard to the second set of questions, we identify the following claims to recognition by the group. During this early phase, it wanted to be recognised for being relentless and perseverant in its struggle. From the outset, it presented itself as 'right-minded', faithful, meek, strong and capable of fight. Al-Zarqāwī himself emphasised these traits in almost all his speeches that circulated as audiotapes both on the internet and on the ground. For example, in his first audio recording from January 2004, entitled *Ilḥaq bi 'l-qāfila* (Join the Caravan), he pledges that his group will 'remain fracturing the throats of the tyrants and a controlling sword on the necks of the oppressors and soldiers for Islam protecting it' (al-Zarqāwī 2004a). In early 2006, the aforementioned self-ascribed traits were extended to include the group's capacity to govern justly.

From the very beginning, the claims to recognition were predominantly directed towards the Sunni population. The group strove to motivate and acquire a broad base in the Sunni population, which was often equated with the whole Muslim community. Al-Zarqāwī emphasised the prominent position of all (Sunni) fighters and asserted their value as 'the chosen few of the *ummah*, its first line of defence, its safety valve and its well-built fortress ... the ever watchful, guardian rock upon which the American arrogance has crumbled' (al-Zarqāwī 2005a). Insisting on the motif of a 'brotherhood of jihad [comprising] both muhājirīn and anṣār [i.e. foreign volunteers and local supporters]', al-Zarqāwī (2004b) also tried to facilitate alliances with other groups, calling on 'the heroes in Iraq, God bless your brothers, rush to their aid. This battle is one of the decisive and historic battles between Islam and the unbelievers [in which] the mujahideen will strike as one' (al-Zarqāwī 2004c). In light of the group's position in the Iraqi Sunni Arab resistance against the US-led occupation and the new government, al-Zarqāwī's rigid interpretation of Islam and his self-ascribed capacity as a vanguard put him and his group in a situation of competition with many Iraqi Sunni scholars. Hence, it is not surprising that he criticised their reluctance to call on the local population to fight on the part of his group. In many of his speeches he accused them of having 'reconciled with the tyrants and handed over the land and the people to the Jews, the Crusaders and their followers among our apostate rulers when you remained silent about their crimes, feared to preach the truth to them, and did not succeed in bearing the banner of jihad and monotheism' (al-Zarqāwī 2004a).

In all this, the group aimed to be recognised as a severe threat to the occupational forces and the newly instated governmental structures: the new government, its administrative, legislative, judicial and executive branches, as well as those religious and/or political groups supporting it. 'To you Bush, you Roman dog, we swear by Allah that you will not enjoy rest or a place of rest, your military will never be able to relax in our lands, as long as blood pulses through our veins and our hearts beat' (al-Zarqāwī 2005a). Similar threats were also directed against the international military coalition in general (al-Zarqāwī 2004b), and against Jews, Shiites and other religious groups (al-Zarqāwī 2006).

This last point reveals that the group also wanted to be recognised as a severe threat to the heterogeneity of Iraq's religious, social and cultural domain by all religious communities other than Sunni, in particular the Shia, which al-Zarqāwī had singled out early as the major 'enemy within' the Islamic community (Günther 2014: 134–138, 165–170; Johannsen 2008: 3–11). This ultimately led him to defend the killing of civilians and call for an 'all-out' war against the Shia as a whole (al-Zarqāwī 2005b, 2005c, 2005d, 2005e).

Phase (B): proto-state (2006–2014)

By 2006, the group's attacks on Shiite civilians in particular were one of many causes of violent civil conflicts that erupted at that point, causing tens of thousands of civilian casualties and massive displacements across the country. However, multinational and Iraqi troops were eager to regain agency and to end the undermining of state authority. To this end, they began large-scale recruitment in predominantly Sunni towns and regions and specifically targeted the leadership of al-Qaeda in Iraq, resulting in the death of its most prominent figure, Abū Muṣʿab al-Zarqāwī, in late 2006. In the light of these developments, we can assume that al-Zarqāwī's heirs were rather forced to act. Against all odds, however, they managed to lay the foundation of what would soon emerge as one of the most powerful social revolutionary movements in the Middle East, presenting the most eminent threat to the integrity of local nation-states: the Islamic State.

In accordance with the general increase in violent struggle during these years, the way the group was perceived and the traits for which it was recognised changed gradually, not substantially. Consequently, the answers to the first set of analytical questions remain largely the same, though there is evidence that the claim to be a state also entailed forms of moderation for which the group sought recognition. In what follows we will highlight changes in nuance and substance in the group's claims to recognition.

In a video released in 2010, excerpts from a lecture by Abū Anas al-Shāmī, one of the group's ideologues, concisely repeated the group's claims and the traits for which it wanted to be recognised:

> We fight until the entire world worships [according to] the sharīʿa of God the Great and the Almighty, until the world is ruled with the Book of God and the Sunna of the Prophet – peace and prayer be upon him – and until Islam extends its rule over the worlds and spreads its wings on earth in the light of the sharīʿa of God the Great and Almighty. (Al-Furqān Media 2010).

This basic doctrinal statement that references Q. 8:39,[3] that is, the claim to disseminate *tawḥīd* (monotheism), exert power according to divine ordinances and fight against anything that diverts from it, constitutes the main line of creedal continuity connecting the Islamic State and any of its predecessors. Particularly in the formative period of the Islamic State in Iraq (ISI) (dawlat al-'Irāq al-islāmīya) from late 2006 onwards, the group elaborated on these principles in various authoritative documents and statements, seeking to underline its claim to legitimacy and fundamental change (al-Baghdādī 2007a; al-Furqān Media 2007).

However, Abū ʿUmar al-Baghdādī, who had succeeded al-Zarqāwī as the leader of al-Qaeda in Iraq and, after the establishment of the ISI, had been inaugurated as *amīr al-muʾminīn* (Leader of the Faithful), emphasised that the organisation's members were responsible for meeting the expectations increased by claiming the rank of a proto-state. In a statement released in April 2007, he addressed the Islamic State's fighters in particular: 'My sons, the soldiers of the Islamic State: Oh mujahideen, do not stop a river you caused to flow by making sacrifices, or demolish an edifice you have raised by your efforts. Do not consider everyone who disagrees with you an adversary, and do not consider everyone who accompanies you a friend. Those who disagree with you may be among your best friends. Be like the sea that is not unsettled by buckets, and be forgiving, for God gives strength and pride to the forgiving' (al-Baghdādī 2007a).

Beyond these invocations, the ISI notably sought to establish forms of rebel governance that could help undergird its claim on transformation into a pristine Islamic order and breathe life into the ISI's claim for a social contract between the *amīr al-muʾminīn* and their subjects. Accordingly, the group's leadership issued several messages between 2007 and 2009 that outlined the institutionalisation of governance structures, and the group's media wings increasingly disseminated footage of governmental services provided by the Islamic State to local populations (Günther 2014: 200–234).

Likewise, while the general goal of uniting the Sunni population remained a core claim of the group, it also already sought recognition for having achieved this to an extent. Abū ʿUmar al-Baghdādī argued in a statement released in April 2007 in which he reviewed the last four years of jihadi activities in Iraq, that the Sunnis had gained 'a clear goal [and many] dividends on the side of monotheism, morals, and worship in general [, because with the help of God] the people of Iraq today are among the greatest peoples on earth in terms of safeguarding monotheism' (al-Baghdādī 2007a). In this speech, al-Baghdādī also promised that the Islamic State would remain (*bāqiya*), thereby portending a keyword that the Islamic State would extol as part of its motto when it rapidly grew in 2014, 'To Remain and Expand' (*bāqiya wa-tatamaddad*).

Together with its increased status as a military power, the group stepped up its claims to recognition by other Sunni rebel groups as the sole legitimate representative. Abū ʿUmar al-Baghdādī repeatedly called on other groups to unite under his command. In a speech of April 2007, shortly after he had been inaugurated as *amīr al-muʾminīn* by the Mujāhidīn Shūrā Council, he directly addressed several of the largest Sunni rebel factions:

> Oh brothers in the Anṣār al-Sunna and of Jaysh al-Mujāhidīn, the friendship between us is deep. The bonds of faith and love are too great and strong to be harmed. Oh my sons in the Jaysh al-Islāmī know that I am prepared to shed my blood to spare yours, and offer my honour to protect yours. By God, you will hear from us only what is good, and you will see from us only what is good. Rest assured, for what is between us is stronger than what some people think, may God forgive them. ... We owe it to God to protect your blood and the blood of every Muslim who has not committed an act of open idolatry or shed blood when he is forbidden to do so. Fear God and do not forget the lofty goal, namely that the word of God prevails, not abhorrent nationalism. (Al-Baghdādī 2007a)

In contrast to his earlier statements, Baghdādī also called on ISI's fighters to strike against those Sunni tribal factions that formed the so-called Awakening Councils (*ṣaḥawāt* or *abnāʾ al-ʿIrāq*) who, encouraged and supported by the US military, had begun to drive back ISI forces from larger areas in western Iraq (al-Baghdādī 2007b): 'We call on all mujahideen to come together under one banner, the banner of "There is no god but God; Muhammad is the messenger of God," one methodology, one *amīr*, in one army, for one purpose: the sovereignty of the *sharīʿa* so that the word of God may be the highest and the word of the infidels the lowest' (al-Baghdādī 2010).

The group's claims to represent a severe threat to the occupying forces and Iraqi government structures were exacerbated over time, with the duration of the struggle becoming a claim to recognition of its own. In the aforementioned audio tape of April 2007, Abū ʿUmar al-Baghdadī outlined 'the thorns that the infidel occupier and his apostate henchmen picked'.

> First: Four years of strikes and humiliation which make some sides here and there sacrifice their honour. The honour of the age's Satan and today's idol, the United States, led by their most stupid obeyed one, Bush, was rolled in the dust. Second: Exhausting the US budget at the expense of social security, health, and education so that the money of the collaborating Gulf governments has failed to meet American needs. ... The collapse of US army morale and the increase of suicide cases and escape attempts, and chronic organic and psychological cases such as permanent tremor. (Al-Baghdādī 2007a)

In the last part of this second phase of the group's existence, it extended its threats to include Syria and the Assad regime, thus adding another element to its claims to recognition by the Sunni populace. In an audiotape that was released on 9 April 2013, Abū Bakr al-Baghdādī, who had succeeded Abū ʿUmar al-Baghdādī as the head of the ISI and been declared *amīr al-muʾminīn* by the organisation's Shūrā Council, proclaimed the establishment of the Islamic State in Iraq and the Levant (dawlat al-islāmīya fi 'l-ʿIrāq wa 'l-Shām; ISIL), bringing with it the entry into the battlegrounds of the Syrian civil war that had begun to unfold two years earlier (al-Baghdādī, 2013). He stated that they would 'extend our wide hands and open our arms and hearts to the factions doing jihād for the sake of God Almighty and the proud tribes in the beloved land of al-Shām to make God's word the highest and that the people and land may be ruled by the laws of God Almighty' (see also al-ʿAdnānī 2014a). Addressing the Sunni population in Syria in January 2014, he said that

> your blood is our blood and your destruction is our destruction. We fight in God's path and for his satisfaction and we do not fear the blame of blamers. Don't be deceived by the media for you will find us the kindest towards you and the harshest towards your enemies. God knows that we tried our best to defend Muslims and then overnight we are accused of making *takfīr*[4] on the Syrian population. (Al-Baghdādī 2014a)

Phase (C): Caliphate (2014–2016)

On 29 June 2014/1 Ramadan 1435h, the ISIL's official spokesman declared the (re-)establishment of the Caliphate for all Muslims (al-ʿAdnānī, 2014b). The document and the claims to recognition it makes represent a significant change in comparison to the group's earlier phases. In what could be termed a dual universalism, the group now claims to be the sole legitimate representative of all Muslims, with Abū Bakr al-Baghdādī being named Caliph Ibrāhīm to whom all Muslims owe an oath of allegiance. The declaration emphasises the state-like qualities of the administration the group exerts and also the personal traits of Abū Bakr that make him worthy of exerting the office of Caliph (see also Turkī al-Bin'alī 2014). At the same time, the group claims universal political significance, which translates into claims of recognition by Western powers and Sunni groups of all kinds in all areas, as well as all of the actors already referred to by the Islamic State in earlier phases. In addition to a broadening of the category of recognition-by-whom, the group broadens its claims to recognition-for-what, when it not only emphasises its military might and religious righteousness as before, but also its global political significance, its unique importance in alleviating social evils besetting the *ummah*, and its ideological and organisational superiority to all other attempts at ameliorating Muslims' plight.

Only two days after al-'Adnānī's proclamation, a speech by Abū Bakr al-Ḥusaynī al-Qurashī al-Baghdādī had been published, who had just been inaugurated Caliph Ibrāhīm by the Islamic State's Shūrā Council. On the one hand, this speech – his inaugural note, one may argue – emphasises the exceptional significance of the holy month for testing one's individual faith, and al-Baghdādī uses it to call for people to join and intensify military jihad. On the other hand, it becomes clear that in this speech al-Baghdādī marks the beginning of a new phase in the Islamic State's evolution. Al-Baghdādī notably widens the Islamic State's focus from Iraq and Syria to ambitions to defend the global Muslim community:

> Muslims' rights are forcibly seized in China, India, Palestine, Somalia, the Arabian Peninsula, the Caucasus, al-Shām, Egypt, Iraq, Indonesia, Afghanistan, the Philippines, Ahvaz, Iran, Pakistan, Tunisia, Libya, Algeria and Morocco, in the East and in the West. So, raise your ambitions, oh soldiers of the Islamic State! For your brothers all over the world are waiting for your rescue and are anticipating your brigades. (Al-Baghdādī 2014b)

In this rhetoric, the Islamic State claims recognition as the spearhead of a global conflict that 'is the Muslims' war altogether. It is the war of every Muslim in every place' (al-Baghdādī 2015). Conversely, this recognition of the plight of Muslims in the countries mentioned by the Islamic State's leadership opens up a host of new venues for recognition of the Islamic State as the legitimate defender of Muslims' rights everywhere, and consequently a significant increase in its global prestige that mirrors its increased sense of political status.

In focusing on global affairs, al-Baghdādī also seeks to shield the Islamic State from accusations of terrorism. While the group's ideologues had always framed their fighters' deeds in light of defence of (and retaliation for) Muslim lives in Iraq and Syria, al-Baghdādī here lists war crimes committed under the pretext of 'counterterrorism' and eventually even adopts the label terrorist, because 'terrorism is to refer to God's law for judgment. Terrorism is to worship God as He ordered you. Terrorism is to refuse humiliation, subjugation, and subordination to the infidels. Terrorism is for the Muslim to live as a Muslim, honourably with might and freedom. Terrorism is to insist upon your rights and not give them up' (al-Baghdādī 2014b). In this instance, the group confronts what it perceives as (normative) mis-recognition and reframes it according to its own goals and justifications.

The change in status the group ascribed to itself by framing itself as the Caliphate opened up new sources for legitimation, and consequently new historical claims to recognition. In his much-noticed public sermon on the first Friday of this Ramadan, al-Baghdādī underlined the claims for acceptance by the Muslim community as he sought to capitalise on the memories of the Caliphate that are an eminent part of the cultural memory in many societies in the Middle East and North Africa region and beyond. He stated that the Islamic State's followers 'declared the Caliphate and instated an imam, and this is a duty upon the Muslims – a duty that has been lost for centuries and absent from the reality of the world and so many Muslims were ignorant of it. The Muslims sin by losing it, and they must always seek to establish it, and they have done so, and all praise is due to God' (al-Furqān Media 2014).

During this phase, the Islamic State not only made significant territorial gains and enjoyed a large clientele, particularly from outside Syria and Iraq. It also notably upgraded its capabilities in partaking in the war of images, feeding the internet and classical media with audiovisual media replete with high-quality pictures that helped to underline the self-image of the Islamic State and earned it (grudging) recognition as a media producer, too (Gruber 2019). The most notable change in topics covered by its media wings in comparison with the above-mentioned phases was intimately tied to the Islamic State's effective exertion of authority over considerable territories in Iraq and Syria. Accordingly, the Islamic State's media extensively covered 'the good life' in the Caliphate, among which the staging of the implementation of an own currency certainly was a capstone in 2015 (see al-Hayat Media Center 2015), as well as other aspects of its rule in photo reports, videos and textual publications. In contrast to the phase between 2006 and 2014, the Islamic State's leadership had institutionalised and bureaucratised its rule in many aspects and wanted this to be recognised.

Al-Baghdādī also notably exacerbated his rhetoric in the upcoming months that saw intensifying fights between the still expanding Islamic State and the Iraqi and Syrian military, their international allies and various non-state actors. The universalist language that had been characteristic of messages by the Islamic State's leadership was gradually superseded by a focus on particularities in terms of battlegrounds and groups referenced in the communiqués (see al-Baghdādī 2015)

Phase (D): rebel group (2016–2018)

Although the group had always relied on the Prophet Muhammad's example, references to his armed conflicts between June 2014 and June 2016 were clearly pushed into the background, and instead his example as head of the early Muslim community was emphasised as the Islamic State referred to itself as *khilāfa ʿalā minhāj al-nubūwa* (Caliphate in the Prophetic Methodology). This changed again when military pressure on the group increased and it had to retreat from its former strongholds across Iraq and Syria by the summer of 2016. At that time there were frequent references to battles in which the Muslim community faced a numerically and materially far superior number of opponents and yet won the battle because of their faith. The so-called 'battle of the trenches' (*maʿrakat al-aḥzāb*), which the Islamic State's leadership and al-Zarqāwī had referred to frequently in the first and second phases mentioned above, recurred even more frequently in the summer of 2016, in particular in analogies likening the battle for Mosul to the battle for Medina between the first Muslim community and tribal forces from Mecca in 627 (see al-Baghdādī 2016). The Islamic State's leadership also referred to territorial losses as a test from God and emphasised that its fighters had to prove values such as steadfastness, endurance and perseverance. Its recognition regime had, by the summer of 2016, hence turned back to an increased emphasis on the military qualities of the group (al-ʿAdnānī 2016; al-Baghdādī 2016, 2017, 2018).

The Islamic State's leadership also constantly called on its (potential) followers to either join the fight on the battlefields in Iraq, Syria, Libya or elsewhere, or to otherwise take action in any location worldwide to terrify their enemies (al-Baghdādī 2017, 2018).

Despite its loss of territory and personnel in this phase, the Islamic State still sought to uphold the image of a well-performing bureaucracy. Particularly in their audiovisual media, the Islamic State's leadership reiterated the differentiated structure of the administrative and bureaucratic apparatus that was the spearhead of fundamentally changing the social, religious, cultural and political sphere in the territories under the Islamic State's control (see al-Furqān Media 2016).

Conclusion

Referring back to the conceptual outline we presented at the outset of this chapter, it becomes clear that the recognition order the Islamic State created for itself changed considerably over time, and in conjunction with its military and political development on the ground. As a result of its rise, it created for itself the image of a universal liberator of the *ummah*, which also changed the traits for which it sought recognition, and the time frame of its narrative. Unsurprisingly, with regard to the second set of questions we proposed, the kind of recognition given by the increasing number of recognition-granters included in the recognition order created by the Islamic State never matched the group's aims, and the mismatch between what the Islamic State wanted to be recognised as and for by all kinds of actors grew as its power grew. At the height of its power, it was almost universally condemned as a terrorist group while its claims to recognition increased beyond comparability with other armed non-state actors. Paradoxically, the very same reasons the Islamic State gave to legitimate its claims to recognition are among the reasons its potential recognition-granters denied the Islamic State the kind of recognition it sought. This is why we see here a case of the 'dark side of recognition', where the conditions for passive recognition not only preclude it from being granted, but also reproduce the conflict underlying the recognition order.

The perspective we employed makes visible that these aspirations for 'thick' recognition (Wendt 2003: 511–512) are accompanied by, and indeed are based on, promises of 'thin' recognition the Islamic State grants groups from which it seeks legitimation, and herein lies the potential for actual matches between the Islamic State as a recognition-seeker and the recognition-granters. Most prominently, this refers to its basic reference group, the *ummah*, which it claims to lift from oppression and poverty, thus guaranteeing the status of the reference group's members (individual Muslims) as 'sovereign person[s] rather than an extension of someone else' (Wendt 2003: 511–512) (e.g. an object of colonial subjugation).

Looking at the development over time, the kinds of recognition the Islamic State or its predecessor groups seek can be roughly characterised as gradual (cf. Biene and Daase 2015), depending on the self-ascribed status as a local, regional or transnational power, and the respective functions and prestige attached to these statuses. At the same time, the change over time in the Islamic State's position and status makes it hard to apply a recognition-theoretical model that is based on a set of ranked positions oriented towards the 'gold standard' of international political recognition.

Our findings imply that the first set of questions can also be framed to guide normative discussions about recognition in that it can be used to focus debates about whether certain actors, such as armed non-state actors, should be recognised: as what, for what, in what capacity and regarding what time frame? With easing of tensions and prevention of (further) violence being general goals of recognition, it is striking that the Islamic State's self-ascribed status often appears as an explicitly violent group praising its ability to exert acts that constitute a priori obstacles to any reconciliation.

The most obvious example is its attempt to justify its status as an Islamic State in Iraq by pointing to its ability to kill soldiers of the US-led coalition occupying Iraq, and its contrasting this with the lack of effective resistance by its competitor groups in Palestine (al-Jubūrī 2006). In our view, this feature of the for-what dimension of the Islamic State's recognition regime makes it hard to believe that, in this particular case, recognition can 'incentivize moderation in means' (Biene and Daase 2015: 222). However, we realise that the idea cannot be ruled out that gradual recognition can be applied to potentially decrease the overall violence exerted by the group and its successor organisation(s), simply because the 'recognition events' (Biene and Daase 2015) that have taken place towards the Islamic State, such as recognising it as a party to a conflict, remain below the threshold of inducing desired behaviour. Still, we see very clear limits to this, since, for instance, recognition of the Islamic State as 'representative of a collective' (Biene and Daase 2015: 224) is hampered by the fact that there is significant overlap in the claims to representation by the group itself and groups that could perform acts of recognition in the first place, that is, groups that represent Sunni Muslims whom the Islamic State claims to represent in their entirety through the entity of the Caliphate. Consequently, we argue that there is significant potential for the 'dark side of recognition' (Hofmann and Görzig 2015) to come to the fore in any attempt at recognising the Islamic State with regard to any of the dimensions discussed in this chapter.

Notes

1 We acknowledge that in order to paint a complete picture of the recognition order in any given case, it would be necessary to extend the view to also include, as a third set of questions, the way in which the group in question acts as a giver of active recognition, and how active and passive recognition influence each other.
2 This classification partly builds on Bunzel (2015).
3 {And fight them until there is no more fitna and the religion [worship] will all be for Allah alone [in the whole of the world]. But if they cease [worshipping others besides Allah], then certainly, Allah is All-Seer of what they do.}
4 The act of declaring someone an unbeliever, hence denying him/her the status of a Muslim, which has a range of ontological and social consequences.

References

Al-ʿAdnānī, A. M. (2014a), *Wa 'l-rāʾid lā yakdhibu ahlihi* [Audiotape], available online: https://shamikh1.info/vb/showthread.php?t=217963 (8 January); last retrieved 20 February 2020.

Al-ʿAdnānī, A. M. (2014b), *Hādha waʿd allāh* [Audio message] (29 June).
Al-ʿAdnānī, A. M. (2016), *Wa-yaḥyā man ḥayy ʿan bayinna* [Audiotape] (21 May).
Al-Baghdādī, A. B. (2013), *Wa-bashshir al-muʿminīn* [Audiotape] (9 April).
Al-Baghdādī, A. B. (2014a), *Wa-Allāh yuʿlam wa-antum lā taʿlamūn* [Audiotape] (19 January).
Al-Baghdādī, A. B. (2014b), *Risāla ilā 'l-mujāhidīn wa-umma al-islāmīya fi-shahr Ramaḍān* [Audiotape] (1 July).
Al-Baghdādī, A. B. (2015), *Infiru khifāfan wa-thiqāla* [Audiotape] (14 May).
Al-Baghdādī, A. B. (2016), *Hādha mā waʿdanā Allāh wa-rasūluhu* [Audiotape] (2 November).
Al-Baghdādī, A. B. (2017), *Wa-kafā bi-rabbika hādiyan wa-naṣīran* [Audiotape] (28 September).
Al-Baghdādī, A. B. (2018), *Wa-bashshir al-ṣābirīn* [Audiotape] (22 August).
Al-Baghdādī, A. U. (2007a), *Ḥaṣād al-sinīn bi-dawlat al-muwaḥḥidīn* [Audiotape] (17 April).
Al-Baghdādī, A. U. (2007b), *Al-dhilla ʿalā 'l-muʿminīn wa ʿizza ʿalā 'l-kāfirīn* [Audiotape] (22 December).
Al-Baghdādī, A. U. (2010), *Jarīma al-intikhabāt al-sharʿīya wa 'l-siyāsīya…wa-wājibnā naḥūhā* [Audiotape] (12 February).
Al-Furqān Media (2007), *Iʿlām al-anām bi-milād dawlat al-Islām.*
Al-Furqān Media (2010), *Intafiḍat hayya* 2 [Video].
Al-Furqān Media (2014), *Taghṭīya khāṣṣa li-khuṭba wa-ṣalāh al-jumaʿa fi 'l-jāmiʿa al-kabīr bi-madīna al-Mūṣil* [Video] (5 July).
Al-Furqān Media (2016), *Ṣarḥ al-khilāfa: The Structure of the Caliphate* (6 July).
Al-Hayat Media Center (2015), *The Rise of the Khilafah: Return of the Gold Dinar.*
Al-Jubūrī A. B. (2006), *Al-iʿlān ʿan qiyām dawlat alʿIrāq al-islāmiyya: Proclaiming the Establishment of the Islamic State of Iraq.*
Al-Zarqāwī, A. M. (2004a) *Ilḥaq bi 'l-qāfila* [Audiotape] (4 January).
Al-Zarqāwī A. M. (2004b), *Ayna ahl al-murūʾāt?* [Audiotape] (11 September).
Al-Zarqāwī, A. M. (2004c), *Risāla ilā al-umma wa 'l-mujāhidīn dākhil al-Fallūja* [Audiotape] (12 November).
Al-Zarqāwī, A. M. (2005a), *Yā ahl al-Islām: Al-shidda al-shidda* [Audiotape] (29 April).
Al-Zarqāwī, A. M. (2005b), *Wa-ʿāda aḥfādh Ibn al-ʿAlqamī* [Audiotape] (18 May).
Al-Zarqāwī, A. M. (2005c), *Ayanquṣ al-dīn wa-anā ḥayy* [Audiotape] (5 July).
Al-Zarqāwī, A. M. (2005d), *Kalima al-Shaykh al-mujāhid Abī Muṣʿab al-Zarqāwī ḥawla aḥdāth Tal ʿAfar* [Audiotape] (11 September).
Al-Zarqāwī, A. M. (2005e), *Hādha bayān li 'l-nās wa-li-yundhirū bihi* [Audiotape] (14 November).
Al-Zarqāwī, A. M. (2006), *Majlis shūrā al-mujāhidīn* [Video message] (21 April).
Biene, J. (2013), 'Internationale Anerkennung: Ein Mittel zur De-Eskalation des Nahostkonflikts?', *Sicherheitskultur im Wandel – Working Paper* 16, 1–42.
Biene, J. and C. Daase (2015), 'Gradual recognition: curbing non-state violence in asymmetric conflicts', in A. Geis, C. Fehl, C. Daase and G. Kolliarakis (eds), *Recognition in International Relations: Rethinking a Political Concept in a Global Context* (Basingstoke: Palgrave Macmillan), pp. 220–236.
Bunzel, C. (2015), *From Paper State to Caliphate: The Ideology of the Islamic State* (Washington, DC: Brookings Institution).

Burns, J. F. (2006), 'After long hunt, U.S. bombs al Qaeda leader in Iraq', *New York Times*, available online: https://nytimes.com/2006/06/09/world/middleeast/09iraq.html (9 June); last retrieved 20 February 2020.

Fisher, I. and E. Wong (2004), 'Iraq's rebellion develops signs of internal rift', *New York Times*, available online: https://nytimes.com/2004/07/11/world/the-reach-of-war-the-insurgency-iraq-s-rebellion-develops-signs-of-internal-rift.html (11 July); last retrieved 20 February 2020.

Geis, A. (2018), 'The ethics of recognition in International Political Theory', in C. Brown and R. Eckersley (eds), *The Oxford Handbook of International Political Theory* (Oxford: Oxford University Press), pp. 612–625.

Gruber, C. (2019), 'The visual culture of ISIS: truculent iconophilia as antagonistic co-evolution', in Isabelle Busch, Uwe Fleckner and Judith Waldmann (eds), *Nähe auf Distanz: Eigendynamik und mobilisierende Kraft politischer Bilder im Internet* (Berlin: De Gruyter), pp. 125–155.

Günther, C. (2014), *Ein zweiter Staat im Zweistromland? Genese und Ideologie des 'Islamischen Staates Irak'* (Würzburg: Ergon).

Günther, C. and T. Kaden (2016), 'The Authority of the Islamic State', *Max Planck Institute for Social Anthropology Working Papers* 169, 1–24.

Hashim, A. (2006), *Insurgency and Counter-insurgency in Iraq* (London: Hurst & Co.).

Hofmann, C. and C. Görzig (2015), 'The dark side of recognition: mutual exclusiveness of passive and active recognition in the Middle East conflict', in A. Geis, C. Fehl, C. Daase and G. Kolliarakis (eds), *Recognition in International Relations: Rethinking a Political Concept in a Global Context* (Basingstoke: Palgrave Macmillan), pp. 237–247.

Johannsen, H. (2008), *Die antischiitische Ideologie von al-Qa'ida im Irak und ihre Akzeptanz in der arabischen Öffentlichkeit* (Tübingen: Eberhard Karls University), available online: https://publikationen.uni-tuebingen.de/xmlui/handle/10900/46426; last retrieved 20 February 2020.

Ritter, S. (2005), 'The risks of the al-Zarqawi myth', *Al-Jazeera*, available online: https://globalpolicy.org/component/content/article/168/37321.html (14 December); last retrieved 20 February 2020.

United States Institute of Peace (2005), *Who Are the Insurgents? Sunni Arab Rebels in Iraq*, USIP Special Report (Washington, DC: USIP).

Turkī al-Binʿalī, A. S. a.-S. (2014), *Maddū 'l-ayādī li-bayʿat al-Baghdādī: Stretch Out Your Hands for an Oath of Allegiance to al-Baghdādī* (Maktabat al-himma).

Warrick, J. (2015), *Black Flags: The Rise of ISIS* (New York, NY: Doubleday Publishing Group).

Weber, M. (1978), *Economy and Society: An Outline of Interpretive Sociology* (Berkeley and Los Angeles, CA, and London: University of California Press).

Wendt, A. (2003), 'Why a world state is inevitable', *European Journal of International Relations* 9:4, 491–542.

Whitaker, B., J. Borger, M. Howard and I. Cobain (2006), 'A remote farm surrounded by date palms: Zarqawi's last hiding place', *The Guardian*, available online: https://theguardian.com/world/2006/jun/09/iraq.brianwhitaker (9 June); last retrieved 20 February 2020.

III

Recognition in conflict stalemates

6

The PKK's zig-zag in its global quest for recognition

Mitja Sienknecht

The (non-)recognition of groups in violent conflicts

The process of recognition establishes a relationship between the subject, who is recognising, and the object, who aims to be recognised. In the realm of world politics, recognition of groups or states is an important tool for states and international organisations (IOs) to distinguish between legitimate and illegitimate actors. Consequently, this relational process is always one that is based on power structures between the one who recognises and the one who is recognised. In the context of intra-state conflicts – an armed conflict in which at least one party is a government – governments frequently refuse to recognise an adversarial group.[1] This non-recognition[2] can inflict harm (Taylor 1992: 25), and it often manifests itself by the exclusion of a specific group from a national political system, meaning 'an active, intentional, and targeted discrimination by the state against group members in the domain of public politics' (Vogt et al. 2015: 1331). This political exclusion and active non-recognition is a major cause for political resistance and a significant factor for the violent escalation of conflicts by armed non-state actors (ANSAs) (Cederman et al. 2010, 2011). The analysis of (non-)recognition processes is therefore significant for a better understanding of how conflicts evolve and can be settled.

When it comes to granting or revoking recognition of domestic groups, governments are the principal actors as they have the direct power to accept a separation from state territory. However, actors of world politics[3] – such as IOs – have steadily gained in relevance in recognition processes of intra-state groups. They can play a decisive role in the recognition or non-recognition of an ANSA, thus influencing the conflict outcome. In one case, the recognition of a group may lead to a separation from a state, while in another the stabilisation of a mis-recognition may result in labelling an ANSA as a terrorist organisation. The recognition attributions towards ANSAs are not permanent and stable, but rather dynamic, as can be seen in the case of the Taliban. In 2018, the US started peace talks (thin recognition), even though the Taliban was previously viewed as a terrorist organisation rather than the governing party in Afghanistan (mis-recognition), which precluded the option of negotiation. This had been a consequence of the attacks of 9/11 and the Taliban's connection to al-Qaeda, for whom they had provided a safe haven and support. However, during the Cold War the West had supported the mujahideen in their struggle against the Soviet invasion of Afghanistan (thick recognition) – and thus the group which provided the ideological grounds as well as some of the personnel for both the Taliban and al-Qaeda. Furthermore, empirical cases such as the recognition policies towards different groups in the Syrian civil war underline that the world political system does not act as a homogeneous bloc, but that different actors acknowledge different actors based on ideological overlaps or strategic interests. (Non-)recognition policies are never stable and differ from actor to actor.

Evidently, recognition processes on the world political level influence intra-state conflicts. They can be diverse in quality, ranging from political statements to active military support of either the ANSA or the government, and influence the outcome of an intra-state conflict accordingly. Up until now, research on recognition processes has mainly focused on domestic affairs – analysing the relationship between governments and groups (Honneth 1995; exceptions are Heins 2010 and Wendt 2003). Studies considering the world political system in recognition processes have mostly analysed them from a top-down perspective, focusing on separatist movements which are somehow dependent on the recognition of the world political system. ANSAs are surprisingly often conceptualised as passive agents – only 'receiving' recognition but not actively seeking it. Arguably, research focuses mainly on one side of the coin while largely neglecting the other. In the present chapter, I argue, first, that ANSAs are, indeed, active agents who lobby actively for their recognition on the world political level in line with global norms (Sienknecht 2018: 123; 2019: 185). Secondly, I will show that (non-) recognition is a dynamic process and that it is subject to constant transformation. Actors of the world political system might revoke their recognition, while ANSAs might change whom they are addressing.

This chapter aims to analyse this triangular relationship between ANSAs, governments and actors of the world political system regarding processes of (non-)recognition. The case of the Kurdistan Workers' Party (Partiya Karkerên Kurdistanê, PKK) and its quest for recognition on the world political level serves as a case in point. The dynamic relationship among the PKK, the Turkish government and the European Union, the latter understood as an

IO of the world political system, is the focus of the analysis. I argue that a shift of global norms led to a shift in the recognition of the PKK by the EU. The analysis is framed by a brief historical review on the international dimension of the conflict, the PKK's early ideological orientation towards the Soviet Union, and an outlook on the changing conditions in the region since the international war against the militants fighting for the Islamic State (IS). I focus on the analysis of the normative structures which enable and restrain the recognition of ANSAs by states and IOs. In order to trace back the PKK's push for recognition and the reaction of the world political level, I conducted interviews with experts, representatives of Kurdish organisations and representatives of European institutions. The case study aims to shed light on (i) the way in which ANSAs actively seek recognition from different international actors; and (ii) how IOs influence intra-state conflicts through their recognition practice.

In the next section, I will introduce my theoretical approach. Then, before focusing in more detail on the period between the 1990s and 2010s and the relationship of Kurds and the Turkish government to the EU, I will discuss the historic dimension of the conflict and the impact of the international community. In the conclusion, I will sum up the findings and discuss their implications for the transformation of the conflict.

Recognition processes between discourse and practice

In order to analyse the triangular relationship between ANSAs, governments and actors of the world political system regarding processes of (non-)recognition, we first need to ask ourselves why conflict parties address the world political system in the first place. To answer this question, we must take a closer look at the conflict structure, as well as the rationales of ANSAs and governments.

Intra-state conflicts are often described as asymmetric, because of the organisational and material advantage the government holds over the ANSA (Münkler 2004: 234–237). Therefore, in addition to a certain organisational structure and common motivation, the group has to acquire financial and material resources in order to be capable of constant fighting (Cederman et al. 2010: 11; Gurr 2000: 70; Tilly and Tarrow 2007: 90). ANSAs are often excluded from the national political system by decisions of the government. From a communicative standpoint, this means that the communication channels on the national political level are blocked for the ANSA. One possibility to attain re-inclusion into the (world) political system and potentially balance the asymmetric relationship with the government is to address actors on the world political level (secondary inclusion) (Sienknecht

2018: 99–100). Therefore, the quest for recognition has a strategic component. If the ANSA receives recognition from actors of the world political system, this reputational resource can help to overcome the political exclusion or even facilitate a separatist process.

Nevertheless, not only ANSAs are striving for international recognition. Since the emergence of the Responsibility to Protect norm and the subsequent softening of the sovereign shell of states, one can observe a particular tendency of governments that are in conflict with an ANSA to avoid overtly contradicting established international norms (Wolf 2011). Frequently, the government's aim is to remain capable of acting while preventing interference from the international community. Most governments strive to become or remain a recognised actor in the world political realm by justifying their use of force against ANSAs via international norms. In order to legitimise their own behaviour, they often mis-recognise ANSAs and label them as terrorists, militia or bandits (Biene and Daase 2015: 220).

The practices of ANSAs seeking recognition do not occur merely out of rationalist reasoning but are embedded in a normative setting. I argue that whether international actors recognise the conflict narratives of ANSAs or governments as legitimate depends on this normative discourse. Seeking recognition by actors of the world political system means framing one's narrative along acknowledged normative discourses – for example, in the case of ANSAs the norm violations in the field of human rights, such as political exclusion or persecution on ethnic or religious grounds – can serve as a normative reference point. Governments, on the other hand, frequently refer to norms connected to combating terrorism in order to legitimate their actions vis-à-vis an ANSA (Toros 2008: 408). In other words, the violation of norms which are upheld by actors of the world political system can serve as a starting point for attaining recognition.

Addressing actors on the world political stage is no new phenomenon in intra-state conflict situations. For example, during the Cold War it was a common strategy for an ANSA to refer to one of the two blocs, framing its conflict narrative according to the respective ideology. The conflict in Angola, for example, was a so-called 'proxy war' in which both the US and the Soviet Union were involved and supported opposing conflict parties (Kalyvas and Balcells 2010: 416). With the end of the Cold War, this phenomenon became less common, and IOs gained in relevance, the United Nations and regional organisations such as the EU or the African Union in particular emerging as crucial players in the world political system. Since then, IOs have had an important role in mediating conflicts and in softening the sovereignty norm in favour of increasingly strong individual rights.[4]

Recognition processes have many different forms and they can materialise in several ways. Biene and Daase (2015) conceptualise recognition and non-recognition as a gradual process on a continuum with two poles. 'This continuum runs from highly formalised to extremely informal modes of recognition, and from the recognition of non-state actors and other political collectives as legitimate negotiating partners to the recognition of entities as sovereign states and as states with specific entitlements' (Geis et al. 2015: 16). Over the decades, IOs have had many different roles in the realm of intra-state conflicts. Concerning recognition processes, one can roughly categorise these roles along three different lines.

First, IOs choose to support an ANSA and recognise its quest by supporting it diplomatically or militarily ('thick recognition'). In such cases, IOs balance the asymmetric power relations between the government and the ANSA by entering the conflict on the side of the ANSA. The dyadic social structure between the conflict parties remains in place, but with a stronger non-state conflict party.

Secondly, IOs choose to stay neutral and act as mediators in order to resolve the conflict. Here, the IO enters the conflict as a third party and changes its social structure from a dyadic to a triadic one (Simmel 1992: 125–150). A third actor opens new possibilities to settle the conflict because the IO can offer guarantees for supervising agreements or ceasefires – for example, diplomatically or militarily by sending peacekeeping or peace enforcement troops ('thin recognition').

A third option for IOs is to support the government in fighting the ANSA, for example by freezing the ANSA's funds or by labelling the ANSA a terrorist organisation ('mis-recognition'). In such cases, the conflict structure remains a dyadic one, and the asymmetric power structure between the conflict parties is stabilised and even strengthened.

In a fourth option, IOs simply do not react to recognition-seekers and non-recognise ANSAs deliberately ('non-recognition').

Table 6.1 broadly summarises the different roles of IOs in intra-state conflict situations. While the table shows the actual practices of recognition from IOs at the world political level, it has already been stated that the practices of recognition are embedded in a normative discourse. This can become problematic when different normative discourses collide. When we think about cases in which both human rights norms and anti-terror norms are referred to by opposing sides, the concrete political practice of the IO must be analysed.

The PKK's quest for recognition on the world political stage

The Kurds experienced political exclusion from the very beginning of the Turkish Republic in 1925 (Patton 2003: 43). Approximately 18 per cent of

Table 6.1 Practices of recognition by IOs of the world political system

Role of the IO	Main addressee	Form of recognition	Conflict structure
Recognition of the quest of the ANSA	Recognition of the ANSA; non-recognition of the government/military	**Thick recognition** Support of the ANSA; military intervention; diplomatic sanctions against the government; etc.	IO as supporter of the ANSA → reinforcement of the dyadic conflict structure, but balancing the asymmetric power structure between ANSA and government
Neutral mediator	Both the ANSA and the government are recognised	**Thin recognition** From facilitative to direct mediation, and high-powered diplomacy	IO as impartial mediator; IO changes the conflict structure to a triadic one
Recognition of the quest of the government	Recognition of the government; mis-recognition of the ANSA	**Mis-recognition** Support of the government; freezing of funds from the ANSA; labelling as terror group; etc.	IO as supporter of the government → reinforcement of the dyadic conflict structure by strengthening the asymmetric structure
Non-recognition of the quest of the ANSA	Non-recognition of the ANSA	**Non-recognition** The IO deliberately withholds or denies the recognition of the ANSA	IO as an observer of the conflict → the dyadic structure of the conflict remains

Source: own illustration based on Sienknecht (2018: 123).

the Turkish population (ca. 20 million people) is Kurdish, thus constituting the biggest ethnic minority in Turkey. Although Kurds are allowed to vote and run for political office, a practice of exclusion was maintained regarding political parties or individuals who emphasised their Kurdish identity (Avci 2006: 74; Kurban and Ensaroğlu 2010: 34). In 1978, the PKK emerged as an organisation that claimed to be the sole and permanent representative of the Kurds, and it quickly entered into a power conflict with the Turkish government. While initially being one organisation among many others that claimed to represent the Kurds, the PKK came to be the dominant representation (also by violent means) in the aftermath of the military coup in Turkey in 1980 (Özcan 2006: 202). The leadership profited from safe havens in neighbouring countries, especially Syria, which bolstered its organisational structure and rendered repression by the Turkish government ineffective (Criss 1995; Imset 1992; Lüdemann-Dundua 2006). 'The small group of armed men and women grew into a tightly-organised guerrilla force of some 15,000, with a 50,000-plus civilian militia in Turkey and tens of thousands of active backers in Europe' (Marcus 2007a: 75). The violent conflict between the Turkish government and the PKK began in 1984 and developed into a full-scale civil war, which to date has led to over 40,000 battle-related deaths (UCDP/PRIO 2017). From the beginning of the conflict, the Turkish government framed it as a mere security problem and mis-recognised the PKK by labelling it a terrorist organisation. The PKK is not recognised by the Turkish government as a legitimate representative of the Kurdish minority (thick recognition), but it is recognised as a conflict party (thin recognition) (Wendt 2003: 511–512).

The conflict between the Turkish government and the PKK has been ongoing for more than thirty years (at different levels of intensity) and has multiple international dimensions, which makes it possible to trace back the active lobbying process of the PKK and the dynamic (non-)recognition from the world political level. For reasons of clarity, I categorise the conflict into five different phases.

Phase 1: the internationalisation of the Kurdish question (1920–1970)

Long before the PKK emerged as the dominant Kurdish actor in the conflict with the Turkish government, the world political system played an important role in setting up the framework of the conflict between the Kurds and the Turkish government. With the end of the First World War and the collapse of the Ottoman Empire, the victorious powers were responsible for the border demarcation of the Turkish Republic (Steinbach 2000: 21). While the Treaty of Sèvres in 1920 promised the right of self-determination to all groups of the former empire (including the Kurds), it was revised by the

Treaty of Lausanne in 1923. The latter changed the territorial border demarcations of the Turkish Republic and recognised only non-Muslim ethnicities (such as Greeks and Armenians) as minorities, granting them minority rights (Bezwan 2008: 271; Özcan 2006: 78). The Kurds were recognised as 'Turkish', whereby they lost their right to their own territory (Strohmeier and Yalçın-Heckmann 2003: 88–97). Subsequently, several Kurdish uprisings took place and the friend–foe dichotomy between Kurdish groups and the Turkish government manifested itself in form of the increasing rejection of the Kurdish identity by the Turkish state. This non-recognition of Kurdish identity by Turkish officials went so far as to prohibit the word 'Kurd' when talking about the ethnic group. Instead, the Kurdish people were officially referred to as 'Mountain Turks' (a reference to their main region of settlement in the southeast of Turkey) (Bezwan 2008: 288; Gunter 2008: 64; Moustakis and Chaudhuri 2005: 81; Somer 2004: 246).

In this early phase of the Turkish Republic, no conflict system with clearly identifiable conflict parties had developed; rather, diffuse and *ad hoc* cleavages characterised relations between the Turkish government and the Kurds, accompanied by forced settlement programmes and assimilation policies, in order to reach a Turkish majority of population on the whole territory of the Turkish Republic (Strohmeier and Yalçın-Heckmann 2003: 100–101; Wimmer 2002: 67). Nevertheless, this early phase served as a reference frame for legitimising Kurdish claims towards the international community. After all, in the Kurdish conflict narrative, the Entente had been responsible for the fact that the Kurds were not recognised as an ethnic group in their own right – neither by the Turkish government nor by the international community. This was a first instance of internationalisation of the Kurdish quest and, still today, serves as a legitimation narrative to hold the international community responsible for the suppression of the Kurdish identity in Turkey.

Phase 2: the emergence of the PKK and its relation to the Soviet Union (1970–1999)

The PKK was formed by Abdullah Öcalan in the 1970s. With the emergence of the PKK, a dyadic conflict structure between the Turkish government and the PKK developed. In the beginning, the PKK was organised along a Marxist-socialist ideology and its overall goal was to create an independent Kurdish state in the southeast of Turkey and parts of the neighbouring countries inhabited by Kurds (Iran, Iraq and Syria). In the beginning, the PKK addressed the Kurdish situation in Turkey with a class-based analysis and fought for the independence and unification of Kurdish people (Bacik and Coskun 2011: 251). The Marxist ideology served as a basis for demanding independence from the 'capitalist' Turkish state and for initiating contacts to other like-minded left-wing groups and gaining recognition from other states. In this regard, the Soviet Union played a decisive role, as it seemed to be a natural supporter of 'national liberation struggles of oppressed people' (Balci 2017: 112). Similar to many other leftist revolutionary organisations, the PKK used its ideological foundation to mobilise supporters (Gurbuz 2015: 9).[5] In order to achieve its goals, the PKK employed a guerrilla strategy, which was very common for leftist groups in the second half of the twentieth century. Although there is no evidence that the Soviet Union recognised the PKK officially or supported it militarily or economically, it played an important role for the ideological base and justification of PKK's conflict narrative (Balci 2017: 113). This underlines the active role of ANSAs in attaching themselves to a normative frame on the world political level. The PKK positioned itself on the side of communism and against US 'imperialism', thus becoming eligible for support from other states and groups of the communist bloc or affiliated with them (Balci 2017: 86). Some authors claim that the PKK was established with the help of Soviet forces and with the aim of balancing the influence of the US within the region (Balci 2017: footnote 7). Another hint for the support of the Soviet Union was the fact that, in the early 1990s, the PKK was in possession of Russian-designed SA-7 Strela shoulder-fired missiles (Marcus 2007b: 188–189). Nevertheless, this could also very well be attributed to the widespread illicit selling of Red Army stocks after the collapse of the Soviet Union.

In Syria, to which the PKK resettled before the military coup in Turkey in 1980, the PKK initiated contacts with other leftist groups, such as the Palestine Liberation Organisation (PLO) and the Armenian Secret Army for the Liberation of Armenia (Criss 1995: 32; Phillips 2015: 55). These groups established contact with IOs and European states to set their quest for self-determination on their respective agendas. For example, relations between the PLO and the EU had already been set up in 1975 as part of the European–Arabic dialogue in the aftermath of the Yom Kippur War. The leadership of the PKK followed this example and in the 1990s initiated protests and campaigns in Europe to attract political attention (Sienknecht 2018: 194). From the 1990s, the PKK began repeatedly underlining the importance of Europe for solving the conflict and tried to initiate and stabilise communication structures to European institutions (Baser 2011: 16).

Phase 3: the turn towards the West (1990s)

The PKK's turn towards the West was accompanied by a change in ideology. With the collapse of the Soviet Union, the PKK moved away from conventional

Marxism in order to reach and attract more supporters (Balci 2017: 135) – within Turkey as well as Europe. The Marxist agenda was transformed into more universal goals, which focused on the individual and the humanisation of society. In 1995, the PKK removed the hammer and sickle from its flag (Balci 2017: 135) and reframed its conflict narrative to fall in line with the norms and values represented by the West, such as human rights and democracy (Rumelili et al. 2011). In this way, the PKK was able to address European institutions that were based on these universal values much more easily. In line with this, the structures of the political work in Europe were professionalised. Several offices, institutes, action groups, the Kurdish National Congress (Kongreya Neteweyî ya Kurdistanê, KNK) as well as an umbrella organisation for coordinating political work abroad (Kongreya Civakên Demokratîk a Kurdîstanîyên Ewrupa, KCD-E)[6] were established in European capitals (Baser 2011: 16; Gunter 2018: 185). By institutionalising political representation in European countries, especially in Brussels and Strasbourg, the PKK set the stage for addressing European institutions and for establishing relationships in the world political system.[7]

Those relationships were grounded on demands for the realisation of basic human rights. The human rights violations such as denial of fair trials, extrajudicial killings, contestation of the prohibition of torture and assimilation politics of the Turkish government towards the Kurds served as communicative reference points and generated support by European authorities, states and civil society for the Kurdish cause (European Commission 1998, 1999, 2000; Interviews 5 and 6).[8] The PKK used its lobby offices, Kurdish institutes and media outlets to initiate contacts with European representatives. Members of the Kurdish diaspora – associated with the PKK – regularly addressed members of leftist parties in the European Parliament or Members of European Parliament with a working focus on human rights (Eccarius-Kelly 2002: 112; Interviews 5 and 6). Kurdish activists enjoyed regular access to European representatives and used these structures to proliferate the PKK's conflict narrative and to receive recognition by European institutions (Interview 4).[9] They provided numerous human rights reports on the situation in southeast Turkey which directly influenced European representatives' stance on the subject (Interview 3).[10]

In the 1990s, there was much support for their fight against the massive human rights violations committed by the Turkish government; meaning the EU recognised the Kurdish demands and supported them diplomatically, while increasingly pressuring the Turkish government via different means (thick recognition). Examples such as the awarding of the Sakharov prize to Leyla Zana (1995) – a Kurdish politician sentenced to fifteen years in prison in Turkey – the suspension of the EU–Turkey Joint Parliamentary Committee for a short period as a reaction to her imprisonment, and the repeated addressing of the Kurdish issue within the Committee, as well as the postponement of the Customs Union between the EU and Turkey in 1994 due to ongoing human rights violations, were clear signs of the recognition of Kurdish grievances by the EU. Particularly beneficial to the Kurdish cause was the initiation of accession talks between the EU and Turkey. As the candidate country must fulfil the Copenhagen Criteria – including the political criteria – the EU had substantial political leverage towards the Turkish government. The Kurds attached huge expectations to the accession process regarding the improvement of their political recognition in Turkey.[11] Even though the Turkish government tried to frame the conflict as a mere security problem and the PKK as a terrorist organisation, the Kurdish organisations were able to frame their quest in line with European norms and values and therefore gained access to the European institutions (Sienknecht 2018).

According to the categorisation of the roles of IOs, one can speak of a thick recognition of the ANSA's quest by the EU in the 1990s. This helped balance the asymmetric relationship in favour of the Kurdish party. However, this was only true for the PKK's agenda, which was by then based on the normative carpet of human rights, and not so much for the organisation itself.

Phase 4: the changing normative discourse and the refusal to recognise the PKK as a legitimate negotiation partner (2000s)

With the capture of Öcalan in 1998, the PKK pushed its strategic-ideological transformation even further. Öcalan no longer demanded independence of the Kurdish state as in the early 1990s but aimed for a democratic solution within the borders of the Turkish state (Balci 2017: 135). A radical democratisation of Turkey was supposed to guarantee the inclusion of Kurdish identity into the Turkish state (Jongerden and Akkaya 2011: 144). The war in Kosovo and the creation of an independent state through the support of Western countries as well as the establishment of an autonomous Kurdish region in northern Iraq reinforced the PKK's claims that its cause for more autonomy within the borders of the Turkish state was just and legitimate. This ideological change went along with a change in means: in 1999, Öcalan decided that the violent struggle had reached its goal and that political developments should now be at the centre of the PKK's development. The abandonment of the armed struggle and the declaration of unilateral ceasefires were manifestations of this development. Öcalan tried to transform the PKK from a revolutionary movement into a democratic one, which was mirrored in transformations of the organisational structure of the PKK and several name changes (in 2002 into the Kurdistan Freedom and Democracy Congress [KADEK], in 2003 into the People's Congress of Kurdistan [Kongra-Gel or KGK], in 2005 into the Kurdistan Democratic Confederation [KKK], and in 2007 into the Kurdistan Communities Union [KCK]).

In the political discourse, the international community continued to refer to the Kurdish ANSA as the PKK. This could be construed as a mis-recognition of the PKK's self-induced democratisation and the attempts of the PKK to receive broad recognition as a legitimate actor. The name changes were not regarded as a new orientation of the ANSA, but rather as an attempt to prevent prosecution. Supporters of the PKK also continued to refer to its original name.

In this period, the EU remained the relevant addressee for lobbying on the world political stage. Several interviews corroborated that the PKK expected to receive recognition as the legitimate negotiating partner for solving the conflict. Öcalan referred to other examples like the Irish Republican Army, the African National Congress and the Basque Country and Freedom (ETA), with whom Western actors had also negotiated to find a conflict solution (Gunter 1998). While support from European actors was rather strong considering the gross human rights violations towards the Kurdish minority in the 1990s, a shift occurred in the early 2000s. This shift went along with an improvement of the basic human rights situation in Turkey and a widening of the Kurdish demands. In connection with the fulfilment of its basic human rights by the Turkish government, the ANSA demanded the realisation of cultural group rights (Kurban 2013). The expectation of an overall recognition of Kurdish identity (including the right to Kurdish-language education and Kurdish media) was brought to the attention of the world political audience. This shift in demands can be explained by a broadening of normative reference points. Especially the political dimension of the Copenhagen Criteria, the Framework Convention for the Protection of National Minorities, and the European Charter for Regional and Minority Languages were referred to on a regular basis (Kurban 2013).[12]

This period was framed by the initialisation of EU accession talks with Turkey. The Turkish government had a strong interest in convincing the European institutions to frame the conflict according to its own interpretation – a mere security problem, with the PKK being a terrorist organisation and the main aggressor. After granting basic rights to the Kurds in the late 1990s and early 2000s, Turkey had somewhat restored its legitimacy on the world political level. This process was accompanied by a norm shift in the early 2000s. The terror attacks in the US in 2001 led to a growing importance of anti-terror norms on the international level and presented a welcome communicative reference point for the Turkish government for legitimising its repressive approach towards the PKK. Again, this policy touches upon the different norms that are prevalent on the world political level. The Turkish government lobbied extensively for its case and its narrative of the conflict on grounds of anti-terror norms and the sovereignty norm (see the session documents of the EU–Turkey Joint Parliamentary Committee 2000–2018). One central aim of Turkey during the accession talks was to convince the European institutions to put the PKK on the European list of terrorist organisations established in 2001. While attempts to delegitimise the PKK had already started back in the 1990s, Turkish officials intensified their efforts towards European institutions to mis-recognise the PKK and label it as a terrorist organisation considering the anti-terror discourse in the early 2000s (Interview 4).

The foreign ministers of the EU member states labelled the PKK as a terrorist organisation in 2002. This move of the PKK's mis-recognition was a success for the Turkish government as it shifted the support of the EU to the acceptance of the conflict narrative of the Turkish government. The renewal of the PKK's labelling as a terrorist organisation by the foreign ministers of the European member states every six months underlines ongoing lobbying efforts by the Turkish government and the stabilisation and reproduction of the mis-recognition. Even though the EU still condemned Turkish human rights violations towards the Kurds in its progress reports and resolutions in the Parliament, its condemnation of the PKK as a terrorist organisation has had considerable effect on the asymmetrical relationship of the conflict system.

This example shows the discrepancy between the discursive support and the practices of an organisation. While both human rights and anti-terror are established norms which guide the political behaviour on the world political level, we can see a certain trade-off between those two discourses when it comes to intra-state conflicts. The political discourse might suggest that both norms are regarded as equally relevant by the IO – in this case the EU; the practices of the organisations (their real decisions) show, however, that they are institutionally not equivalent, but that they affect the power relationship between the two conflict parties.

The decision of the EU led to a two-fold exclusion of the PKK, both from the national and the world political system. Regardless of their attempts to democratise and to frame their demands in the coat of international norm discourses, in this phase the EU only recognised the quest for basic human rights as legitimate but not the PKK's quest for being recognised as a legitimate representative of the Kurdish people (Sienknecht 2018). This led to a discursive recognition of the general aims of the Kurdish minority and a support of the Turkish government, but a practical mis-recognition of the ANSA itself.

Phase 5: renewed recognition (2013–2019)?

Starting in 2013, the ascendance of IS resulted in a re-evaluation of the Kurdish role – at least in some parts of society. While city after city fell under the rule of IS and European cities suffered horrendous terrorist attacks, Kurdish groups gained prominence and were praised as one of the few who actually fought IS on the ground (Seufert 2015: 73).

In Iraq, the West allied with the Kurdistan Democratic Party and the Patriotic Union of Kurdistan by conducting military training and by supplying arms and equipment to the Peshmerga (military unit of the Kurds in Iraq) from 2014. In Syria, the US proactively supported the Democratic Union Party (Partiya Yekîtiya Demokrat, PYD) – the Syrian sister party of the PKK. By supporting the People's Protection Units (Yekîneyên Parastina Gel, YPG, the PYD's military arm) from 2014, the US had contributed to transforming a guerrilla unit built by the PKK into a semi-regular and well-organised army (Seufert 2015: 73). In 2017, US president Trump authorised arms supplies to the YPG.[13] The Kurds in Syria have some historical and ideological ties with the PKK, as Abdullah Öcalan operated for almost twenty years from Syrian territory when training and educating PKK fighters.

The cooperation between PKK-affiliated troops and the international community, as well as the Kurds' secular ideology, renewed the question of how to deal with the PKK – should it be removed from the list of terrorist organisations, against the will of NATO member Turkey? Voices from leftist organisations and parties in Europe demanded the withdrawal of the PKK from the list of terrorist organisations (e.g. die Linke, the leftist German party, filed an unsuccessful request to repeal the listing of the PKK as a terrorist organisation in the German Bundestag in 2014). European institutions also started to rethink their labelling of the PKK in the face of IS atrocities. The Parliamentary Assembly of the Council of Europe (PACE) decided to remove the PKK from the list of terrorist organisations in April 2013. In Resolution 1925 (2013) of the Post-Monitoring Dialogue with Turkey, PACE speaks of a 'conflict between the Turkish state and the PKK' and no longer of a 'fight against terrorism'.[14]

Yet still today, most states and organisations have not recognised the PKK or its sister parties as legitimate negotiation partners. So, while the political recognition of the PKK seems to remain elusive given the concerted and continued effort of the Turkish government, the fight against IS has diversified the discourse about the PKK. But in the end, the PKK is not recognised as the legitimate representative of the Kurdish people. On the contrary, the decision of the US to withdraw from Syria in 2019 and allow Turkish troops to march in Kurdish-controlled areas in the north strengthens the perception that the mis-recognition of the PKK as a terrorist organisation radiates to affiliated groups as well. While the West still debates how to deal with the PKK and affiliated groups, the Kurdish administration in northern Syria requested, and received, military support from the Syrian government in reaction to the military invasion by Turkish troops and the withdrawal of the US. Those developments underline the (necessary) strategic alignment of the Kurdish groups, which otherwise would have been overrun by Turkish troops. The cooperation with the Assad regime and Russia in light of the prevailing mis-recognition by the West characterises the situation in Syria since 2015.[15]

It remains to be seen what the struggle against IS will ultimately mean for the Kurdish quest for recognition on the world political level. This fifth phase clearly demonstrates two things: on the one hand, the changing course of the West towards the PKK and affiliated groups, and, on the other hand, the (necessary) flexibility in the group's strategic orientation within the world political system.

Conclusion: reconsidering (non-)recognition

The goal of this chapter was to show that ANSAs lobby actively for their recognition on the world political level along global norms and that (non-) recognition processes are subject to constant transformation, depending on the dominant normative structures which enable and restrain the recognition of ANSAs by states and, in particular, by IOs. The analysis has shown that the PKK's quest for recognition has led the organisation in multiple directions over the years. While the conflict featured an international dimension from its very beginning, the emergence of the PKK as a conflict party has led to the development of international relations with several actors of the world political system. The PKK initially addressed the Soviet Union on grounds of a shared socialist ideology with the expectation that it would be a supporter of the Kurdish national liberation struggle. Additionally, the PKK developed relations with other leftist groups and copied several strategies – for example, the guerrilla tactic in its military fight, but also the reference to IOs as part of its political work. The subsequent turn towards the West in the 1990s demonstrates that the quest for recognition by an ANSA does not have to be tied to a single actor. After the collapse of the Soviet Union, the PKK framed its struggle against the Turkish state in terms of human rights and democratic principles, represented by Western actors. The analysis of the PKK's practices towards international actors supports the assumption of ANSAs being active agents in recognition processes. The PKK lobbied directly for its case by framing its conflict narrative along the respective normative discourse and adjusting it according to the respective international actor.

Furthermore, the analysis has shown that the recognition of ANSAs by IOs is dependent on a normative discourse, which can change over time. In the 1990s, the normative discourse was especially characterised by the acknowledgement and enforcement of basic human rights, which made the rights-based claims of the PKK appear in a favourable light on the international stage. After 9/11, the anti-terror norms gained in relevance and opened avenues for the recognition of the Turkish government by European institutions. With the labelling as a terrorist organisation, the PKK faced a double mis-recognition – on both the national and the world political level. This stresses an important aspect of recognition processes, as it demonstrates that, considering potential norm collisions, IOs might distinguish between the ANSA itself and its specific agenda to remain capable of acting. In consequence, the ANSA was non-recognised while its political goals remained compatible at the same time.

The case study revealed another interesting aspect of recognition processes, namely that the same normative discourse can yield grounds for both the recognition and non-recognition of the same ANSA. The anti-terror discourse provided the normative framework for branding the PKK as terrorists, leading to a restriction of its scope of action in several ways. Just a couple of years later, in face of the violent onslaught of IS, this same discourse served for the legitimation of renewed calls for the re-recognition of the PKK in the international sphere. In other words, the anti-terror discourse – in the early 2000s deployed to non-recognise the PKK – offered new points of reference once a more menacing threat appeared, in the fight against which the PKK-affiliated organisations and the Western states were aligned.

According to the four ideal role types of IOs in intra-state conflict situations, one must state that the categorisation is not as clear-cut as theory might suggest. We can see an overlap between the support of broader goals of the ANSA's and the Turkish government's demands by the EU. In doing so, the EU does not enter the conflict on one or the other side and neither does it act as a neutral mediator. One can observe a fifth role of the EU, in which it is involved in the conflict, which changes the social structure into a triadic one, but it is not able to act as a neutral mediator. Both sides address the EU in order to receive political support, and both demands are recognised as legitimate, at least to a certain degree. The EU delegitimised the use of violent means and blamed the PKK for the renewed fighting in 2005 but supported the broader goals the PKK claimed to represent. While this might work as a strategy in theory, in the case of the PKK it led to a gradual withdrawal from the European stage and subsequently to a reduced ability for the EU to contribute to conflict settlement. This became obvious when the Turkish government initiated peace talks with the PKK in 2009 without including the EU. Recognising the political goals without recognising the ANSA as a legitimate negotiation partner in order to solve the conflict seems to hinder a conflict settlement – at least in this specific case.

This chapter has demonstrated two things. First, ANSAs are active agents in lobbying for their recognition on the world stage; secondly, the process of recognition and non-recognition is dynamic. Both aspects are very important for the question of how to deal with ANSAs and how to reach conflict settlements. Unless the involved conflict parties are recognised as negotiation partners – and that does not necessarily mean recognising and legitimising their methods – a conflict settlement is impossible. The international community and IOs in particular should be aware of this and should try to keep their potential influence in asymmetric intra-state conflict situations by acting as mediators – a role the EU could have played much better in light of the Turkish interest in accessing the EU and an interest of the PKK in being recognised as the representative of the Kurdish people.

Notes

1 An intra-state conflict is 'a contested incompatibility that concerns government and/or territory where the use of armed force between two parties, of which at least one is the government of a state, results in at least twenty-five battle related deaths in one calendar year' (UCDP/PRIO (2017) definitions). Sixty-four per cent of the current intra-state conflicts are so-called 'ethnic conflicts' (Denny and Walter 2014: 199).

2 The concept of non-recognition is defined as the deliberate withholding or denial of recognition (see Clément et al. in this volume).

3 Since the seventeenth century, the political system of world society has been differentiated by segmentation into territorial states (Luhmann 2013: 98). Characterised by the emergence of IOs, non-governmental organisations, international treaties and regimes, global structures were institutionalised and led to the development of the system of world politics (Albert 2016: 89).

4 To assure individual humanitarian rights and to prevent genocides, some IOs, such as the UN or the Council of Europe, developed certain strategies such as early warning systems to be able to react swiftly to possibly escalating conflict situations. They constantly scan their environment for norm violations and potentially escalating factors and try to settle conflicts as early as possible.

5 Unlike Gurbuz (2015: 9), I assume that changes in the world political system are an essential driving factor for gradual changes in revolutionary ideologies. In the following pages, I will show that changes on the global level are leading to a change in ideologies of the PKK – from demanding independence to autonomy within the borders of the Turkish state. However, this does not mean that local conditions lack a comparably high influence on changing the ideology.

6 Until 2014, the KCD-E was named the Confederation of Kurdish Associations in Europe (*Konfederasyona Komelên Kurd Li Avrupa,* KON-KURD).

7 Interview with a Member of the KNK in Brussels conducted in Brussels in June 2013 (Interview 2).
8 Interview with a Member of the European Parliament (MEP), Group of the European People's Party (Christian Democrats) and European Democrats, Committee on Foreign Affairs, Subcommittee on Human Rights conducted in Strasbourg in January 2012 (Interview 5); Interview with an MEP, Group of the European People's Party (Christian Democrats) and European Democrats, Member of the EU–Turkey Joint Parliamentary Committee conducted in Strasbourg in January 2012 (Interview 6).
9 Interview with a former MEP (2002–2009), Group of the Greens/European Free Alliance, EU–Turkey Joint Parliamentary Committee conducted in Istanbul in May 2012 (Interview 4).
10 Interview with an expert on Turkey conducted in Berlin in June 2013 (Interview 3).
11 Interview with a member of a civil society organisation conducted in Diyarbakır in May 2012 (Interview 1).
12 Until 1999, the PKK had demanded separation from the Turkish state; since then, however, it has lobbied for a unified Turkish state with the recognition of political, cultural and social rights for the Kurds.
13 In light of the Syrian war, an assembly of Kurdish, Turkmen, Assyrian and Arab delegates proclaimed the Democratic Federation of Northern Syria (better known as Rojava), controlled by the PYD. Rojava literally means 'west', or 'where the sun sets', and refers to western Kurdistan. It includes three self-declared autonomous 'cantons' (Afrin, Kobane and Hasaka) and came into being after the withdrawal of Assad's forces in 2011 (Pollock 2016: 2).
14 From 2013 until 2015, Turkey engaged in peace talks with the PKK. In this time, Turkey invited PYD officials to Ankara for official talks. With the ending of the peace talks, the ties between Turkey and the PYD also changed, becoming more hostile and clashing when Turkey invaded north Syria (Pollock 2016: 3).
15 See for a description of the historical ties between Russia and the Kurds Borshchevskaya (2016).

References

Albert, M. (2016), *A Theory of World Politics* (Cambridge: Cambridge University Press).

Avci, G. (2006), 'Turkey's EU politics: consolidating democracy through enlargement?', in H. Sjursen (ed.), *Questioning EU Enlargement: Europe in Search of Identity* (London and New York, NY: Routledge), pp. 62–68.

Bacik, G. and B. B. Coskun (2011), 'The PKK problem: explaining Turkey's failure to develop a political solution', *Studies in Conflict and Terrorism* 34, 248–265.

Balci, A. (2017), *The PKK–Kurdistan Workers' Party's Regional Politics: During and After the Cold War* (Cham: Springer International Publishing).

Baser, B. (2011), *Kurdish Diaspora Political Activism in Europe with a Particular Focus on Great Britain* (Berlin and Luzern: Berghof Peace Support and Centre for Just Peace and Democracy).

Bezwan, N. (2008), *Türkei und Europa: Die Staatsdoktrin der Türkischen Republik, ihre Aufnahme in die EU und die kurdische Nationalfrage* (Baden-Baden: Nomos).
Biene, J. and C. Daase (2015), 'Gradual recognition: curbing non-state violence in asymmetric conflicts', in A. Geis, C. Fehl, C. Daase and G. Kolliarakis (eds), *Recognition in International Relations: Rethinking a Political Concept in a Global Context* (London: Palgrave Macmillan), pp. 220–236.
Borshchevskaya, A. (2016), *Russia in the Middle East: Motives, Consequences, Prospects* (Washington, DC: The Washington Institute for Near East Policy).
Cederman, L.-E., N. B. Weidmann and K. S. Gleditsch (2011), 'Horizontal inequalities and ethnonationalist civil war: a global comparison', *American Political Science Review* 105:3, 478–495.
Cederman, L.-E., A. Wimmer and B. Min (2010), 'Why do ethnic groups rebel? New data and analysis', *World Politics* 62:1, 1–50.
Criss, N. B. (1995), 'The nature of PKK terrorism in Turkey', *Studies in Conflict and Terrorism* 18:1, 17–37.
Denny, E. K. and B. F. Walter (2014), 'Ethnicity and civil war', *Journal of Peace Research* 51:2, 199–212.
Eccarius-Kelly, V. (2002), 'Political movements and leverage points: Kurdish activism in the European diaspora', *Journal of Muslim Minority Affairs* 22:1, 91–118.
European Commission (1998), *Progress Report Turkey 1998*, available online: http://ec.europa.eu/enlargement/archives/pdf/key_documents/1998/turkey_en.pdf; last retrieved 20 February 2020.
European Commission (1999), *Progress Report Turkey 1999*, available online: http://ec.europa.eu/enlargement/archives/pdf/key_documents/1999/turkey_en.pdf; last retrieved 20 February 2020.
European Commission (2000), *Progress Report Turkey 2000*, available online: http://ec.europa.eu/enlargement/archives/pdf/key_documents/2000/tu_en.pdf; last retrieved 20 February 2020.
Geis, A., C. Fehl, C. Daase and G. Kolliarakis (2015), 'Gradual processes, ambiguous consequences: rethinking recognition in international relations', in C. Daase, A. Geis, C. Fehl and G. Kolliarakis (eds), *Recognition in International Relations: Rethinking a Political Concept in a Global Context* (London: Palgrave Macmillan), pp. 3–26.
Gunter, M. M. (1998), 'An interview with the PKK's Abdullah Ocalan', *Journal of Conflict Studies* 18:2, 1–7.
Gunter, M. M. (2008), *The Kurds Ascending: The Evolving Solution to the Kurdish Problem in Iraq and Turkey* (New York, NY: Palgrave Macmillan).
Gunter, M. M. (2018), *Historical Dictionary of the Kurds* (Lanham, MD: Rowman & Littlefield).
Gurbuz, M. E. (2015), 'Ideology in action: symbolic localization of Kurdistan Workers' Party in Turkey', *Sociological Inquiry* 85:1, 1–27.
Gurr, T. R. (2000), *Peoples Versus States: Minorities at Risk in the New Century* (Washington, DC: United States Institute of Peace Press).
Heins, V. (2010), 'Of persons and peoples: internationalizing the critical theory of recognition', *Contemporary Political Theory* 9:2, 149–170.
Honneth, A. (1995), *The Struggle for Recognition: The Moral Grammar of Social Conflicts* (Cambridge, MA: MIT Press).
Imset, I. G. (1992), *The PKK: A Report on Separatist Violence in Turkey (1973–1992)* (Istanbul: Turkish Daily News Publications).

Jongerden, J. and A. H. Akkaya (2011), 'Born from the left: the making of the PKK', in M. Casier and J. Jongerden (eds), *Nationalisms and Politics in Turkey: Political Islam, Kemalism, and the Kurdish Issue* (Abingdon and New York, NY: Routledge), pp. 123–142.

Kalyvas, S. N. and L. Balcells (2010), 'International system and technologies of rebellion: how the end of the Cold War shaped internal conflict', *American Political Science Review* 104:3, 415–429.

Kurban, D. (2013), 'To Europe and back: the three decades of Kurdish struggle in Turkey', available online: www.iai.it/sites/default/files/GTE_PB_07.pdf; last retrieved 20 February 2020.

Kurban, D. and Y. Ensaroğlu (eds) (2010), *Towards a Solution to the Kurdish Question: Constitutional and Legal Recommendations* (Istanbul: TESEV Publications).

Lüdemann-Dundua, A. (2006), 'Kurden in der Türkei: Die Gewaltordnung der PKK', in J. Bakonyi, S. Hensell and J. Siegelberg (eds), *Gewaltordnungen bewaffneter Gruppen: Ökonomie und Herrschaft nichtstaatlicher Akteure in den Kriegen der Gegenwart* (Baden-Baden: Nomos), pp. 193–203.

Luhmann, N. (2013), *Theory of Society: Volume 2, translated by Rhodes Barrett* (Stanford, CA: Stanford University Press).

Marcus, A. (2007a), 'Turkey's PKK: rise, fall, rise again?', *World Policy Journal* 24:1, 75–84.

Marcus, A. (2007b), *Blood and Belief: The PKK and the Kurdish Fight for Independence* (New York, NY: New York University Press).

Moustakis, F. and R. Chaudhuri (2005), 'Turkish–Kurdish relations and the European Union: an unprecedented shift in the Kemalist paradigm?', *Mediterranean Quarterly* 16:4, 77–89.

Münkler, H. (2004), 'Krieg', in G. Göhler, M. Iser and I. Kerner (eds), *Politische Theorie: 22 umkämpfte Begriffe zur Einführung* (Wiesbaden: VS Verlag für Sozialwissenschaften), pp. 227–243.

Özcan, A. K. (2006), *Turkey's Kurds: A Theoretical Analysis of the PKK and Abdullah Öcalan* (London: Routledge).

Patton, M. J. (2003), 'Voices from Turkey's Southeast', *Middle East Report* 227, 42–45.

Phillips, D. L. (2015), *The Kurdish Spring: A New Map of the Middle East* (London and New York, NY: Routledge).

Pollock, D. (2016), 'Making Rojava more like the KRG', in P. Clawson (ed.), *Syrian Kurds as a U.S. Ally: Cooperation and Complications* (Washington, DC: Washington Institute for Near East Policy), pp. 1–11.

Rumelili, B., F. Keyman and B. Isyar (2011), 'Multilayered citizenship in extended European orders: Kurds acting as European citizens', *Journal of Common Market Studies* 49:6, 1295–1316.

Seufert, G. (2015), 'Die Kurden als zentraler Faktor der politischen Entwicklung in der Türkei: Wie weiter mit dem PKK-Verbot?', in G. Seufert (ed.), *Der Aufschwung der kurdischen Politik: Zur Lage der Kurden in Irak, Syrien und der Türkei. SWP-Studie* (Berlin: Stiftung Wissenschaft und Politik), pp. 61–76.

Sienknecht, M. (2018), *Entgrenzte Konflikte in der Weltgesellschaft: Zur Inklusion internationaler Organisationen in innerstaatliche Konfliktsysteme* (Wiesbaden: Springer VS).

Sienknecht, M. (2019), 'Conflict diplomacy – political de-bordering strategies in intrastate conflicts', *Special Issue: ZefKo: Studying Micro Dynamics in Civil Wars*, guest editors: R. van der Haer, J. Vüllers and N. Weidmann, 8:2, 183–211.

Simmel, G. (1992), *Georg Simmel Gesamtausgabe Bd. 11 Soziologie: Untersuchungen über die Formen der Vergesellschaftung* (Frankfurt am Main: Suhrkamp).
Somer, M. (2004), 'Turkey's Kurdish conflict: changing context, and domestic and regional implications', *Middle East Journal* 58:2, 235–253.
Steinbach, U. (2000), *Geschichte der Türkei* (Munich: Beck).
Strohmeier, M. and L. Yalçın-Heckmann (2003), *Die Kurden: Geschichte, Politik, Kultur* (Munich: Beck).
Taylor, C. (1992), 'The politics of recognition', in A. Gutmann (ed.), *Multiculturalism: Examining the Politics of Recognition* (Princeton, MA: Princeton University Press), pp. 25–73.
Tilly, C. and S. G. Tarrow (2007), *Contentious Politics* (Boulder, CO: Paradigm Publishers).
Toros, H. (2008), '"We don't negotiate with terrorists!": legitimacy and complexity in terrorist conflicts', *Security Dialogue* 39:4, 407–426.
UCDP/PRIO (2017), 'Armed conflict dataset, 1946–2016', available online: http://pcr.uu.se/research/ucdp/datasets/ucdp_prio_armed_conflict_dataset/; last retrieved 20 February 2020.
Vogt, M., N.-C. Bormann, S. Rüegger, et al. (2015), 'Integration data on ethnicity, geography, and conflict: the ethnic power relations dataset family', *Journal of Conflict Resolution* 59:7, 1327–1342.
Wendt, A. (2003), 'Why a world state is inevitable', *European Journal of International Relations* 9:4, 491–542.
Wimmer, A. (2002), *Nationalist Exclusion and Ethnic Conflict: Shadows of Modernity* (Cambridge and New York, NY: Cambridge University Press).
Wolf, R. (2011), 'Respect and disrespect in international politics: the significance of status recognition', *International Theory* 3:1, 105–142.

7

Recognition, respect and identity in the discourse of China's Uyghur problem

Chien-peng Chung

Introduction

Covering an area of 1.66 million square kilometres, Xinjiang (Uyghur) Autonomous Region is the largest provincial-level unit in the People's Republic of China (PRC). It contains some 23 million people, about 60 per cent of whom are from ethnic groups other than the Han-Chinese, who are the predominant people of China (An 2017). About 45 per cent of Xinjiang's population is constituted by the Uyghurs, a Turkic-speaking people who mostly practise Sunni Islam and are the largest ethnic group in the region; 10 per cent by the Turkic Muslim Kazaks, and 40 per cent by the Han. Xinjiang's history of short-lived Uyghur independence movements in the 1930s and 1940s has inflamed the passions of some Uyghur militants to realise an independent Xinjiang, which they refer to as Uyghuristan or, more commonly, East Turkestan. Others typically want a minimum of recognition from the Chinese state that Xinjiang should be considered the historic homeland of the Uyghurs. For top officials in Xinjiang, the biggest challenge has been to prevent terrorist activities by alleged Uyghur separatist groups, as the region has been considered by the national leadership as China's frontline in the fight against terrorism. This has particularly been the case since the early 1990s, with the collapse of the Soviet Union and the independence of its Turkic Muslim Central Asian republics serving as an example for the Uyghur militants (Dillon 2018; Jacobs 2017).

This chapter analyses the Chinese government's practices towards the Uyghurs as a form of mis-recognition. In particular, it argues that, while the government has granted the Uyghurs some forms of economic participation and pursued policies of affirmative action, the dominant strategy remains that of delegitimising the Uyghurs' identity claims. The chapter unfolds its argument by engaging different concepts of (mis-)recognition for analysing the

Chinese government's behaviour towards the Uyghurs. First, it introduces the concepts of mis-recognition and labelling and contextualises them with the broader recognition literature. It demonstrates how the Chinese government made use of the terrorism label in order to delegitimise the Uyghurs' political grievances. Then it discusses the notion of respect and disrespect, and the dichotomy between recognition and redistribution, arguing that the latter cannot replace the former and may even amount to mis-recognition: the framing of the Uyghurs' problem as economic grievances precisely undermines their quest for recognition as an indigenous Turkic Muslim community in China's Xinjiang region. As the next part argues, being recognised in terms of one's own identity is essential to transforming Uyghur armed non-state actors (ANSAs) into non-violent actors. In the final part of the chapter, the question of whether or not to talk to ANSAs among the Uyghurs will be discussed and, based on this, policy recommendations will be given.

Defining (mis-)recognition and labelling terrorism

Recognition may be regarded as the acceptance, and indication of the acceptance, of another human entity's construction and perception of its own identity. Mis-recognition, or that which is perceived as a lack of due recognition, experienced by individuals or collective actors as humiliation, disrespect or false representation of their identity, is seen as a major cause of political discontent and resistance. Acts of mis-recognition constitute acts of injustice when they impede people from becoming full, and equal, members of a social collective (Geis 2018: 614). When recognition is partially or wholly denied, an individual or social group perceives its identity to be threatened (Clément 2014: 429). As such, continuous or recurring acts of mis-recognition are capable of generating conflicts, especially when minority groups in a society must struggle for the recognition of their rights and identities. Struggles for recognition can thus be interpreted as a way in which stigmatised and oppressed groups seek to maintain collective self-respect (Honneth 1995: 156).

While mis-recognition may cause conflicts, recognition is considered a potential key to promoting conflict transformation. It may help parties to achieve peace by modifying their images of one another and of the problem, rather than just reaching an uneasy compromise that may not last. Recognition is divided in critical International Relations theory into 'thin' and 'thick' forms of recognition. Thin recognition implies the acknowledgement of the existence of an independent legal subject (Wendt 2003: 511–512), such as an ANSA as a party in a conflict. Thick recognition points to recognising and thus accepting differences (Honneth 1995: 122), which includes understanding another's fundamental features of identity in relation to one's own and respecting the features that make a subject unique (Moller 2007: 60; Wendt 2003: 511). It would imply acknowledging the 'other' as part of a larger collective identity whose social standing matters to the 'self'.

However, rather than being granted thin or thick recognition by a state or other collective political actor, ANSAs are often referred to by governments as groups engaging in terrorism, or simply terrorist groups. Since at the state level, relationships of recognition are always relationships of power (Iser 2013: 27), for a government to label a violent group 'terrorists' is meant to delegitimise the actor, if not to downright demonise it. Framing a group in such a derogatory term would allow the authorities to adopt repressive counterterrorist measures such as law enforcement, counterinsurgency or outright military action to criminalise and suppress the group so officially designated. Repressive measures often result in the radicalisation of non-state actors. However, by provoking the use of violence by radicals, the government and its security apparatus will have even more justification to suppress them.

China has a broad definition of what constitutes terrorism. The PRC Counterterrorism Law (Chapter 1, Article 2), promulgated in 2016, defines terrorism as '[a]ny advocacy or activity that, by means of violence, sabotage, or threat, aims to create social panic, undermine public safety, infringe on personal and property rights, or coerce a state organ or an international organisation, in order to achieve political, ideological, or other objectives'. Thus, even slogan-shouting, flag-burning, fruit-throwing or self-immolation, often considered victimless acts of civil disobedience in liberal societies, may under the Counterterrorism Law be designated by the PRC government as acts of terrorism, and individuals or groups of individuals committing those acts as terrorists, for instigating violent disturbances or undermining social stability.

The present Chinese authorities believe that half-hearted responses to organised violence will only encourage more violence, while resolute suppression ensures stability. The Chinese government is confident that its physical domination of Xinjiang is so overriding that there is no necessity to reach for reconciliation with the discontented minorities there. Apart from recognising the existence of a couple of ANSAs in Xinjiang, all the more to delegitimise them and focus public energy on destroying them, no further forms of recognition have been put in place by the government.

(Dis)respect and (mal)distribution in the (mis-)recognition debate

Struggling for recognition is a way for marginalised and discontented groups to obtain respect from other individuals and groups, and to maintain collective self-respect. Respect reflects one's sense of entitlement that others must show consideration confirming one's importance (Wolf 2011: 107). As a value, respect pertains to the affirmation of the existence and uniqueness of the identity of a people. Since the idea of universal human rights was established in modernity, and particularly after the Second World War, assigning and receiving equal dignity or respect is commonly thought to be the central dimension of recognition (Iser 2013: 11). As citizens are supposed to hold equal rights and duties under the law, being arbitrarily denied some of these rights can harm people's self-respect, as it is implied that they are merely second-class citizens (Wolf 2011: 110), bereft of respect from the rest of the citizenry. Because a state institution expresses, and reinforces, underlying attitudes of those who design or reproduce it (Iser 2013: 7), as institutions reflect the values and identities of groups who control them, it can disrespect people or make them feel disrespected.

Being disrespected or humiliated can cause frustration and anger on the part of the individual. Arrogant or condescending treatment from outsiders tends to increase one's attachment to the in-group, dependence on its affirmation and confidence in its values, which comes at the price of blocking the unbiased appreciation of out-group arguments (Wolf 2011: 125). Furthermore, if a person perceives that her collective is under constant threat, that person tends to be highly aware of her membership in the group at all times (Strömbom 2014: 173). Threats to stable boundaries which demarcate groups from one another will often result in efforts to secure the boundaries of the self (Strömbom 2014: 175), crystallising psychological defences and separating the self from others. Patterns of disrespect, if similarly experienced by a large number of individuals in a community, turn victims of discrimination into social movements contesting for recognition of their equal rights (Wolf 2011: 110).

'Peoples', or nations, nationalities or ethnic groups, as they are variously referred to, seek recognition as identifiable, bounded, self-determining political communities (Heins 2010: 161). The desire of individuals to be part of a collective of 'people', and recognised as such, shows no signs of waning or vanishing in the contemporary world. Thus, the struggle for recognition is also about reputation and status (Biene and Daase 2015: 221), and they in turn relate to respect or esteem by others for individual or collective capabilities and accomplishments. Sovereign statehood or independence may be desired because states alone are given recognition by the international community and international law to possess a monopoly in the use of force, which a people may feel they would need to defend themselves and their values and interests. It may also be sought and cherished by human communities as an end in itself, as the highest form of recognition by themselves and outsiders as a 'people' (Honneth 1995: chapter 6).

Citizenship in the Chinese state is legally or constitutionally equal. However, for the ruling Communist Party of China (CPC), whose legitimacy lies with a mechanism of authorisation that consists not of free elections but some sort of hierarchical consultation (Heins 2010: 158), pursuing domestic peace means seeking the consent of major actors and bureaucracies in supporting its authoritarian one-party-state political system. Since ethnicity or religion can always form the basis for political association and mobilisation, the CPC has no wish to see ethnic or religious identities politicised, particularly by groups it could not control, which might then conceivably threaten its monopoly on power. The Chinese government thus in its policies and actions inadvertently or otherwise privileges certain groups, namely CPC cadres, and highlights the cultural attributes of certain communities such as the majority Han-Chinese, while downplaying those of others. Nonetheless, disrespect could also be the product of wilful ignorance – not worth taking the trouble to find out about other peoples, and some people seek recognition as members of an ethnic majority group to acquire what they believe to be a privileged status that enables them to shrug off respect for ethnic minority groups. Many people in the country even consider minorities as exotica having few values or interests worth respecting or preserving. In China, such racist and xenophobic attitudes, referred to as manifestations of 'Great Han Chauvinism', are officially frowned upon, but still afflict many Han-Chinese (Leibold 2013).

Respect in the Western philosophical tradition comes in both equal, universal respect and respect for differences (Onuf 2015: 275). The Chinese government expresses neither type towards Uyghur or other ethnic minorities considered especially troublesome, such as the Tibetans. This could be because in traditional Han-Chinese thought, law functions as a regulatory mechanism rather than a bearer of rights, certainly not political rights. Furthermore, although Han-Chinese overall do not have a problem recognising other human beings as autonomous and rational subjects and according them common courtesy, respect conferred on individuals is differentiated depending on their achievements and position on the social pyramid. Given such an understanding, it is perhaps not surprising that the liberal argument of deriving for persons a sense of equal dignity or respect from a legal or human rights perspective is not well accepted in Han-Chinese political conceptualisations. Since the discourse of respect for Han-Chinese overall pertains to hierarchy and order, minorities who insist on emphasising the saliences of their own characteristics are considered to be (potentially) disruptive to social stability and existing status-ordering.

Some Uyghurs desire to see more decision-making rights to be given to Uyghur officials: a reduction in the number of Han-Chinese migrating to, or residing in, 'their' Xinjiang; and less government interference in religious practices (Clarke 2015). The PRC government unilaterally altered the Uyghur writing script from traditional modified Arabic to Latin in 1965 and back to modified Arabic in 1982, and in the mid-2000s encouraged the merging of Uyghur- and Chinese-language kindergartens and elementary schools into bilingual ones in which Chinese is the main language of instruction (Hamut and Joniak-Lüthi 2015). Since self-rule, demography, religion and language are salient expressions of ethnic identity, their neglect, suppression or alteration by the authorities may very well engender feelings of disrespect for the community concerned. The experiences of disrespect may be severe, prolonged or repetitive enough to bring about violent conflicts in cases where a rational calculation of material risks would rule out mutual escalation (Fearon 1995). They might result in attacks by ANSAs directed chiefly against not so much objects with strategic value but rather targets of symbolic meaning (Wolf 2011: 113), such as party, government and public security buildings, railway stations, bazaars and buses in Xinjiang and elsewhere in China.

As far as the CPC and Chinese government are concerned, self-governing rights have been sufficiently accorded to ethnic minorities in the Constitution of the PRC and legal provisions for regional autonomy. To redress unemployment among the Uyghurs and other non-Han ethnic groups, and the difficulties that they generally have with the Chinese language, the Chinese government has engaged in material redistribution to benefit them by instituting affirmative action policies, such as reserving favourable quotas for government jobs, giving additional points for college admission, and providing long-term low-interest loans to small businesses and poor farmers, for ethnic minorities in their own ethnic autonomous region, prefecture or county. Given such self-perceived generosity on the part of the authorities, unrest in Xinjiang or terrorist attacks by Uyghurs are thus officially considered a question of economic underdevelopment and material inequality exploited by troublemakers (Barabantseva 2009), not identity mis-recognition by the state or systemic discrimination by the ethnic Han-Chinese majority. This perspective, although unsurprising given that a Marxist-Leninist regime might wish to privilege dialectic materialism over dialectic idealism, warrants self-re-examination by the Han-Chinese and the Chinese state. Even if affirmative action policies are deemed necessary to raise the living standards of Uyghurs, can the government, for the sake of greater fairness, allow them to be applied to a Uyghur wherever she or he resides in China instead of just in Xinjiang? Are such policies sufficient to address the discontentment acted upon by Uyghur ANSAs? No less a personage than the secretary-general of the CPC–cum president of the PRC himself, Xi Jinping, in 2014 warned against any 'ethnic melting-pot' thinking or calls for changing any policy associated with regional autonomy or affirmative actions for the country's ethnic minorities (BBC

2017). This is for fear of adverse reaction from some minorities who are beneficiaries of the redistribution system and the bureaucratic interests that administer to their needs.

The relationship between redistribution and recognition is at the heart of the debate between the two preeminent contemporary social thinkers Nancy Fraser and Axel Honneth. Fraser proposes a 'dualist perspective' that considers economic (mal)distribution and cultural (mis-)recognition as two separate axes of (in)justice; neither of which is reducible to the other (Ohlström et al. 2011: 206), for 'we cannot remedy cultural injustices with a politics of redistribution or economic injustices with identity politics' (Ohlström et al. 2011: 217). For Honneth, recognition is the key concept which structures normative life of society; as reciprocal recognition between subjects is a necessary precondition for unimpeded identity-formation and self-realisation (Fraser and Honneth 2003: 125–134). He takes disrespect as experienced by subjects themselves, by allowing subjects' experiences to enter social struggles purely at face value, not discriminating between warranted and unwarranted claims (Ohlström et al. 2011: 208). This is Fraser's main critique of Honneth's perspective. To Honneth, what motivates individuals or social groups to question the prevailing social order and engage in practical resistance is the moral conviction that, with respect to their own situations or particularities, the recognition principles are incorrectly or inadequately applied; therefore, redistributive conflicts also belong to the sphere of struggles for recognition (Ohlström et al. 2011: 213). This is Honneth's essential point of disagreement with Fraser. The economy cannot be considered as a sphere apart from the normative processes of recognition, for the rules organising the distribution of goods relate to the degree of social respect which a social group can enjoy within a society, according to the normative hierarchies and orders of values institutionalised in that society (Ohlström et al. 2011: 218–220).

It may be unfair to say that material redistribution as an answer to recognition claims constitutes a form of 'maldistribution' or 'mis-recognition'. If one buys into Fraser's argument, it is a separate issue from recognition; for a Honneth follower, subordinated groups motivated by feelings of disrespect could be expected to invoke 'the hardly disputable assertion that members of society can only make actual use of their legally guaranteed autonomy if they are assured a minimum of economic resources' (Fraser and Honneth 2003: 149). The problem with material redistribution is that it is grossly inadequate as a means of addressing recognition claims. At best, economic development and redistribution comprise the bases for groups with their own cultural identities or superstructures to manifest; they do not prescribe the recognition and respect for a group's identity by another group or by the state or make up for the lack thereof.

It is conceivable that different regime types – democratic, authoritarian or autocratic – might adopt or prioritise different strategies in dealing with an ANSA. It might well be that a political regime which requires less public approval or electoral legitimacy, such as that of China, will have more manoeuvring space in both applying coercion or offering concessions to ANSAs. This merits further research.

(Mis-)recognition: a matter of identity

The struggle for recognition, which relates to demands for respect or redistribution or both, is ultimately about the affirmation of one's own identity by others. Group identities are translated into nationalist demands through the expressions of commemorative narratives, which are stories based on the shared collective memories of a people to stake, support or contest a political or territorial claim. As 'nationalist movements are often saviours of one people and destroyer of another' (Strömbom 2014: 180), vested political interests may work to uphold the master commemorative narrative of the victorious nationalist group, as there is concern, not altogether illegitimate, that expression of contrition by the victors or victimisers may allow the vanquished or victims to demand stringent terms of redress and compensation.

China, in its essence, is a Han-Chinese state, as the Han ethnic group makes up 90 per cent of the country's population. Dominant Han-Chinese collective identity constructions rely heavily on one master commemorative narrative: China was a once great civilisation which had over-awed and acculturated its surrounding peoples, but became a victim of intrigues and invasions by foreign imperialist powers in the twentieth century which encouraged separatism by its frontier ethnic minorities to split and weaken the Chinese state. Brief but major insurrections by separatist Turkic Muslims which engulfed large areas of Xinjiang in the early 1930s and middle 1940s were blamed on machinations on the part of British India and Soviet Russia respectively. This narrative has lately revealed itself in Chinese voices against China's so-called 'liberal' decade of the 1980s, which blames subsequent Uyghur unrest on heightened self-identification resulting from the excessive building of mosques and publication of Uyghur literature in Xinjiang by the government to appease Uyghur sentiments. In any case, the Chinese government does not see itself as a victimiser of the Uyghurs in Xinjiang. Contra Allan and Keller (2006: 199), it believes that acknowledging and accepting the identity of the 'other' is a zero-sum game, for this may mean having to divide and yield territory and resources, particularly if it admits the 'other' as a victim. Recognising the identity of a separatist ANSA threatens not only the control of the Chinese party-state over parts or all of China, but the Party's identity as well, since the CPC is supposed to represent all fifty-six officially recognised ethnic groups existing in China today. At the risk of simplification, since the Chinese generally fear chaos and thus place much trust in authority, denying counter-narratives serves the silencing or suppression of centrifugal tendencies that may lead to disorder.

The core identity of a group of people would be the set of salient characteristics or features possessed by members of this community that defines this community to its membership and to outsiders. Certainly, the core identity of a Uyghur involves being a Muslim of Turkic origin, just as that of a Tibetan involves being a Buddhist, with their particular customs and systems of writing. All of these make them very different from the Han-Chinese. However, it seems far-fetched to think that by recognising and accommodating a minority nationality's core identity, the core identity of China's overwhelming majority Han-Chinese nationality will be undercut or destroyed. Yet, discerning what is the core identity of the Han-Chinese is not an easy matter, as the CPC has swept away many aspects of traditional Chinese culture since coming to power in 1949. If the Han-Chinese are not sure what constitutes their own core identity, apart from perhaps reification of 'their' state, they may be reluctant to recognise that there could or should be any core identity for minority communities, or entertain the notion that these communities may embrace different histories, aspirations or existential purposes for themselves.

For survival, an ANSA may try to resolve its subnational identity into a transnational one, as it responds to authorities' framing and labelling by changing its self-identification. Uyghur extremists have referred to Han-Chinese as *kaffir*, or non-Muslim infidels, in order to appeal to the world Muslim *ummah*, or fellowship. To broaden their base of support and in appealing for sympathy from Muslims in Central Asia and worldwide, these extremists have portrayed themselves as victims of attacks on Islam by the Han-Chinese state (Lee 2015).

It is not that the Chinese state deliberately refrained from providing recognition to the Uyghurs as a distinct ethnic community, but rather seemed to have offered mis-recognition that consisted of much form but little substance, which may be taken by the Uyghurs as signs of disrespect for their identity and, as such, cause further political resistance and conflict escalation. The government has officially designated Xinjiang as Xinjiang (Uyghur) Autonomous Region for the Uyghurs and instituted affirmative action programmes to benefit them through material redistribution, yet denied them a voice or meaningful participation in the political processes of their region and the country. Although the right to hold religious beliefs is guaranteed by the PRC Constitution, more than a million Uyghurs accused of exhibiting 'deviant' talk or overly religious (though not necessarily violent) behaviour, as defined by the authorities, have since 2017 been hauled off by these authorities to attend political re-education, 'vocational training' and Han-Chinese language classes with indefinite periods of confinement (Radio Free Asia 2018). The authorities have also prohibited face-covering veils (*hijab*) for women, long beards for men and certain Muslim names to be given to babies, in an attempt to ward off or minimise the transnationalisation or 'Arabisation' of the discourse of the Uyghurs' Muslim identity. A major part of this identity penetration is the increasing popularisation among Uyghurs of the 'Wahhabi tradition' of Islam from Saudi Arabia. Wahhabism considers its religious doctrine not as a school of thought within Islam, but as Islam itself, and the only Muslim way of life. Wahhabism is also attached to egalitarianism, meaning that every *imam* has the right to declare jihad against a perceived danger to the Muslim community (Clément 2015: 435). This would include a government of the state in which a Wahhabi community resides. Religious intolerance and Middle Eastern orientation for the Uyghurs are the direct product of their feelings of political helplessness, cultural marginalisation and besieged identity.

While the Chinese state would not accept that it has 'mis-recognised' the Uyghurs by offering them economic development and material redistribution rather than respect for their identity and political participation, ironically the Han-Chinese believe that they themselves are victims of 'mis-recognition' by Westerners, in the sense employed by Gustafsson (2016: 617) that their state is being recognised, or understood, in a way that is not in line with how they see its identity. How, then, do the Han-Chinese see their state's proper identity? To the Han-Chinese, China's historical narrative of victimisation by foreign imperialists has been largely overcome. However, status recognition of China's greatness as a civilisation and country is slow and sparing from Western countries and peoples, including respect for the Chinese mode of governance and management of ethnic minority relations. Sensitive to the slightest perceived words or acts of disrespect from others, the Han-Chinese will see foreign entreaties or pressure to negotiate and compromise with its domestic ANSAs, even the offer of good offices for mediation purposes, as unacceptable Western interference. The Chinese state realises full well that the principle of recognition is now embedded in the language of human rights, and is acquainted with the argument that massive human rights violation may entitle outsiders to intervene in other states' internal affairs on behalf of the victims, implying the notion of 'international responsibility' (Honneth 1997: 172). As such, China is all the more reluctant to legitimise the involvement of officials from foreign countries that are unaccountable to it as the final arbiters of its domestic ethnic and human rights condition. In response to the passing of the Uyghur Human Rights

Policy Act of 2018 by the United States Congress committing the American government to sanction Chinese officials involved in the detentions of Uyghurs, Chinese authorities have countered that the internment policy is needed to combat the spread of extremist religious ideology and terrorism through re-education (Churchill 2018). When the Party secretary and three top officials of Xinjiang were denied visas to the US in July 2020 under this Act, China reciprocated in kind against one White House official, two US senators and one US congressman (Ministry 2020).

To challenge the discourse of the Han-Chinese and the Chinese state, Uyghur diaspora organisations in Western countries, such as the World Uyghur Congress in Munich, Germany, and the Uyghur American Association in Washington, DC, have disavowed violence and framed their struggle in human rights terms. However, they face an uphill battle getting their message across to the world audience. This is perhaps to be expected, given the legacy of the 9/11 attacks, the activities of global Islamist ANSAs and the sensitivities of the Chinese government.

Talks with ANSAs: for and against

Many states adhere at least publicly to a 'no-negotiations policy' with terrorists, for the very act of engaging with an ANSA may be construed by the ANSA, third parties or even some members of the government as formally recognising to some degree the legitimacy of terrorists or their causes. However, governments may have felt pressured by third parties into negotiating with an ANSA. They may also have recognised an ANSA for the sole purpose of suppressing it. This is the case with China.

To the Chinese Communist authorities, religion is an unenlightened feudal relic, ethnic consciousness is parochial and separatism is treason. As such, Uyghur separatists who highlight the ethnic and religious characteristics of their people risk being labelled terrorists, and therefore a violent uncompromising enemy to be crushed by the government. China's war against terrorism, particularly shadowy Uyghur ANSAs such as the East Turkestan Islamic Movement (ETIM) and East Turkestan Liberation Organisation (ETLO), is fought in the context of battling the 'Three Evils' of separatism, terrorism and religious fundamentalism. This condemnatory three-in-one designation was devised in the late 1990s, for the specific purpose of combating what the authorities consider to be a religion-driven separatist agenda conducted through terrorist means by Uyghurs in Xinjiang, to detach the region from China (Human Rights Watch 2006).

In the unlikely event that negotiations were to take place between the Chinese government and the Uyghur ANSAs, this would imply preparedness on the part of both sides to make and meet concessions to achieve an agreement. Yet, given the overwhelming military strength and police vigilance of the state, the Chinese authorities do not feel a need to make concessions, while the Uyghur ANSAs have no chance to force negotiations. Besides, apart from securing peace, which is only sporadically but not greatly disturbed, there are hardly any other overlapping interests or concerns for both sides to engage in talk or negotiations. Certainly, the government would prefer the ANSAs to give up their struggle, while the ANSAs could attempt to broadcast their cause by engaging in more frequent and larger-scale violent activities. However, both sides are nowhere near a 'mutually hurting stalemate' which might compel them to sit together and try to resolve their conflict (Miller 2011, 175; cf. Görzig in this volume). Still, the presence of closed-circuit television, metal detectors and neighbourhood police posts on the streets and in many public buildings of cities and towns in Xinjiang demonstrate the government's awareness that the threat from Uyghur militants and ANSAs is very much alive.

Three arguments in favour of a state authority talking to or negotiating with its ANSAs were identified by Toros (2008: 413). First, negotiations may eliminate the rationales for the insurgents to engage in violence in the first place, by providing them an outlet to voice their grievances. Secondly, negotiations may strengthen the faction in the insurgent group that is in favour of non-violent engagement. Thirdly, negotiations may draw violent groups down a path of change or transformation towards non-violence.

Regarding the first point, the key to conflict resolution is to overcome the sense of exclusion, humiliation and impotence through engagement, which involves the state acknowledging that a terrorist group represents a valid claim and recognising its goals as legitimate, while making known that its means are unacceptable (Ignatieff 2004: 88). The crux of the matter is: what are these claims and goals, and can the state accept the claims or goals of what it deems to be a terrorist group as valid or legitimate? Uyghur separatists consider Xinjiang, or, as they refer to it, East Turkestan, the homeland of the Uyghurs and their Turkic ancestors. The Chinese government, however, regards Xinjiang as the common domain of all ethnic groups in the country and asserts that Han-Chinese have been dwelling there for as long as the Uyghurs or even before. Uyghur ANSAs demand secession or at least complete internal self-government for Xinjiang. For the CPC authorities, either option would be out of the question, as the territorial integrity and unity of China is non-negotiable for this regime which is concerned about separatist sentiments in Tibet and trying to recover Taiwan. This reveals different identity narratives for different ethnic groups, from which commonalities will have to be located for mutual recognition and respect to occur, before any talk or negotiation can take place.

Regarding the second point, with whom, which subgroup or faction of a group, should the authorities negotiate? It may not be easy even to recognise a particular ANSA as a dialogue partner, as there may in a conflict be many 'teams' of ANSAs that are (squad-level) small, (territorially) diffused and (operationally) independent, who just happen to be like-minded. Recognising an ANSA, or even a faction that eschews violence, may legitimise demands to which authorities are not prepared to yield and raise expectations for the ANSA that may be hard to satisfy. Still, if there is an interest and a will by the authorities to negotiate, peace talks are possible, as long as local grievances remain the prime focus of the group (Toros 2008: 420). This is the case even though the ANSA or one of its factions is affiliated to, training with or supported by the Taliban at the Afghanistan–Pakistan frontier or transnational structures such as al-Qaeda or Islamic State (IS). When IS supported ETIM's claim that some Uyghurs have found their way to the Middle East to fight under IS, both ETIM and IS were probably making use of one another to broadcast their Islamic linkage and propagandise their supposed far-reaching influence. In any case, the strength of IS in the Middle East has been greatly diminished (see Kaden and Guenther in this volume). Most importantly, ethno-nationalist groups like ETIM and ETLO are principally focused on the local situation and status of Uyghurs in Xinjiang.

Regarding the third point, having labelled a violent group 'terrorists' renders it especially difficult for a government to initiate talks or negotiations with the group. The government involved in such a conflict also faces another consideration, and that is: will recognition of an ANSA lead not to less but more violence, if it is seen as confirmation of the efficacy of the use of violence to coerce compromises and concessions, and thus encourage other groups to engage in similar activities? Even if the Chinese government were amenable to negotiations, it would not refer to domestic ANSAs as 'insurgents', or members of an organised movement that aims to overthrow the political order within a given territory (Miller 2011: 134). This is because to do so would imply accepting these actors as combatants in a civil or guerilla war with a political cause to promote. However, if the authorities are prepared to (re)consider terrorism an issue of criminal justice rather than war (Crelinsten 2002: 84–87), and start referring to the ANSAs or terrorist groups as 'criminal organisations', this may signal a willingness to open talks. Demonstrating and publicising the humane treatment of terrorist detainees and involving rehabilitated terrorists in reaching out to these 'criminal organisations' may encourage existing 'law-breakers' to pursue the path of non-violence.

Assuming the authorities are disposed to holding talks with an ANSA, or at least meet with its representatives, non-state actors can seek recognition strategically, gradually and step by step, in what Onuf (2015: 276) refers to as four levels of 'graduated reciprocity' engagement. First step: gaining thin recognition as a party to a conflict. Second step: gaining acceptance as a participant in informal talks and thus recognition of its relevance for the successful management of the conflict. Third step: gaining invitation to participate in formal talks, which indicates that the state acknowledges that the non-state actor has legitimate claims for negotiation. Final step: gaining recognition as the legitimate political representative of a collective with the capacity to enforce binding agreements (Biene and Daase 2015: 224–225).

How well does the Chinese/Uyghur case measure up to the four levels of 'graduated reciprocity' engagement? Step one has been infamously achieved by the East Turkestan Islamic Movement (subsequently renamed the Turkistan Independence Party), which has been officially designated by the Chinese government, US government and United Nations as a terrorist group since the 9/11 attacks. China considers another group – ETLO – to be a terrorist organisation, but it has not been recognised as such by the US or UN. Step two has not occurred for the Uyghur ANSAs but has been accomplished by the personal emissaries of the exiled Dalai Lama of Tibet, who have succeeded in meeting Chinese officials several times in Beijing, although the last fruitless meeting was held in 2008. The Chinese may not consider the Dalai Lama and his self-proclaimed government-in-exile in India an ANSA, but it is definitely to Beijing an INSA – an Infuriating Non-State Actor. For Step three to occur, international pressure, encouragement or mediation may be necessary, but so far, no Uyghur ANSA or diaspora group has received formal recognition from a foreign government or international organisation of states. Engaging in violence, or being involved with al-Qaeda and IS, have not earned the Uyghur cause much sympathy in the eyes of non-Muslims. Step four is most unlikely: the CPC considers itself the sole political representative of the Uyghur and other peoples of Xinjiang and throughout mainland China.

All these issues beg the question: are the Uyghur ANSAs even aiming at negotiations with the authorities, or simply trying to voice grievances on behalf of their community with the intermittent use of violence, hoping that so doing will make the authorities change their ways in dealing with the Uyghurs? Engaging in terrorist activities is a low-cost strategy, given the terrorists' limited organisational strength and lack of sophisticated weapons (e.g. knives, dynamite and cars are most often used in attacks), which yields a comparatively high return when attacks are widely reported in the domestic and international mass media. The computer, mobile phone and other up-to-date telecommunication devices, by offering instantaneous access to information to many individuals simultaneously, are giving non-state, non-territory-based actors increasing and prominent agency in gathering and mobilising resources. These same technologies are also giving the state greater abilities to detect, monitor and censor electronic communications (and vehicles registered in Xinjiang are required to instal China's *Beidou* (North Star) Global Positioning System for them to be tracked anytime), but their appearance has offered more and faster ways for the ANSAs to act. The Uyghur rioters which caused the death of some two hundred people in Xinjiang's capital of Urumqi in July 2009 reportedly assembled through short messages sent over mobile phones and the internet, which led to their temporary blockage by the authorities after the riot (Dillon 2018).

Tolerance as a basis of recognition

The incorporation of the other's narrative, together with their accommodation of one's own, might lead to narratives that can co-exist, although they are built upon differing experiences and perspectives (Strömbom 2014: 176). In the interest of promoting peace, a state should as much as possible strive to integrate and harmonise the norms and identities of its ethnic majority with those of its ethnic minorities. The purpose of so doing is to advance mutual respect and derive an enlarged consciousness encompassing both collectives. Perhaps the Chinese authorities can tout the correspondence between Xinjiang's main Sufi Muslim tradition and Mahayana Buddhism, which is a major religion of the Han-Chinese, Tibetans and Mongolians. The government can highlight the fact that Mahayana Buddhism was the traditional faith of the Uyghur people before their adoption of Islam from the eleventh to the fourteenth century, and that it shares similar reverence for saints and emphasis on meditation as Sufism. Justice, charity and cleanliness are basic tenets of Islam, but they can easily be adopted by the Chinese government and incorporated into a civic code for the entire country. Still, the root of respect is toleration of differences. The Uyghurs under confinement should be released unless there are grounds for the authorities to charge or hold them for engaging in acts of violence or separatism. With the Han-Chinese, preserving and respecting minorities' salient ethno-cultural-religious characteristics, or at least certain aspects of them, are tolerable, provided these characteristics are not politicised or susceptible to politicisation. To show that it is not against Islam *per se*, but only the use of religion to politicise an ethnic identity, the Chinese government has very much left the Han-Chinese Muslims, called 'Hui', alone to practise their religion.

Identities, as with most things in the human world, are not set in stone. The reconstruction of identity is a regular, ongoing process in the life of any national group (Allan and Keller 2006: 199). Shifting recognition through altering the construction of identity and thus transforming political realities may steer the whole dynamics of a conflict in either peaceful or violent directions (Strömbom 2014: 173). Hence, a strategy of delegitimising violent means should be accompanied by a strategy of giving recognition to the identities and goals represented by an ANSA, and the causes which gave rise to the discontent behind it ought to be clearly understood by the state. The Chinese government may not for political reasons care to offer 'thin' formal recognition of domestic ANSAs, but it should engage in the hard work of tendering 'thick' recognition of the causes or grievances which have led to violence, in order to rectify or at least minimise them and eliminate the reasons for further bloodshed.

Ultimately, a government's problem with a domestic ANSA is the country's internal issue to be resolved between the two parties, and the key to the resolution is the toleration of diversity. Toleration is the liberal state's approach to recognising and respecting differences but, as argued by Allan and Keller (2006: 212–213), toleration does rest on a distinction between majority norms and minority deviance and implies official preference for a particular way of life. Rather than just toleration, then, to advance inter-ethnic harmony, we should strive for acceptance of differences. At the minimum, top Han-Chinese state leaders can demonstrate symbolic acts of recognition by shaking hands with, visiting the homes of and having meals with, the humblest Uyghur villagers in Xinjiang, or, better still, speaking some words of Uyghur in public or when visiting mosques. Non-Uyghur students in Xinjiang should be actively encouraged by the government to enrol in Uyghur language classes, and a public statement should be made to the effect that the religious beliefs of party and state officials should not be an issue as long as they are not employed for policy advocacy. Since the Han-Chinese consider Xinjiang as part of China, and the Uyghurs generally refer to their homeland as East Turkestan, it may be a mutually satisfying discursive act to have the region officially designated as Chinese Turkestan (Zhonghua Tukesitan). Most importantly, even if members of the majority cannot for the moment completely accept the norms and values of the minorities, they should at least tolerate the ways of life of others. We need not embrace unfamiliar ways of life, but there is no reason to suppress them, as long as they are not forced upon us.

References

Allan, P. and A. Keller (2006), 'The concept of a just peace, or achieving peace through recognition, renouncement, and rule', in P. Allan and A. Keller (eds), *What is a Just Peace?* (Oxford: Oxford University Press), pp. 185–215.

An, B. (2017), '"Cherish ethnic unity", president tells Xinjiang', *China Daily*, available online: www.chinadaily.com.cn/china/2017twosession/2017–03/11/content_28515253.htm; last retrieved 15 February 2020.
Barabantseva, E. (2009), 'Development as localization', *Critical Asian Studies* 41:2, 225–254.
BBC (British Broadcasting Corporation) (2017), 'Xi Jinping de Zhongguo meng: zhu xuanluu yu shaoshu minzu wenhua [Xin Jinping's China dream: main themes and ethnic minorities' cultures]', available online: www.bbc.com/zhongwen/simp/chinese-news-41781666 (27 October); last retrieved 15 February 2020.
Biene, J. and C. Daase (2015), 'Gradual recognition: curbing non-state violence in asymmetrical conflicts', in C. Daase, C. Fehl, A. Geis and G. Kolliarakis (eds), *Recognition in International Relations* (Basingstoke: Palgrave Macmillan), pp. 220–236.
Churchill, O. (2018), 'Global coalition of scholars calls for added pressure on China over Uygur internment camps in Xinjiang', *South China Morning Post*, available online: www.scmp.com/news/china/politics/article/2175120/global-coalition-scholars-calls-added-pressure-china-over-uygur; last retrieved 15 February 2020.
Clarke, M. (2015), 'China and the Uyghurs: the "Palestinization" of Xinjiang?', *Middle East Policy* 22:3, 127–146.
Clément, M. (2014), 'Al-Muhajiroun in the United Kingdom: the role of international non-recognition in heightened radicalization dynamics', *Global Discourse* 4:4, 428–443.
Crelinsten, R. (2002), 'Analysing terrorism and counter-terrorism: a communication model', *Terrorism and Political Violence* 14:2, 77–122.
Dillon, M. (2018), *Xinjiang in the Twenty-first Century: Islam, Ethnicity and Resistance* (London and New York, NY: Routledge).
Fearon, J. (1995), 'Rationalist explanations for war', *International Organization* 49:3, 379–414.
Fraser, N. and A. Honneth (2003), *Redistribution or Recognition? A Political-Philosophical Exchange* (London: Verso).
Geis, A. (2018), 'The ethics of recognition in International Political Theory', in C. Brown and R. Eckersley (eds), *The Oxford Handbook of International Political Theory* (Oxford: Oxford University Press), pp. 612–625.
Gustafsson, K. (2016), 'Routinized recognition and anxiety: understanding the deterioration in Sino-Japanese relations', *Review of International Studies* 42:4, 613–633.
Hamut, B. and A. Joniak-Lüthi (2015), 'The language choices and script debates among the Uyghur in Xinjiang Uyghur Autonomous Region, China', *Linguistik Online* 70:1, 111–124.
Heins, V. (2010), 'Of persons and peoples: internationalizing the critical theory of recognition', *Contemporary Political Theory* 9:2, 149–170.
Honneth, A. (1995), *The Struggle of Recognition: The Moral Grammar of Social Conflicts* (Cambridge: Polity).
Honneth, A. (1997), 'Is universalism a moral trap? The presuppositions and limits of a politics of human rights', in J. Bohman and M. Lutz-Bachmann (eds), *Perpetual Peace: Essays on Kant's Cosmopolitan Ideal* (Cambridge, MA: MIT Press), pp. 155–178.
Human Rights Watch (2006), *Eurasia: Uphold Human Rights in Combating Terrorism*, available online: www.hrw.org/news/2006/06/14/eurasia-uphold-human-rights-combating-terrorism; last retrieved 15 February 2020.

Ignatieff, M. (2004), *The Lesser Evil: Political Ethics in an Age of Terror* (Princeton, NJ: Princeton University Press).
Iser, M. (2013), 'Recognition', in Edward Zalta (ed.), *Stanford Encyclopedia of Philosophy*, available online: http://plato.stanford.edu/entries/recognition/; last retrieved 15 February 2020.
Jacobs, J. (2017), *Xinjiang and the Modern Chinese State* (Seattle, WA: University of Washington Press).
Lee, Y. E. (2015), 'Behaviorist fundamentalism turns radical: ETIM/ TIP's Islamic fundamentalist representations and narratives', *Journal of Middle Eastern and Islamic Studies* 9:4, 85–99.
Leibold, J. (2013), *Ethnic Policy in China: Is Reform Inevitable?* (Honolulu, HI: East-West Center).
Miller, C. (2011), 'Is it possible and preferable to negotiate with terrorists?', *Defence Studies* 11:1, 145–185.
Ministry of Foreign Affairs of the People's Republic of China (2020), *Foreign Ministry Spokesperson Hua Chunying's Regular Press Conference on July 13, 2020*, available online: www.fmprc.gov.cn/mfa_eng/xwfw_665399/s2510_665401/2511_665403/t1797455.shtml; last retrieved 24 August 2020.
Moller, U. (2007), *The Prospects of Security Cooperation: A Matter of Relative Gains or Recognition* (Goteborg: Goteborg Studies in Politics).
Ohlström, M., M. Solinas and O. Voirol (2011), 'On Nancy Fraser and Axel Honneth's "Redistribution or Recognition? A Political-Philosophical Exchange"', *Iris: European Journal of Philosophy and Public Debate* 3:5, 205–221.
Onuf, N. (2015), 'Acts of recognition, shades of respect', in C. Daase, C. Fehl, A. Geis and G. Kolliarakis (eds), *Recognition in International Relations* (Basingstoke: Palgrave Macmillan), pp. 265–278.
Radio Free Asia (2018), 'Survey: three million, mostly Uyghurs, in some form of political "re-education" in Xinjiang', available online: www.rfa.org/english/news/uyghur/millions-08032018142025.html; last retrieved 15 February 2020.
Standing Committee of the National People's Congress (2016), *Order No. 36 of the President: Counterterrorism Law of the People's Republic of China*, available online: http://en.pkulaw.cn/display.aspx?cgid=261788&lib=law; last retrieved 15 February 2020.
Strömbom, L. (2014), 'Thick recognition: advancing theory on identity change in intractable conflicts', *European Journal of International Relations* 20:1, 168–191.
Toros, H. (2008), '"We don't negotiate with terrorists!": legitimacy and complexity in terrorist conflicts', *Security Dialogue* 39:4, 407–426.
Wendt, A. (2003), 'Why a world state is inevitable: teleology and the logic of anarchy', *European Journal of International Relations* 9:4, 491–542.
Wolf, R. (2011), 'Respect and disrespect in international politics: the significance of status recognition', *International Theory* 3:1, 105–141.

8

Recognition dynamics and Lebanese Hezbollah's role in regional conflicts

*Hanna Pfeifer**

Introduction

On 3 January 2020, Iranian general Qassem Soleimani was killed in a US drone strike in Baghdad in a targeted killing operation. Besides being a general in the Iranian military forces, he is also considered to have been the second most important political figure in Iranian leadership after Ayatollah Ali Khamenei. At the same time, however, he was the head of the Islamic Revolutionary Guard Corps's (IRGC's) Quds Force (QF). While the QF had been sanctioned as a terrorist entity since October 2007, it was only the Trump administration that put the IRGC on the list of terror organisations in April 2019.[1] Iran immediately responded by designating US military forces a terrorist entity.[2]

Observers have warned against the consequences of such listings for state sovereignty and political legitimacy.[3] Some perceive the upholding of Iran's recognition as a state *and* simultaneous mis-recognition of its armed forces as a terrorist organisation to be a severe disruption of previously established inter-state practices. But the case may not be so unique after all. This chapter argues that similar patterns of hybrid recognition practices can also be found in the case of Lebanese Hezbollah. It explores how the recognition of Hezbollah as a somewhat legitimate part, or at least a major player, of Lebanese society and Middle Eastern politics *and* simultaneous mis-recognition as a transnational terrorist organisation influence conflict dynamics in the region. It analyses Hezbollah's recognition claims directed at three different audiences, that is, the Lebanese people, regional actors and publics, and the international community and particularly Western states, and traces Hezbollah's discursive strategy with regard to acts it perceives as mis-recognition. It thereby aims at investigating how hybrid recognition practices may impact armed non-state actors' (ANSAs') identity construction and, in the long run, conflict dynamics.

By hybrid recognition, I refer to the simultaneous occurrence of recognition and mis-recognition practices by different granters, but sometimes also by one and the same actor. Depending on the respective recognition-granter, Hezbollah's recognition may be more (Lebanese domestic context, population in the Arab world) or less (global context) 'thick' (Allan and Keller 2006; see introductory chapter to this volume). Moreover, recognition practices change over time (Biene and Daase 2015); addressees of recognition claims may gradually grant, but also withdraw recognition. Following the editors' conceptualisation, mis-recognition is understood as humiliation, disrespect or false representations of a collective identity, where the labelling as a terrorist organisation is one possible form (see also Dudouet in this volume). Finally, and this is particularly relevant with regard to Hezbollah, I understand an ANSA's identity and the practices of recognition with which it is met as mutually constitutive. This means that claims to the recognition of a certain identity may be rejected or acknowledged, which feeds back into how an ANSA (re-)casts its identity. Conversely, recognition-granters may actively label an ANSA, thereby trying to (re-)shape or undermine its identity, which may or may not entail a reframing of recognition claims on the part of the recognition-seeker. The most important label in the case of Hezbollah is 'terrorism', but 'sectarianism' and 'foreignness' (see also Toros and Sugal in this volume) play an important role, too.

The chapter does not attempt to position itself in terms of an 'objective' classification of Hezbollah but focuses on the discursive struggles over what this ANSA wants to be recognised, and is recognised, as, and how that plays out in conflict dynamics. Notably, this also means that Hezbollah's characterisation as a 'hybrid' actor (Azani 2013) in the academic literature is not taken as a given ontological quality, but rather as a product of a political power-play (Armborst 2017) or, more specifically, hybrid recognition dynamics. While the chapter also takes into account reactions (formal and discursive acts) of recognition-granters, its main empirical focus is the recognition claims put forward by Hezbollah as a recognition-seeker, as well as its reactions to recognition-granting and -denying, and mis-recognition (discursive acts).

The chapter briefly touches upon Hezbollah's emergence and historical development, as they are at the basis of its contemporary recognition claims. The main section is divided into three parts, each of which addresses Hezbollah's recognition claims as formulated vis-à-vis different (potential) recognition-granters (1) in Lebanese society, (2) in the Middle East and (3) among a global audience, in particular Western states. The final section summarises the results and sketches out implications for local and regional conflict dynamics.

Hezbollah between ANSA and Lebanese party

Lebanese Hezbollah emerged in 1982, that is, in the middle of the Lebanese civil war. While its foundation was directly linked to Israel's invasion of the Lebanese South, it needs to be put in the broader context of Shiite social mobilisation in the 1970s which, among others, spurred demands for more political rights in the sects-based Lebanese political system. This politicisation was reinforced by Shiite clerics who had been sent to *hawzat* (Shiite seminaries) in Najaf (Iraq) and Qom (Iran) and introduced an activist, revolutionist spirit to the movement. In 1978, with the mysterious disappearance of its founder Musa as-Sadr, the Shiite movement lacked a unifying religious-political leadership and experienced a split into two camps. On the one hand, some within the leadership were following a secular and rather moderate path of internal reform and change of the Lebanese state and regime. On the other hand, a militant wing called for violent resistance against foreign aggression, emphasising the necessity of individual sacrifices and social solidarity. After the Islamic revolution in Iran in 1979, a few hundred Iranian Revolutionary Guards were sent to Lebanon in order to support the emerging Islamic militants in their fight against Israel and spread the teachings of the Islamic revolution (Azani 2011: 47–74). It is from this milieu that Hezbollah emerged.

Officially founded in 1982, Hezbollah only consolidated with its *Open Letter Addressed to the Oppressed in Lebanon and the World* in 1985 (Alagha 2011: 39–55). At this point, Hezbollah's platform revolved around resistance to the Israeli occupation of Lebanon and Palestine, as well as to any kind of oppression, emphasising 'its identity as an Islamic jihadi movement struggling to address and redress the injustices that the oppressed suffer … irrespective of their color, race, or religion' (Alagha 2011: 16). This idea of solidarity addressed mainly those in the Global South suffering from the US–USSR struggle for influence, both of which were perceived as hegemonic powers. Finally, the letter called for establishment of an Islamic state along the Iranian model.

While the ideas of resistance (*moqawama*) against occupation and struggle against oppression remained at the core of Hezbollah's programme, it changed other parts of its platform. In 1992, Hezbollah had decided to enter the Lebanese political system as a party. This came to be known as the *infitah* (opening-up) policy and the 'Lebanonisation' of Hezbollah (Alagha 2011: 160, 188–189). Its new secretary-general, Hassan Nasrallah, pursued the path of political inclusion and prepared the party for elections. He put an emphasis on Hezbollah's rootedness in Lebanese society, thereby countering the claim that it was an 'imported' phenomenon, and foregrounded the movement's priority: resistance against Israel. Hezbollah obtained eight parliamentary seats and thus had considerable success in the elections of 1992. In 2009, Hezbollah issued a new Manifesto which shifted some of the *Open Letter's* foci. It developed a more nuanced stance towards European countries, warning them against US leadership and encouraging them instead to embrace a 'moderate drift' (quoted in Alagha 2011: 31). Moreover, Hezbollah formally declared a refrain from pursuing an Islamic state in Lebanon. Instead, it called for a strong state which would eventually abolish political sectarianism.

Besides this political reorientation, Hezbollah kept pursuing its resistance agenda, primarily targeting the Israeli Defence Forces (IDF) in Lebanon, but also was a party to the conflict in the Lebanese civil war which ended in 1990. The post-war Taif Agreement (1991) stipulated the disarmament of all non-state militias. However, Syria was able to put through Hezbollah's exemption from this. Rather than being treated as a militia, Hezbollah was declared a resistance movement and thus a necessary force to end Israeli occupation which was allowed to keep its weapons (Salem 2017: 1522–1524). Against the Taif Agreement's provisions regarding the withdrawal of foreign forces, Israeli and Syrian occupation forces remained in the country. Even though the document called for 'fully eliminating the Israeli occupation'[4] with the support of forces of the United Nations Interim Force in Lebanon (UNIFIL), Israel would not retreat until 2000. Hezbollah pursued its violent resistance over the following years and many parts of the Arab world accredited Hezbollah with the success of the eventual Israeli withdrawal (Salem 2017: 1530). It put an end to occupation – except for a piece of land in the Golan Heights, the Shebaa Farms, which Lebanon claims as belonging to its national territory. Still today, this serves as a justification for Hezbollah's continued activity as a militant, armed resistance. Few Lebanese voices raised doubts about this state of affairs (Azani 2011: 173). Except for minor episodes of violence in the Shebaa Farms, the period from 2000–2006 can be qualified as relatively calm.

Syrian forces, too, remained on Lebanese territory. Tensions over their continued presence grew stronger in Lebanese society in the early 2000s. In addition, with the beginning of the 'global war on terror', international pressure rose, given that the US had denounced Syria as being part of 'the axis of evil'. Supported by the US and France, then-prime minister Rafiq al-Hariri formed an inter-sectarian, anti-Syrian alliance in Lebanon. In 2005, Hariri and more than twenty other persons died in a massive car bomb explosion in the centre of Beirut. As many Lebanese anti-Syrian politicians and large parts of the population, as well as international actors, suspected Syria and Hezbollah to be directly involved in the attack, pressure on Syrian forces to leave Lebanon became still higher. On 14 March, more than one million people demonstrated against the Syrian occupation of Lebanon in

Beirut's Martyrs' Square. Six days earlier, that is, on 8 March, Hezbollah and allied groups had organised a protest supporting the Syrian presence. In April, this culminated in anti-Syrian protests and the withdrawal of Syrian forces after twenty-nine years of occupation (Salem 2017: 1531–1534).

The political landscape after the Cedar Revolution was marked by the polarisation between two blocs, the March-14 and the March-8 Alliances, giving rise to 'a new cleavage in Lebanon in which political contestation … takes place' (Nagle 2016: 1149): They cut across the classical sectarian boundaries between Muslims and Christians, but have created new tension between Sunnis and Shiites. This tension is reinforced by the regional support for both groups, with Saudi Arabia assisting the Sunni Future Movement and Iran supporting Hezbollah and, to a lesser degree, Amal. The assassination of Hariri and the subsequent revolution also had international ramifications. In 2007, the UN Security Council adopted resolution 1757, thereby creating the Special Tribunal for Lebanon (STL) which aims at investigating the Hariri assassination and whose work is still ongoing.

Meanwhile, occasional border incidents escalated in July 2006. Hezbollah militants attacked a patrol on Israeli soil, killing three and capturing two Israeli soldiers. The IDF launched what came to be known as the July War, leaving over 1100 Lebanese and over 40 Israeli civilians dead and several hundreds of thousands of people displaced in both countries. The Lebanese South as well as the *Dahiyeh* were devastated (Norton 2014: 132–143). Despite the success of Hezbollah in fighting back against the IDF, debates in Lebanon about the power of Hezbollah and the question of disarmament re-emerged, and tensions grew to a new level in 2008. Under the leadership of Rafiq al-Hariri's son Saad al-Hariri, the Lebanese government decided to investigate Hezbollah's independent telecommunications system with the purpose of removing it. Hezbollah reacted by blocking the road to the airport and seizing control over West Beirut. Both the prime minister's private militia and the Sunni-dominated Internal Security Forces could not defy Hezbollah and allied armed groups. Fearing an internal sectarian split, the military forces did not intervene in the conflict.

The period of analysis for this chapter begins with the Arab uprisings of 2010 and 2011 as experienced by many of the Middle East and North Africa (MENA) republics. It coincided with the collapse of the national unity government in Lebanon that Saad al-Hariri had formed in 2009. In reaction to the first indictments issued by the STL against Hezbollah members, eleven ministers from the March-8 alliance resigned. In June 2011, a new government was formed – without the participation of March-14 and allegedly dominated by Hezbollah, which had two ministers in the cabinet (Fakhoury 2016: 24–25). Not even two years later, this government collapsed and was followed by a new national unity government, putting an end to ten months of political stalemate (Wählisch and Felsch 2016: 5). After years of negotiations over the new Lebanese president, parties finally reached an agreement that involved yet another re-formation of government at the end of 2016, with Saad al-Hariri becoming prime minister again. Under massive anti-government protests, the cabinet resigned in October 2019. This most recent popular uprising is directed against the political class as a whole, thereby transcending both sectarian dividing lines and the March-8–March-14 alliance logic. As of February 2020, protests are continuing, despite the formation of a supposedly 'neutral' technocratic government under the independent prime minister Hassan Diab in January 2020.[5]

Hezbollah's recognition claims vis-à-vis different recognition-granters

For the breadth and diversity of its repertoire, Hezbollah has sometimes been called a 'hybrid terrorist organisation' because it has 'three complementary, related areas of activity: *da'wa* and social welfare, military resistance (*jihad*), and political activity' (Azani 2013: 902). Indeed, the three areas of activity go hand in hand with recognition claims addressed to at least three audiences: first, the Lebanese people, particularly the Shiite community, and political adversaries and allies; secondly, on the regional level, Arab publics, like-minded resistance movements, and Arab states and governments; and finally, a global audience. Hezbollah's recognition claims refer to its own identity, its claim to representing the Shiite community in Lebanon *and* the interests of an imagined Arab-Islamic community in the broader Middle East, as well as the legitimacy of their resort to violent means, in particular in contrast to other actors' use of force.

The analysis is based on sixty-five speeches by Secretary-General Hassan Nasrallah between 2011 and 2016, as well as interviews conducted in 2014 and 2015 with Lebanese journalists, think-tank members, researchers, and representatives of research and media institutions close to Hezbollah. The study focuses on Nasrallah because he is Hezbollah's clear and uncontested leader, and sets the tone in both political and military affairs. Other voices from within the party are present, but do not challenge Nasrallah's views. Rather, they are in line with the official party platform as defined by Nasrallah, which is one indicator of the party's strictly hierarchical organisation. The empirical study is a discourse analysis. Mis-recognition as perceived by Hezbollah can be identified whenever there is an emphatic, sometimes even emotional discursive act of rejection, directed against claims about identity, acts and goals 'falsely' attributed to Hezbollah. Those are usually followed by positive recognition claims which aim at correcting the misrepresentation. Sometimes, however, recognition claims are formulated more proactively, without being a direct reaction to an act of perceived mis-recognition.

Domestic recognition games: between Lebaneseness and resistance exceptionalism

Hezbollah's recognition claims in the Lebanese context address two audiences: the Shiite community and its own supporters, and the general Lebanese public, including political adversaries. The latter audience is more prominent in Nasrallah's speeches. The main recognition claim concerns Hezbollah's cause: the necessity and legitimacy of resistance against Israel and, more generally, oppression. Derived from this are three interlinked recognition claims regarding Hezbollah's identity as an actor: it wants to be recognised (1) as a genuinely Lebanese actor; (2) as a non-sectarian, honest and constructive political player; and (3) as the defender of the Lebanese people.

The Lebaneseness of Hezbollah is a recurring theme in its discourse and addresses three forms of mis-recognition. The first is the allegation that Hezbollah is controlled from outside and part of a would-be 'Shiite expansion' (Nasrallah 2012a) project led by Iran that supposedly aims at Shiite dominance in Lebanon, Yemen, Palestine and Iraq. According to Hezbollah, the goal behind the narrative of the Shiite crescent, the demonisation of Iran as a global threat and the misrepresentation of Hezbollah as its puppet is to instigate intra-Muslim tensions and incite Sunnis against Shiites, as well as Arabs against Persians. Secondly, Hezbollah's adversaries regularly present it as a globally operating terror organisation whose agenda reaches far beyond the Lebanese and Middle Eastern context. For instance, it was claimed that Hezbollah's military activity covered places like Iran, Libya, Yemen, Bahrain, Egypt, India, Georgia, Thailand, Latin America, West Africa and Azerbaijan as well as Bulgaria. Nasrallah's reactions to these claims used humour in order to display their absurdity: 'If only we were as such. … If only we had this expansion and presence. That would have made us feel strong and efficient' (Nasrallah 2012c). Finally, Hezbollah also feels mis-recognised as an actor that operates with a secret agenda to take over the state and Islamise Lebanon, pulling the strings of government behind the scenes. According to Nasrallah (2015d), this 'psychological warfare' is waged by parts of the March-14 bloc, but also the media, and is supported by Israel and America who spend huge amounts of money to harm the reputation of Hezbollah and the resistance, and to mislead public opinion.

Against these allegations, Hezbollah emphasises, first, that it is a genuinely Lebanese actor that acts in the interest of the Lebanese nation, has for a long time abandoned its agenda to establish an Islamic state, and 'entered deeper into the Lebanese status quo' (Nasrallah 2012a). It insists on democratic, legitimate political institutions and has a firm belief in democratic procedures. Secondly, Hezbollah seeks recognition for its role as an honest and constructive political partner with a decidedly anti-sectarian agenda. Nasrallah regularly expressed sympathy for fears of other religious communities, especially in the context of reforming the Lebanese electoral system and against the backdrop of increased sectarian violence in Syria. Despite the respect for religious pluralism in Lebanon, Hezbollah has the vision to build one Lebanese 'community and … a nation as a prelude for building a state for it later on' (Nasrallah 2012a), eventually abandoning the sectarian basis of Lebanese politics. As proof of these intentions, Nasrallah points to Hezbollah's demonstrated willingness for dialogue and compromise with political adversaries. It thereby seeks to prove that it is a rational, ethical and responsible actor, an honest broker for Lebanese interests. The basis for this ethical stance is a commitment to truthfulness, which is at the core of Nasrallah's public image. He presents himself and, indeed, is widely perceived as a man who is capable of logical argumentation and clear-sighted political analysis, and who keeps his word (Interviews 1 and 2).

Finally, Hezbollah clearly identifies armed resistance as the one field where there is no room for concessions or negotiation. Being recognised as a defender of Lebanese sovereignty against Israel's aggressions and, later on, what Hezbollah calls the 'Takfirist threat' spilling over from Syria is the most important claim the party makes vis-à-vis the Lebanese public (Nasrallah 2014a, 2015e, 2016b). It calls upon the Lebanese to acknowledge the (Islamic) resistance's success in restoring the rights, land and dignity of the Lebanese people against the Israeli invasion and occupation. Neither the Lebanese army nor UNIFIL had been capable of protecting Lebanon in the past. In this situation, the resistance stepped up and took over the task of Lebanese self-defence. Even though the Israeli occupation ended in 2000, its massive attacks in 2006, as well as the fact that it still occupies the Shebaa Farms, are manifestations of the persistent Israeli threat, which makes continued resistance indispensable. In 2013, Nasrallah also added 'Takfirism', that is, Salafi-jihadi groups such as ISIS, to the resistance's list of enemies and its agenda of self-defence, portraying it as an imminent threat to all Lebanese.

Emphasising the non-sectarian, patriotic character of the resistance is central to Hezbollah's recognition claims vis-à-vis the broad public: solidarity with the resistance is part of the Lebanese nation-building project. This does not mean that everyone has to fight – even though there is a multi-confessional brigade within the resistance (Alagha 2011: 160, 188–189) –, but rather support it mentally and morally. At the same time, however, Nasrallah also seeks recognition for the main burden the resistance carried in defending the country and the sacrifices that were made by the Shiite community. Its 'steadfastness' and 'courage' (Nasrallah 2015a) brought Lebanon liberation and peace, 'which all the Lebanese are enjoying, regardless of having paid the price for it or not' (Nasrallah 2014a). The oscillation between both arguments, that is, the trans-sectarian nature and deep anchoring of the resistance in the broad population, and the tribute to the *Islamic* resistance and gratefulness towards the Shiite community, is an expression of Hezbollah's struggle to gain legitimacy among all the Lebanese and keep up the resistance spirit among its own adherents and fighters. This became significantly more difficult with its military engagement in Syria (see next section).

Besides emphasising the immediate security interests of all Lebanese being jeopardised by the conflict dynamics in Syria, one discursive strategy Hezbollah employed was to regularly evoke the so-called 'army–people–resistance formula' (Nasrallah 2011b). As the army is not strong enough to defend Lebanese sovereignty, and the state has proven to be too naïve to recognise and effectively tackle external threats from early on, Hezbollah, as an auxiliary, regularly steps up to support the army in its efforts. This burden-sharing is completed by the popular resistance, which refers to 'laymen' that are willing to protect their country and people against hegemonic schemes, side by side with the army and the organised resistance. At the same time, however, Nasrallah calls for an enhancement of the military's strength, so as to make the resistance's support dispensable in the future. This goes hand in hand with Hezbollah's urges to build a stronger Lebanese state. But this claim is yet another manifestation of the hybrid character of recognition practices around Hezbollah. While it does seek recognition as a legitimate and somewhat normal part of Lebanese politics, as well as a 'patriotic' defender of national interests and sovereignty, Nasrallah regularly detaches Hezbollah from the Lebanese state, which he portrays as weak, sometimes as corrupt and inefficient, and as based on precarious sectarian foundations. He seeks recognition for Hezbollah's autonomy, not least in taking such decisions as intervening in neighbouring Syria, keeping its weapons and communication systems, and getting involved in regional politics as a non-state actor. Separating itself from the state in this way not only ignores the ways in which Hezbollah contributes to undermining state authority and power itself. It is also a way of absolving itself from the responsibility of implementing effective policies, even though Hezbollah has been part of the government over the whole period between 2011 and 2016. In a way, it is Hezbollah's ambiguous recognition claims that are answered with similarly ambivalent (discursive) acts of recognition and mis-recognition: its adversaries, notably from the March-14 bloc, cooperate with it pragmatically on an everyday basis, but still engage in discourses that portray Hezbollah as an outsider, threat to Lebanese security or transnationally rooted terrorist actor. This phenomenon of hybrid recognition claims and responses is even more pronounced on the regional level.

Regional recognition practices: between defender of the oppressed and terrorist organisation

On the regional level, Hezbollah seeks recognition from two main recognition-granters: (1) Arab and Muslim publics in the MENA and (2) state actors. In both cases, it tries to portray itself as a core part of the transnational resistance against Israel and, more generally, oppression and hegemony, and thus the (only remaining) honest broker for Arab and Muslim interests. When Nasrallah addresses the people of the region, he tries to gain recognition for Hezbollah as a core part of the axis of resistance. It consists of two 'steadfast' countries, Iran and Syria, that have not submitted to the international pressure of normalising relations with Israel, as well as the armed resistances in Lebanon and Palestine (Hamas). To Nasrallah, the axis of resistance is the only defender of Arab sovereignty in the face of Israeli aggression, the continued occupation of Palestine as *the* Arab–Muslim cause, and global hegemonic schemes devised for the broader region. While the focus of Hezbollah's activity within the axis of resistance used to be the fight against Israel, two additional causes were added in the aftermath of the Arab uprising and subsequent regional dynamics: the struggle against oppressive Arab regimes and the fight against 'Takfirism'. For Hezbollah, both are at the core of Arab–Muslim shared interests.

The Israeli occupation and the deprivation of Palestinians' rights are simultaneously a humiliation of all Muslims and Arabs. This is why the only legitimate choice is resistance; any government in the MENA should be judged according to its stance on the Palestinian cause which is 'the ruling norm in this time' (Nasrallah 2012b). It is governments' obligation to show solidarity with the transnational resistance. However, the only countries to have constantly supported the struggle, even in times of severe crisis and pressure, are Iran and Syria. According to Hezbollah, without their financial support, weapons deliveries and unconditional solidarity, neither the Lebanese nor the Palestinian resistance could have achieved success. Hezbollah thus seeks recognition as the key actor of the resistance, but also for the Palestinian question as the one true Arab and Muslim cause. Calling for solidarity among Arabs and Muslims, Nasrallah (e.g. 2012b) also wants them to acknowledge the merits Hezbollah has in fighting for this common cause without asking anything in return. Its military success is all the more laudable as it is the only Arab actor ever to have defeated Israel.

While this role as 'the last man standing' against the common enemy has always been central to Hezbollah's discourse, the Israeli–Palestinian conflict became relatively less important once the Syrian civil war started. As soon as the Arab uprisings began in late 2010, Hezbollah needed to formulate a position on the popular protests and, later in 2011, the ousting of some of the authoritarian leaders. Nasrallah interpreted the events not only as a popular demand for freedom, but also took them as an expression of Arabs' discontent with the regimes' submissiveness to Israel and abandonment of the Palestinian cause. Both motivations deserved Hezbollah's full solidarity, and thus Nasrallah lauded the Tunisians, Egyptians, Bahrainis, Yemenis and Libyans for their courage and readiness to sacrifice for the revolutions. He also expressed the hope that successive leaders would strengthen the resistance and allow for 'Iran and Syria to gain new allies, advocates and members in this axis' (Nasrallah 2011b). But it turned out that the Israeli–Palestinian question would not be prominent on the agenda of new or old political elites. Rather, some of the post-uprising societies were drawn into civil wars – a development for the *ummah* which, according to Nasrallah, 'is the most dangerous situation ever since the occupation of Palestine' (Nasrallah 2014b).

Hezbollah's stance on the uprisings was more ambivalent when it came to the Syrian situation. Initially, it insisted that the Assad regime was trying to establish political dialogue and push for reform. But these efforts were undermined by the interests of international actors. According to Nasrallah, and as opposed to the situation in other countries, there was a Western–Israeli-led and Gulf-supported agenda to topple the Syrian regime so as to break the axis of resistance. Imposing war on the country was part of this plan. As a consequence, Hezbollah came to a different judgement for Syria than with regard to other countries affected by the Arab uprisings. Both the regime's supposed will for reforms and its merits in supporting the Palestinian cause justified Hezbollah's continued support for Assad: 'Syria has been the cherisher of the Resistance, so the Resistance can't stand still while that cherisher is being ruined' (Nasrallah 2013). Against this backdrop, Hezbollah's attempt to be recognised by the peoples of the region as the voice – and hand – of the oppressed against oppressors became increasingly implausible. While it had tried to show itself as the advocate of the people who had been oppressed by their own governments for years, its stance on Syria made this narrative increasingly hard to sell.

This became even clearer after Hezbollah had officially started intervening in the Syrian conflict in spring 2013, at the request of the regime. At that point, it had become clear to the party that 'the Takfiri current is dominant among the Syrian opposition' (Nasrallah 2013). In this initial phase, Nasrallah claimed that an intervention became necessary, first, because solidarity with the Syrians had to be demonstrated and the axis of resistance needed to be protected. Nasrallah also tried to establish a tight link between the survival of the Syrian regime and the struggle for Palestine, and thus the resistance project in the narrow sense: 'For sure the road to al-Quds [Jerusalem] passes through Qalamoun, Zabadani, Homs, Aleppo, Daraa, Sweidaa and Sasakeh …; that's because if Syria is lost, Palestine would be lost too' (Nasrallah 2015e). Secondly, Hezbollah emphasised that Lebanon's security was jeopardised by potential spill-overs from its neighbour country. Indeed, several border assaults by Syrian rebel groups, and particularly jihadi groups, occurred in 2013 and 2014. Through these arguments, Hezbollah sought recognition, yet again, as a defender of Lebanese sovereignty among its compatriots, but also as a firm believer in, and protector of, the resistance project against Israel. The latter claim was directed at the broader Arab public, but also a signal to Iran and Syria that they could count on Hezbollah.

In contrast to this narrative, Hezbollah's Lebanese adversaries claimed that its military engagement had given rise to jihadi attacks on Lebanon in the first place. But critics increasingly also emerged from within the Shiite community. This is why Nasrallah shifted the focus of justification to the fight against 'Takfirism' as a global threat against the Muslim *ummah* and the Middle East as a whole. He portrayed Hezbollah as the only clear-sighted actor that had understood and acted upon the 'Takfiri' threat. The severity of this danger called for joint action in Syria and Iraq, and Nasrallah encouraged fellow Muslim actors and Arab states to support Hezbollah in fighting ISIS and other Salafi jihadists. But even if no one were to respond to these calls, Hezbollah would always be 'assuming this responsibility on both levels', that is, against Israel and the 'Takfirists' (Nasrallah 2015f).

In that sense, Hezbollah tried to gain recognition as a responsible actor that engaged in Arab self-defence where necessary. In 2014 and 2015, when ISIS had risen to the top of the global security agenda, Nasrallah increasingly made the case that fighting 'Takfirism' was not only a matter of security for the whole region, especially the Levant, but also elevated it to a religious duty. Protecting the Muslim *ummah*, Shiites as much as Sunnis, as well as Islam itself against terrorists was declared a priority. However, actors such as ISIS also threatened the broader cultural and political make-up of the region and the people living in it, 'their civilization, their history, their diversity, their right to live a dignified peaceful life, their right to partnership, and their right to free expression' (Nasrallah 2015f). Nasrallah tried to convey an image of Hezbollah that emphasised its non-sectarian, tolerant and pluralist nature, as well as its commitment to preserving unity among Middle Eastern peoples. To this end, he also emphasised that Hezbollah only stepped up to fulfil its 'jihadi, religious, and historic responsibilities' (Nasrallah 2016c) where it had been asked for help prior to its respective military engagements, such as in the cases of Syria and Iraq.

These attempts to be granted recognition as a non-sectarian and non-divisive actor must also be seen in the context of an increasingly hostile anti-Shiite discourse which was reinforced by the Gulf countries and in particular Saudi Arabia from 2015. Nasrallah's rhetoric had always been critical towards these countries, but a whole new tone was set when the Saudi-led coalition started its military intervention in Yemen in March 2015. By engaging in this brutal war, 'the Kingdom of "Benevolence"' (Nasrallah 2015c) had now started to show its real face. Nasrallah tried to reveal the intimate connection that exists between Wahhabist ideology and 'Takfirism' – and, thus, between Saudi and Salafi-jihadist practices. By this, Nasrallah aimed, on the one hand, at establishing that the situations in Yemen and Syria/Iraq should be seen as very similar, with the 'real' enemy in both cases being a child of Wahhabism. On the other hand, he also tried to put the terrorism label on both Saudi Arabia and 'Takfirist' groups. This escalation is a reaction to the discursive, but also legal mis-recognition acts pushed for by Saudi Arabia. The Gulf Cooperation Council and the Arab League had agreed to list Hezbollah as a terrorist group in early 2016. The party answered by painting an image of the 'real' terrorist connection between the Gulf and 'Takfirist' groups all over the MENA region, emerging from the same intellectual tradition and aiming at the annihilation of religious and cultural pluralism: 'The entire world is now … well aware that all the terrorism in this world and in any corner in the world is due to the intellect and money of the [Saudis]' (Nasrallah 2016d).

Nasrallah then tried to re-embed this narrative in the broader framework of oppressors vs oppressed. He pointed out the cynicism by which such countries as Saudi Arabia and the United Arab Emirates intervened with the purpose of establishing legitimacy, freedom or democracy, reminding his audience of the authoritarian, brutal and oppressive nature of these regimes. He also painted rich rhetorical images, opposing 'a self-indulgent prince who lives in luxury' to 'a prideful, poor, oppressed, struggling and striving people' (Nasrallah 2015b), an army of cowards that 'will get the Pakistanis, the Egyptians, and the Jordanians to fight for them' (Nasrallah 2015b) to the 'bravery and courage' (Nasrallah 2015a) as well as steadfastness of the resistance movements all over the Middle East. Indeed, he also tried to gain recognition for the Lebanese model of resistance where, according to Nasrallah, the organised resistance fights side by side with the armed forces and the popular resistance (see previous section). He not only considers the effectiveness of this arrangement to have been proven in the fight against Israel and in Syria, but he also sees that the Iraqis adopted the model in their fight against ISIS and the Yemenis in the face of US–Saudi aggression. Establishing this model all over the MENA promises success in fighting off hegemonic, oppressive plans: 'This is the formula of victory. This is the deterrence formula' (Nasrallah 2015d).

International mis-recognition: between demonisation and pragmatism

With regard to the international level, Hezbollah's recognition claims remain moderate (see also Dudouet in this volume). This can partly be explained through its listing as a terrorist organisation in most Western countries; it has been designated so by the USA since 1995 and several Western states have followed. However, it seems that Hezbollah seeks recognition from Western states, at least in some respects, too. Most of Hezbollah's discourse on international matters revolves around the West, the liberal world order and its institutions, and how they interact with regional actors and interfere in MENA affairs (Pfeifer 2017). Three recognition claims can be identified that are directed at Western recognition-granters: (1) Hezbollah wants Lebanon to be recognised as a sovereign country and its internal affairs to be respected; (2) it wants to be recognised as an actor with a legitimate cause and a commitment to rules and norms as stipulated by international law; and (3) it wants to be recognised for its success in fighting the 'Takfirist threat'. This last claim is tightly connected to the perceived mis-recognition as a terrorist group.

According to Hezbollah, Western states – in particular the US and France – constantly try to meddle with Lebanese domestic affairs. Given its weakness, the state cannot stand up against these acts of interference. One example is the establishment of the STL due to US and French pressure. But Western hegemony goes far beyond Lebanon: through bringing docile dictators to power and spreading chaos and conflict, the West tries to make Arabs 'singers and dancers' (Nasrallah 2012b). Even though Nasrallah holds that liberal norms are the product of 'political considerations' rather than expressing 'rights and values' (Nasrallah 2011a), it is noteworthy that Hezbollah has always committed to some international norms, notably regarding international humanitarian law. Since 1996, it has refrained from attacking civilians (Dionigi 2014: 157). In his assessments of the wars waged in Yemen, Syria and Iraq, Nasrallah also regularly commented on illegitimate and legitimate uses of force, often using similar argumentation to that found in just war theory (Kızılkaya 2017; Pfeifer 2017: 282–302). It is remarkable that Hezbollah sets itself clear limits on the use of violence and also regularly comments on infringements on human rights and international law as committed by other actors, including ISIS and Saudi Arabia, but also Western states. Nasrallah happily points to the hypocrisy of the West and its so-called 'universal values'. The West 'gives lectures … on civilization, democracy and the will of the majority' (Nasrallah 2011a), yet forgets about human rights when Israel attacks Palestinians and does not 'have any problem when the ruler wears a crown [or] a turban' (Nasrallah 2012a).

However, since it has been cooperating side by side with the Assad regime and, since its intervention, Russia in Syria, Hezbollah's commitment to human rights norms becomes more and more questionable. The void on human rights violations and war crimes committed by these actors in Nasrallah's discourse can be seen as indicating a predicament (Khatib and Matar 2014): on the one hand, Hezbollah's core interest of keeping the axis of resistance makes this cooperation necessary; on the other hand, it makes the party vulnerable to allegations of being an irrational, immoral actor whose violence is simply unjustified. But what all of this shows is that there is *some* desire to be recognised by an international audience as a rational actor bound by certain norms – and thus be distinguished from such actors as ISIS. Being labelled a terrorist organisation was perceived as particularly unwarranted against the backdrop of Hezbollah's fight against ISIS in Syria, which involved heavy losses. While the West only became militarily active in 2015, Hezbollah had started its armed struggle against ISIS two years earlier. But instead of showing gratefulness, the West keeps, and some Arab states started, demonising Hezbollah: '[W]e are fighting the terrorist organization which is labeled by the world as a terrorist organization. How come we are labeled as terrorists? How come we are condemned?' (Nasrallah 2016a).

For Hezbollah, the West's declared fight against ISIS should not be bought into. Rather, the US has a strong interest in bringing further chaos upon the region. They do so via their 'puppet regimes' (Nasrallah 2013) in the Gulf. The eventual goal the US and its allies pursue is, according to Nasrallah, the toppling of all regimes loyal to the transnational resistance against Israel. The international will to 'forcefully frustrate' the transnational resistance grew stronger in the post-Arab uprising era, as the US, Israel and Western states at large, and the Gulf states realised that the popular revolutions might bring about resistance-friendly regimes and thus a new 'peak of the resistance project on the level of the nation' (Nasrallah 2016b). Creating chaos could serve the counter-resistance purpose: first, the US and its allies ruin the region, in order to later reintroduce themselves as heroes and liberators 'from outside' (Nasrallah 2015d). Hezbollah's interpretation of the situation in 2016 is that there is a more or less coordinated 'US, "Israeli", Takfiri, Saudi scheme that wants to practise hegemony and control, and drive away and expel the other' (Nasrallah 2016c). While not suspecting a direct, open US involvement with 'Takfirist' groups, Nasrallah does seem to think that letting ISIS grow was a calculated risk the US took – that would later overwhelm and surprise the West. Hezbollah's discourse oscillates between, on the one hand, a claim to being recognised as something entirely different from other violent groups – especially 'Takfirist' groups – and, on the other hand, the suggestion that in the end Hezbollah does not care about what Western actors think about it, given that they are caught up in their hegemonic, self-interested schemes and, as a consequence, are not to be trusted anyway.

Conclusion

As this chapter showed, Hezbollah dynamically reacts to practices it perceives to be mis-recognition by developing new, or re-emphasising old, recognition claims, re-interpreting its own identity and role in conflicts, and by withdrawing recognition from actors, for example the Saudi regime. Both its claims as a recognition-seeker and the reactions by its (potential) recognition-granters are hybrid, and sometimes contradictory: they combine practices of recognition with mis-recognition.

In the Lebanese context, Hezbollah defends itself against mis-recognition as a foreign-controlled, sectarian, irrationally violent actor by emphasising its patriotism, readiness for dialogue and sacrifices made for all Lebanese in the face of external threat. Indeed, Hezbollah's discursive practices within Lebanon tend to aim at calming sectarian tensions, finding compromise and avoiding open conflict, especially with violent means. How it will react to the non-sectarian protests of 2019 and 2020 which are directed against the Lebanese political class as a whole is not yet fully clear – a new narrative needs to be found, as Hezbollah, too, is denounced as keeping up a corrupt system that has led the country into economic and social catastrophe. Seeking recognition as key actor in the transnational resistance against Israel will certainly not suffice to calm the public.

On a regional level, Hezbollah claims recognition as a core actor for the most important common Arab–Muslim cause: the transnational resistance and liberation of Palestine. Later on, it also claimed to be a forerunner in the defence of Middle Eastern civilisation and Islam against the 'Takfirist threat', thereby fighting for both pluralism and unity in the region. Confronted with an increasingly hostile anti-Shiite discourse and being labelled a terrorist organisation by its 'fellow' Arabs and Muslims, that is, several states from the Gulf and regional organisations, Hezbollah tried to establish that the real terrorist connection has its origin in Wahhabi ideology and consists of both 'Takfirist' actors and Saudi Arabia. This labelling and counter-labelling, or struggle over who is the 'real terrorist', reinforces existing cleavages between what is often perceived as a sectarian conflict between Shiites and Sunnis, but is more complex by far. Hezbollah's attempt to 'sell' its success model of the golden formula of resistance to other places in the MENA is not only a form of recognition-seeking; it can also be seen as a recipe for practically countering Western-supported, high-tech warfare as led in Yemen. In this sense, Hezbollah seeks recognition not so much for the Shiite, but the resistance model *per se*, as a form and means of legitimate struggle against hegemonic projects.

Finally, Hezbollah's recognition claims are moderate with regard to the West – certainly because its hopes of cracking the wall of Western counterterrorism policies are rather low. Still, it does want to be perceived as a rational actor that complies with certain norms and is qualitatively different from ISIS. Hezbollah's discourse oscillates between, on the one hand, a claim to being recognised as something entirely different from other violent groups – especially jihadi groups – and, on the other hand, suggesting that in the end Hezbollah does not care what Western actors think about it, given that they are caught up in their hegemonic, self-interested schemes and, as a consequence, are not to be trusted.

This oscillation is also mirrored in the diverging practices of recognition that Western actors show towards this ANSA. While the US is very clear in listing the entirety of Hezbollah, including its media outlets, as a terrorist organisation and imposes strict financial sanctions, the European position is much more mixed. Many European countries and the EU have decided to only designate Hezbollah's armed wing as a terrorist organisation, but recognise its political wing as a party and a part of the Lebanese political system. It thus keeps open a door for negotiations and transformation. However, the distinction between 'two wings' obviously matches neither Hezbollah's self-perception nor the functioning of its organisation. For instance, despite the pragmatically motivated recognition of Hezbollah as an essential part of Lebanese society, its military capabilities were significantly enhanced after 2011 (O'Sullivan 2013). At the same time, for those who list the whole organisation, the question might be of how to seek ways around the state and official Lebanese government, which Hezbollah has been part of for almost a decade now. By sidelining these institutions, the Lebanese state may be weakened further. Moreover, as the above analysis showed, practices of mis-recognition are usually met by new discursive efforts to present an alternative image. These re-interpretations of the self and how it is positioned in regional conflict dynamics are motivated by a struggle for survival through recognition, at least among some audiences. Raising pressure on actors will not lead to their submission to external recognition 'offers', that is, an acceptance of being a terrorist, an outsider, and so on. Rather, more hostile rhetoric and spirals of mis-recognition may be the consequence.

Notes

* For helpful comments on earlier versions of this chapter, I am grateful to Maéva Clément, Anna Geis and Franz Xaver Schießleder.

1 www.state.gov/designation-of-the-islamic-revolutionary-guard-corps/; last retrieved 3 April 2020.
2 www.reuters.com/article/us-usa-iran/in-unprecedented-move-u-s-names-irans-revolutionary-guards-a-terrorist-group-idUSKCN1RK1NY; last retrieved 3 April 2020.
3 https://augengeradeaus.net/2020/01/sicherheitshalber-der-podcast-folge-23-live-usa-vs-iran-und-kampfflugzeug-der-zukunft/; https://smallwarsjournal.com/blog/are-we-prematurely-designating-irans-revolutionary-guards-as-criminal-soldiers; www.ejiltalk.org/the-killing-of-soleimani-and-international-law/; last retrieved 3 April 2020.
4 www.presidency.gov.lb/Arabic/LebaneseSystem/Documents/TaefAgreementEn.pdf; last retrieved 3 April 2020.
5 https://foreignpolicy.com/2020/01/22/lebanons-halloween-government/; last retrieved 3 April 2020.

References

Alagha, J. (2011), *Hizbullah's Documents from the 1985 Open Letter to the 2009 Manifesto* (Amsterdam: Pallas Publications).

Allan, P. and A. Keller (2006), 'The concept of a just peace, or achieving peace through recognition, renouncement, and rule', in P. Allan and A. Keller (eds), *What is a Just Peace?* (Oxford: Oxford University Press), pp. 185–215.

Armborst, A. (2017), 'Conceptualizing political violence of non-state actors in international security research', in A. Kruck and A. Schneiker (eds), *Researching Non-state Actors in International Security: Theory and Practice* (Abingdon and New York, NY: Routledge), pp. 14–28.

Azani, E. (2011), *Hezbollah: The Story of the Party of God. From Revolution to Institutionalization* (Basingstoke: Palgrave Macmillan).

Azani, E. (2013), 'The hybrid terrorist organization: Hezbollah as a case study', *Studies in Conflict & Terrorism* 36:11, 899–916.

Biene, J. and C. Daase (2015), 'Gradual recognition: curbing non-state violence in asymmetric conflict', in C. Daase, C. Fehl, A. Geis and G. Kolliarakis (eds), *Recognition in International Relations* (Basingstoke: Palgrave Macmillan), pp. 220–236.

Dionigi, F. (2014), *Hezbollah, Islamist Politics, and International Society* (New York, NY: Palgrave Macmillan).

Fakhoury, T. (2016), 'Lebanon's consociational politics in the post-2011 Middle East: the paradox of resilience', in M. Felsch and M. Wählisch (eds), *Lebanon and the Arab Uprisings: In the Eye of the Hurricane* (Abingdon and New York, NY: Routledge), pp. 21–30.

Khatib, L. and D. Matar (2014), 'Conclusion: Hizbullah at a crossroads', in L. Khatib, D. Matar and A. Alshaer (eds), *The Hizbullah Phenomenon: Politics and Communication* (New York, NY: Oxford University Press), pp. 181–190.

Kızılkaya, Z. (2017), 'Hizbullah's moral justification of its military intervention in the Syrian civil war', *Middle East Journal* 71:2, 211–228.

Nagle, J. (2016), 'Between entrenchment, reform and transformation: ethnicity and Lebanon's consociational democracy', *Democratization* 23:7, 1144–1161.

Norton, A. R. (2014), *Hezbollah: A Short History* (Princeton, NJ: Princeton University Press).
O'Sullivan, D. (2013), 'Road to proscription: the EU and Hezbollah since the Arab Spring', *College of Europe EU Diplomacy Papers* 7, 1–34.
Pfeifer, H. (2017), *Discursive Struggles over World Order: Exploring Encounters between Islamists and the West* (Hamburg: Helmut Schmidt University / University of the Federal Armed Forces, PhD Dissertation).
Salem, P. (2017), 'Lebanon', in E. Lust (ed.), *The Middle East: 14th Edition* (Electronic iBooks Edition, Thousand Oaks, CA and London: Sage), pp. 1497–1571.
Wählisch, M. and M. Felsch (2016), 'Lebanon and the Arab uprisings: in the eye of the hurricane', in M. Wählisch and M. Felsch (eds), *Lebanon and the Arab Uprisings: In the Eye of the Hurricane* (Abingdon and New York, NY: Routledge), pp. 1–18.

Interviews and primary sources

Interview 1 with a journalist from l'Orient le Jour, Baabda (16 March 2015).
Interview 2 with a free journalist and author, Beirut (28 March 2015).
Nasrallah, H. (2011a), *Hizbullah SG Sayyed Hassan Nasrallah Speech on Arbaeen of Imam Hussein in Baalbeck* (25 January).
Nasrallah, H. (2011b), *Speech Delivered by Hizbullah Secretary General Sayyed Hassan Nasrallah on the occasion of the Martyr's Day held by Hezbollah at Sayyed Ashuhada (pbuh) Compound in Rweiss* (11 November).
Nasrallah, H. (2012a), *Speech Delivered by Hizbullah Secretary General Sayyed Hassan Nasrallah during the Ceremony Held to Commemorate the Blessed Birthday of the Holy Prophet Mohammad (Peace be upon him and his Household) and the Islamic Unity Week Held in Sayyed Ashuhada Compound – Rweiss* (7 February).
Nasrallah, H. (2012b), *Speech Delivered by Hizbullah Secretary General Sayyed Hassan Nasrallah during the Ceremony of Loyalty to the Leader Martyrs* (16 February).
Nasrallah, H. (2012c), *Political Section of the Speech Delivered by Hizbullah Secretary General Sayyed Hassan Nasrallah during the Ceremony Commemorating the Leader Martyrs' Day Held in Nabi Sheath* (24 February).
Nasrallah, H. (2013), *Sayyed Nasrallah Delivers Speech on Resistance and Liberation Day* (15 May).
Nasrallah, H. (2014a), *Full Speech Delivered by Hizbullah Secretary General, His Eminence Sayyed Hassan Nasrallah, via Al Manar Channel Marking the Anniversary of the Martyr Leaders* (16 February).
Nasrallah, H. (2014b), *Full Speech Delivered by Hizbullah Secretary General, His Eminence, Sayyed Hassan Nasrallah, during al-Quds Day Ceremony held by Hizbullah in Sayyed al-Shuhada Complex in Rweiss* (25 July).
Nasrallah, H. (2015a), *Full Speech Delivered by Hizbullah Secretary General His Eminence Sayyed Hassan Nasrallah during the Memorial Ceremony in Honor of the Great Quneitra Martyrs Held* (30 January).
Nasrallah, H. (2015b), *Full Televised Speech Delivered by Hizbullah Secretary General, His Eminence Sayyed Hassan Nasrallah* (27 March).
Nasrallah, H. (2015c), *Sayyed Nasrallah's Full Speech on April 17 over Yemen* (17 April).

Nasrallah, H. (2015d), *Full Speech Delivered by Hizbullah Secretary General Sayyed Hassan Nasrallah on the Day of Resistance and Liberation held in Nabatiyeh* (24 May).
Nasrallah, H. (2015e), *Full Speech Delivered by Hizbullah Secretary General His Eminence Sayyed Hassan Nasrallah on al-Quds International Day* (10 July).
Nasrallah, H. (2015f), *Full Speech Delivered by Hizbullah Secretary General, His Eminence Sayyed Nasrallah, in the Ceremony Held to Mark a Week on the Martyrdom of Hassan al Hajj in Lweizeh* (18 October).
Nasrallah, H. (2016a), *Full Speech Delivered by Hizbullah Secretary General, His Eminence Sayyed Nasrallah, on the First Week Commemoration Ceremony Held in Honor of Martyr Leader Ali Ahmad Fayyad [Alaa of Bosnia] in Ansar Village* (6 March).
Nasrallah, H. (2016b), *Full Televised Speech Delivered by Hizbullah Secretary General Sayyed Hassan Nasrallah on al-Quds Day* (2 July).
Nasrallah, H. (2016c), *Full Speech Delivered by Hizbullah Secretary General, His Eminence Sayyed Nasrallah, during the Memorial Held to Honor Martyr Leader Sayyed Mustafa Badreddine* (20 May).
Nasrallah, H. (2016d), *Speech Delivered by Hizbullah Secretary General Sayyed Hassan Nasrallah on the Tenth Night of Muharram during the Central Council Held in Sayyed Ashuhada [pbuh] Complex* (11 November).

IV

Recognition in mediation and peace processes

9

Ripe through recognition? The case of the Provisional Irish Republican Army

*Carolin Görzig**

Introduction

The Provisional Irish Republican Army (PIRA) began fighting for the reunification of Ireland in 1969.[1] It reached a turning point nearly three decades later when it called a final ceasefire in 1997, supported the Good Friday Agreement in 1998 and disarmed in 2005. Since then, the PIRA has become a role model for other groups around the world (Dixon 2006), a development that has contributed to the group's 'self-esteem' (Interview 8), as an interviewee describes it:

> So, if the president of Colombia says I want to ask my friend Martin McGuinness for advice on how to deal with the FARC. That's kind of cool. Right? If he says I wanna fly you over first class. Or if you know, if someone says can you come and give a speech at the UN, we fly you over when you do it. You can say well, no we're giving that up and I'm going back to being on the run and living in like slightly shady circumstances, but it's kind of quite nice to be treated seriously. You become a world statesman. (Interview 1)

Ringmar has stated that 'few things matter more than the identities we put together for ourselves since, without an identity, we have no idea of who we are' (Ringmar 2011: 3). The PIRA developed a new idea of who they were as an organisation when they contributed to peace, saw their leaders turn into 'world's statesmen' and became a global role model. Being recognised as a role model is only half of the story, however; the other half consists of recognising others, a step undertaken by the PIRA as well. Thus, they realised that 'the most important lesson of all, is to realise exactly that … this Northern Ireland is not Irish, it is not British, it is both' (Interview 4). To some observers this was the real turning point: 'The fundamental change, I would argue, … is the idea that the British and Irish governments have a shared problem here' (Interview 5).

According to William Zartman's ripeness theory (see below), which is much cited in conflict transformation literature, a conflict becomes ripe for resolution when the conflict parties perceive a mutually hurting stalemate and a way out. The PIRA perceived a hurting stalemate as well as a way out of the conflict when it was recognised by others and when it recognised others, two dynamics that went hand in hand. Commonly, 'putting together an identity is quite a struggle' (Ringmar 2011: 3). This struggle – the complex combination of seeking and granting recognition – is the topic of this chapter, that answers the question of how one party to the Northern Ireland conflict, the PIRA, became ripe through recognition. While ripeness relates to the conflict and includes both sides in a conflict, this chapter looks at one party in the Northern Ireland conflict in particular in order to discern how it arrived at the ripe moment. The chapter contributes to ripeness theory by investigating a case study in which a hurting stalemate and a way out were perceived by PIRA leaders when they acknowledged friends and enemies and in which PIRA leaders negotiated 'ripeness' internally by winning the recognition of their followers.

The chapter will proceed by spelling out the argument, followed by operationalising the different levels of recognition-granters and -seekers, detailing the case study and concluding with final observations.

The conceptual framework: ripeness theory and identity transformation

According to ripeness theory, a conflict becomes ripe for resolution when a mutually hurting stalemate coincides with a way out. William Zartman explained that conflict actors aim at conflict resolution when they are in a costly predicament, a 'ripe' moment, and therefore seek a way out: 'The mutually hurting stalemate is grounded in cost–benefit analysis. It is fully consistent with public-choice notions of rationality' (Zartman 2001: 8). William Zartman further explains that ripeness is a matter of subjective perception: 'If the parties do not recognize "clear evidence"... that they are at an impasse, a mutually hurting stalemate has not yet occurred, and if they do perceive themselves to be in such a situation, no matter how flimsy the "evidence", the mutually hurting stalemate is present' (Zartman 2001: 9).

The mutually hurting stalemate must moreover be accompanied by a way out. Without such a way out, 'the mutually hurting stalemate would leave the parties with nowhere to go' (Zartman 2001: 9). However, as this chapter argues, the perception of a mutually hurting stalemate and a way out might be based on cost–benefit analysis on the one hand, but both are also related to identity transformation on the part of the actors involved, on the other. As Zartman has put it, both parties to a conflict need to perceive the 'ripeness' of a conflict situation. In fact, acknowledgement of the other is crucial to the perception of ripeness. Acknowledgement and recognition can be gradual and can take different forms. '"Recognition" is a fuzzy term that is used quite differently by authors and speakers … [Among other things] the term can be used as a synonym for … "*acknowledgement*"; this implies recognition having "*evaluative or normative entities or facts* as its objects, so that we can acknowledge something as valuable, as valid, as giving reasons, and so forth"' (Clement et al. in this volume, p. 5). While the perception of ripeness is connected with the acknowledgement, for example, of the facts 'on the ground' or of the enemy as having a valid impact, perceiving a ripe moment not only comes along with acknowledging and recognising others but also with being recognised by others. Our understanding of the situation we are in and the options we have in this situation is connected to our self-perception and our perception of and by others. This implies that we can ask ourselves whether we start by telling stories about ourselves and then test these stories on others, or whether we acquire a story through others in the first place.[2] As Mead (1934) suggested, people cannot see themselves without relating to how others see them. Alexander Wendt explained accordingly that 'one cannot be a teacher without recognition by students, a husband without recognition by a wife, a citizen without recognition by other citizens' (Wendt 2003: 559).

However, when does this interactive process lead to identity transformation and when to identity confirmation? In the empirical case of peaceful transformation in this chapter, the non-state armed actor first changed its identity and then had its new identity confirmed by significant others. Accordingly, the chapter deals with a non-state armed group that became ripe for identity change: the Provisional Irish Republican Army. Based on field research in Northern Ireland this study of the PIRA helps to paint a differentiated picture of ripeness theory. PIRA leaders acknowledged friends and enemies and therewith became themselves 'ripe' to question their identity. Thus, acknowledging enemies such as the UK and the Unionists – who favour the political union between Ireland and Great Britain and are mostly from Protestant backgrounds – contributed to the PIRA's perception of a hurting stalemate. Recognising friends like South Africa's African National Congress (ANC) in turn helped PIRA leaders to recognise a way out.

Furthermore, both the hurting stalemate and the way out had to be 'sold' by the leaders to their follower base. The rational cost–benefit approach that underlies ripeness theory comes along with a tendency to neglect those actors. Breaking up this 'black box' and looking inside organisations helps us to understand how 'ripeness' is negotiated internally. If leaders of a group perceive a hurting stalemate and a way out, they have to 'sell' that perception to their followers. The internal negotiations of the PIRA are a case in point. The recognition of PIRA leaders as role models around the world thereby contributed to their capacity to convince PIRA followers. Recognising friends and enemies externally, and being recognised by followers internally, made PIRA leaders 'ripe' for transformation. This case study helps us to understand how ripeness is realised and negotiated when friends and enemies are acknowledged and the recognition by followers is won. It helps us to grasp the complexities of ripeness by complementing ripeness theory with a view of how an armed non-state group acknowledged and recognised itself and others.

Studying recognition in the case of the PIRA

Levels of analysis

The interplay between recognition-seekers and recognition-granters is complex: '[s]ocial actors always want to be recognised as and/or for something by other (groups of) actors … diverse actors are involved in such dynamics' (Clement et al. in this volume, p. 10). The empirical case that will be examined in this chapter problematises several external and internal sources of recognition-granting and -seeking. In order to clarify these sources, different levels of analysis are helpful. Analyses of armed non-state actors frequently neglect them in much the same way that states are often 'black boxed'. Several authors have called for looking inside this black box. Differentiating between leaders and followers helps to solve the problem of the anthropomorphisation of a collective actor (Wendt 2004). However, analyses that focus only on the micro level can also come with limitations, namely the examination of the organisation in isolation from its environment. Erik Ringmar describes how our stories are related to our affiliations in the environment: 'our stories make statements about our affiliations – they place us in an affective field made up of friends and enemies' (Ringmar 2011: 7). Armed non-state actors are placed in an affective field of friends and enemies when it comes to other armed non-state actors (the meso level) as well as the state (the macro level).

Black-boxing the armed non-state actor or seeing it in isolation from the environment has certain limitations: neither can explain the interrelation between the micro, meso and macro levels or account for empirical complexity. In order to understand this complexity, the concept of recognition can serve as a helpful analytical lens. Lindemann has written about the political person who is by definition preoccupied with self-image: 'His electoral survival depends, for a large part, on the opinions expressed by other important people and as a consequence on his symbolic capital' (Lindemann 2010: 2). Looking at the leaders of armed non-state actors and how they relate, internally, to followers (micro level) on the one hand, and, externally, at other allied or competing organisations (meso level) as well as to the state (macro level) on the other hand, makes it possible to interrelate the different levels.

When contemplating the complexity of the levels of analysis, the question arises whether they can be categorised according to their impact on the transformation of the PIRA, that is, whether a hierarchy of impact can be discerned. As the case study of the PIRA will subsequently reveal, a difference of granting recognition to enemies and to friends can be observed, as well as a difference of granting recognition and seeking recognition. The different levels of analysis can be visualised in Figure 9.1.

In the following, the change from violence to non-violent means in the PIRA is analysed. In this case study, granting recognition to external actors led to the leaders perceiving a ripe moment, and the micro level became a source for seeking followers' recognition of the new approach. The case study is based on field research and the collection of interviews and analysis of primary sources. Interviews were conducted with six experts and two former PIRA members. It was noteworthy that the interview partners in Belfast were comfortable expressing themselves with terms like 'tactics' and 'strategy' or 'ends' and 'means', but could not immediately relate to the term 'recognition'. When the author asked the interviewees about recognition, they replied that recognition was not their primary purpose. However, they usually associated the question with recognition as role models. They emphasised that being recognised as role models was only secondary. They found it, however, important to talk about their legacy, emphasising the change they brought about and implying the significance of recognition for

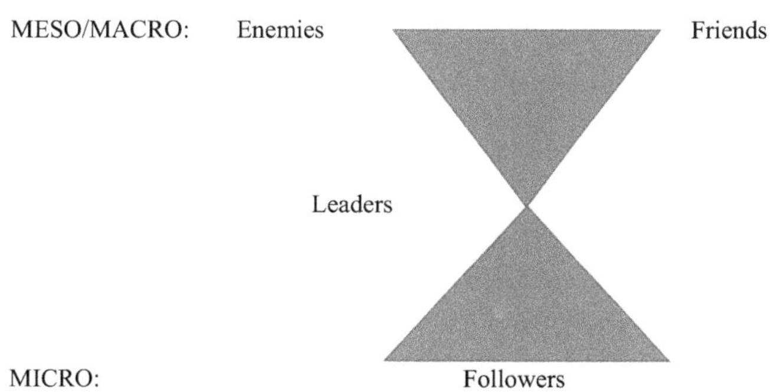

Figure 9.1 Levels of analysis regarding the sources of recognition-granting and -seeking

that. Hence, the term 'recognition' used to evaluate the empirical data in this chapter is an interpretation by the author.

The transformation of the Provisional Irish Republican Army

The conflict in Northern Ireland has been described as a result of a 'self-sustaining process of tit-for-tat' (Interview 1). Accordingly, an interviewee describes a reason why the conflict persisted:

> Northern Ireland was a conflict which no one was going to win in a neat way, so the demography of Northern Ireland hasn't got a big enough majority one to win, the British state was never going to do what the Sri Lankan state did to the Tamil Tigers and kill thousands of people, 'cause it's not that kind of stage and the IRA never had the capacity to win militarily, but it had the resilience not to lose, it was a game of chess and either side could finally lose. (Interview 1)

This quote demonstrates that there was no easy conflict exit, suggesting instead that all conflict players played the 'chess game' with vigour. The 'self-sustaining process of tit-for-tat' was eventually halted and the conflicting parties created a momentum for peace. The result of this momentum, the transformation of the PIRA[3] in the wake of the peace process (Archik 2005; Hayes 1998), turned the group into a role model worldwide, raising the question of how the PIRA arrived at this situation. Capturing the development of the PIRA in a few pages is a daunting task, however. In order to make sense of the complexity of the Northern Irish conflict, it is useful to point out the multitude of causes and changing motivations of the PIRA, the long history of the PIRA throughout which different dynamics unfolded and that saw the adoption of changing strategies, and the multiplicity of actors involved that substantially complicated conflict transformation.

Although the conflict in Northern Ireland 'at its most basic can be seen as a struggle between those who wish to see Northern Ireland remain part of the United Kingdom and those who wish to see the reunification of the whole island of Ireland …, the conflict in its present form is in fact "a tangle of interrelated questions"' (Cairns and Darby 1998: 754). Among those interrelated questions, causal factors can be attributed to history, nationalism, inequality, repression and theology (although theology figures among the least important factors) (Cairns and Darby 1998). According to Robert White (1989: 1277) 'quantitative examination of the development of the IRA … shows that state repression, not economic deprivation, was the major determinant of this violence'. As a reaction to these causal factors, as well as to the changing environment and context, the PIRA adopted different ideological colours for its struggle, including nationalism and

Marxism. It exhibited a certain pragmatism, especially when it came to its relations with other actors who could support its goals, a pragmatism that helped the group to transform, as will be shown further below. This pragmatism might also partially explain why the PIRA adopted several strategies along the way, ranging from the shift from short-term struggle to the war of attrition over the decision to adopt the armalite and ballot box strategy, and finally the decision to abandon the armed struggle.

These shifts reflected dynamics that unfolded between the PIRA and its external environment, as well as between PIRA leaders and their followers and popular support. The decision to emphasise the political course, for example, was influenced by the public will. The electorate of Sinn Féin favoured a political over a military course and the PIRA realised this (Richards 2001). The multi-layered context of the PIRA's struggle has been characterised by a multitude of actors. According to Ronald Francisco, '(i)n Northern Ireland at least three sides battle one another. There are republican protesters, their loyalist counterparts, and the state … Within each community there are several splinter groups that engage in internecine conflict' (Francisco 1996: 1196). Did the complexity of the Northern Irish conflict and of the PIRA's development complicate conflict transformation? The PIRA created a momentum for peace and managed to turn the complexity of actors into a source for conflict transformation. It achieved this when granting recognition to external enemies and friends led to the perception of a ripe moment and when seeking recognition from followers helped to 'sell' the new approach. This process is depicted in the following section.

Granting recognition and self-recognition

Referring to lessons drawn from Vietnam, a former PIRA member stated in an interview: '[W]e quite literally had the impression that we were gonna militarily force the British out of Ireland' (Interview 8). Emulating what happened in Vietnam, Gerry Adams (the president of Sinn Féin since 1983) had adopted the strategy of a war of attrition. However, in the late 1980s things changed. When the leaders of the PIRA started to acknowledge the British state and its presence in Northern Ireland they realised that the British were not going to leave. The PIRA had cultivated a narrative of an anti-colonial struggle against Britain. It saw itself as being in the same boat as other anti-colonial liberation movements around the world and sought to draw legitimacy from that.

However, by the end of the 1980s they had realised that 'Northern Ireland was different to other colonial contexts' (Interview 4). Senior leaders had realised that the PIRA could not win.

> Adams, McGuinness and others, they're saying: We are as good as we're ever gonna get at this and we're still not winning. You know, we can't get any better than we are. This is learning from failure and it's learning from the limitations of militarism, it's learning and recognising that you can be technically good at this, but still, still not much ... we're still not driving the British out. (Interview 2)

According to Anup Phayal, that realisation was connected to increasing pressures on the PIRA by the British military, domestic actors such as non-governmental organisations and moderate political parties, and the international environment (Phayal 2011: 1).[4] However, neither side could win. The British state recognised that it could not win against the PIRA[5] and the Provisionals in turn recognised that they could not win against the British state. The self-sustaining process of tit-for-tat that kept the conflict going turned into a gradual recognition that one's respective counterpart had an interest in peace as well,

> there is an inevitability about peace after conflict, or even during the conflict, you'd always be hoping for it, but at the end of it would have to be conditional on certain things. I mean, nobody wants to be fighting. So, the prospect, the peace was good, but at one stage we just didn't see it coming. We didn't see it ... hope for it. But obviously, when the British government made their momentous statement in the late 1980s, about having no strategic interest, the British secretary of state here made a statement about 1989, 1990 that the British government had no longer any strategic, economic, or some other interest in remaining on the island of Ireland. That was a major turning point within our mentality. Well everybody wants peace, but it has to be the right type of peace ... I could just tell you we all wanted peace, but not at any price. (Interview 8)

The PIRA gradually started to recognise the British state and its real interests, such as Britain's interest in peace. The PIRA's recognition of Britain that came along with the realisation of the limits of its previous understanding of its enemy was also closely related to recognising the real nature of the Unionists (Farrington 2006). PIRA leaders started to realise that the Unionists were serious about their identity and that they were the main obstacle to a United Ireland and not just a by-product of the British state. While PIRA leaders had previously referred to Unionists as 'puppets of the British state' and believed Unionists would accept a United Ireland if the British state left, their attitudes evolved and they started to recognise the identity of the Unionists: 'their identity was real and genuine and passionate and it was just as important as PIRA's identity of nationalists ... the most important lesson of all, is to realise exactly that ... this Northern Ireland is not Irish, it is not British, it is both' (Interview 4). Importantly, they realised that the Unionists were the reason Britain could not just leave even if it wanted to. Indeed, 'Northern Ireland was different to other colonial contexts' (Interview 4). This recognition-granting led to the recognition by PIRA leaders of a hurting stalemate. They realised the limits of their struggle and became more realistic.

Granting recognition to enemies and competitors made PIRA leaders aware of the limits of their previous understanding of the nature of the conflict and the impasse they were in. An ex-PIRA member recalls that 'Adams and McGuinness decided that they were going nowhere. They believed that it was time to engage with other people. The PIRA came to a point where a lot of people were tired, people were looking for a way out of it' (cited in the workshop summary by Ranstorp and Brun 2013: 44). PIRA leaders found a way out when they turned to friends and supporters. What they learned from enemies provides only half of the story. While enemies and competitors contributed to the self-recognition of the PIRA in terms of their weaknesses and limits, friends and supporters contributed to PIRA leaders' recognition of their possibilities and strengths.

As Ringmar stated, 'our stories make statements about our affiliations – they place us in an affective field made up of friends and enemies' (Ringmar 2011: 7). However, we also draw our stories from our affective field. One interviewee described the affective field of the PIRA with the observation, 'ideas travel'. An illustration of how ideas travel is how the Catholics in Northern Ireland saw themselves as analogous to South Africa's black population and the Protestants as analogous to South Africa's white population:

> there's been a crude equation in Northern Ireland that Catholics are South Africa's black people and Protestants are South Africa's white people. In a way there's another crude equation that Catholics are Israel's Palestinians and Protestants are Israel's Jews, that loose cultural equation where sub-ordered groups identify with sub-ordered groups, dominant groups identify with dominant groups. Now of course, ... Mandela's particular vision of a non-violent peaceful transition that delivers social justice and human rights impacted on Sinn Féin in particular. (Interview 3)

PIRA leaders realised their strengths and possibilities from their affiliations with groups like the ANC, the PLO and ETA, or from contrasting themselves with the Red Army Faction (RAF) and the Tamil Tigers. While they emulated the successes of role models like the ANC, they also realised their own strengths in contradistinction to less successful groups like the RAF and the Tamil Tigers. The recognition of the ANC as a role model, particularly a role model for peaceful transformation, facilitated PIRA leaders' ideas on how to realise change. Friends like the ANC showed the PIRA leaders a way out. In fact, you see depictions of Nelson Mandela everywhere when you go around Belfast. The ANC also became a role model because they 'got more and more through negotiations' (Interview 8). The success of the ANC made PIRA leaders realise that they could win without violence, that change was possible. The ANC thereby served not only as a role model but also as a direct mentor for change. The problems with unity and splits in the past and the question of 'how far you can lead' were issues PIRA leaders had to solve, and the assistance of the ANC made solutions seem possible:

> once those international actors came on to the scene, it acknowledged us … Not only did they go into the prisons and talk to the prisoners, encouraging an acceptance of a change in strategy, but they also engaged in talks on the outside with activists. We had senior, senior ANC leaders coming over here. Giving their experience, not telling us what to do, but giving their experiences. (Interview 7)

While PIRA leaders recognised their own strengths and possibilities when recognising role models, they also realised what they could do in contradistinction to the Tamil Tigers and the RAF. In an interview a former PIRA member reported on the experience of consulting the Tamil Tigers, stating that the Tamil Tigers' lack of insight into the reality of the situation in Sri Lanka was frustrating: 'they had no sense of the moment, of what was happening, of global politics … that the world was changing. … And they were slaughtered' (Interview 8). The experience with the Tamil Tigers contributed to PIRA leaders' realisation of their own strengths. When asked about the Red Army Faction, a former PIRA member emphasised 'we had a different image of ourselves. We never considered ourselves to be in the same boat with the likes of the Red Army Faction' (Interview 8). The main reason given for lack of identification is the lack of support that the Red Army Faction had.[6] For PIRA members it was clear that they had a cause as well as a community of support. In fact, their self-perception as a movement with mass support was essential also for their positioning vis-a-vis the British state:

> The British just could not believe it, because they assumed the Provisional IRA was like the Baader Meinhof gang … It was a famous German novelist to describe the war of the Red Army Faction,[7] it's the war of 6 against 60 million. So, the assumption of the IRA was like the Red Army Faction or like the Red Brigades in Italy and that it was basically a fringe violent movement without any support. That was … what people on the mainland assumed. And then the discovery that they had mass support amongst Catholics in Northern Ireland was a deep, deep shock to the British and it led to changes in policy, to the assumption that … things had to change. And it led to the Anglo-Irish Agreement, it led to … it opened the way. (Interview 6)

Granting recognition opened new opportunities on both sides. Granting recognition to enemies and friends led to a new perception among the PIRA leaders of a situation that was leading nowhere. When they transformed their understanding of their enemies and friends, they found a new self-perception, a new identity. They recognised their own weaknesses and limits through interaction with enemies and they recognised their own strengths and possibilities through interaction with friends. While enemies contributed to PIRA leaders' perception of a hurting stalemate, friends showed them a way out.

Negotiating 'ripeness': how the leaders sought recognition by the followers

Leaders of armed groups usually seek confirmation from their followers. The PIRA's active members did not exceed a few hundred at any one time; however, its support network consisted of thousands throughout the thirty-two counties. PIRA's members are also referred to as volunteers. There were part-time volunteers who held regular work positions and full-time volunteers without other jobs who received a weekly allowance from the organisation. Volunteers were of different ages and backgrounds. Most were male and roughly range from fifteen to forty years. Small groups such as the RAF, where members or cells had a high degree of autonomy, stand in contrast to the centrally and hierarchically organised PIRA. In the PIRA, decision-making was centralised and the followers, comprising the active members of the organisation, had little effect on the decision-making process (Horgan and Taylor 1997: 25). However, the degree of violence employed by the PIRA had an effect on the group's members, including the followers, as well as on broader public support. Accordingly, an interviewee emphasised that the audience of violence is always your own community 'so that the limitation is what your own community will tolerate' (Interview 3). Sanchez-Cuenca (2007), examining the war of attrition strategy of ETA and the IRA, concludes that popularity constraints and the moderate preferences of supporters limited the violence of these organisations. Public support can constrain the employment of violence by organisations if it does not tolerate an excess thereof because non-state armed actors also depend on the public, for example for shelter. On the other hand, it is public support itself that can lead to the radicalisation of non-state armed groups. Hayes and McAllister, for example, state that 'one of the reasons for the intractability of the conflict is widespread exposure to political violence among the civil population' (Hayes and McAllister 2001: 901). They argue that exposure to violence increased the support for military groups and decreased chances of decommissioning weapons in Northern Ireland.

While employing violence can create an impetus for gaining public support, persuading the group's own followers to give up the struggle arguably also needs an impetus. While in hierarchically structured organisations decision-making runs top-down, the leaders nevertheless need to convince the followers of their idea. The leaders of the PIRA found an impetus in the electoral successes of Sinn Féin. Sinn Féin is frequently labelled the political arm of the IRA. The success of Sinn Féin also signalled to the PIRA that the pendulum of public support was swinging from the military to the political side. However, as another interviewee pointed out, 'the difficulty is that momentum is hard to sustain … they have to keep delivering progress … how can you make this week better than last week' (Interview 1). Furthermore, even if peace is the preferred option for the public and followers, the will for peace is not always enough – as an interviewee pointed out:

> You could say in a very simple analysis, to say well, the majority always wanted that. But that didn't stop things, right. 'Cause even if the majority wanted peace, lots of people still profoundly disagreed on really important issues. And then there were people who were just extreme, who would just disagree no matter what the issue was. So, I think it's too simple to say the public opinion got tired or persuaded the militants to give up. I think it's part of the process, you know, that conflict could have continued for a good while longer, I believe. A majority believed in peace, but they didn't agree on the way to establish peace. (Interview 5)

People disagreed over what peace should look like and when PIRA leaders found their version of peace they had to 'sell' it to their followers: 'something like 95 per cent of negotiations were with their own base' (Interview 8). As an interviewee quoted earlier remarked, all wanted peace, but not at any price. PIRA leaders had to find arguments that would convince their followers that the price paid would not be too high. While success in elections was one of the arguments PIRA leaders could draw upon, they put forward further arguments in order for their new approach to be recognised by their followers.

Granting recognition to enemies and friends, as described above, enabled them to collect more such arguments. The statement by the British state that it could not win against the PIRA and that it had no selfish interest in Northern Ireland could be used by PIRA leaders to convince followers by telling them: look, it is not surrender. The British state gave them a face-saving exit option.[8] A positive self-image thereby also becomes an argument that can gather support, a tool for self-realisation. While recognising enemies leads to self-recognition of limitations, getting recognised by followers is facilitated when granting recognition to enemies can be explained to followers and turned into an argument. In this case the face-saving exit supported the leaders' argument for stopping violence.

Granting recognition to friends delivered further supporting arguments because it showed a way out. Looking at the ANC made PIRA leaders realise 'how to move violence to politics and keep your support unified' (Interview 4). The success of the ANC helped PIRA leaders argue that politics is not surrender, that it is not defeat but a change of tactics to achieve the same goal. That argument helped to keep the support unified: 'What they learned from their revolutionary brothers in arms is how to bring your whole group behind you' (Interview 4). When ANC representatives were brought into prisons in Northern Ireland as dialogue partners, PIRA prisoners engaged with them and could 'question and listen to their advice about moving forward' (Interview 8). A former PIRA member accordingly states, 'that for me was a big, big thing. 'Cause I understood then, look we can do this. We can end the armed conflict. And we can move ahead with confidence' (Interview 8).

While the affective field of friends and enemies yielded arguments that PIRA leaders could employ to develop a convincing story for their followers, the peace process also turned into a model for other conflicting parties all over the world. PIRA leaders also had their story heard. This self-realisation has been perceived differently by different interviewees. One academic argues that PIRA leaders see their role in the context of a moral responsibility, an ethical commitment, as 'putting something back' (Interview 3). Another academic emphasises that the new role gave more momentum to the peace process: 'What the IRA is selling is, we're a successful terrorist group who have done a successful peace process, how can we help you?' Clearly, 'you become a world's statesman' (Interview 1). This room for self-realisation through being recognised reinforced PIRA leaders in their new role as politicians. For the followers, the recognition of the peace process 'gave acknowledgement, a degree of legitimacy' (Interview 8), as a senior member explains. To him, the interest of others contributed 'to a degree, to our self-esteem' (Interview 8).

Conclusion

PIRA leaders granted recognition to enemies and friends and recognised their own strengths and weaknesses as a consequence. Their new perception of reality and of what was possible and what was not possible had to be implemented and 'sold' to their followers. The leaders wanted and needed the recognition of their followers. While the leaders got their story externally, learning about strengths and weaknesses from other organisations and the British state, they got their story *right* internally, seeking confirmation from followers. The perception of a hurting stalemate and a way out, and the selling of a moment of ripeness internally, complemented each other, and the success of the peace process can be explained by their mutual reinforcement. Granting recognition yielded arguments that supported the search for recognition of the new approach by the followers, and seeking recognition by the followers reinforced the insights gained through granting recognition. The leaders of the PIRA emphasised that they wanted new means to an old end and that their change of strategy was not surrender. These arguments helped the leaders to take a face-saving exit. Arguments gathered externally – such as the way out shown by the ANC – helped PIRA leaders to take the face-saving exit internally. Without granting recognition they could not have developed the arguments needed to successfully seek recognition internally, and without being recognised by their followers, their ambitions would have remained unfulfilled and arguably would have led them down a different path. As a result, the peace process in Northern Ireland became a model for the whole world. The leaders who translated processes between the internal and external realm of the PIRA were 'incredible leaders' who knew 'how far they can lead' (Interview 4).

However, the interviews could also be seen as serving positive retrospect self-rationalisation. As the interviewer, the author's approach to critical distancing towards the interviewees was supported by her experience in other contexts. The author's investigation of several case studies makes it possible to discern similarities and differences between non-state armed actors who operate in different geographical regions and conflict contexts. The case of PIRA is telling as to how its leaders negotiated between the internal and external domains. Although the description of the leaders as 'world's statesmen' might be a positive evaluation, particularly in retrospect, it is indeed a skill to change direction and take one's followers along.

The openness of PIRA members towards members of the ANC and the acknowledgment of the Unionists speak to the group's ability to learn. In contrast, it has been argued that Islamist terrorist groups are not able to learn. Mohammed Hafez has stated that Islamist terrorist groups generally are unable to learn because they frame the world in terms of friend and foe and fight their Muslim brethren instead of uniting with them (Hafez 2018). The so-called Islamic State, for example, has not been able to learn from its environment, also because of the insularity of al-Baghdadi, the group's leader. That raises the question whether ethno-nationalist groups like the PIRA have a greater ability to learn than Islamist groups. The case of the Egyptian Islamist terrorist group Gamaa Islamiya hints otherwise. It is remarkable that members of the Gamaa Islamiya argued very similarly to the members of the PIRA. Members of both groups problematised means and ends relationships, arguing for employing new means to an old end. Furthermore, the case of Gamaa Islamiya is revealing with regards to how its leaders dealt internally with their followers and externally with critical voices and more radical groups like al-Qaeda.

It is apparent that non-state armed actors who embark on a new course have to justify their approach, especially when they distance themselves from their core. It is indeed important that leaders know 'how far they can lead'. Otherwise they risk losing their followers. In some cases, the impetus for change comes from the followers themselves. The leadership of Boko Haram in Niger has been challenged by group members because they considered that the indiscriminate violence of the leadership against Muslims implied that the group went too far from its core goal, which was to establish Sharia law for Muslims. In fact, when groups acknowledge that they have gone too far and that their violence has corrupted their original goals, they can become ripe for change. Both radicalisation and deradicalisation come along with moving away from a starting point and such a move has to be negotiated internally. The case of the PIRA is an example where the leaders have been especially successful in that negotiation.

This case study demonstrates how leaders translated recognition-granting of the external affective field of enemies and friends into arguments for seeking recognition by the internal base. It demonstrates how recognition-granting and -seeking went hand in hand in creating ripeness.

The leaders of the PIRA were flexible when it came to questioning their approach to violence and their perception of their enemies. Some have argued that the longevity of the group can be explained by its willingness to adapt its ideological outlook:

> The IRA were a broad church, so some of them more Marxist and some of them less, some of them more devoutly Catholics, some of them less. Many of them became less Catholic over the struggle, became less believers towards the end than they were in the beginning, but I think they were adaptive and I think that their ideology was one which was flexible, so broadly speaking a separatist nationalist movement, but a nationalism that drew very heavily on Catholic tradition and identity, a nationalism that for a while for some of them was very left-wing. ... So there is enough in the ideological box for them to keep going. (Interview 1)

Furthermore, the group was quite pragmatic when it came to choosing friends. For example, although they sympathised with the Colombians, they maintained distance after they recognised that FARC (see the chapter by Boesten and Idler, this volume) had a serious enemy in the USA, for the PIRA did not want to be at war with America. While there was enough in the ideological box to ensure longevity and adaptation to circumstances, the flexibility of the PIRA also facilitated its recognition of new circumstances and of their affective field of enemies and friends. Pragmatism was related to the recognition of a new reality.

Interestingly, the in-group identification was more robust. Referring to the use of group members for bomb construction and attack execution, one PIRA member emphasised:

> No, no, the IRA never would have had too many expendables. Yeah, probably a close examination of the IRA would indicate that it was very much an organisation of equals. You didn't have Colonel sitting behind the desk somewhere sending the sheep out to get slaughtered, you know. It was, if things were happening it was all hands on deck. You know, there's no, there are no expendables. (Interview 7)

This statement confirms the strong in-group identification. Furthermore, interviewed PIRA members stated that the prisoners at the time of negotiations were not to be used as a bargaining tool and that the deal was to be made without them. While PIRA leaders were flexible externally and granted recognition to enemies and friends, therewith transforming their perception of the situation, their internal recognition interests were not that flexible and served to confirm their new perception. The perception of a hurting stalemate and a way out was above all influenced by the acknowledgement of external enemies and friends. Internally the leaders sold the moment of ripeness.

Regarding whether certain recognition needs were more important than others, a senior member of the PIRA was asked by the author whose recognition he sought the most. He pointed to the legacy of the PIRA: 'this place is unrecognisable compared to what it was' (Interview 8). PIRA members take pride in their influence on the affairs of Northern Ireland. The leaders of the PIRA created a legacy, taking responsibility for subsequent generations:

> I think part of it certainly was generational in that … I think for people like Martin McGuinness or Gerry Adams who'd been involved in armed struggle all of their lives. The realisation, they're becoming grandparents, you know and, so by the time the peace process is starting to emerge, you know, their own kids are growing up and then another generation of kids are coming along. … Martin McGuiness, he suddenly realises, you know there has to be a way out of this, like there has to be a way that the next two generations don't end up doing the same thing that we did, you know. So I think the generational aspect of it was important, in terms of that. (Interview 2)

The evolution and the transformation of the PIRA spanned several generations. When are leaders ready to recognise their enemies and which generation does it take to become open to identity transformation? As the quote above demonstrates, the responsibility for the next generation has been seen as part of the leaders' turnabout. The responsibility, the legacy of the PIRA leaders has been part of their self-realisation. They wanted to be recognised as responsible for peace and they found the arguments to convince others of peace when they granted recognition to their enemies and friends. This case illustrates the complexity of recognition. The peace process and the legacy of PIRA tell the story of how its members recognised themselves by recognising others. This self-recognition led to the perception of a ripe moment, a moment PIRA leaders seized and sold to their followers. While leaders of the Provisional IRA thereby granted recognition to other organisations and the British state, they sought recognition by their followers. PIRA leaders got their story externally and got their story *right* internally. PIRA leaders were thereby flexible in their perception of enemies and friends.

Furthermore, granting recognition to enemies and friends differed in their impact on forms of self-recognition, at least in this case. Recognising enemies leads to new insights into one's weaknesses and hence reality. Thereby granting recognition to enemies led to the PIRA's perception of a hurting stalemate. As Ringmar has stated, 'putting together an identity is quite a struggle' (Ringmar 2011: 3). Arguably, transforming their identity was the real struggle for PIRA leaders. Recognising that they had misunderstood the nature of their enemies needed a certain courage, the will to face a new reality. This courage was facilitated when the PIRA leaders recognised friends, leading to the self-recognition of their strengths and possibilities and therewith a way out. Insights into both limits and possibilities form part of identity transformation, of the story we create about ourselves.

The second differentiation concerns the sources of recognition. Externally, PIRA leaders granted recognition (meso, macro). Internally, PIRA leaders sought recognition (micro). Therewith external sources became a base for self-recognition and internal sources became a source for self-realisation (Figure 9.2).

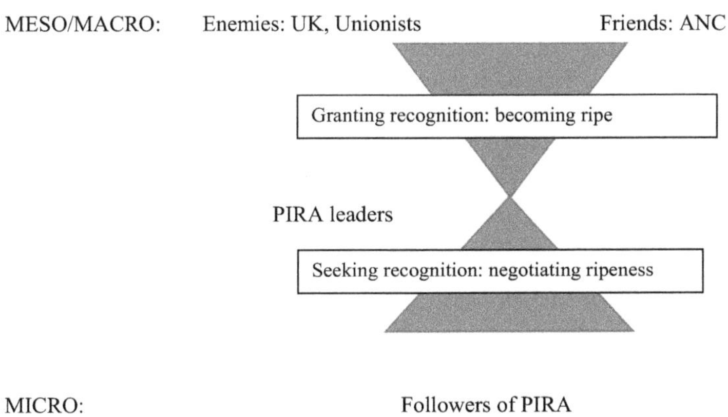

Figure 9.2 Levels of analysis, recognition acts

The empirical case in this chapter illustrates how an armed non-state actor first transformed its identity and then had its new identity confirmed. Instead of asking whether we start by telling stories about ourselves and then test these stories on others or whether we acquire a story through others in the first place, this case illustrates that the two processes need to complement each other. While armed non-state actors change as a result of recognition, they are also confirmed by it. Since '[t]he quest for a stable and just peace ... requires "thick" recognition among the conflicting parties, including an understanding of *one's own identity*' (Clément et al. in this volume, p. 00), it can be argued that PIRA's transformation of its self-understanding is directly related to the Northern Irish peace process. William Zartman envisions a ripe moment as a condition for conflict resolution. While reaching a ripe moment is an interactive process, this chapter looked at just one party to the Northern Irish conflict in order to grasp what happens inside the black box of one non-state armed actor who nevertheless is part of the overall conflict equation. This research could be expanded upon by asking how the self-understanding of one conflict party interacts with the self-understanding of the other conflict party/ies. Such research would take full account of William Zartman's concept of a mutual process.

Notes

* The interviews cited in this chapter were collected during a two-week field research stay in Belfast. Interviews were conducted with former PIRA members and academics/experts on the topic. This research is part of the author's comparative work on tactical and strategic learning of terrorist groups. She and her research group have conducted field research in Egypt, Syria, Turkey, Colombia, Northern Ireland, Spain, Palestine, Niger and Kyrgyzstan.

1 Members of the Provisional Irish Republican Army refer to their organisation simply as the Irish Republican Army (IRA) which they saw as the direct continuation of the Army of the Irish Republic which fought for the Independence of Ireland from 1916 to 1922.

2 While some authors argue for the former (Ringmar 1996), others argue for the latter (Agné et al. 2013; Honneth 2012).

3 For a history of the IRA see English (2012, 2019), Bishop and Mallie (1989) and Moloney (2007).

4 In terms of changes in the international environment, Jonathan Stevenson (1998: 41) emphasises that 'the drive toward European integration and unity has eroded national borders and the notions of sovereignty that underpin them, it also has undermined the beliefs and the support that gave voice and strength to Northern Ireland's most stubborn politicians'.

5 In 1989 Northern Ireland Secretary Peter Brooke said that the IRA could not be defeated entirely. On 9 November 1990 he gave a speech stating that Britain had

no 'selfish strategic or economic interest' in Northern Ireland and would accept unification if the people wished it.

6 Tangen Page and Smith (2000) introduce their article 'War by other means' with the formal announcement that the Red Army Faction made in 1998. Therein the RAF explains its failure as the result of it not having built a parallel political structure. Tangen Page and Smith argue that this insight also came from the RAF's observation of the role political organisations played in the conflict in Northern Ireland.

7 Referring to Heinrich Böll, 'Will Ulrike Gnade oder freies Geleit?' *Der* Spiegel, 10 January 1972.

8 See also Lindemann (2010).

References

Agné, H., J. Bartelson, E. Erman, et al. (2013), '*Symposium* "The politics of international recognition"', *International Theory*, 5:1, 94–107.

Archik, K. (2005), 'Northern Ireland: the peace process', *CRS Report for Congress* (26 April).

Bishop, P. and E. Mallie (1989), *The Provisional IRA* (London: Transworld Publishers Ltd.).

Cairns, E. and J. Darby (1998), 'The conflict in Northern Ireland: causes, consequences and controls', *Psychologist* 53:7, 754–760.

Dixon, P. (2006), 'Performing the Northern Ireland peace process on the world stage', *Political Science Quarterly* 121:1, 61–91.

English, R. (2012), *Armed Struggle: The History of the IRA* (Oxford: Oxford University Press).

English, R. (2019), *Does Terrorism Work? A History* (Oxford: Oxford University Press).

Farrington, C. (2006), 'Unionism and the Peace Process in Northern Ireland', *British Journal of Politics and International Relations* 8:2, 277–294.

Francisco, R. A. (1996), 'Coercion and protest: an empirical test in two democratic states', *American Journal of Political Science* 40:4, 1179–1204.

Hafez, M. M. (2018), 'Fratricidal jihadists: why Islamists keep losing their civil wars', *Middle East Policy* 25:2, 86–99.

Hayes, B. C. and I. McAllister (2001), 'Sowing dragon's teeth: public support for political violence and paramilitarism in Northern Ireland', *Political Studies* 49:5, 901–922.

Hayes, M. (1998), 'The evolution of Republican strategy and the "peace process" in Ireland', *Race and Class* 39:3, 21–39.

Honneth, A. (2012), 'Recognition between states', in T. Lindemann and E. Ringmar (eds), *The International Politics of Recognition* (Boulder, CO: Paradigm), pp. 25–38.

Horgan, J. and M. Taylor (1997), 'The Provisional Irish Republican Army: command and functional structure', *Terrorism and Political Violence* 9:3, 1–32.

Lindemann, T. (2010) *Causes of War: The Struggle of Recognition* (Colchester: ECPR Press).

Mead, G. (1934), *Mind, Self, and Society* (Chicago: University of Chicago Press).

Moloney, E. (2007), *A Secret History of the IRA* (New York, NY: W. W. Norton and Company).
Phayal, A. (2011), 'Cost of violence and the peaceful way out: a comparison of the Provisional Irish Republican Army and the Communist Party of Nepal (Maoists)', *Dynamics of Asymmetric Conflict* 4:1, 1–20.
Ranstorp, M. and H. Brun (2013), 'Terrorism learning and innovation: lessons from PIRA in Northern Ireland', *Center for Asymmetric Threat Studies: Closed Workshop Summary* (Stockholm: Swedish National Defence College).
Richards, A. (2001), 'Terrorist groups and political fronts: the IRA, Sinn Fein, the peace process and democracy', *Terrorism and Political Violence* 13:4, 72–89.
Ringmar, E. (1996), *Identity, Interest and Action* (London: Cambridge University Press).
Ringmar, E. (2011), 'Introduction', in T. Lindemann and E. Ringmar (eds), *The International Politics of Recognition* (Boulder, CO: Paradigm), pp. 3–24.
Sanchez-Cuenca, I. (2007), 'The dynamics of nationalism: ETA and the IRA', *Terrorism and Political Violence* 19:3, 289–306.
Stevenson, J. (1998), 'Peace in Northern Ireland: why now?', *Foreign Policy* 112, 41–54.
Tangen Page, M. and M. L. R. Smith (2000), 'War by other means: the problem of political control in Irish republican strategy', *Armed Forces & Society* 27:1, 79–104.
Wendt, A. (2003), 'Why a world state is inevitable: teleology and the logic of anarchy', *European Journal of International Relations* 9:4, 539–590.
Wendt, A. (2004), 'The state as person in international theory', *Review of International Studies* 30, 289–316.
White, R. (1989), 'From peaceful protest to guerrilla war: micromobilization of the Provisional Irish Republican Army', *American Journal of Sociology* 94:6, 1277–1302.
Zartman, I. W. (2001), 'The timing of peace initiatives: hurting stalemates and ripe moments', *Global Review of Ethnopolitics* 1:1, 8–18.

Interviews

Interview 1 with an expert, Belfast (June 2017).
Interview 2 with an expert, Belfast (June 2017).
Interview 3 with an expert, Belfast (June 2017).
Interview 4 with an expert, Belfast (June 2017).
Interview 5 with an expert, Belfast (June 2017).
Interview 6 with an expert, Belfast (June 2017).
Interview 7 with a former PIRA member, Belfast (June 2017).
Interview 8 with a former PIRA member, Belfast (June 2017).

10

Norms and recognition in mediation processes: promoting inclusivity in the mediation of the Intergovernmental Authority on Development in South Sudan

*Jamie Pring**

Introduction

Full-scale violence once again erupted in Juba, the capital of South Sudan, on 15 December 2013, barely three years after the country's independence from Sudan. It was the culmination of mounting political tensions among key members of South Sudan's ruling party, the Sudan People's Liberation Movement/Army (SPLM/A). The SPLM ran the government almost exclusively, being the party that negotiated the autonomy of South Sudan from the Government of Sudan (GoS) in 2005 under the Comprehensive Peace Agreement (CPA) that led to South Sudan's independence in 2011. The implosion of the SPLM not only meant the collapse of the Government of the Republic of South Sudan (GRSS), but also the return of armed conflict, this time with no northern adversary, but among South Sudanese who have been fighting each other for almost as long as they have been fighting the North.

As the CPA recognised one representative of the south at the expense of other armed groups that were also operating, long-time observers of the two Sudans were not blindsided by the re-eruption of violence. They argued that the bilateral framing of the CPA and its focus on power-sharing had ignored other actors and aspects of the conflict, and hence recurrence of violence was imminent (Jok 2015). In response to the revived scepticism, the Intergovernmental Authority on Development (IGAD), the regional body in the Horn of Africa, mandated a mediation mission that aims to provide 'a conducive environment for all stakeholders to participate and determine(d) that face-to-face talks by all stakeholders in the conflict' will be conducted (IGAD 2013:4). While the parties signed an agreement in August 2015, entitled *Agreement on the Resolution of the Conflict in South Sudan* (ARCSS), fighting restarted in July 2016, and the GRSS and the Sudan People's Liberation Movement-in-Opposition (SPLM-IO) further splintered.

The events described above illustrate two salient themes in the practice of mediation. First, the recurrence of violence came as no surprise to mediation practitioners and researchers familiar with arguments for greater inclusivity in international peace mediation. Research has shown that armed non-state actors (ANSAs) excluded in the negotiations may become spoilers of the peace process by resorting to or intensifying violence in order to derail the ongoing negotiations or the implementation of the peace agreement (Blaydes and de Maio 2010). Meanwhile, civil society participation in the peace process has been linked to a more sustainable peace agreement (Paffenholz 2014a; Paffenholz and Ross 2015; Wanis-St John 2008) and hence their exclusion contributed to the collapse of the peace. Secondly and relatedly, the IGAD-led mediation reflects the current mediation practice of promoting certain norms, defined as 'collective expectations about proper behaviour for a given identity' (Katzenstein 1996: 5). These norms, such as transitional justice and gender equality, are in addition to their main mandate of assisting conflict parties towards a peacefully negotiated agreement. The norm most salient in this case is inclusivity, defined as 'the extent and manner in which the views and needs of conflict parties and other stakeholders are represented and integrated into the process and outcome of a mediation effort' (United Nations 2012: 11). While 'inclusion' and 'inclusivity' are used interchangeably in policy discourse, the term 'inclusivity' is employed in this contribution to refer to the *quality* ('extent and manner') of incorporating stakeholders and the *norm* prescribing their incorporation. Meanwhile, 'inclusion' is used here as the *act* of incorporating a broader set of actors.

However, despite attempts at greater inclusivity, incorporating armed and non-armed groups alike, the peace in the 2015 agreement was short-lived and armed groups fragmented after it was signed. The South Sudan case illustrates that the relationship between greater inclusivity and the non-recurrence of violent conflict is not as straightforward as currently theorised in mediation research. With this in mind, this contribution probes the question of why ANSAs continue to use violence during and after the peace mediation despite their inclusion. The analysis draws on recognition theory, particularly the concept of mis-recognition, to further nuance the relationship between inclusivity in mediation processes and the recurrence of violent conflict. The general trend of recognition studies is that recognition practices aim for the inclusion of actors. However, there have also been instances of incompatibility between the two, where recognition has enabled different forms of exclusion (Bartelson 2013).

Examining the mediators as recognition-granters of ANSAs, the main argument of this chapter is two-fold. First, it forwards that understanding the relationship between inclusivity and recognition in mediation processes can better capture inclusivity's relationship with the non-recurrence of violence.

These relationships are more complicated than popularly depicted. Parties desiring recognition may indeed aim to be included in the peace process, but mere inclusion is not enough. Inclusivity, the quality of inclusion, reflects which identity or traits are being recognised in the process of inclusion. Since recognition is more about which traits are acknowledged and does not necessarily improve with more actors, greater inclusion may also lead to insufficient recognition or mis-recognition. Secondly, norms inherent in mediation and the norms of the mediating organisation shape recognition processes by setting the standards for selecting who is recognised, which might not always be responsive to the identity claims of ANSAs.

In the case of South Sudan, the IGAD mediation's desire to protect regional ownership guided the promotion of inclusivity in both the 2005 CPA and the 2015 ARCSS mediation. In the 2005 CPA process, subsuming other ANSAs under the GoS or the SPLM delegations undermined key identity differences between them and the two delegations that contributed to the peace agreement's collapse in 2013. In the 2015 ARCSS process, having a broader set of stakeholders, especially with the inclusion of civil society and other unarmed groups, undermined the SPLM-IO's claim as the only credible counterpart of the government. Hence, greater inclusion altered the standards of who gets to talk to the government, mis-recognising the SPLM-IO relative to its claim by relegating it as only one of the many counterparts. In order to regain their aspired kind of recognition, the SPLM-IO capitalised on its armed identity by escalating its violence. Within the SPLM-IO, the position compromises by Riek Machar led to divergences in key positions and contributed to the splintering of the delegation and the proliferation of more armed groups after the 2015 peace agreement.

I pursue the two-fold argument in four parts. The first part connects concepts on recognition, norms and inclusivity to formulate a conceptual framework. The second part describes how the exclusive CPA negotiations mis-recognised ANSAs and caused their forced marriage with the SPLM. The third part explains how, despite attempts at greater inclusivity, mis-recognition continued in the ARCSS negotiations, and violent conflict recurred in July 2016. The fourth part provides a summary of the main arguments, supporting evidence and a conclusion.

Conceptual framework

Inclusivity in mediation processes

Two types of actor have been studied separately in examining inclusivity in mediation: armed actors and civil society. Research on spoilers, fragmentation, multilateral negotiations and recognition processes examined the inclusion of armed actors, but rarely in studies on inclusivity, which centre on the inclusion of civil society (Hellmüller 2019). The dilemma of including armed actors, particularly ANSAs, is generally portrayed as binary, as a choice between 'two risky roads' between inclusion and exclusion (Lanz 2011). As mentioned earlier, arguments in favour forward that ANSA's inclusion minimises the risk of having violent spoilers (Blaydes and de Maio 2010). Arguments against their inclusion note that inclusion prolongs and exacerbates violence by encouraging the formation of splinter groups by actors seeking to have greater influence in the peace process (Cunningham 2013; Tull and Mehler 2005). Furthermore, a smaller set of actors more easily arrive at solutions, are more manageable and entail fewer costs (Axelrod 1997; Raiffa et al. 2007).

While there is a debate on whether the inclusion of ANSAs minimises violence, there is broader agreement on a positive relation between civil society inclusion and long-term peace. The premise is that civil society represents a broader set of interests in the conflict. Hence, including civil society would in principle increase the buy-in and national ownership needed to implement the peace agreement. During the talks, civil society can also direct attention to broader issues of governance and justice that armed groups tend to ignore or downplay, but are considered important for the full recovery and restructuring of society (Paffenholz 2014a; Paffenholz and Ross 2015; Wanis-St. John 2008; Wanis-St. John and Kew 2008).

With the aim of nuancing the binary dilemma of ANSA inclusion, Hellmüller examines the dynamics of including armed actors in the Democratic Republic of the Congo (DRC) and argues that 'violence often does not directly depend on exclusion or inclusion, but that it is influenced by the underlying *motivations* of armed actors to be included and their corresponding *strategies*' (Hellmüller 2019: 3). While her work focuses on recognition-seekers in the DRC, this contribution, in contrast, focuses on the recognition-granters' considerations. In particular, it examines how the normative priorities of mediators shape how the mediation process (mis-) recognises seekers' motivations and strategies, which may lead to violence escalation despite inclusivity.

Recognition, mis-recognition and the role of norms

The typology of recognition relevant for this chapter is Wendt's 'thin' and 'thick' recognition. Thin recognition refers to the acknowledgement of shared identity or full membership in a community. Meanwhile, thick recognition entails acknowledging the unique traits of the entity being recognised.

Different aspects of identity are salient depending on the kind of recognition being practised (Geis 2018; Wendt 2003).

As mentioned in the introductory chapter, violence has been viewed as one of the patterns of coping with lack of recognition. Current empirical research explores the link between non-state actors' violence and recognition, for example in asymmetrical conflicts and deradicalisation (Biene and Daase 2015; Clément 2014). In mediation, Aggestam (2015) identifies ways in which recognition hinders efficient diplomacy and peace processes, while Toros examines recognition dynamics in negotiating with terrorists (Toros 2008, 2012).

In between full or mutual recognition and non-recognition, the concept of mis-recognition connotes a somewhat imperfect form of recognition and, so far, has received less scholarly attention. Mis-recognition may also be taken to mean a perversion of recognition that involves ridicule or other forms of humiliation. As summarised in the introductory chapter, mis-recognition constitutes 'acts of injustice in so far as they violate personal integrity and impede people from becoming full members of a social collective'. Laitinen, furthermore, specifies that '*mis*recognition (including nonrecognition) is a matter of inadequate responsiveness to the normatively relevant features of someone (their personhood, merits, needs, etc.), *and* if the kind of mistreatment in question obeys the general dynamic or "logic" of mutual recognition and relations-to-self' (Laitinen 2012: 25; emphasis added). Laitinen's 'narrow' view of mis-recognition implies that mis-recognition acts must be underpinned by logic that goes against the recognition-seekers' full claim.

These conceptualisations point to *a priori* standards of the social collective that determine what a 'full' claim and 'full' membership mean, what justice and being a peer in such a society look like, and how violations are judged as such. As Laitinen argues, mis-recognition assumes a minimal level of objectivism because it relies on both the 'fact [of] (mis)recognition and what is "subjectively" *taken to be* (mis)recognition. ... For some "takes" to be "mistakes", there must be some fact of the matter or a "correct take" that differs from a "mistake"' (Laitinen 2012: 32). In this regard, norms can set such standards to which recognition-seekers and -granters can refer in recognition processes.

At the same time, norms can also be the 'systematic bias in applying the principle' of recognition (Laitinen 2012: 31). For the recognition-granter, norms may disable the recognition of certain features or claims of actors. As an example, sovereignty is a norm still highly valued in the international system and hinders international recognition of domestic challenges to ruling governments. International recognition and action have been invoked in these cases, however, but upon the consent of the government concerned and/or after linking such issues to other international norms, such as international humanitarian and criminal law, which are gradually gaining acceptance as a qualifier for sovereignty.

In short, norms are a dual-edged sword. On the one hand, they help achieve minimal objectivism by guiding both recognition-seekers and -granters in formulating 'reasonable' expectations of the full extent of recognition. On the other hand, they can contribute to mis-recognition as part of the systematic bias in recognising features and claims of actors. In both these cases, norms are invoked not only due to actors' belief in the norms' inherent value, or their appropriateness. They may also be used as part of a strategy in pursuing actors' interests (March and Olsen 1998).

Norms in the IGAD-led mediation

Norms inherent or 'definitional' in mediation processes and the norms held by the mediator or mediating organisation are two sources of norms that facilitate reasonable expectations or form part of a systematic bias in recognising actors in the mediation context.

Definitional norms in mediation

Norms that underpin the very definition of a mediation process are called definitional norms and are considered necessary preconditions for a process to be regarded as mediation. Examples of definitional norms are the right to life and the peaceful settlement of disputes. Another is the consent of the parties, without which a process would not be considered as mediation, but as another form of third-party engagement, such as sanctions, high-powered diplomacy or a judicial decision (Hellmüller et al. 2015).

These prioritised norms imply a preference for expediency and efficiency as well as a focus on taming the armed actors. Mediators are thus expected to ensure that those with arms are engaged in the process (Hellmüller et al. 2015). One way of ensuring such is through consolidation, where mediators assist in forming a coalition of armed groups to be represented by one delegation. Through consolidation, mediators can maintain efficiency by being able to hold many groups accountable through the principals, and overall have a semblance of inclusivity (Watkins 2003).

The conflict context in this case study all the more reinforces the legitimacy of arms. Having taken up arms is regarded as a patriotic act and entitles the former combatant to current rewards. '[Using arms] was their way for generations, and then suddenly … you have to tell them [that] sorry, you're no longer allowed to do that' (Interview 1).

Norms in African Union and IGAD mediation

Furthermore, the organisation mandating the mediation also advocates specific norms that may not be as mandatory as in other mediating organisations.

First, as one of the Regional Economic Communities of the African Union (AU), IGAD member states observe the AU prohibition of unconstitutional changes of government. This implies that the AU will not recognise any solution that would condone ousting an incumbent through force. This norm makes the environment unfavourable for ANSAs that aspire to the overthrow of incumbent governments (Nathan 2012, 2017). Secondly, IGAD values regional ownership in peace processes. In 1996, IGAD chartered the aspiration to 'create mechanisms *within* the sub-region for the prevention, management, and resolution of inter and intra-State conflicts through dialogue' (IGAD 1996: 7; emphasis added). IGAD member states also agreed to 'deal with disputes between the member states within this sub-regional mechanism before they are referred to other regional or international organisations' (IGAD 1996: 16).

Conceptual framework: linking inclusivity, recognition and other norms in mediation processes

Synthesising mediation and recognition research, the contribution focuses on three sites where mediators' recognition of ANSAs can be observed, namely the narrative of the conflict, the process design and the contents of the peace agreement. Here the difference between inclusivity and recognition can be observed.

The narrative of the conflict in the official mediation mandate is an important site to observe which aspects of the conflict the mediation recognises (Nathan 2017; Pring 2017). The similarity between the narratives of the recognition-granter, the mediator and the recognition-seeker, in this case the ANSA (or its leader), points to the mediation's recognition of the latter's needs and motivations. This narrative, however, may not be inclusive in that it does not need to reverberate with the wider public opinion or identify a broad range of actors and agenda.

In the process of negotiating an agreement and the agreement's content, recognition involves both the *act* of recognition, which could entail (but is not limited to) inclusion, plus the *logic* of recognition that responds (adequately or not) to the identity claims relevant to the kind of recognition sought. Full recognition may be ideally manifested in the congruence among the kind and level of an ANSA's participation, the mediation's reasons for inclusion, and the status and identity traits which the ANSAs claim. Meanwhile, inclusivity may be manifested in a multi-party negotiation process as well as in the expansive scope of an agenda reflecting the interest of a broad set of stakeholders, including ANSAs and civil society. However, the reasons for having such high inclusivity need not meet all parties' identity claims.

Given the difference between inclusivity and recognition, ANSAs may seek to be recognised in a way that jeopardises greater inclusivity. Their inclusion may be direct participation, but the reasons behind their inclusion, the logic of recognition, may not acknowledge their identity claims and may inspire them to resort to violence despite their inclusion in the peace process. Mis-recognition may be linked to the norms being espoused in the peace process. This hypothesised relationship drawn from recognition theory contributes to understanding the complexity of the relationship between inclusivity and the recurrence of violent conflict (Table 10.1).

Mis-recognition despite inclusion: the South Sudan Defence Forces and the 2005 CPA negotiations

During the fifty-year-long war against Sudan, the SPLM was not the only ANSA with effective control of territories in then southern Sudan. Initially, these other militias were focused on protecting their immediate communities and 'never developed to the stage of being liberation armies or forming viable political parties' (Young 2006: 15). Nonetheless, to the extent they had political positions, they deviated from the SPLM in that while then SPLM leader John Garang advocated for a united Sudan under the 'New Sudan' programme, these groups were for the separation of the South. Most prominent among these other groups that took up a political character was the South Sudan Defence Forces (SSDF), which consolidated many of these militias, controlled a significant swathe of territory and posed a serious military threat to the SPLM. Many battles in the two Sudans were by southerners fighting each other (Arnold 2007; Young 2006).

The absence of the SSDF in the narrative of the conflict in the CPA

The narrative of a fragmented South was not fully recognised in the CPA negotiations as it recognised only two parties: the GoS and the SPLM. One reason for downplaying the SSDF's role was its confusing relationship with the GoS. The SSDF and the GoS signed the Khartoum Peace Agreement in 1997, which stopped the clashes between the two and bound them to work on southern self-determination. Khartoum conceded to this as it found a practical ally in the SSDF given its strength to challenge and destabilise the SPLM. However, this union was troublesome and merely tactical (Arnold 2007).

Mis-recognition despite inclusion in the process design

The SPLM/A and the GoS did not want the mediation to involve other armed groups, including the SSDF, in the CPA. Several SSDF personalities

Table 10.1 Ideal-type links among norms, inclusivity and ANSA recognition in mediation

	Norms Publicly available reference for reasonable expectations of full recognition and/or Systematic bias in recognising actors' features and claims	Inclusivity The quality of inclusion	ANSA recognition The act of recognition + the logic of recognition
Narrative of the conflict at the start of mediation	• Definitional norms – peaceful settlement of disputes and protecting the right to life • Norms of the mandating organisation such as the AU Prohibition of Unconstitutional Changes of Government, and IGAD regional ownership of peace processes	The mediation's narrative of the conflict identifies with and includes a broad range of actors, not just ANSAs	The mediation's narrative of the conflict is the same as the ANSAs' narrative and motivations, not necessarily resonating with a wider set of actors
Process design		The process design is a spectrum from direct participation to observer status (Paffenholz, 2014b), independent of the design's acknowledgement of identity claims	The process design acknowledges the traits (identity, motivations, strategies) the ANSAs seek to be recognised
Content of the final agreement		The agreement includes the agenda of the ANSAs, along with other actors'	The agreement reflects the agenda and solutions of the ANSAs but also that their role in the agreement implementation matches their identity claims

Source: the author.

negotiated on the side of the GoS, but at the same time the SSDF called for its separate representation at the table. In an interview in 2002, Martin Kenyi, the military leader of one of the components of the SSDF, clarified its position in the following:

> Our relations with the GoS are guided by the [1997] Khartoum Peace Agreement and, as a result, we have to cooperate with the government in every way – security, political, etc – to defend the agreement. It is wrong to conclude that this cooperation makes the SSDF into stooges. …
>
> We took up arms to fight the government [of Sudan] when it was not willing to have a dialogue and when other avenues of communication were closed. The 1997 agreement signed with the GoS was a step in ending the war, with the aim of achieving our political objectives through the right of self-determination determined by a referendum. … Today the SPLA is negotiating a peace agreement with the GoS. We are not opposed to such a process because after all these years the SPLA has come to follow our example. … If the SSDF is excluded from the IGAD negotiations, then we are not parties to the agreement. We will then not be responsible if anything happens in terms of fighting with the GoS or SPLA and the peace process is de-railed. (Cited in Institute for Security Studies 2003: 3–4)

The GoS and the SPLM's desire to keep the process bilateral was reinforced by equal resistance from the mediation team to expand the process beyond the two parties. Noting the SSDF's alliance with Sudan, the mediation and the international community did not recognise the SSDF as a separate entity and subsumed it under the GoS delegation. The mediation believed that the additional actors might make the process unworkable and open a floodgate of participants. General Sumbeiywo, the lead mediator for the CPA mediation, and his secretariat thought that 'small was good', to keep the participation manageable (Young 2007: 25).

In addition to efficiency reasons, the bilateral framing of the issue reinforced IGAD's highly regarded norm of regional ownership of the peace agreement as it provided a semblance of continued IGAD performance that helped keep parallel initiatives at bay (Francis 2005; Healy 2015).

Mis-recognition in the CPA content and the CPA's dangerous legacy

What resulted in the 2005 CPA was a security arrangements agreement that called for the dissolution of Other Armed Groups (OAGs) that were not a party to the CPA (Young 2007, 2015). This then *de facto* nullified the 1997 Khartoum Agreement and called for the dissolution of the SSDF. The recognition of the SPLM and the primacy of the CPA were at the cost of not recognising the Khartoum Agreement on which the SSDF and OAGs relied.

Although there was indeed some level of recognition of the SSDF as an entity, the logic behind this did not fully recognise its historical identity claims. Mis-recognition processes included subsuming the SSDF into the GoS despite the former's claim to be treated individually, undermining the Khartoum Peace Agreement, and labelling them as OAGs called to integrate with the SPLM. To use Alexander Wendt's typology of recognition, the SSDF was only 'thinly' recognised, as one of the conflict actors, despite aspiring to 'thick' recognition based on distinctive traits that could warrant its own delegation.

An excluded SSDF would have been a recipe for disaster were the SPLM still being led by John Garang, given the SSDF's ideological differences with and history of fighting against Garang. However, Garang's death and the succession of Salva Kiir opened avenues for unification. Under the 'Big Tent Strategy', Salva Kiir issued a Juba Declaration in 2006 that invited all OAGs to join the ranks of the SPLM. Key leaders from these groups have also obtained higher positions to attract them into joining. Salva Kiir also continued to offer amnesties to rebel groups under this strategy.

However, this unification was mostly in terms of incorporating OAGs into the SPLM payroll while command and control structures were retained. Top SSDF officials that were appointed in high-ranking SPLM positions were given only a *de facto* 'ceremonial' role (Arnold 2007; Young 2006). Granting amnesties and the lack of further force integration seemed to merely hide the historical animosity between the SPLM and SSDF in this Big Tent, drawing enemies in close proximity. One interviewee described: 'imagine the person that led the raid of your village and killed your families is living and sleeping opposite your barracks … how can you work with them?' (Interview 2).

Mis-recognition despite greater inclusivity: the SPLM-IO and the 2015 ARCSS

After the CPA, peace from the unification of the OAGs with the SPLM under the 'Big Tent' did not last long. The lack of genuine reforms beyond mere incorporation in the payroll and the dominance of SPLM in the government contributed to dissatisfaction among the incorporated armed groups. This dissatisfaction, along with the long history of fighting against one another, fortified divisions within the SPLM based mainly on pre-CPA alliances, which is a combination of personal/political allegiances and ethnic grouping. The fighting in December 2013 started between guards loyal to Kiir and Machar respectively, but it was a culmination of the mounting dissatisfaction and tensions within the expanded SPLM. The killing of civilian

Nuer in Juba was incited by rhetoric building up before December that inspired the Dinkas to band together, and the news of Nuers massacred in Juba inspired Nuers to carry out retaliatory killings in areas where they are dominant. These aspects generated different narratives of what the conflict was all about, entailing different process design options and agendas for negotiations.

The narrative of the conflict and the formation of the SPLM-IO

There were three different explanations as to why the December 2013 violence broke out and at such a fast pace. First, the Government of South Sudan accused Machar of launching a coup against the president. Buying into this narrative would mean that the opposition violated the AU prohibition of unconstitutional changes of government and could even merit an international military action on the opposing forces (Interview 3). Secondly, the violence started between guards of the two highest SPLM officials. Since the conflict started within the SPLM, it can be solved by unifying the party. Thirdly and lastly, the fighting guards were also divided into the two dominant ethnicities, Dinka and Nuer, and triggered a reaction beyond Juba that included civilians. The clash reflected deeper-rooted causes of the conflict and the need for national reconciliation.

At the Meeting of the Heads of State and Government immediately after, most of the IGAD Heads of State were convinced that there was no coup attempt and thereby no violation of the AU prohibition. Nonetheless, to respond to the revived scepticism about the IGAD's credibility as a peacemaker, IGAD mandated an inclusive process beyond the SPLM, which was a break from the bilateral CPA (Interviews 3 and 4). The Heads of State noted that the mediation should open the opportunity of nation-building that was denied South Sudan given the speedy transition from the CPA to its independence. The speed at which the violence spread in the country indicated the need to have a broader approach to the conflict, one that addresses the root causes, such as long-standing grievances, injustice and the lack of representation of marginalised groups, particularly civil society (Interview 5). While motivated by IGAD's credibility, the narrative adopted at the Heads of State meeting was in line with the claims of armed opposition groups beyond the SPLM.

With the division of the SPLM in December 2013 came the reactivation of old alliances including the SSDF. Former vice-president Machar was a former commander-in-chief of the SSDF in 1997 before returning to the SPLM in 2002. While he was fleeing Juba and the country for his own life in December 2013, local commanders who were senior SSDF officers restarted fighting in their home towns. It was questionable whether Machar had control of these groups. According to Young, '[w]ithout any formal leadership structures and little to unite them beyond anger, the desire for revenge, and a strong sense of Nuer solidarity, they fought the government and the Ugandan army' (Young 2015: 15).

The mediation nonetheless proceeded with getting Machar on board with the process. What eventually became the SPLM-IO senior military command was made up mostly of officers from the SSDF. The opposition gravitated towards Machar as the focal point for three reasons. First, he was the front-runner opposition to the president before the 2013 crisis broke out. His ideas of reform and critique of the president appealed to many in the SSDF. Secondly, he had allies in the SSDF as he shared a history and ethnic group with most of them. Lastly, he was recognised as such by the international community (Interview 6). The IGAD, partner countries and other international organisations made sure to liaise with him on the premise that he could unite the opposition (Young 2015).

There are also factors that render Machar's unifying ability doubtful. While those in Machar's faction overall shared the desire for justice for the Nuer, they were divided regarding the solutions for achieving this. Two popular positions were prominent. First, many of the SPLM-IO members wanted a solution that would oust the current president. Any post-agreement that involved Salva Kiir was considered by some a mere continuation of the status quo. Secondly, most of the commanders, especially in the early days of the conflict, did not favour any affiliation or unification with the SPLM. Due to historical animosities and ideational differences with the late John Garang, several senior SSDF members did not join the SPLM under the 2006 Big Tent Strategy, even though they joined the SPLM-IO military wing. They nonetheless went on with Machar as the chairman of the SPLM-IO and the principal of the SPLM-IO delegation in Addis Ababa (Interview 6).

An inclusive mediation was guided by the need to defend IGAD's ownership of mediation processes in the Horn of Africa amid the criticism of the CPA's exclusivity. This narrative of the conflict recognised the motivations of the SPLM-IO (that included armed groups beyond the SPLM) and enabled their inclusion. The next expansion of the talks, however, was not as responsive to the SPLM-IO's identity claims.

Mis-recognising the SPLM-IO through a more inclusive process design

The focus on getting the GRSS and the SPLM-IO on board with the mediation process was to set the ground for a more inclusive process (Interview 3). On 23 January 2014, the two warring parties signed the Cessation of Hostilities Agreement and the Agreement on the Status of Detainees, which provided for the release of key SPLM stalwarts that the government had detained during December 2013. However, the detainees decided not to join either of the two parties and formed their own, named the SPLM Former Detainees. Here, the international community saw an opportunity for the Former Detainees to be an alternative to both warring parties. While opposing the government similarly to the SPLM-IO, they did not command any army and highlighted this choice of non-violence to differentiate themselves from the SPLM-IO.

In April, the warring parties signed the Agreement to Resolve the Crisis in South Sudan. The agreement stipulated that other actors would be involved thereon, such as the Former Detainees (under the name, 'SPLM Leaders'), political parties, civil society and faith-based leaders. The agreement furthermore stated that 'these other stakeholders shall participate in negotiations on transitional governance, the permanent constitution, and any other items that concern the political future of the country and reconciliation of South Sudanese communities' (IGAD 2014: 2).

The inclusion of the former detainees, political parties and civil society gave a voice to non-violent actors, against which the GRSS and the SPLM-IO vehemently protested. When talking about these non-armed groups, both the government and SPLM-IO respondents doubted their inclusion on the basis that they did not command an army. They argued for continued primacy to be given to them as they were the ones with troops on the ground (Interview 7). To differentiate themselves and prove that they were the only credible challenger to the government, the SPLM-IO intensified their military operations in South Sudan while negotiating in Addis Ababa. Frustrated with the continuous ceasefire violations, one interviewee from the mediation remarked that one would know the day after who won in the battlefield by how they acted with superiority during the negotiations (Interview 4). To keep the process alive, most of the might of the mediation concentrated on the two warring parties. Unarmed groups were more cooperative and provided their proposals, but final decisions and key issues remained within the GRSS and SPLM-IO (Interview 3).

Hence, the kind of SPLM-IO inclusion remained the same, but they continued their armed operations to protest the emerging logic of recognition that implied equality between them and non-armed groups. While there was will for the mediation to expand its focus beyond the warring parties, the warring parties held the mediation to ransom by intensifying their military campaign, undermining the protection of the right to life 'definitional' (Hellmüller et al. 2015) in mediation. Greater inclusivity contributed to the SPLM-IO's drive to differentiate itself from the other voices against the government by intensifying one key trait of its identity, the command of arms.

Mis-recognition in the content and the proliferation of new groups

Following most SPLM-IO members' positions, the SPLM-IO delegation initially called for the resignation of the president as part of the peace agreement. The IGAD mediators did not find this acceptable as any resolution that would result in the ousting of an incumbent president would violate the AU prohibition on unconstitutional changes of government (Interviews 3 and 4). The mediators also noted that if this solution were entertained at all, it should be compensated with Machar not being part of the transitional arrangements. As this did not appeal to Machar, the SPLM-IO delegation soon dropped this proposal, to the dissatisfaction of many of its members. Another contentious issue within the SPLM-IO was the proposed reunification with the SPLM. Hardline SSDF stalwarts did not approve, but the SPLM-IO delegation continued to participate in SPLM intra-party talks in Arusha and signed the agreement to reunify the party (Young 2015). Given these rifts, months before the signing, several members left the SPLM-IO and formed their own armed group. These members no longer recognised Machar as their leader.

International peace process supporters noted that in addition to soliciting the recognition of the mediators, Machar was also trying to appeal to another group of recognition-granters, namely Machar's own officials within the coalition of armed groups under the SPLM-IO. In many meetings between the international community and the SPLM-IO, the internationals would notice that often Machar was not speaking to the international community when making his claim. Instead, it seemed he was addressing and appealing to the personalities on his own side of the table (Interview 8).

However, as the members splintered from the SPLM-IO at a time when an agreement was in sight, the mediation did not accommodate these groups and focused on Machar as the armed opposition leader. The preamble identifying the parties in the final version was changed last-minute to state, 'South Sudan Armed Opposition' instead of 'SPLM-IO' as reflected in many of the previous drafts (IGAD 2015). At this point, there was 'thin' recognition that other armed opposition groups existed but not 'thick' recognition in terms of several armed groups' distinctive traits (aversion to joining the SPLM and the retention of the president). However, in signing the agreement Machar changed this name back to SPLM/A-IO, citing that he was not the leader of the South Sudan Armed Opposition but the chairman of this particular group (IGAD 2016). This handwritten amendment is shown in Figure 10.1.

The resulting ARCSS contents oscillated between inclusivity and continued dominance of the warring parties. Power was divided among armed and unarmed actors, but the former, particularly the SPLM armed actors, still

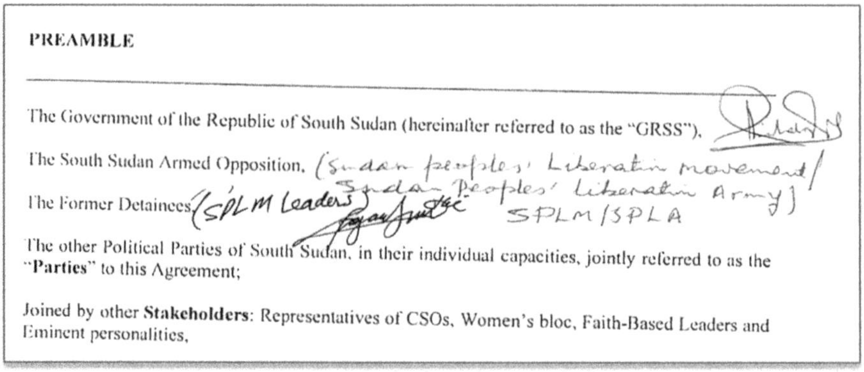

PREAMBLE

The Government of the Republic of South Sudan (hereinafter referred to as the "GRSS"),

The South Sudan Armed Opposition, (Sudan Peoples' Liberation movement/ Sudan Peoples' Liberation Army) SPLM/SPLA

The Former Detainees (SPLM Leaders)

The other Political Parties of South Sudan, in their individual capacities, jointly referred to as the "**Parties**" to this Agreement;

Joined by other **Stakeholders**: Representatives of CSOs, Women's bloc, Faith-Based Leaders and Eminent personalities,

Figure 10.1 Signature of the main parties in the Preamble in the 2015 Agreement on the Resolution of the Conflict in South Sudan. 'The South Sudan Armed Opposition' was signed by Machar. Source: United Nations Peacemaker, available at: https://peacemaker.un.org/node/2676.

retained most of the positions in the transitional government. Nonetheless, several roles were defined for civil society, especially in transitional justice and gender aspects of the peace agreement. The agreement's contents on paper expanded governance to a broader set of stakeholders compared with the CPA.

However, one year later, in July 2016, fighting once again erupted in Juba between the forces of President Kiir and then First Vice-President Machar; the return and reinstatement of the latter were in fulfilment of the ARCSS. After the outbreak of violence, other armed groups, allied with neither the government nor the SPLM-IO, also intensified their operations.

Conclusion

The peace process in South Sudan illustrated the difference between inclusivity and recognition, as well as their close interrelationship. During the CPA negotiations, the SSDF were thinly recognised despite their calls for thick recognition. SSDF commanders were indeed able to participate in the negotiations, but as they were under the GoS delegation, the mediation process and the resulting agreement did not recognise their identity claim as a separate key actor in the post-agreement setting. The way the SSDF was included, subsumed as part of the GoS delegation, reflected mis-recognition in the process and content. Unresolved divisions between these armed groups and the SPLM made the post-CPA peace fragile.

During the ARCSS negotiations, the mediation's intention to promote greater inclusivity entailed treating non-armed groups as independent and equal to the government and SPLM-IO. This logic was counter to the SPLM-IO's identity claims and encouraged its intensification of armed operations to bolster its claim as the GRSS's only counterpart. Here, greater inclusivity did not contribute to peace during the talks. Moreover, the mediation recognised only one representative and thereby one delegation of the armed opposition. While the armed opposition did rally behind Machar initially, his concessions were against key positions by several members, leading to the delegation's breakdown. These events showed that recognition consists of more than one act, and is an ongoing process. Even while inclusion stayed the same, recognition dynamics were more vulnerable to developments.

In both negotiations, mis-recognition, or the failure to meet the kind of recognition aspired to by the ANSA, was fuelled by norms definitional in mediation and valuable to the mediating organisation. The protection of the right to life, the IGAD's regional ownership and the AU prohibition served as systematic biases in choosing to keep the CPA process bilateral, the SPLM-IO engaged and the GRSS in power. Meanwhile, the global trend for inclusivity served as a publicly available reference for recognition, but it was a standard to which the SPLM-IO objected through violence. Table 10.2 summarises the main empirical points of this chapter. It is also worth noting that these norms are invoked both for their appropriateness but also for instrumental reasons, such as to gain political and financial support.

With insights from the concept of mis-recognition, this analysis aspired to further examine the relationship between inclusivity and violence. The analysis developed does not discount the instrumental use of norms and identity claims or the strategic motivations behind their invocation. However, the analysis in this chapter begins *after* the invocation of such norms and identity claims, and it asks how these claims, once made, may be (mis)recognised in the mediation process, leading to recurrence of violence. Moreover, the intention is not to eliminate other explanations such as splintering of armed groups or spoilers. However, through recognition dynamics the analysis identifies structural conditions or identity-focused explanations for such splintering or spoiling despite the inclusion of ANSAs. With regard to policy practices, this contribution shows the need for a more careful application of inclusive processes. Mediation training manuals highlight the importance of the 'who' or 'how' of inclusivity (diverse stakeholders, levels of participation, process design, etc.), but recognition studies add the importance of the logic of recognition behind the inclusion, or the 'why'.

Table 10.2 Summary of empirical findings

	CPA 2005 mediation			ARCSS 2015 mediation		
	Inclusive of ANSAs?	Recognising ANSAs?	Salient norms	Inclusive of ANSAs?	Recognising ANSAs?	Salient norms
Narrative of the conflict at the start of the mediation	Excluded other ANSAs in the interpretation of the conflict	Non-recognition; North–South division between GoS and the SPLM-IO only	IGAD Ownership	Inclusive	Recognised the president, vice-president and 'All the actors critical to bringing peace…' and aimed to address the root causes of the conflict	IGAD ownership
Process design	ANSAs subsumed as part of the government delegation	Misrecognition – other non-SPLM ANSAs as part of the government		ANSAs as part of the consolidated opposition under SPLM-IO leader Machar	Misrecognition: ANSAs as a united entity with the same claims SPLM-IO's association with unarmed actors recognises its existence but undermines its armed identity	Legitimacy of arms
Content	No role in transitional arrangements, told to consolidate with the SPLM	Misrecognition as OAGs		Nominal role in transitional arrangements, still under SPLM-IO as the main signatory Provisions on Transitional Justice	Nominal recognition but subsumed in SPLM-IO Justice provisions were addressed, but two key claims by non-SPLM-IO ANSAs were ignored	AU prohibition of unconstitutional changes of government

Source: the author.

Notes

* This contribution is based on the author's research under the Swiss National Science Foundation's research programme *Are Mediators Norm Entrepreneurs? The Role of Norms in International Peace Mediation.* The author conducted 128 interviews in Addis Ababa, Ethiopia, Juba, South Sudan and Nairobi, Kenya in 2017 and 2018, involving participants in the mediation process on South Sudan led by the Inter-governmental Authority on Development that lasted from 2013 to 2015.

References

Aggestam, K. (2015), 'Peace mediation and the minefield of international recognition games', *International Negotiation* 20:3, 494–514.

Arnold, M. (2007), 'The South Sudan Defence Force: patriots, collaborators or spoilers?', *Journal of Modern African Studies* 45:4, 489–516.

Axelrod, R. (1997), *The Complexity of Cooperation: Agent-Based Models of Competition and Collaboration* (Princeton, NJ and Chichester: Princeton University Press).

Bartelson, J. (2013), 'Three concepts of recognition', *International Theory* 5:1, 107–129.

Biene, J. and C. Daase (2015), 'Gradual recognition: curbing non-state violence in asymmetric conflict', in C. Daase, C. Fehl, A. Geis and G. Kolliarakis (eds), *Recognition in International Relations* (Basingstoke: Palgrave Macmillan), pp. 220–236.

Blaydes, L. and J. de Maio (2010), 'Spoiling the peace? Peace process exclusivity and political violence in North-Central Africa', *Civil Wars* 12:1–2, 3–28.

Clément M. (2014), 'Al-Muhajiroun in the United Kingdom: the role of international non-recognition in heightened radicalization dynamics', *Global Discourse* 4:4, 428–443.

Cunningham, K. (2013), 'Understanding strategic choice', *Journal of Peace Research* 50:3, 291–304.

Francis, D. (2005), *Uniting Africa: Building Regional Peace and Security Systems* (Hampshire: Ashgate Publishing Limited).

Geis, A. (2018), 'The ethics of recognition in international political theory', in C. Brown and R. Eckersley (eds), *The Oxford Handbook of International Political Theory* (Oxford: Oxford University Press), pp. 612–625.

Healy, S. (2015), 'Peacemaking in the midst of war', *Crisis States Research Centre – Working Paper* 59, 1–22.

Hellmüller, S. (2019), 'A global and inclusive agreement? Participation of armed actors in the inter-Congolese dialogue and its impact on local violence', *International Negotiation* 24:1, 1–23.

Hellmüller, S., J. Palmiano-Federer and M. Zeller (2015), *The Role of Norms in International Peace Mediation* (Bern: swisspeace).

Institute for Security Studies (2003), 'Interview with Martin Kenyi and Garoth Garkuoth of the South Sudan Defence Force', *African Security Analysis Programme*, available online: https://files.ethz.ch/isn/137116/SUDANJUN03A.PDF; last retrieved 3 April 2020.

IGAD (1996), *Agreement Establishing the Inter-governmental Authority on Development* (Nairobi: IGAD).
IGAD (2013), *Communiqué of the 23rd Extra-ordinary Session of the IGAD Assembly of Heads of State and Government on the Situation in South Sudan* (Nairobi: IGAD).
IGAD (2014), *Agreement to Resolve the Crisis in South Sudan* (Addis Ababa: IGAD).
IGAD (2015), *Agreement on the Resolution of the Conflict in the Republic of South Sudan* (Addis Ababa: IGAD).
IGAD (2016), *Report of the Special Envoys on the Conclusion of the IGAD-Led Mediation to Resolve the Conflict in the Republic of South Sudan (2013–2015)* (Addis Ababa: IGAD).
Jok, M. (2015), *Negotiating an End to the Current Civil War in South Sudan: What Lessons Can Sudan's Comprehensive Peace Agreement Offer?* (Berlin: Inclusive Political Settlements Papers).
Katzenstein, P. (ed.) (1996), *The Culture of National Security: Norms and Identity in World Politics* (New York, NY: Columbia University Press).
Laitinen, A. (2012), 'Misrecognition, misrecognition, and fallibility', *Res Publica* 18:1, 25–38.
Lanz, D. (2011), 'Who gets a seat at the table? A framework for understanding the dynamics of inclusion and exclusion in peace negotiations', *International Negotiation* 16:2, 275–295.
March, J. G. and J. P. Olsen (1998), 'The institutional dynamics of international political orders', *International Organization* 52:4, 943–969.
Nathan, L. (2012), *Community of Insecurity: SADC's Struggle for Peace and Security in Southern Africa* (Farnham: Ashgate Publishing, Ltd).
Nathan, L. (2017), 'Marching orders: exploring the mediation mandate', *African Security* 10:3–4, 1–21.
Paffenholz, T. (2014a), 'Civil society and peace negotiations: beyond the inclusion–exclusion dichotomy', *Negotiation Journal* 30:1, 69–91.
Paffenholz, T. (2014b), *Broadening Participation in Peace Processes: Dilemmas and Options for Mediators*, available online: http://hdcentre.org/wp-content/uploads/2016/07/MPS4-Broadening-participation-in-peace-processes-July-2014.pdf; last retrieved 3 April 2020.
Paffenholz, T. and N. Ross (2015), *Inclusive Peace Processes: An Introduction*, available online: http://daghammarskjold.se/wp-content/uploads/2016/01/DHF_DD63_p28–37.pdf; last retrieved 3 April 2020.
Pring, J. (2017), 'Including or excluding civil society? The role of the mediation mandate for South Sudan (2013–2015) and Zimbabwe (2008–2009)', *African Security* 10:3–4, 223–238.
Raiffa, H., J. Richardson and D. Metcalfe (2007), *Negotiation Analysis: The Science and Art of Collaborative Decision-Making* (Cambridge, MA and London: The Belknap Press of Harvard University Press).
Toros, H. (2008), '"We don't negotiate with terrorists!" Legitimacy and complexity in terrorist conflicts', *Security Dialogue* 39:4, 407–426.
Toros, H. (2012), *Terrorism, Talking and Transformation: A Critical Approach* (Abingdon: Routledge).
Tull, D. and A. Mehler (2005), 'The hidden costs of power-sharing: reproducing insurgent violence in Africa', *African Affairs* 104:416, 375–398.
United Nations (2012), *United Nations Guidance for Effective Mediation* (New York, NY: United Nations).

Wanis-St. John, A. (2008), 'Peace processes, secret negotiations and civil society: dynamics of inclusion and exclusion', *International Negotiation* 13, 1–9.

Wanis-St. John, A. and D. Kew (2008), 'Civil society and peace negotiations: confronting exclusion', *International Negotiation* 13:1, 11–36.

Watkins, M. (2003), 'Strategic simplification: toward a theory of modular design in negotiation', *International Negotiation* 8:1, 149–167.

Wendt, A. (2003), 'Why a world state is inevitable', *European Journal of International Relations* 9:4, 491–542.

Young, J. (2006), *The South Sudan Defence Forces in the Wake of the Juba Declaration* (Geneva: Small Arms Survey).

Young, J. (2007), 'Sudan IGAD peace process', *Sudan Tribune*, available online: www.sudantribune.com/spip.php?article24243 (15 October); last retrieved 3 April 2020.

Young, J. (2015), *A Fractious Rebellion inside the SPLM-IO* (Geneva: Small Arms Survey).

Interviews

Interview 1 with advisor to the churches, Juba (March 2017).
Interview 2 with civil society representative, Juba (March 2017).
Interview 3 with mediation team member 1, Addis Ababa (July 2016).
Interview 4 with mediation team member 2, Nairobi (April 2017).
Interview 5 with mediation team member 3, Addis Ababa (July 2016).
Interview 6 with SPLM-IO negotiating team member, Nairobi (April 2017).
Interview 7 with government negotiating team member, Juba (March 2017).
Interview 8 with international peace process supporter, Washington, DC (April 2018).

11

Mutual recognition in the context of contested statehood: evidence from Tumaco, Colombia

Jan Boesten and Annette Idler

Introduction

> If I had to choose between paramilitaries and guerrillas, I would choose the guerrillas. *Toda la vida*!'[1]

This somewhat surprising statement of a cleric from the port city of Tumaco on the Southern Pacific coast in Colombia confirms recent analyses from the literature on internal conflict processes: there is variation in how local civilian populations perceive behaviour of different violent non-state actors that operate in the same generic context (Arjona 2016; Gutiérrez Sanín 2008; Gutiérrez Sanín and Wood 2014; Kalyvas 2006; Weinstein 2007; Wood 2015). Exploring the reasons for this preference provides an intriguing entry point for recognition-based analyses of violent non-state actors. An important focus of recognition-based research has been transitional processes from internal conflict to post-conflict societies and the reintegration of demobilised combatants into civil society (Geis 2018). We aim to contribute to this body of research by highlighting that a successful transition, aiming to construct effective (civilian) state institutions in marginalised regions, requires understanding pre-peace accord relations between armed actors and local communities.

Our approach takes insights from Conflict Studies to the study of recognition. Specifically, the recent 'local turn' in studies of conflict and armed non-state actors (ANSAs) has highlighted that civil war zones often appear orderly rather than anarchic (Arjona 2016). Conventionally, recognition-based research in International Relations focuses on the recognition of ANSAs by states in the context of peace processes. To expand, we hold that recent transition processes in Colombia show that recognition also exists between local civilians and the ANSA. Appreciating these modes of recognition in the context of non-state order has institutional ramifications that the state needs to address in order to construct effective post-accord (local) institutions.

In this chapter, we explore how divergent behaviour of non-state armed actors is either conducive or detrimental to the recognition of collective agency of local communities in conflict zones. Specifically: if the mutual recognition of equals is constitutive for subjectivity (Fraser 2003), we ponder whether the different experiences of guerrilla and paramilitary order in Colombia are indicative of differing effects of vertical and horizontal organisational structures and behavioural patterns of the armed group on the ability to recognise and be recognised.

We argue that in the context of non-state order during armed conflict (particularly when the line between crime and conflict is blurred), recognition is contingent on the existence of institutions. In the context of states, institutions are the formal and informal rules that structure actors' behaviour (Hall and Taylor 1996; Helmke and Levitsky 2004; North 1991). In the context of non-state order, we mean locally constructed *and* accepted procedures that result from behavioural patterns and provide avenues to structure behaviour.[2] Essential to our argument is that the expressed preference for the Fuerzas Armadas Revolucionarias de Colombia – Ejercito Popular (Revolutionary Armed Forces of Colombia – People's Army; FARC)[3] preponderance as dominant non-state order over paramilitary preponderance is not surprising because, as others have shown, everyday life under FARC preponderance is often considered to be less brutal and arbitrary (see for example Arjona 2016; Gutiérrez Sanín 2003, 2008).[4] This is related to a number of differences between the guerrillas and the paramilitaries of the Autodefensas Unidas de Colombia (United Self-Defence Forces of Colombia; AUC), ranging from the social base of their combatants, recruitment and enumeration, ideology, organisational structure and repertoire of violence (see discussion below).

The organisational structure and behavioural patterns that we hold responsible for enabling a degree of mutual recognition between armed actor and local community are of two types: the coherence of the internal organisational structure of the armed actor enables procedures for recognition by the community (they know who to talk to); and the space the armed actor allows for local communities to express their grievances indicates recognition of the community by the armed actor (providing space for input). Hence, post-conflict institutions should fulfil those two conditions: coherent, enduring structures (organisation) and space for voicing grievances that results in action (input and responsiveness).

We proceed by first outlining our conceptualisation for connecting recognition with non-state order. We briefly discuss the nature of trust relations between non-state actor and community – an issue we explore in more detail elsewhere (Idler and Boesten 2018). Our empirical evaluation first leads to an exploration of the differences between the FARC and the AUC; with a specific focus on the systematic differences scholars have documented. We then shift the analytical lens to the community-level perspective, providing our own empirical analysis, based on in-depth interviews from Tumaco and qualitative conflict data (disaggregated homicide rates and risk reports by the Colombian Ombudsman Office for Human Rights). Our conclusion highlights the implications for state institutions in the post-accord context in Colombia.

Institutions and recognition

The editors of this volume state that 'recognition [is] a process ... a social interaction' (this volume p. 6). If we take this ontology of recognition seriously, we must additionally appreciate that recognition is the result of an *intersubjective* process. We see that recognition in a multi-actor conflict – with multiple ANSAs vying for control – as a two-pronged process that is in its first instance functional, as it is contingent on the ability to exercise a sufficient degree of territorial control, and in its second instance political, as it is contingent on space for community agency. Territorial control usually comes with some stability in applicable rules. This does not imply ideological convergence between the community and the armed actor, but represents the condition for community members to have some confidence to engage in social action in the first place. Our exploration of the Colombian case shows, however, that the plain functionality of territorial control is not sufficient for recognition. Rather, FARC control had some institutional caveats that communities utilised to voice their own grievances and coordinate their daily quotidian affairs. We argue that recognition-based research is useful to highlight these differences between different ANSAs active in the same territories.

Recognition is 'an ideal reciprocal relation between subjects in which each sees the other as its equal and also separate from it', and therefore 'constitutive for subjectivity' (Fraser 2003: 10). The intersubjective nature of recognition is contingent on an ideal-type speech situation that implies rights and duties for participants and requires uncoerced deliberation among equals in order to validate ideas and identities. In states, spaces for contestation can be institutionalised and tied to collective decision-making processes. In the context of contested statehood, the monopoly over coercive means is at stake, meaning that this possibility is not as easily transferable to the context of conflict zones. Recent research has shown, however, that conflict zones with non-state armed actors are not as anarchic as intuitively perceived, but are relatively orderly (Arjona 2016; Idler and Boesten 2018). We argue that in some cases, the order resulting from the preponderance of an armed actor is conducive for letting collective agency develop among community members because the resulting regularised procedures allow for an increase in human interaction and productivity.

To diffuse any doubt over the deliberative nature of recognition, Nancy Fraser continues arguing 'one becomes an individual subject only in virtue of recognising, and being recognised by, another subject' (2003: 10). The deliberative nature becomes even more pronounced if we transfer the act of recognition from the micro, individual level to the formation of communities' collective identities. Habermas writes that self-recognition and the transformation of that ego identity into a group identity are only plausible in the context of discourse. He argues that the identity of a collective group results when 'the members can utter an emphatic "we"; it is not an ego identity writ large but rather supplements the individual's identity' with selectively chosen 'native traditions' that determine how 'we recognize ourselves' and would like to be recognised as citizens (1996: 160). The transformation of an ego identity that feeds from personal experiences to a collective presupposes an exchange between members of a community as to what the key native traditions are.

Deliberative processes that lead to agreements over collective identities and the (self-) recognition of these identities are contingent on the absence of coercion. Intersubjectivity relies on our ability to place ourselves in the situation of any other person (Arendt 1958) and is only possible in 'structures of undamaged intersubjectivity found in non-distorted communication' (Habermas 1996: 148). Understanding recognition in the context of contested statehood therefore requires identifying potential conditions that create space for communication among community members.

This is where what Idler terms 'shadow citizenship' comes into play: 'clusters of illegal institutionalised organisational structures that guide behaviour in illicitly controlled territory' (Idler 2012; Idler and Boesten 2018). We analyse the relation between shadow citizenship and recognition in the context of contested statehood via exploring the effects of armed actor preponderance on local communities. Specifically, when we take the community perspective, we can, with the help of sociological conceptualisations of complexity-coping mechanisms, explore how non-state order can inhibit or facilitate productive interaction among agents.

To explain briefly, uncertainty arises from the fact that the future contains many possibilities. Our reaction to the increase of possibilities is contingent on how we process information: if we fear the multitude of future possibilities, we remain in a familiar world anxious of the other; if we recognise future possibilities as threats to a desired outcome, we can contain these and build confidence based on observable patterns; if we understand future possibilities as calculable risks, we can venture a risky investment that exposes us to the malfeasance of third parties or, in other words, place trust in an outcome (Gambetta 1988; Giddens 1990: 36; Luhmann 1988). In the context of internal armed conflict, where violent death is one future possibility, remaining in the familiar lifeworld and reducing interaction with others – that is, outsiders to the in-group experience – is not only plausible but also rational. The implication is, though, that practices that could facilitate recognition are also severely constrained: if recognition is contingent on exposing oneself to the outsider experience, uncertainty, constraining the individual to the familiar lifeworld, undercuts the possibility of that experience.

We therefore argue that recognition in a situation of internal armed conflict can only arise in the context of confidence in reoccurring patterns, such as the facilitation of safe passages through a territory by an armed actor. Elsewhere, we trace the effects of the regularity of outcomes in non-state order on community attitudes, arguing that a certain stability of conduct can generate confidence in the stability of those very procedures (Idler and Boesten 2018). In such cases, the mere regularity of specific interactions and outcomes signals a shift from anxiety about future possibilities to threats to a desired outcome (amenable to confidence-building). If recognition is an intersubjective and deliberative process, as the theory suggests, confidence is a necessary condition for affirming one's own subjectivity.

There is more, though. Just as with guerrilla preponderance, paramilitary preponderance induces a regularity of procedures and establishes clear rules of conduct – often imposing extremely draconian punishment for digressions (Duncan 2006; Romero 2003). Therefore, there needs to be more than simply imposition of a regularity of rules that gives rise to the apparent preference of the guerrillas over the paramilitaries. We propose that the answer lies in the groups' behaviour vis-à-vis local communities. The FARC instrumentalised local institutions, such as communal councils, and coercively imposed rules on the activities of community members – all, to be sure, for the primary reason to exert and retain territorial control. Nevertheless, it thereby also opened spaces for the recognition of collective agency of local communities as well as of armed actors' social recognition by the local population in conflict zones.

The relevance of these sociological concepts for our understanding of non-state actors' behaviour and recognition becomes clearer if we relate this to our understanding of institutions. The neo-institutionalist literature in comparative politics – in the context of established statehood – defines institutions as '*relatively enduring* features of political and social life (rules, norms, procedures) that structure behaviour and that cannot be changed easily or instantaneously' (Mahoney and Thelen 2010: 4; see also Hall and

Taylor 1996). We stated that the recurrence of patterns – driven by armed actors' behavioural patterns – generates confidence in the regularity of these patterns. Note, however, that this cannot be equated with institutions in the conventional sense because these patterns are not subjecting the armed groups themselves to specific constraints. They are not the rules of the game because the coercive actor can, and often does, change the rules of the game.

The quality of the definition of institutions that we want to raise for our argument is their '*relatively enduring*' nature. The endurance of rules as the defining feature of institutions connects with recent advances in democratic theory that disaggregate democratic practices to provide more fine-grained assessments of these practices. It also connects with our observation that recurring behavioural patterns by armed groups generate confidence among community members. Such established patterns of behaviour have spin-off effects. Mark Warren argues, 'binding qualities of collective decision-making capacities can follow from non-state-based incentives, such as capturing economic benefits or avoiding the costs of externalities *and uncertainties, including war*' (Warren 2017: 45; italics added). Behavioural patterns of armed groups strive to avoid the externalities of war.

We propose that the apparent preference of the guerrillas over the paramilitaries goes beyond the functional avoidance of uncertainties and implies an attitude of legitimacy towards the group (see also Idler et al. 2018). Again, we can return to Warren. He argues, 'performance legitimacy (often called output legitimacy)' is tied up with collective decision-making and 'contingent upon organisational systems that translate decisions into collective responsiveness' (2017: 46). Thus, for there to be an attitude that goes beyond accepting the facts (i.e. the dominance of one group), there needs to be a connection between making a (collective) claim and a response to that claim. We argue that FARC domination in Nariño reduced uncertainty and contributed to generating confidence among local community members. What apparently set them apart from paramilitary domination was the inclusion of the community in specifically delegated spaces. In sum: recognition in the context of FARC preponderance was a function of the FARC's ability to coerce and create predictable procedures, coupled with their (at least somewhat) responsive behaviour vis-à-vis local communities – that is, the emergence of shadow citizenship.

The next section details the differences between AUC paramilitaries and FARC guerrillas documented in the literature. This indicates our contribution by shifting the analytical lens to the community perspective. Our own empirical investigation then shows that clarity of rules of conduct, clear organisational structures within the FARC and, importantly, spaces delegated to community affairs allowed local communities to assert their own subjectivity.

Paramilitaries and the guerrilla in Colombia's armed conflict

Recent conflict research has taken a turn to focusing on local dynamics, exploring order in intra-state conflicts and civilian agency vis-à-vis armed actors (Arjona 2016; Hallward et al. 2017; Idler and Boesten 2018; Kaplan 2017). The Colombian case has played a key role in this turn to the local, providing ample empirical variations to test the most cutting-edge theories of conflict research. This is because, in Colombia's long history of violence, various non-state armed actors that operate in the same context where crime and conflict often converge share several characteristics, including their involvement in the international cocaine trade as a source of funding, but differ in other aspects, most importantly their ideology, and related issues such as technical expertise in the illicit economy, recruitment of fighters and, not least, behaviour towards local communities. The preference expressed at the beginning of this chapter reflects this variation between the FARC and the AUC paramilitaries, but we contend that the research has focused on characteristics of the armed actors themselves and paid less attention to the effects on communities. The next section shows evidence of the importance of the community perspective as it holds epistemological contributions for a more fine-grained assessment of non-state order in conflict zones.

Appreciating the link between recognition and informal institutions that guide behaviour patterns under shadow citizenship in the Colombian conflict requires accounting for the historical complexity of the conflict itself. At least three major actors have played a role in violence in Colombia: leftist guerrillas, the state forces and right-wing paramilitary forces (Duncan 2006; López 2010; Martínez and Fernando 2010; Romero 2003). Adding to the complexity is that throughout the more than six decades of civil strife, there were not solely guerrilla or paramilitary groups operating at the same time, but various armed actors on each side with shifting alliances. Among the guerrillas, the FARC and the Ejército de Liberación Nacional (National Liberation Army; ELN) were the strongest, while the AUC were an umbrella organisation of various regional paramilitary groups financed partly by rural elites and drug traffickers.

Further compounding the intricateness of armed actors is the longevity of the conflict and the accompanying transformations each group has undergone. Manuel Marulanda Vélez and Jacobo Arenas formed the FARC out of a small band of liberal militias in 1964 and moulded them into a Castro-inspired rebel group that remained active, but relatively small. Yet, at the zenith of its power in the early 2000s, it had an estimated fighting force of around 20,000 troops and significantly threatened to turn Colombia into a failed state (McLean 2002). Its 'success' for maintaining control and authority over large swathes of Colombia's rural areas is at least partly rooted in a decision from 1982 to strategically expand into cocaine-producing areas and become an important actor for facilitating cocaine-trafficking routes (Gutiérrez Sanín and Barón 2006).

The paramilitaries grew out of the large drug cartels in Colombia's urban hubs, Medellin and Cali, in convergence with landowner interest in rural Colombia. The cartels' mid-level enforcers used profits from the drug economy to buy rural land, thereby joining the traditional rural land-owning class. After the Seventh Guerrilla Conference in 1982, landowners and ranchers had felt the effects of FARC offensives first and welcomed the arrival of resourceful new actors (Gutiérrez Sanín and Vargas 2017). It created a heterogeneous armed alliance with mutual benefits: traditional elites provided status in the social fabric of rural society to otherwise criminal actors, while aspiring drug lords provided the resources to mount private armies to counter guerrilla insurgences. The inaccessible context of rural Colombia, characterised by state absence, supplied the opportunities to expand the control of territory (a key factor for success in the illicit economy), while at the same time served as a justification to utilise coercion as a measure of self-defence (Duncan 2006; Gutiérrez Sanín and Barón 2006: 44; Romero 2000).[5]

The dismantling of the large cartels of the 1980s in the mid-1990s precipitated key changes in the political economy of the drug business, creating opportunities for actors with a territorial base. The rising demand of cocaine on US and European markets and 'war on drugs' incentivised the production and export of coca paste through rural territory over the monopolisation of the entire production and distribution chain in urban hubs (McDermott 2018). As a consequence, guerrillas consolidated their presence in major coca production regions where they levied taxes on coca and coca paste, whereas paramilitaries expanded into key trafficking routes connecting the coca laboratories in the Colombian jungle with export points on the coast and in border areas. The paramilitaries were further helped with public policies that legalised the creation of private security groups as a counter-insurgency measure. Most regional blocs of the AUC were private vigilante groups under the CONVIVIR programme institutionalised under the Gaviria and Samper administrations (1994–1998; Martínez and Fernando 2010). In sum, the paramilitary project 'united a good sector of Colombian society: *ganaderos* (agro industrialists), industrialists, narco-traffickers, militaries, some national politicians, and the entire regions and locales where they had dominated before' (Martínez and Fernando 2010: 120).

The period from the second part of the 1990s through to the early 2000s was one of the most violent in Colombia's history, with both paramilitaries and guerrillas utilising indiscriminate violence and committing large-scale atrocities.[6] This was also the period when the extent of territory in Colombia living under non-state order was most extensive, as the FARC and the AUC were at the peak of their power. The AUC officially demobilised between 2003 and 2006, with new smaller criminal enterprises forming from its remnants (so-called Bandas Criminales, or 'Criminal Bands', known by the acronym BACRIM). The FARC outlasted the paramilitaries and formally began peace negotiations with the Colombian government in 2012, resulting in the Havana peace agreement and the transformation of the FARC from an armed actor into a political party in 2017.

Despite a number of similarities, including their involvement in the international cocaine economy, the FARC and the AUC displayed significantly different behaviour vis-à-vis local communities (Gutiérrez Sanín 2008). Moreover, these differences appeared to be driven by variation in their ideology, social composition, internal organisational structures, recruitment techniques and technical expertise in the cocaine business (Saab and Taylor 2009).

First, the social composition mirrors the ideological orientation and origin of each group. Evidence from internal databases taken from computers confiscated by the Colombian state[7] shows that FARC combatants were more often peasants, included more females and were generally less educated, while the AUC paramilitaries comprised landowners at the leadership level and often recruited mid-level commanders from the armed forces and combatants from common delinquents. Generally speaking, the social differentiation between leadership and combatants was higher within the AUC than in the FARC (Arjona 2016; Gutiérrez Sanín 2008; Romero 2003).

Fighters in each group signed up for very different lives. Internally, a strict vertical hierarchy placed command firmly in the hands of commanders of the FARC.[8] However, despite the large sums handled by the guerrillas, neither the leadership nor the recruits personally profited. FARC recruits did not receive payments and tightly integrated into a chain of command (Arjona 2016). Insubordination was punishable with death, with the result that looting for individual benefit was virtually non-existent among lower ranks. Harassment of local populations did occur, but 'basically if they [were] ordered to do so' (Gutiérrez Sanín 2008: 13). The same is true for commanders in leadership positions. Cases of personal enrichment were very rare. What is more, we have evidence of a case where a mid-ranking commander shortly before the commencement of the demobilisation process of the FARC was getting more deeply involved in the drug trade and was acting abusively towards local civilians. The FARC declared him no longer FARC and assassinated him. The AUC, on the other hand, operated on 'the continuous and grand offer of selective incentives' (Gutiérrez Sanín 2008: 19). This left much more space for lower-ranking commanders to exploit the riches of the territory under their control (it also opened the flood gates of abuse; see below on the repertoire of violence). In fact, allowing lower-ranking files to exploit rents was a key currency for commanders to increase their power. It buttressed a 'system [based on] territorial delegation, where each commander [gave] a zone to a sub-commander, who has latitude to impose his own rules' (Gutiérrez Sanín and Barón 2006: 24). The result was a much more decentralised command structure, where even the most prominent commanders never fully exhorted their authority over regional blocs. In fact, the AUC internally fractured as a consequence of centrifugal forces set in motion by disagreement over the role of narco-profits for financing the organisation.

The criminality of the Colombian context has blurred the line between crime and conflict since the 1970s (Idler 2012). Hence, it also created actors with specific expertise in the drug business and, as a consequence, different functions within the illicit economy. Saab and Taylor write that even in a highly criminalised context such as the Colombian, 'group goals, the political environment, and membership strongly influence the types of criminal activities a given armed group undertakes' (2009: 455). First, technical limitations inherited from the origin of a group's membership also limit the criminal activities in which it can engage now. Since the FARC often operated in remote and ragged (jungle) territory, it had an advantage in overseeing the production of coca paste. It did not, however, directly possess distribution networks in key export markets. As explained above, the AUC (and its successor organisations) evolved from the ranks of the large cartels of the 1980s. They had developed networks in key export.

There are also political constraints affecting involvement in the illicit economy. The AUC had fewer difficulties in defending its well-known involvement in the drug economy. For the longest time, it successfully claimed that it was only the business of rogue elements within the organisation. In addition, the linkages with the political class that surfaced after the demobilisation of the AUC in the so-called *parapolítica* scandal shielded paramilitaries from legal exposure. In effect, they only became a military target after their demobilisation (López 2010; Restrepo et al, 2006). In the second part of the 1990s and early 2000s, they could rely on their alliances with local business, political and military elites (see Duncan 2006; López 2010; Romero 2000). The FARC, as an insurgency group, on the other hand, faced the prospect that accusations of a deepening involvement in the drug economy could, first, result in fiercer military responses, and, secondly, undermine its political claims. Considering the highly demanding recruitment explained above, the FARC was sensitive to accusations that it was simply a drug-trafficking enterprise, and not a valid political project (Saab and Taylor 2009).

Notwithstanding the importance of these findings for our understanding of conflict zones, ultimately the foci have been the actors themselves: their internal organisation, expertise. The effects on community or civilians have usually been traced only indirectly. A final, and important, feature differentiating the paramilitaries and guerrillas – their respective repertoires of violence – goes some way towards incorporating community perspectives, since violence ultimately connects to questions of governance; yet, it still problematises the violence directed *against* communities. The AUC, due to its linkages with Colombia's rural ruling class, had used kidnapping much more sparingly as a strategy to extract resources, but used massacres to instil fear and co-opt local populations into submission much more liberally than the guerrillas (Gutiérrez Sanín 2008; López 2010; Romero 2003). Over time, it had to adapt its violence regimes, as for example, the paramilitaries switched to a more selective repertoire of violence (but maintaining hit lists that differentiated between 'killable categories', ranging from common criminals, traitors, alleged guerrilla collaborators and social leaders).

The fact that an armed actor must attune the use of violence in order to make its domination over a territory and important sectors of an illicit economy finally raises the issue of governance. Governance, notwithstanding the complexity of the term (Fukuyama 2013), always implies a relational component between different parties. The next section documents evidence of differing governance systems of armed groups in Tumaco, Colombia. It documents the civilian or community perspective to those systems and highlights the importance of specific spaces for civilian agency that facilitate recognition between community and armed actor.

Recognition and institutions of non-state order in Tumaco

The evidence that we provide here has two parts. The first part outlines the general security situation in Tumaco, Nariño, where our interviewees were based. The second part moves to discussing the interview data displaying different attitudes local civilians espoused towards the guerrillas and paramilitaries.

The fieldwork took place in some of Colombia's most marginalised conflict-affected regions during crucial moments of transition: when armed conflict with the FARC was ongoing and before the formal peace talks started (2011–2012); while the peace talks were ongoing (2016), during the transition period when FARC demobilised (2017) and once the demobilisation had been completed (2018). It consists of an extensive database of 606 interviews for context and a focus on data from an overall number of around twenty semi-structured interviews carried out in Tumaco.[9] To ensure triangulation of data sources, interviewees included community leaders, clerics, civil society representatives, staff members of non-governmental organisations (NGOs) and international organisations, ex-combatants, indigenous leaders, members of state forces and government officials (see Idler 2019: 347). This data collection method was complemented by reviews of documents, most notably the risk reports of the Colombian Ombudsman's Office ranging back to the early 2000s and disaggregated conflict data (regional and national homicide rates from the Legal Medicine and Forensic Sciences Office, Medicina Legal y Ciencas Forenses; see Table 11.1).

We show that local community members experienced a wide variety of violent non-state actors in their territory, encompassing various guerrilla groups (FARC, ELN), paramilitary groups (AUC), post-demobilisation groups and small criminal groups, as well as the effects of army offensives. Moreover, the evidence also portrays different types of non-state order, ranging from preponderance of some actors through unstable alliances to open confrontation between non-state armed actors (see Idler 2019). For the purpose of our argument: the first part demonstrates that the presence of numerous non-state actors correlates with a generic sense of uncertainty (documented with extremely high levels of homicide rates); the second part documents evidence from interview subjects relating the ability to recognise an armed group with its internal organisation, and the potential for being recognised with spaces allowing for voice of grievances. Both together ensure a degree of responsiveness on part of the armed group to community demands that cannot be explained with coercive capacities alone. Future recognition-based research should therefore focus on the relations between communities and armed actors; specifically, the spaces delegated to the former for voicing grievances and the internal cohesion of the latter as a condition for being recognised by local civilians.

Context: the security situation in Tomaco

In the early 2000s, 'Plan Colombia', including aerial fumigations and the state forces' military operations in neighbouring department Putumayo, pushed coca cultivation and armed groups operating in the drug economy westwards to Nariño and the port of Tumaco. As a consequence, the AUC, FARC and ELN repeatedly clashed in battles for territorial control between Pasto and Tumaco, an important corridor for the illicit cocaine economy.[10] The civilian population was often caught between the warring factions of various violent non-state groups vying for territorial control and state forces' offensives against insurgent groups.[11] In 2005, the AUC began the demobilisation process of the Justice and Peace Process. By April 2005, the ELN and FARC had begun to target previous AUC strongholds.[12] At the same time, some former members of the Bloque de Libertadores del Sur tried to link up with narco-traffickers to counter the guerrilla offensive, resulting in an

Table 11.1 Homicide rates per 100,000 people per year, 1999–2017

Year	Tumaco	Nariño	Colombia
1999		22	56.00
2000	90.00		61.00
2001	121.00	30.00	64.00
2002	113.00	38.00	65.00
2003	n.a.	n.a.	50.00
2004	61.00	19.40	42.00
2005	112.00	29.00	41.00
2006	151.00	36.00	38.00
2007	163.00	36.00	37.00
2008	100.00	27.00	34.00
2009	174.00	38.35	39.00
2010	136.87	29.95	38.36
2011	136.06	30.06	35.95
2012	140.00	31.06	33.76
2013	112.96	27.15	30.33
2014	72.66	19.39	26.49
2015	65.61	16.17	24.03
2016	75.01	18.52	23.66
2017	100.81	19.86	23.07

Source: Republic of Colombia, Instituto Nacional de Medicina Legal y Ciencias Forenses. Forensis 1999–2017.

increase of assassinations, threats and terror against civilians (including the public display of mutilated bodies).[13] The homicide rates for Tumaco show two identifiable commencement points of an upward slope in 2000 and 2005 reflecting these developments (see Table 11.1).

Two years later, in 2007, the remnants of previous AUC groups fully consolidated into post-demobilisation groups, or so-called BACRIM.[14] The Colombian Ombudsman's Office for Human Rights reported the presence of the Autodefensas Campesinas, Águilas Negras and Rastrojos in Tumaco, Pasto, Samaniego, Barbacoas and Ricaurte, all vying for territorial control of key trafficking routes.[15] In addition, the increasingly (and much more purely) criminal context produced counterintuitive alliances and enmities. The FARC began attacking the ELN, while the latter cooperated with the Rastrojos.[16] The impact on the civilian population was immense as all groups utilised repressive strategies to exert control. Thus, the homicide rates for Nariño and Tumaco increased drastically from 2008 to 2009, reaching acute crisis levels in the port city (174 per 100 000; see Table 11.1). Only in 2009 did both insurgent groups sign a non-aggression pact.

The context somewhat eased in 2010: the alliance between the ELN and the Rastrojos against the FARC terminated, the two guerrilla groups had signed a non-aggression pact, and the Rastrojos apparently fused with another post-demobilisation BACRIM, the Autodefensas Campesinas.[17] The calm was only relative, though, as homicides remained high, and another post-demobilisation group, the Águilas Negras, made its presence evident in 2011.[18] Only after 2013 did homicide rates for Nariño and Tumaco noticeably recede (see Table 11.1). This coincided with a reduction in the number of violent non-state groups present. The non-aggression pact between the FARC and the ELN contained the advancement of the armed forces and prevented the entry of other illegal armed groups.[19] In fact, both groups, the FARC and the ELN, deepened their territorial control: the FARC in previous Rastrojos areas, and the ELN in important corridors on the north coast of Nariño. In addition, the FARC gained access to beaches and established militia presence in municipal capitals, and its 29th Front extended corridors up the coast and into the interior to the Pan-American highway.

By the end of 2013, the Águilas Negras had disappeared and by 2015 the Rastrojos had also been displaced from the region.[20] Even though their disappearance opened space for new, and only very loosely organised, criminal gangs with no apparent affiliation with other illegal armed groups, the guerrillas contained and targeted them if they appeared to offset established structures of the status quo. Additional structures from Cauca (FARC Front 60) and Putumayo (FARC Front 48) occasionally entered the department to secure mobility corridors.[21] Mapping ELN presence during the same period shows that the two rebel groups partly occupied the same territory. In some of these regions, FARC and ELN engaged in a strategic alliance and in others operated in pacific coexistence to share mobility corridors, strategic for their wider operations in Colombia (Idler 2019). Throughout this period, violence reduced notably from 140 to 65 homicides per 100 000 and 31 to 16 per 100 000 people in Tumaco and all of Nariño, respectively (Table 11.1). Being preponderant in remote and hardly accessible regions with a strong social base allowed the FARC to benefit from controlling areas of coca cultivation and from engaging with other groups in stable transactional supply chain relationships.

Conditions for recognition: evidence from Tumaco

The previous section explained the context of conflict in Nariño since the early 2000s and, in the course of the analysis, showed a correlation between uncertainty/insecurity for communities and the presence of various armed actors. Here, we used homicide rates as an indicator for insecurity, but elsewhere we also trace the effects on attitudes among community members with our interview data (Idler and Boesten 2018). However, certainty itself does not suffice to explain the preference for the FARC over the AUC. After all, when the paramilitaries asserted their domination and established relative control, they, too, provided the clarity of rules that is essential for generating confidence in procedures. In the words of a representative of a humanitarian organisation based in Pasto, Colombia, in 2011: 'Technically, moving around where there is only one armed actor is much easier than moving in a scenario where there are more armed actors present.'[22] What we add here is that the FARC – with the intent to control territory – attempted to co-opt local populations with the help of spaces that gave voice and a minimum degree of autonomy to communities and their leaders. In other words, these institutions helped communities to assert their subjectivity vis-à-vis the armed actor.

To begin, we explore in more detail the citation quoted at the beginning of this chapter:

> If I have to choose between paramilitaries and guerrillas, I would choose the guerrillas. *Toda la vida*! The paramilitaries have come to defend the interests of a few families with a lot of money, while the guerrillas were born to defend peasant interests that had been violated. ... But I do not choose either one or the other because both, by using weapons and violence, they are against the people.[23]

The interview includes a sober reminder that with all the differences between the FARC and the AUC (and other post-demobilisation groups), the context remains one of violence. The normative connotations of this exploration of armed groups governance should not be misread as assigning generic benevolence on the part of the FARC. In fact, the imposition of domination typically occurred through extremely repressive means, as several subjects, who said they preferred the FARC over paramilitary groups, insisted. Conflict zones leave a very limited choice.[24] One interviewee, for example, stated that the FARC 'is an armed actor, [who] is generating a kind of control; it should not exercise that kind of control, there are activities that citizens normally do, and usually have been doing, but an armed actor comes to impose certain orders.'[25] In addition, the interview appears to confirm that guerrillas and paramilitaries have a different social base, with the implication that the nature of the support base also affects behaviour.

Despite the predatory nature of the FARC, the group's (partial) responsiveness made it easier for locals to address the group – and ultimately be heard by the armed group. A representative of an indigenous population, the Awá in Nariño, explained: it is easier to coordinate with the FARC, 'because in some way it is known that they have an organisational branch and that there is a Secretariat'.[26] The reference to the Secretariat relates to the organisational coherence of the FARC. This reference, though, has two implications: it is easier for a community to address the group, and decisions by the leadership are more fluidly passed down the chain of command. Confirmation comes from a staff member of a Colombian international organisation who explained that paramilitaries[27] and 'those groups that the government calls BACRIM, are extremely volatile in their conformation and dynamics'.[28] The second implication of the reference to the 'Secretariat' is that internal coherence increased the likelihood of responsiveness. Another interviewee explained more explicitly that with 'the ELN or the FARC, there is a kind of surveillance by the Secretariat, but in the case of these paramilitary groups, the level of control that can be exercised is not so clear'.[29] Together, these points link up with Gutiérrez Sanín's contention that the FARC was characterised by a strict verticalism whereas the paramilitaries functioned on a system based on regional delegation of authority (2008; see also López 2010). This shows that the internal organisational structure of the armed group matters greatly for the local civilian population. Without a hierarchical structure, or only in diminished form, this 'relating',[30] as an international organisation staff member referred to it in a curious acknowledgement of the recognition vocabulary, is only possible in diminished form.

The second hypothesis arising from our analyses requires appreciating the behavioural patterns of the FARC and their effects on local communities. Here, a quotation from an indigenous leader of the Awá in Nariño is telling. He explained that 'especially the AUC, from 1999 to 2006 and after that the Los Rastrojos, until 2013–14, intimidated the people, created the law of silence, [and] recruited young people'.[31] Control over the local population essentially equalled coercion and violence (note that the AUC and Los Rastrojos did not differ in that respect). They evidence very little interest in the community interests and did not recognise them as a separate collective.

The FARC took a different route. Another international organisation staff member explains, 'they [the FARC] also commit atrocious violations of [international humanitarian law], without a doubt' but at the same time have shown 'a certain respect to the leaders of the communities'.[32] Another respondent confirmed: 'according to my analysis, the guerrillas are more interested in having better relations with the community'.[33] What is more, such relations with communities built on specifically delegated spaces that let the communities view the FARC as a force that helped to manage quotidian affairs: 'They used peace judges because the guerrillas settled disputes in that area, settled even marital disputes, land disputes, or even such things as alleged disrespect of elders.'[34] This played a crucial rule for the FARC to become 'an authority for the community. Many of the community conflicts are mediated by them, in their own way obviously, [but] if you have problems, they solve them.'[35] A leader of an Afro-Colombian community stated that 'the FARC not only enforces itself with violence, homicides and displacement. ... They create their own community councils and meetings.'[36] In sum, there should be no mistaking that the spaces the FARC delegated to local communities ultimately had very utilitarian purposes: exert and maintain territorial control. Such spaces, nevertheless, offered possibilities to utter grievances and, thereby, opened opportunities for the community to be recognised by the armed actor.

Conclusion

Social leaders and civil society representatives often lament the inadequate presence of the state. This is not surprising given the longevity of the Colombian conflict, the multitude of different violent actors, and the intricate relations between them – ranging from cooperation to armed confrontation. Often, though, they utter their discontent more specifically than that, as, for example, the aforementioned Colombian NGO staff member: 'state presence is often limited to military presence, and that is not enough; the great challenge is to also reach civic authorities.'[37] The history of past (failed) peace processes in Colombia does indeed tell a narrative of the militarised outreach of the state to marginalised regions at the neglect of creating effective civilian institutions that protect local communities. It is in that respect that our methodological shift to the community perspective has a normative implication that echoes the intergovernmental organisation staff grievance on the militarisation of state responses.

To put it in the context of this volume: in order to construct effective post-conflict institutions, the state should recognise civil leadership by local communities. The major deficiency of the Colombian state, especially in those regions affected by the violence, has been the sporadic civilian presence of those structures. While not having to replicate the structure of the FARC that enabled recognition of the armed group by the community, the state must replicate the *permanence* of those state structures, police and civil, to be an effective facilitator of recognition. Secondly, by facilitating participatory mechanisms to coordinate in local decision-making processes, the state acts as a recognition-granter and satisfies communities' status as recognition-seekers.

While the implications are normative, we reach this conclusion via an empirical analysis of non-state order. To reiterate our interviewees, the preference articulated in the quotation at the beginning of this chapter is neither normative embrace nor ideological inclination towards the political goals of the FARC. It is resultant of a behaviour that leaves more space for local communities than paramilitary order tended to do.

The first part of our argument rests on theoretical implications. A standard definition of recognition – an ideal-type reciprocal relationship between equals that recognises different subjectivities (Fraser 2003) – implies the ideal-type configuration of deliberative spaces, in which agents can assert and mutually observe their subjective identities. We make the argument that recognition is an intersubjective process because a 'collective we' requires communication over what that 'collective we' entails. We inferred for the purposes of our analysis that recognition in the context of non-state order then relies on some degree of security from violent death and behavioural patterns that delegated spaces with the potential to recognise and be recognised.

We built on the documented evidence that traced systematic differences between the FARC and the AUC paramilitaries. This research has produced findings of how each group differed from each other, but the focus remains on the armed actors themselves (their social composition, sources of resources, organisation, etc.). The turn towards community perspective allows us to propose conditions for recognition in armed conflict. First, we established the necessity of observable patterns that reduce the fear of violent death and facilitate confidence to explore interaction with others. We hold that there must be a certain degree of preponderance of *one* actor (and not competition among several actors for control) to reduce uncertainty in outcomes. This is purely functional and does not fully explain the preference for the FARC over the AUC, because both established clear and strictly enforced codes of conduct.

Our second hypothesis arrives via an analysis of our data from conflict zones in Nariño. Our interview subject highlighted two specific characteristics of FARC preponderance: itsinternal cohesion and the instrumental utilisation of informal spaces to maintain preponderance. What scholars have referred to as 'strict verticalism' inside the FARC had two implications for local communities: 1) it was easier to address the relevant people within the FARC; 2) there was also a higher likelihood that the assurances communities received were in fact enforced. The final part of our chapter was devoted to detailing how subjects in zones under guerrilla control experienced interactions in regulated spaces. To be sure, the FARC tightly controlled these spaces and they served a clearly instrumental purpose. Nevertheless, this space allowed communities to voice their grievances – even if these related to quotidian aspects of life. It was for that reason that they argued the FARC cared more about civil leaders of communities. In sum, this leads us to conclude that recognising civil authorities of local communities entails, at a minimum, enduring structures (organisation) and space for voicing grievances that results in action (input and responsiveness).

Notes

1 Interview with cleric, Tumaco, November 2016.
2 For the concept of non-state order see Idler (2019).
3 Conventionally, the FARC is referred to in papers without the appendix 'EP' for *Ejercito Popular* (Popular Army). Given that its nature fundamentally changed in the transformation from guerrilla group to political party, but the acronym remained the same (FARC now standing for Fuerza Alternativa Revolucionaria del Común, or Alternative Force for the Common Good), the inclusion of the appendix 'EP' distinguishes the FARC guerrilla group from the FARC political party. Since we are only problematising governance issues of the FARC as a guerrilla group, we use FARC in the traditional way as the acronym for the armed group, *not* the political party.
4 For a discussion of 'preponderance' in the context of violent non-state groups see Idler (2019).
5 A demobilised paramilitary reported that 'the cattle rancher cannot maintain let's say 500 people, medicines for combatants, uniforms, clothes, he simply does not have the capacity' (cited in Gutiérrez Sanín and Barón 2006: 13).
6 In 1997, for example, a total of 193 massacres were registered in Colombia. Antioquia was the hardest hit, with 75 massacres, followed by Cesar (19), Magdalena (15) and Bolivar (13). Several human rights organisations and the Interamerican Court for Human Rights have condemned the close cooperation between armed forces and the CONVIVIR paramilitary groups in those crimes (see Human Rights Watch 1997, 1998; Inter-American Court of Human Rights, *Caso de las Massacres de Ituango vs. Colombia 2006*; Martínez and Fernando 2010: 113).
7 The hard drives seized after a raid on Raul Reyes's camp in 2008 in Ecuador on the FARC side and the Jorge 40 computer seized in the course of the parapolítica investigations on the AUC side.
8 FARC is organised hierarchically into Central High Command, the Estado Mayor Central, and into Blocks with several Fronts that include Columns with Companies, Guerrillas and Squads.
9 For details on the full database see Idler (2019). For the data analysis, we drew on NVivo software. We coded the interview transcripts on the basis of a pre-designed list of codes that aimed to look for attitudes about the security landscape, differentiating between expressions that reflect attitudes of confidence or lack thereof in the security situation. During the data analysis process, we added In Vivo codes to reflect the themes that emerged from the interviews around confident or non-confident attitudes. In this second data analysis process emerged a picture of institutional caveats that either facilitated or damaged confidence in benevolent outcomes.
10 Defensoría del Pueblo de Colombia. Sistemas de Alertas Tempranas – SAT. Informe de riesgo No. 024-03 AI, 27 March 2003.
11 Defensoría del Pueblo de Colombia. Sistemas de Alertas Tempranas – SAT. Informe de riesgo No. 06-04, 12 August 2004.

12 Defensoría del Pueblo de Colombia. Sistemas de Alertas Tempranas – SAT. Informe de riesgo No. 036-05, 9 August 2005.
13 Defensoría del Pueblo de Colombia. Sistemas de Alertas Tempranas – SAT. Informe de riesgo No. 065-05, 28 December 2005.
14 Defensoría del Pueblo de Colombia. Sistemas de Alertas Tempranas – SAT. Informe de riesgo No. 010-07, 23 May 2007.
15 Defensoría del Pueblo de Colombia. Sistemas de Alertas Tempranas – SAT. Informe de riesgo No. 016-07, 29 June 2007.
16 Defensoría del Pueblo de Colombia. Sistemas de Alertas Tempranas – SAT. Nota de seguimiento No. 008-10, 30 April 2010: 2.
17 Defensoría del Pueblo de Colombia. Sistemas de Alertas Tempranas – SAT. Nota de seguimiento No. 020-10, 24 August 2010: 4.
18 Defensoría del Pueblo de Colombia. Sistemas de Alertas Tempranas – SAT. Nota de seguimiento No 007-11, 7 April 2011: 3.
19 Defensoría del Pueblo de Colombia. Sistemas de Alertas Tempranas – SAT. Informe de riesgo No. 027-13 AI, 20 August 2013: 11.
20 Defensoría del Pueblo de Colombia. Sistemas de Alertas Tempranas – SAT. Nota de seguimiento No. 017-13, 16 December 2013: 4.
21 Defensoría del Pueblo de Colombia. Sistemas de Alertas Tempranas – SAT. Nota de seguimiento No. 020-15, 18 September 2015: 4.
22 Interview with representative of a humanitarian organisation, Pasto, 2011.
23 Interview with cleric, Tumaco, 2016.
24 Interview with NGO staff member, Pasto, 2011.
25 Interview with male international organisation staff member, Pasto, 2011.
26 Interview with female international organisation staff member 2, Pasto, 2011.
27 Interview with indigenous leader, Tumaco, 2016.
28 Interview with female international organisation staff member 1, Pasto, 2011.
29 Interview with female international organisation staff member 2, Pasto, 2011. Interestingly, the FARC asserted the internal hierarchy until shortly before the official commencement of the re-integration process, ordering the assassination of a commander that had gone rogue in Nariño (Interview with cleric, Tumaco, 2016).
30 Interview with international organisation staff member 1, Pasto, 2011.
31 Interview with indigenous leader, Tumaco, 2016.
32 Interview with international organisation staff member 2, Pasto, 2011.
33 Interview with international organisation staff member 3, Pasto, 2011.
34 Interview with civil society representative, Pasto, 2011.
35 Interview with international organisation staff member 4, Pasto, 2011.
36 Interview with civil society representative, Tumaco, 2011.
37 Interview with female international organisation staff member 1, Pasto, 2011.

References

Arendt, H. (1958), *The Human Condition* (Chicago: University of Chicago Press).
Arjona, A. (2016), *Rebelocracy* (Cambridge: Cambridge University Press).

Duncan, G. (2006), *Los Señores de la Guerra: De Paramilitares, Mafiosos y Autodefensas en Colombia* (Bogota: Editorial Planeta Colombiana).

Fraser, N. (2003), 'Redistribution or recognition? A critique of justice truncated', in N. Fraser and A. Honneth (eds), *Redistribution or Recognition? A Political-Philosophical Exchange* (London: Verso), pp. 7–88.

Fukuyama, F. (2013), 'What is governance?', *Governance* 26:3, 347–368.

Gambetta, D. (ed.) (1988), *Trust: Making and Breaking Cooperative Relations* (Oxford and Cambridge: Blackwell).

Geis, A. (2018), 'The ethics of recognition in International Political Theory', in C. Brown and R. Eckersley (eds), *The Oxford Handbook of International Political Theory* (Oxford: Oxford University Press), pp. 612–625.

Giddens, A. (1990), *The Consequences of Modernity* (Cambridge: Polity Press).

Gutiérrez Sanín, F. (2003), 'Criminal rebels? A discussion of civil war and criminality from the Colombian experience', *Crisis States Research Centre Working Papers Series 1* 27, 1–26.

Gutiérrez Sanín, F. (2008), 'Telling the difference: guerrillas and paramilitaries in the Colombian war', *Politics & Society* 36:1, 3–34.

Gutiérrez Sanín, F. and M. Barón (2006), *Re-stating the State: Paramilitary Territorial Control and Political Order in Colombia (1978–2004)* (London: Crisis States Research Centre, DESTIN, LSE).

Gutiérrez Sanín, F. and J. Vargas (2017), 'Agrarian elite participation in Colombia's civil war', *Journal of Agrarian Change*, 17:4, 739–748.

Gutiérrez Sanín, F. and E. J. Wood (2014), 'Ideology in civil war: instrumental adoption and beyond', *Journal of Peace Research* 51:2, 213–226.

Habermas, J. (1996), *Between Facts and Norms: Contributions to a Discourse Theory of Law and Democracy* (Cambridge, MA: MIT University Press).

Hall, P. A. and R. C. R. Taylor (1996), 'Political science and the three new institutionalisms', *Political Studies*, 44:5, 936–957.

Hallward, M., J. Masullo and C. Mouly (2017), 'Civil resistance in armed conflict: leveraging nonviolent action to navigate war, oppose violence and confront oppression', *Journal of Peacebuilding and Development* 12:3, 1–9.

Helmke, G. and S. Levitsky (2004), 'Informal institutions and comparative politics: a research agenda', *Perspectives on Politics* 2:4, 725–740.

Human Rights Watch (1997), *Human Rights Watch World Report 1997* (New York: Human Rights Watch).

Human Rights Watch (1998), *Human Rights Watch World Report 1998* (New York: Human Rights Watch).

Idler, A. (2012), 'Arrangements of convenience in Colombia's borderlands: an invisible threat to citizen security?', *St Antony's International Review* 7:2, 93–119.

Idler, A. (2019), *Borderland Battles: Violence, Crime, and Governance at the Edges of Colombia's War* (Oxford: Oxford University Press).

Idler, A. and J. Boesten (2018), 'Bringing citizens back in: uncertainty in Colombia's changing security landscape', paper presented at the *International Studies Association Annual Meeting San Francisco*, March.

Idler, A., C. Mouly and M. Belén Garrido (2018), 'Between shadow citizenship and civil resistance: shifting local orders in a Colombian war-torn community', in L. E. Hancock and C. Mitchell (eds), *Local Peacebuilding and Legitimacy: Interactions between National and Local Levels* (Abingdon: Routledge), pp. 43–62.

Kalyvas, S. N. (2006), *The Logic of Violence in Civil Wars* (Cambridge: Cambridge University Press).

Kaplan, O. (2017), *Resisting War: How Communities Protect Themselves* (Cambridge: Cambridge University Press).
López, C. H. (2010), *Y Refundaron La Patria… De Cómo Mafiosos Y Políticos Reconfiguraron El Estado Colombiano* (Barcelona: Debate).
Luhmann, N. (1988), 'Familiarity, confidence, trust: problems and alternatives', in D. Gambetta (ed.), *Trust: Making and Breaking Cooperative Relations* (Hoboken, NJ: Blackwell Publishers), pp. 94–107.
Mahoney, J. and K. Thelen (2010), 'A theory of gradual institutional change', in J. Mahoney and K. Thelen (eds), *Explaining Institutional Change: Ambiguity, Agency, and Power* (Cambridge: Cambridge University Press), pp. 1–37.
Martínez, Á. and A. Fernando (2010), 'Injerencia política de los grupos armados ilegales', in C. H. López (ed.), *Y Refundaron la Patria: De Cómo Mafiosos y Politicos Reconfiguraron el Estado Colombiano* (Bogotá: Corporación Nuevo Arco Iris), pp. 79–215.
McDermott, J. (2018), *La Nueva Generación de Narcotraficantes Colombianos Post-FARC: 'Los Invisibles'* (Bogota: InsightCrime.org).
McLean, P. (2002), 'Colombia: failed, failing, or just weak?' *Washington Quarterly* 25:3, 123–134.
North, D. C. (1991), 'Institutions', *Journal of Economic Perspectives* 5:1, 97–112.
Restrepo, J., M. Spagat and J. Vargas (2006), 'El conflicto en Colombia: quién hizo qué a quién? Un enfoque cuantitativo', in F. Gutiérrez Sanín et al. (eds), *Nuestra Guerra Sin Nombre: Transformaciones Del Conflicto En Colombia* (Bogotá: Grupo Editorial Norma), pp. 505–540.
Romero, M. (2000), 'Changing identities and contested settings: regional elites and the paramilitaries in Colombia', *International Journal of Politics, Culture and Society* 14:1, 51–69.
Romero, M. (2003), *Paramilitares Y Autodefensas, 1982–2003* (Barcelona: Temas de Hoy).
Saab, B. and A. Taylor (2009), 'Criminality and armed groups: a comparative study of FARC and paramilitary groups in Colombia', *Studies in Conflict & Terrorism* 32:6, 455–475.
Warren, M. (2017), 'A problem-based approach to democratic theory', *American Political Science Review* 111:1, 39–53.
Weinstein, J. M. (2007), *Inside Rebellion: The Politics of Insurgent Violence* (Cambridge: Cambridge University Press).
Wood, E. J. (2015), 'Conflict-related sexual violence and the policy implications of recent research', *International Review of the Red Cross* 96:894, 457–478.

V

Practising recognition: concluding outlook

12

From rebels to violent extremists: evolving conflict trends and implications for the recognition of armed non-state actors

Véronique Dudouet

Introduction

Armed non-state actors (ANSAs) are active in most contemporary violent conflicts. For instance, the Uppsala Conflict Data Programme found that forty-eight countries were affected by an internal violent conflict between state authorities and one or several ANSAs in 2017 (Pettersson and Eck 2018). In some of the most intense ongoing conflicts – from Syria and Iraq to Afghanistan, Somalia and Nigeria – these actors are characterised, especially in media depiction, by their radical religious beliefs rooted in Salafi-based Islamism and the brutality of their tactics. In 2015, the Islamic State (IS), al-Qaeda and their affiliates represented 25 out of 45 ANSAs active in intra-state armed conflicts and accounted for more than half of all deaths caused by organised violence (66,000 out of 118,000) (Melander et al. 2016). Based on these trends, one could argue that the 2010s have seen the emergence of a new phenomenon, often labelled in media and policy circles as the era of 'violent extremism'. However, labels such as 'terrorism' or 'violent extremism' are not only historically contingent but also normatively charged, by enabling certain practices and kinds of behaviour towards ANSAs while precluding others. In this sense, how ANSAs are labelled has important ramifications for whether their claims to recognition can be met. Whether or not 'violent extremists' constitute a novel form of ANSAs remains an open question: do they display a new type of behaviour or is this new label merely a way of recognising (and engaging with) some actors while not recognising or marginalising others?

This chapter adopts a more practitioner-oriented perspective in order to explore the purpose of, dilemmas in, and options for the recognition of ANSAs through soft-power engagement by governments or third-party actors (state or non-state). The arguments developed here build on the author's past research on the political transformation of ANSAs (Dudouet 2009, 2012), the impact of counterterrorism on peace processes (Dudouet 2010, 2011), and the challenges and opportunities for third-party engagement with Salafi-jihadi armed groups in Mali, Syria and Somalia (Göldner-Ebenthal and Dudouet 2019). The chapter also draws on anecdotes and stories collected through participation in various policy meetings as well as training and dialogue support activities conducted by the Berghof Foundation, a conflict resolution non-governmental organisation (NGO) based in Berlin.

The chapter offers a broad perspective on several ANSAs active in various conflicts and world regions. It traces the labels given to ANSAs historically and analyses the practices of engagement related to them. As the term 'recognition' has not so far entered the conceptual world of practitioners in the field of conflict transformation, the chapter evaluates the extent to which it is a useful conceptual addition. In particular, it aims to delimit recognition from engagement, as well as to explore how the two concepts relate to one another. Finally, the conclusion reconsiders critically the novelty of the label 'violent extremism' and provides an outlook on how the concept of recognition could be used in dealing with the actors under consideration.

From rebels to terrorists to violent extremists: the 'new frontiers' for the engagement and recognition of ANSAs

As argued by Hensell and Schlichte in this volume, the politics of recognition is strongly influenced by ANSAs' geo-political environment and the global order of the day. In this section, I draw on recent trends within what they call the (post-Cold War) 'age of humanitarianism and multilateral intervention' (Hensell and Schlichte in this volume, p. 35) and examine the ramifications of the 'global war on terrorism' on the nature of contemporary ANSAs and their recognition claims, and, in turn, on the attitudes and behaviour of state and international agencies towards these actors. I will do so by describing a double semantic shift, from rebels and insurgents to terrorists (shift 1) and into the more recent era of 'violent extremists' (shift 2).

Rebels and insurgents vs terrorists

Ever since the Second World War, many ANSAs have successfully pursued a 'politics of legitimacy' (Geis et al. 2012; Schlichte and Schneckener 2015) by gaining international recognition as valid political interlocutors and rightful representatives of their (claimed) constituency. From the 1980s until the end of the twentieth century, groups such as the Farabundo Martí National Liberation Front (FMLN) in El Salvador, the African National Congress in

South Africa, the Kosovo Liberation Army in Kosovo and the Revolutionary Front for an Independent East Timor in Timor-Leste managed to garner significant international backing, including support from the USA and Western European states. For example, the FMLN was recognised in 1981 by the French and Mexican governments as a legitimate 'representative political force' (Dudouet et al. 2012: 10).[1] Such diplomatic recognition helped these groups to leverage power during political negotiations with their opponents and/or to gain important positions in post-war governance, with their leaders sometimes becoming successful politicians and heads of state.

The factors that contributed to such international backing were manifold. First, ANSAs themselves undertook action to demonstrate their adherence to international codes of conduct (e.g. international humanitarian law, in the following: IHL) in their relations with the civilian population, or to pursue claims of legitimate struggle against an oppressive regime or illegal foreign occupation under international law. They also pursued effective 'rebel diplomacy' strategies by adapting their framing of the conflict and lobbying efforts to evolving global norms. For example, the Zapatista armed movement in Mexico effectively shifted its ideological claims from an orthodox Marxist-Leninist agenda, aiming to take over the state, to a participatory democratic ideal focusing on indigenous rights in order to follow regional trends across Latin America and global trends at the United Nations since the 1990s (Rovira 2015). In Indonesia, the separatist Free Aceh Movement also progressively left aside its Islamist claims to focus on a human rights discourse, prompted by the post-2001 US-led 'global war on terror' dominating the international agenda (Dudouet 2009).

This latter example brings to the fore the importance of the 9/11 attacks in the United States as a critical juncture in the politics of recognition of armed non-state actors. Of course, the label 'terrorism' pre-dates 2001, and many ANSAs were consistently labelled as terrorist organisations by governments long before the so-called 'war on terror', including violent state challengers in Northern Ireland, Turkey, Spain, Sri Lanka, the Palestinian territories, and so on. As will be argued below, the characterisation of these struggles through the terminology of terrorism has had a major impact on prospects for resolution through a negotiated settlement, given the widely held view that 'one cannot negotiate with terrorists'. This argument, as documented by previous studies (Miller 2011; Toros 2008), is often grounded in the belief that dialogue with terrorism-labelled ANSAs would automatically result in the recognition, and hence the legitimation, of their violent means of action and their (contested) political claims.

Yet, if the depiction of various ANSAs as terrorist organisations pre-dates 9/11, the counterterrorism policies introduced after 2001 have added further obstacles to the dialogical settlement of armed conflicts. In particular, the terrorism proscription regimes put in place by the EU, the USA and most UN member states, which have been aimed at isolating and criminalising listed armed groups, have negatively affected ANSAs' interest and ability to transform into peaceful political actors, and directly contributed to the breakdown of several peace processes (Dudouet 2011).[2] For example, the Communist Party of the Philippines (CPP) and its New People's Army were added to the US Foreign Terrorist Organisations list in 2002 during a phase of peace negotiations with the Philippine government. This ill-timed decision struck a severe blow to confidence-building. The CPP withdrew from the peace talks and demanded that the government work towards its removal from the list as a precondition for renewed dialogue. Meanwhile, the government felt encouraged to reactivate a counterinsurgency campaign against the CPP, with US military assistance (Dudouet 2011: 6).

The new frontier: the era of 'violent extremism'

The terminology 'violent extremism' has become increasingly used in media and policy circles in the last decade, especially since the UN Security Council adopted it in 2014.[3] Arguably, the negative connotations associated with the term 'terrorism' have been the main driving force behind the rise of the label 'violent extremism', which is – even though just as vague, politicised and under-defined – considered to be more neutral. In fact, the UN leaves it to its member states to define both 'terrorism' and 'violent extremism', and calls on them to develop their own national countering violent extremism (CVE) programmes aligned to the biggest threat in each state and region. UN statements have consistently evoked the fact that 'the threat of violent extremism is not limited to any one religion, nationality or ethnic group'.[4] However, the term is consistently associated with Salafi-jihadi armed groups such as IS, al-Qaeda, Boko Haram and al-Shabaab. One might hence argue that the introduction of the term 'violent extremism' has helped draw a line between the 'old terrorism' of secular rebels and revolutionaries, and the 'new terrorism' of radical religious (and especially Islamist) armed actors.

There is indeed a broad understanding that Islamist jihadis form part of a new generation of ANSAs, which require new tools and approaches by the international community. For example, according to a report by the UN System Staff College, the transnational Islamist threat – along with other 'hybrid armed groups' such as criminal actors (gangs, drug cartels, pirates, etc.) – 'presents novel analytical and practical challenges for the United Nations, as these groups differ substantially from the traditional ones active in civil conflicts' (Javan and Wieland-Karimi 2015: 7). The Global Extremism Monitor, designed by the Tony Blair Institute, also states that 'extremism based on a perversion of the religion of Islam – the turning of religious belief into a totalitarian political ideology – remains the most potent global security threat'.[5] This international attention to Islamist armed actors is empirically justified; according to a recent study by the International Committee of the Red Cross (ICRC 2018: 14), 40 per cent of states experiencing armed conflict in 2017 were confronting jihadi groups. But how exactly do they differ from 'traditional' ANSAs?

A number of typologies have been proposed by scholars, that either seek to distinguish Islamist jihadi groups from other actors (e.g. Bellamy 2016) or examine the wide spectrum of Islamist ANSAs, based on their particular aspirations, their modes of action, or their relationship to society and territory. For example, typologies often characterise Salafi-jihadi armed groups by their rejection of the Weberian nation-state model (Hegghammer 2014; Maher 2016). This echoes policy assumptions on the perceived exceptionalism of 'violent extremist organisations' (VEOs)[6] in view of their radical, maximalist and non-negotiable goals – such as the IS organisation's aim to establish a Caliphate. These actors are assumed to uniformly reject the Weberian model and accept only God's sovereignty above any man-made laws or states that gain their legitimacy from the people they govern. Hence, their political claims are denied or dismissed as being irrational, in comparison to those of secular armed groups fighting for government overthrow or self-determination. While the general argument in relation to 'conventional' ANSAs is that they commit violence as a means to a political end, and would be ready to de-escalate violence in exchange for political concessions (Dudouet 2009), VEOs are often portrayed as having little interest in political transformation and democratic governance.

In terms of their behavioural features or modus operandi, Islamist groups are most known for their extreme tactics such as mass atrocity crimes and indiscriminate or sectarian violence, which would distinguish them from armed groups that conduct acts of (self-limited) violence against strategic (often non-civilian) targets through guerrilla insurgency or quasi-conventional warfare. Their tactics and strategies are the most common arguments used by policy-makers to justify the primacy of hard-power approaches to counter these groups and to reject any possibility of dialogue, let alone negotiation. In recent research conducted on de-escalation options for Salafi-jihadi armed groups, Göldner-Ebenthal and Dudouet (2019) asked various diplomats about their government's red lines for dialogue engagement. Many cited ANSAs which have 'blood on their hands' or which use 'terrorism as a means rather than as an end' (i.e. violence for the sake of violence) as being 'beyond the pale', that is, ANSAs with which no dialogue could be envisaged under any circumstances (Göldner-Ebenthal and Dudouet 2019: 10).

When it comes to organisational matters around leadership and command-and-control structure, previous research on ANSAs shows that identifying and engaging with leaders who have a high degree of internal legitimacy and authority (including over 'hardliners') might be central to ensuring the successful implementation of a peace settlement (Dudouet 2009). However, VEOs are typically described as decentralised network-based organisations, with fragmented self-governing cells (e.g. ICRC 2018). For instance, al-Qaeda is known for its horizontal and overlapping networks that operate across countries. This feature, as well as the fluidity of group membership, pose a challenge for humanitarian actors or mediators, who may face difficulties in identifying their interlocutors prior to any dialogue engagement (Toros 2008).

Finally, regarding issues around representation, one may argue that it is far easier for governments and international mediation teams to harness public support (both on the ground and at home) for negotiations with ANSAs which mobilise a large social constituency and are considered legitimate representatives of social groups' grievances and interests, than to justify engagement with VEOs committing mass atrocity crimes against civilians in the territories under their control.

However, these various assumptions on VEOs – both on their perceived homogeneity and on their distinctiveness from other ANSAs – do not match the complex reality of contemporary conflicts. When looking at individual cases, one finds many more commonalities between jihadi organisations and the previous generations of nationalists and revolutionaries (Glazzard et al. 2017; Göldner-Ebenthal and Dudouet 2019; Kalyvas 2018). For example, even the most ruthless VEOs are likely to show an interest in developing governance functions to gain social support and legitimacy. Indeed, it is hardly possible for any ANSA to hold territory exclusively through fear and coercion, especially over the long run. One could argue that a group like IS could not have taken over a large city such as Mosul (1.5 million inhabitants), with only two thousand fighters, without some degree of local support and acquiescence (Powell 2015). Indeed, all ANSAs, be they primarily ideologically, ethnically or religiously motivated, are to some degree locally embedded, and they draw on popular support by capitalising on structural grievances such as marginalisation, economic deprivation, social inequalities and the absence of, or mismanagement by, the state.

Violent extremist organisations: no interest in state and/or international recognition?

Further, the lower prospects for negotiated conflict settlements with such actors than with other ANSAs are rooted in the assumption that, just as governments do not want to recognise and thereby legitimise VEOs, neither are VEOs interested in seeking recognition. For instance, Salafi-jihadis such as IS- or al-Qaeda-affiliated groups' rejection of dialogue with all external actors who do not share their worldview can easily lead to the conclusion that there is no solution beyond military confrontation or a hardline counterterrorism approach. Moreover, their apparent lack of interest in gaining international support presents serious obstacles for humanitarian actors or diplomats seeking to convince these groups of the ethical or strategic benefits of reducing violence and abiding by IHL, as the appeal of international recognition cannot be used as an effective incentive to curb human rights violations. Yet, in my view, rather than ruling out prospects for negotiation, these challenges underscore the need to adopt context-specific, tailored approaches to dialogue through credible local interlocutors.

The depiction of all Westerners as 'crusaders' and portrayal of the dominant world order as an enemy image does not necessarily mean that VEOs do not seek international recognition. When Hezbollah leaders take pride in being labelled and listed as a terrorist organisation by the US government (as asserted in private conversations[7]), does it not signal an interest in being recognised as a valid conflict party by their self-declared enemy? Similarly, if IS takes so much care in staging and publicising its fighters' gruesome acts of extreme violence, one might argue that it is actively seeking recognition by its opponents as a powerful agent.

'Engagement without recognition'? Disaggregating types, degrees and aims of engagement

Following this brief overview of the evolution of (Western) state policy and media perceptions of ANSAs' claims to recognition, I will turn to the challenges and opportunities of soft-power dialogue engagement with ANSAs, and the linkages between engagement and recognition. I will summarise the (well-known) arguments for or against engagement, before connecting this debate to the concept of recognition, by reviewing how different forms of engagement relate to types of recognition.

The case for and against engagement

As I argued in a 2010 report synthesising findings from an international policy workshop on mediation with proscribed armed groups (Dudouet 2010), arguments favouring dialogue engagement with ANSAs encompass both pragmatic and moral perspectives. First, with regards to ANSAs in general, it is almost a truism in the field of mediation that an agreement that does not include the main conflict stakeholders is unlikely to hold. Groups representing societal grievances and/or with the power to continue a conflict must be party to its resolution. Otherwise, they may use their power to spoil the agreement and prevent sustainable peace – as illustrated by the case of the Afghan Taliban following their exclusion from the 2001 Bonn agreement. Moreover, peaceful forms of engagement tend to strengthen 'accommodationists' (Toros 2008: 415) and pro-dialogue parties within ANSAs, while their absence tends to strengthen hardliners by removing viable alternatives to violence.

Secondly, at an ethical level, a key argument is that any chance of reducing violence should be seized, for even if dialogue attempts do not result in a settlement, they can address humanitarian concerns and save civilian lives. One might argue that such dividends, in case dialogue succeeds in reducing violence or bringing about peace, are far more important than the possible risk of prolonging conflict if the parties are not serious about dialogue. By contrast, there is consistent empirical evidence pointing to the human costs of hard-power approaches. In Sri Lanka, the Liberation Tigers of Tamil Eelam was defeated militarily after the failure of a negotiated settlement, but the pure use of force led to devastating consequences for civilians – with a credible estimate of 40,000 people killed towards the end of the conflict (United Nations Secretary-General (UNSG) 2011). This does not necessarily mean that dialogue should replace security approaches (military, judiciary, policing) but that dialogue should be one element of the intervention toolbox that needs to be given due consideration, as early as possible – including as a preventive strategy.

The risks, pitfalls and possible side effects of engagement also need to be considered and mitigated. An argument often made by those cautioning against dialogue with ANSAs is that talking is rarely cost-free (Dudouet 2010: 4). No matter how carefully engagement is framed, some parties are likely to perceive it as conferring some legitimacy on the parties engaged. Engagement with armed or extremist actors might also risk marginalising moderates and non-violent resistance groups, which have opted for peaceful means. Moreover, although humanitarian engagement, including ceasefires, might save lives in the short term, it could contribute to extending the conflict if parties use it to buy time or strengthen themselves militarily. In this regard, humanitarian action could reduce the pressure to resolve a conflict. Opening talks with armed groups might also cause them to split or proliferate, as was seen in Darfur, Mali and Myanmar. More fundamentally, engagement that seems to reward violence infringes ethical imperatives. Hence, any third-party actor contemplating opening dialogue channels with an ANSA should seek to maximise the benefit of engagement while minimising its potential costs. Having reviewed why engagement is desirable from a pragmatic and ethical standpoint, I now turn to the modalities of engagement and their implications for recognition theory.

Types of engagement and recognition

The literature on recognition, and contributions throughout this volume, have shown that far from representing a binary category, recognition comes in many shades and may be more accurately described as a continuum, along a spectrum ranging from thin to thick (Biene and Daase 2015), informal to formal or unofficial to official, indirect to direct (Clément et al. in this volume), and tactical to strategic ('mixed motive' game, Miller 2011) forms of recognition. The same logic applies to engagement with ANSAs, and in this section three types of engagement will be described, according to the degree of (state/international) recognition they confer on ANSAs.

'Engagement without recognition'

This term was coined by the Council of the European Union in the context of the South Caucasus to justify its relations with *de facto* authorities in Abkhazia and South Ossetia without having to question the territorial integrity of Georgia. This is effectively described as a two-pillar policy for dealing with secessionist regions by 'being firm on principle and pragmatic in practice': on the one hand, it reaffirms the 'non-recognition' of their independence to avoid being seen as granting them legitimacy and, on the other, it practices 'engagement' with their self-proclaimed authorities in order to encourage dialogue and reconciliation efforts in the region (Ashik 2017). This logic may be applied to various ANSAs, regardless of their territorial, revolutionary or religious aspirations, even though some governments demand from their adversaries that they recognise their authority and legitimacy as a precondition for engaging in dialogue with them – as documented by Aggestam (2015) in the Israeli–Palestinian case.

In practice, there are many forms and purposes of engagement with ANSAs – including so-called VEOs – which do not necessarily imply a dialogue, and which are not conditioned by the recognition of their interlocutor as a legitimate party to the conflict. For example, talking to members or 'proxies' of ANSAs may help develop a greater understanding of their motives and interests and, in turn, might socialise them to the importance and intricacies of dialogue and negotiations. Engagement might also offer opportunities to build trust with armed groups, and to 'encourage the group to reflect on entrenched positions and/or prevent its immersion in a logic that is a consequence of its isolation and pursuit of armed struggle' (Whitfield 2010: 10). Such trust may also allow mediators or other external third parties to build an armed group's capacity to engage in political dialogue in the future, by pulling it into the logic of negotiations, or, in other words, by enhancing its 'negotiability' (Lustenberger 2012).

Tactical recognition through humanitarian engagement

Informal engagement with ANSAs also contributes to short-term humanitarian goals such as violence reduction, prisoner exchange or gaining access for the delivery of aid or medical assistance to needy populations under their control. Indeed, humanitarian organisations such as UN agencies, the ICRC and international NGOs such as Doctors without Borders or Geneva Call are often at the front line of engagement with ANSAs. In the case of Salafi-jihadi armed groups, humanitarian engagement is usually conducted through trusted local intermediaries, such as religious clerics, community members, former militants who retain some degree of trust by the group, or locally embedded humanitarian organisations. Their action is often motivated by a logic of 'socialisation' of ANSAs to incentivise them to abide by IHL standards (Hofmann and Schneckener 2011).

In a recent research report, the ICRC identified the importance of informal socialisation in driving armed groups to restrain their behaviour, by depicting the influence of local social networks on the patterns of violence of decentralised armed non-state actors (ICRC 2018). In certain cases, humanitarian engagement might even contribute to localised informal ceasefire deals with local commanders, with or without leadership endorsement. For instance, a study on local truces in the Syrian civil war highlights the role of local aid workers in facilitating informal de-escalation mechanisms with Salafi-jihadi armed groups (Hall et al. 2019). While this form of engagement suggests a tactical or tacit recognition of ANSAs as valid and credible interlocutors who are able to abide by their commitments, it does not imply the legitimation of their ideology and political claims.

Strategic recognition through formal negotiations

As demonstrated by the scholarship on conflict resolution and recognition (Clément et al. in this volume) and the empirical contributions in this volume, mutual recognition between the disputants is a crucial factor for successful political negotiations to come about. It can, however, take several years of tactical, informal and sometimes clandestine engagement before the parties (especially the government) become ready to formally and publicly move to this stage. The Norwegian facilitators in the Havana peace process (private conversation[8]) argue that the secret pre-negotiation phase was extremely important for the success of the peace process between the Colombian government and the Revolutionary Armed Forces of Colombia (FARC). It provides both parties with sufficient time to build trust and test each other's commitment to the process.

While negotiated agreements are the modus operandi for peaceful conflict transformation with most ANSAs, there are very few instances of formal negotiations involving so-called VEOs such as Salafi-jihadi armed groups. Instead, the focus is placed on preventive action by engaging individuals 'at risk' before they radicalise into violent extremist behaviour,[9] or on rehabilitating disengaged individuals (Ashour 2009; Gunaratna 2017). In particular, government-led or international CVE initiatives seek to incentivise the defection and breakaway of disenchanted members from ANSAs, by luring them through attractive rehabilitation programmes. This approach follows a logic of engaging with individuals seen as moderates in order to isolate and weaken the radicals (Zartman and Alfredson 2010). However, if one looks at past examples of jihadi groups which moved away from violence and demobilised, cohesion and discipline were key factors in their collective shift towards demobilisation. For example, the group al-Jama'a al-Islamiyyah in Egypt offers one of the clearest instances of intentional violence de-escalation by a Salafi armed group. The organisation not only stopped its attacks and explicitly renounced violence, but it revised its ideology and completely re-invented itself, transforming into a political party after the fall of Mubarak (Ashour 2015). Accordingly, looking forward we need to consider not only the opportunities for negotiated settlements but also the transformation implied for the groups in order to enhance stabilisation and sustainable peace (Göldner-Ebenthal and Dudouet 2019: 57). The realistic prospects for a political agreement between the Taliban and Afghan government could provide a breakthrough for other conflicts involving Islamist ANSAs by breaking the taboo of recognition around 'violent extremists'.

Labelling as pathway or obstacle to the (de)legitimisation of engagement

Among the many challenges precluding mutual engagement with most contemporary ANSAs, the practices of labelling and proscription have serious ramifications for the politics of recognition. As the brief overview of the historical evolution of naming ANSAs demonstrates, the way we name actors matters and impacts the ways in which we can engage them. Indeed, the politics of labelling plays a crucial role in legitimising or delegitimising an ANSA, as well as in the decision to engage or isolate them. As labels evolve over time, so do 'red lines' once drawn for restricting options for dealing with ANSAs. In this section, I will use examples from several armed conflicts in order to trace practices of labelling and un-labelling, as well as their expected and actual consequences. Indeed, as many examples show, labelling practices sometimes entail unintentional and unexpected results; they may escape the full control of those who introduce them and even result in paradoxical situations.

Two contemporary cases illustrate how the politics of labelling is used to justify strategic or tactical choices to engage with or to isolate ANSAs. They also show how the 'red lines' of (non-)recognition evolve constantly, according to the political preferences of the day. In Mali, the UN Stabilisation Mission classifies various ANSAs contesting state authority – be they Tuareg-led separatist movements or Islamist jihadi groups – into so-called 'compliant' vs 'terrorist' armed groups. The label aims to distinguish between ANSAs which were invited to participate in the inter-Malian negotiations that led to the 2014 Algiers peace accord and those which were excluded, or which excluded themselves, from the talks. The latter category is also often subdivided between home-grown 'terrorists' and international jihadists. The signing of the Algiers accord led to the introduction of new nuances such as 'compliant non-signatory armed groups' when an ANSA splintered into various factions and new entities competed over influence and resources in post-agreement processes. All armed groups are also understood to have overlapping allegiances and various connections with organised crime, with 'criminal armed groups' forming yet another category of Malian ANSAs. However, given the fluidity in ANSAs' leadership, with high-ranking members often moving from one group to another based on opportunity, analysts stress the blurring of lines between these multiple labels (Boutellis 2015: 65).

In Syria as well, members of the international coalition against IS and other Salafi-jihadi ANSAs have tried to come up with a consensual list of terrorist organisations, but failed to do so, due to their diverging strategic interests and ideological biases.[10] The 2016 ceasefire at the beginning of the Geneva Peace Talks was considered by many diplomats as a marker helping to draw the line between 'legitimate actors' abiding by its terms and 'legitimate targets' with whom no dialogue would be possible.[11] There as well, the red line for engagement keeps evolving according to the realignment of tactical alliances. For instance, the former al-Qaeda affiliate Jabhat al-Nusra became labelled 'moderate extremists' in US counterterrorism circles and media statements when it became seen as a possible ally in the fight against IS (Watts 2015).

If the terrorist or VEO label aims to signal one's refusal to recognise an ANSA as a legitimate dialogue interlocutor, how do diplomats reverse their stance when their strategic interests and/or a new recognition regime favour engagement? First, it is worth mentioning that some experts do not find terrorist labelling and engagement as being antithetical. As highlighted by a leading conflict resolution scholar, 'it is very common for governments to say they "will not talk to terrorists", but to then establish secret channels of communication. This is normal politics, and there is no other way, especially given the public stance that needs to be taken towards groups that engage in barbarous practices. … All governments establish such channels, even where they have simultaneous counter-terrorism operations.'[12] Others have documented the practice of 'un-labelling' ANSAs to legitimate their decision to engage in peace talks in the eyes of the public. This was done successfully in Northern Ireland, where 'British officials stopped using the term "terrorist" when [IRA] republicans came to be seen as political actors that one could engage with on terms other than through legal or violent counterterrorism' (Toros 2012: 97).

On the other hand, labels can sometimes become 'sticky'. Indeed, the 'demonisation of the enemy' which accompanies terrorism and counterterrorism approaches has a severe consequence for the prospect of conflict resolution, as it delegitimises dialogue. Such a paradigm might be challenging to reverse as villains need to be 'devillainised' for talking to begin. In a previous publication (Haspeslagh and Dudouet 2015), a colleague and I examined the implications of terrorist labelling for the resolution of the conflicts with ANSAs in Colombia and the Basque Country/Spain – respectively the FARC and Euskadi Ta Askatasuna (Basque Country and Freedom; ETA). In both contexts, semantic shifts took place during (pre-)negotiation phases, with government officials signalling their readiness to engage in peace talks by softening their language vis-à-vis their armed opponents. In Colombia, President Santos was seen to engage in a 'linguistic ceasefire' during the Havana talks, while in Spain, Prime Minister Aznar addressed separatist leaders as the 'Basque National Liberation Movement' to signal his interest in dialogue in 1999, while Batasuna's leader Otegi became a 'man of peace' in the words of his successor Zapatero (Aiartza and Zabalo 2010).

However, the persistent 'either with us or against us' mentality imparted upon public opinion during these conflicts led to increased polarisation over the issue of negotiations. This posed an acute challenge during peace talks, since the vilifying label used to depict the groups made it hard for governments to convince the public that they could become legitimate interlocutors. Indeed, the level of social polarisation fed by state media can become so acute that it proves challenging to get the public to follow this discursive reversal and the paradigm shift that it underscores. In Spain, the terrorism label imposed on all social and political entities endorsing a Basque nationalist agenda deeply influenced the minds of citizens and strengthened the hardliner position of terrorist victims' associations. Such dynamics have prevented the political establishment from engaging in formal negotiations with ETA even when they were prepared to do so, as they feared that their constituency might respond negatively – especially in (pre-)electoral periods. Interestingly, since my co-author and I published this analysis in 2015, both ANSAs have been formally dismantled – through a peace accord in Colombia and a unilateral demobilisation process in the Basque Country. However, the acute social polarisation prompted by political labelling largely contributed to the 'no' vote in the peace referendum in Colombia and negatively impacts efforts to start a process of reconciliation in both countries (see also Boesten and Idler in this volume).

Terrorism and VEO labels may also cause 'collateral damage' to other actors, by criminalising any attempt to engage ANSAs in dialogue by local or international peacebuilding practitioners. In particular, local civil society activists and 'bridge-builders' are under constant threat of arrest for engaging in illegal activities by meeting with proscribed or publicly shunned ANSAs. This leads to particular difficulties in the pre-negotiation phase where local groups and individuals – who often build their engagement on pre-existing links with ANSA members such as kinship or shared religion/ideology – play an essential role in coaxing armed groups to embrace a non-violent solution to the conflict (Haspeslagh and Yousuf 2015). Physically accessing actors proscribed as terrorist entities or even their banned social and political allies – a necessary precondition for conflict resolution practitioners – has become increasingly difficult and dangerous. Recent research on Mali found that most local 'bridge-builders' such as tribal, traditional or religious leaders have been targeted by counterterrorism operations, mainly by the French military, signalling that they were not identified as impartial third parties but as accomplices of VEOs. This has severely reduced the number of individuals who may still be able to facilitate engagement with such groups (Göldner-Ebenthal and Dudouet 2019). Elsewhere, religious clerics, such as members of the Afghan Ulema Council, have been killed by ANSAs because of their participation in, or perceived endorsement of, foreign-led CVE programmes. These various examples show that local peacebuilders are becoming increasingly victimised by all sides in polarised conflict constellations, as a result of the securitisation of outreach programmes and the terrorist/violent extremist label being used expansively.

Finally, it is worth noting that the timing of terrorist proscription may be at odds with the dynamics and necessities of peace processes, resulting in a contradictory and counterproductive approach to the politics of recognition. The example of the CPP cited earlier is far from being an exception; many other cases of ill-timed bans and proscriptions against alleged terrorist organisations have had negative repercussions on the peaceful resolution of armed conflicts. In Turkey, the Kurdish organisation Partiya Karkeren Kurdistan (Kurdistan Workers Party; PKK) was placed on the EU terrorist list in May 2002, despite the fact that it had silenced its guns for several years and that its leaders had recently announced their decision to dissolve and reorganise their work 'using entirely peaceful and democratic methods' (Dudouet 2011: 8; see also Sienknecht in this volume). This surprising move by the EU, which signalled its member states' refusal to recognise its peaceful overture, may have fuelled the PKK's eventual return to violence.[13] In the Palestinian Territories, international opposition to the Hamas movement (especially from Europe and North America) went so far as rejecting the electoral results that recognised its political legitimacy in 2006, placing both its political and military branches on the EU terrorist list. Some argue that the perceived unfairness of these sanctions has also led to its re-radicalisation and a weakening of moderate forces within the movement (Hovdenak 2009).

Conclusion

Several conclusions can be drawn for peace and conflict researchers but also and especially for peace practitioners. First, with regards to the question raised in the introductory chapter, has the past decade given rise to new types of ANSA, which both resemble each other and are distinct from secular (nationalist/ethnic/revolutionary) armed groups? The analysis of the behavioural, organisational and ideological features of so-called 'violent extremist organisations' shows that they have much more in common with all other ANSAs than is often assumed or portrayed in media and policy discourses. Salafi-jihadi armed groups – such as al-Qaeda affiliates in Syria, Mali and Somalia – also exhibit significant *differences* between them, including when it comes to the claims and practices of recognition. Government and international forces are prone to recognising their value as dialogue interlocutors if and when it serves their own strategic interests, or to vilify them as terrorists 'beyond the pale' when the tide turns in their disfavour. In Mali, jihadist leader Iyad ag Ghali is treated as a 'son of the Nation' who deserves engagement by Malian government officials but as a pariah with whom no dialogue will ever be possible by their French military allies (see also Toros and Sugal in this volume). VEOs have diverging interests in external engagement – from those adamantly refusing to deal with non-Salafi apostates, to groups such as Ahrar al-Sham in Syria or the Taliban in Afghanistan, which opened political representation offices (in Istanbul and Doha respectively) to formalise their engagement with Western diplomats.

Secondly, I argued that the framing of ANSAs in contemporary conflicts as terrorists or VEOs has deeply affected not only the character of those conflicts but also their possible resolution. The vilification by governments of their armed challengers through 'sticky' terrorist or VEO labels has shaped domestic public opinion for years to come, stigmatising whole communities and making conflict resolution approaches unpopular and risky. In essence, the dynamics of (counter)terrorism distort the classical conflict resolution paradigm of inter-party negotiations between adversaries bound by a mutually hurting stalemate and the acknowledgement of each other's relative power parity. The terrorism framing accentuates the acute asymmetry between an internationally recognised state and its non-recognised challenger (Haspeslagh and Dudouet 2015).

Finally, examining contemporary conflict trends through the lens of recognition theory also brings to light a number of lessons learnt for conflict resolution practitioners. A recognition frame helps to spell out the implications of various dialogue approaches (engagement without recognition, tactical recognition through humanitarian engagement, strategic recognition through peace talks). It also calls attention to the need for fine-grained analysis of ANSAs in order to better understand the contours of their own recognition claims and practices, as well as their sources of social legitimacy, as potential entry points for humanitarian or political engagement or as sources of leverage for incentivising behavioural de-escalation. Given the variety of ANSAs, including those rooted in a radical interpretation of Islam, they should be analysed in all their (military, social, charitable, religious and political) dimensions. For example, practitioners seeking to prevent or mitigate violent extremism should seek to identify VEOs' intra-group, societal and transnational legitimacy claims, by asking questions such as: what drove their radicalisation? Did they intensify the use of violence against civilians as a core part of their ideology, or because of their isolation, competition with other groups (outbidding), internal splits or as a result of state repression? Do they attempt to justify these tactics by invoking religious texts or other forms of cultural legitimation? Do they have any moral barriers associated with their particular ideology and worldview? Do they perceive all Western diplomats and/or international NGOs indiscriminately as their enemies? Depending on the answers, practitioners may also find suitable and trusted entry points for engagement through, for example, religious clerics, local commanders or even business leaders to induce these groups to disengage from indiscriminate violence against civilians.

Given the potential pitfalls of engagement mentioned earlier, including the risk of legitimising human rights violators, it is also crucially important for diplomats and humanitarian actors considering soft-power engagement with VEOs to emphasise very clearly and transparently that their primary goal is to reduce violence and suffering; and to start with very discreet encounters, hoping that the process will eventually result in acceptance by domestic and local constituencies for reducing human rights violations and paving the way towards peaceful conflict transformation.

Notes

1 Ironically, the FMLN was later on retroactively added to databases of terrorist organisations, such as the 'global terrorism' database set up by the US Department for Homeland Security at Maryland University, or the RAND Corporation's statistical study 'How terrorist groups end' (Jones and Libicki 2008).

2 Labelling may also lead to the labelled party not wanting to be recognised (any longer) under the current order (see Clément 2014; and Kaden and Günther in this volume).

3 'Violent extremism' became part of the official UN counterterrorism vocabulary after UNSCR 2170 (2014), which established the contours of the UN response to the phenomenon of foreign terrorist fighters volunteering to join the Islamic State of Iraq and the Levant (ISIL) in Syria and Iraq.

4 Speech by Under-Secretary-General Jeffrey Feltman on 8 April 2016, Geneva Conference on Preventing Violent Extremism, available online at: www.un.org/undpa/en/speeches-statements/07042016/Preventing-Violent-Extremism (last retrieved 20 February 2020).

5 See *Global Extremism Monitor: Violent Islamist Extremism in 2017*, available online: http://institute.global/sites/default/files/inline-files/Global%20Extremism%20Monitor%202017.pdf; last retrieved 20 February 2020).

6 This term and its acronym have become commonly used among US defence, intelligence and law enforcement officials since 2011 (see Liebl 2019).

7 Phone conversation with Hezbollah representative, February 2006.

8 Private conversation, Oslo, June 2018.

9 For example, the 2015 UN secretary-general's action plan on preventing violent extremism recognises the value of engaging 'potential terrorists' (i.e. vulnerable individuals or groups) through dialogue, mediation and arbitration to prevent or counter violence (UNSG 2015).

10 As stated, for instance, by the Russian International Affairs Council, 'many countries, primarily Russia, have time and again emphasised the need to form a single list of terrorist groups. Since different actors have different views of the current situation, they have failed to arrive at a consensus' (Egorov et al. 2016).

11 Interviews with UN Syria office staff, Geneva, November 2018.

12 Interview with I. William Zartman, Washington DC, June 2018.

13 The listing of the PKK as a terrorist organisation has been contested by several judicial bodies. In November 2018, the Court of Justice of the European Union (CJEU 2018) stated that the continued listing of the PKK was unlawful – a judgment based on the insufficiency of the proof provided concerning the organisation's terrorist character. In January 2020, the Belgian Court of Cassation also ruled that the conflict involving the PKK in Turkey is an 'internal armed conflict' and, as such, the group cannot be considered a terrorist organisation (Brussels Times 2020).

References

Aggestam, K. (2015), 'Peace mediation and the minefield of international recognition games', *International Negotiation* 20:3, 494–514.

Aiartza, U. and J. Zabalo (2010), *The Basque Country: The Long Walk to a Democratic Scenario* (Berlin: Berghof Foundation).

Ashik, K. C. (2017), 'EU's policy of non-recognition and engagement in Georgia's secessionist conflicts', *Tensions: Online Magazine on Post-Soviet Affairs*, available online: http://postsoviet.eu/2017/05/15/eus-policy-of-non-recognition-and-engagement-in-georgias-secessionist-conflicts/ (15 May); last retrieved 20 February 2020.

Ashour, O. (2009), *The De-radicalization of Jihadists: Transforming Armed Islamist Movements* (New York, NY: Routledge).

Ashour, O. (2015), 'Egypt's revolution and the transformation of armed Islamist movements towards unarmed activism', in V. Dudouet (ed.), *Civil Resistance and Conflict Transformation: Transitions from Armed to Nonviolent Struggle* (London: Routledge), pp. 173–189.

Bellamy, A. J. (2016), 'Non-state armed groups and the responsibility to protect', discussion paper for the seminar *Fulfilling the Responsibility to Protect: The Threat of Non-state Armed Groups and Their Increased Role in Perpetrating Atrocity Crimes*, Brussels, 22 March.

Biene, J. and C. Daase (2015), 'Gradual recognition: curbing non-state violence in asymmetric conflicts', in C. Daase, A. Geis, C. Fehl and G. Kolliarakis (eds), *Recognition in International Relations: Rethinking a Political Concept in a Global Context* (Houndmills: Palgrave Macmillan), pp. 220–236.

Boutellis, A. (2015), 'Armed groups in Mali and implications for the UN Stabilization Mission', in UN System Staff College (ed.), *Understanding a New Generation of Non-state Armed Groups* (Turin: UN System Staff College), pp. 59–72.

Brussels Times (2020), 'Belgian court decision on PKK is "unacceptable" says Turkey', available online: www.brusselstimes.com/all-news/belgium-all-news/94135/belgian-court-decision-on-pkk-is-unacceptable-says-turkey-kurdish-workers-party-terrorist-organisation-geens-goffin (8 February); last retrieved 20 February 2020.

CJEU (2018), 'Judgment of the General Court (Third Chamber, Extended Composition) in Case T-316/14', available online: http://curia.europa.eu/juris/document/document.jsf?docid=207801&text=&dir=&doclang=EN&part=1&occ=first&mode=lst&pageIndex=0&cid=7235776 (15.11.2018); last retrieved 20 February 2020.

Clément, M. (2014), 'Al-Muhajiroun in the United Kingdom: the role of international non-recognition in heightened radicalization dynamics', *Global Discourse*, 4:4, 428–443.

Dudouet, V. (2009), *From War to Politics: Resistance/Liberation Movements in Transition* (Berlin: Berghof Foundation).

Dudouet, V. (2010), *Mediating Peace with Proscribed Armed Groups* (Washington, DC: United States Institute of Peace).

Dudouet, V. (2011), *Anti-terrorism Legislation: Impediments to Conflict Transformation* (Berlin: Berghof Foundation).

Dudouet, V. (2012), 'Intra-party dynamics and the political transformation of non-state armed groups', *International Journal of Conflict and Violence* 6:1, 96–108.

Dudouet, V., H.-J. Giessmann and K. Planta (2012), *From Combatants to Peacebuilders: A Case for Inclusive, Participatory and Holistic Security Transitions*, policy report (Berlin: Berghof Foundation).

Egorov, O., D. Narmania and R. Mamedov (2016), 'Anti-government extremist organizations in Syria: a brief overview of the main groups and their leaders', *Russian International Affairs Council Reader*, available online: https://russiancouncil.ru/en/syria-extremism; last retrieved 20 February 2020.

Geis, A., F. Nullmeier and C. Daase (eds) (2012), *Aufstieg der Legitimitätspolitik: Rechtfertigung und Kritik politisch-ökonomischer Ordnungen* (Baden-Baden: Nomos).
Glazzard, A., S. Jesperson, T. Maguire and E. Winterbotham (2017), 'Islamist violent extremism: a new form of conflict or business as usual?', *Stability: International Journal of Security and Development* 6:1, 1–19.
Göldner-Ebenthal, K. and V. Dudouet (2019), *Dialogue with SalafiJihadi Armed Groups: Challenges and Opportunities for Conflict De-escalation* (Berlin: Berghof Foundation).
Gunaratna, R. (2017), 'The changing threat landscape: countering terrorism in Singapore', in S. N. Romaniuk, F. Grice, D. Irrera and S. Webb (eds), *The Palgrave Handbook of Global Counterterrorism Policy* (London: Palgrave Macmillan), pp. 749–770.
Hall, N., B. Smith and T. McGee (2019), 'Local cross-line coordination in Syria', *Peaceworks* 152, 1–36.
Haspeslagh, S. and V. Dudouet (2015), 'Conflict resolution practice in conflicts marked by terrorist violence: a scholar-practitioner perspective', in I. Tellidis and H. Toros (eds), *Researching Terrorism, Peace and Conflict Studies: Interaction, Synthesis, and Opposition* (London and New York, NY: Routledge), pp. 103–123.
Haspeslagh, S. and Z. Yousuf (eds) (2015), 'Local engagement with armed groups: in the midst of violence', *Accord Insight: An International Review of Peace Initiatives* 2 1–40.
Hegghammer, T. (2014), 'Jihadi-Salafis or revolutionaries?', in R. Meijer (ed.), *Global Salafism: Islam's New Religious Movement* (Oxford: Oxford University Press), pp. 244–266.
Hofmann, C. and U. Schneckener (2011), 'Engaging non-state armed actors in state- and peace-building: options and strategies', *International Review of the Red Cross* 93:883, 603–621.
Hovdenak, A. (2009), 'Hamas in transition: the failure of sanctions', *Democratization*, 16:1, 59–80.
ICRC (2018), *The Roots of Restraint in War* (Geneva: International Committee of the Red Cross).
Javan, J. and A. Wieland-Karimi (2015), 'Foreword', in UN System Staff College (ed.), *Understanding a New Generation of Non-state Armed Groups* (Turin: UN System Staff College), pp. 5–8.
Jones, S. and M. Libicki (2008), *How Terrorist Groups End: Lessons for Countering al Qa'ida* (Washington, DC: RAND Corporation).
Kalyvas, S. (2018), 'Jihadi rebels in civil war', *Daedalus* 147:1, 36–47.
Liebl, V. (2019), 'Violent Extremist Organizations (VEOs): the strategic importance of defining the enemy', *Strategic Multilayer Assessment*, 11 December, 1–17.
Lustenberger, P. (2012), *A Time to Fight, and a Time to Talk? Negotiability of Armed Groups* (Bern: swisspeace).
Maher, S. (2016), *Salafi-Jihadism: The History of an Idea* (Oxford: Oxford University Press).
Melander, E., T. Pettersson and L. Themnér (2016), 'Organized violence, 1989–2015', *Journal of Peace Research* 53:5, 727–742.
Miller, C. (2011), 'Is it possible and preferable to negotiate with terrorists?', *Defence Studies* 11:1, 145–185.
Pettersson, T. and K. Eck (2018), 'Organized violence, 1989–2017', *Journal of Peace Research* 55:4, 535–547.

Powell, J. (2015), 'Negotiating with ISIS', *The Atlantic*, available online: www.theatlantic.com/international/archive/2015/12/negotiate-with-isis/419157/ (7 December); last retrieved 20 February 2020.
Rovira, G. (2015), 'From armed struggle to interaction with civil society: Chiapas' Zapatista National Liberation Army', in V. Dudouet (ed.), *Civil Resistance and Conflict Transformation: Transitions from Armed to Nonviolent Struggle* (London: Routledge), pp. 126–153.
Schlichte, K. and U. Schneckener (2015), 'Armed groups and the politics of legitimacy', *Civil Wars* 17:4, 409–424.
Toros, H. (2008), '"We don't negotiate with terrorists!": legitimacy and complexity in terrorist conflicts', *Security Dialogue* 39:4, 407–426.
Toros, H. (2012), *Terrorism, Talking and Transformation: A Critical Approach* (Abingdon: Routledge).
UNSG (2011), *Report of the Secretary-General's Panel of Experts on Accountability in Sri Lanka*, available online: www.securitycouncilreport.org/atf/cf/%7B65BFCF9B-6D27–4E9C-8CD3-CF6E4FF96FF9%7D/POC%20Rep%20on%20Account%20in%20Sri%20Lanka.pdf (31 March); last retrieved 20 February 2020.
UNSG (2015), *Plan of Action to Prevent Violent Extremism*, available online: www.un.org/en/ga/search/view_doc.asp?symbol=A/70/674 (24 December); last retrieved 20 February 2020.
Watts, C. (2015), 'Should the United States negotiate with terrorists?', *Brookings Institute*, available online: www.brookings.edu/blogs/markaz/posts/2015/08/17-us-negotiate-with-terrorists-nusra (17 August); last retrieved 20 February 2020.
Whitfield, T. (2010), 'Engaging with armed groups: dilemmas and options for mediators', *Mediation Practice Series of the Center for Humanitarian Dialogue* 2, 1–39.
Zartman, W. I. and T. Alfredson (2010), 'Negotiating with terrorists and the tactical question', in R. Reuveny and W. R. Thompson (eds), *Coping with Terrorism: Origins, Escalation, Counterstrategies, and Responses* (Albania, NY: State University of New York Press), pp. 247–283.

13

Recognition of armed non-state actors: what we have learned and what lies ahead

*Harold Trinkunas**

Introduction

As the introductory chapter of this volume highlights, in February 2020 the US government signed a deal with the Taliban, an insurgent movement that the US and its allies had been fighting in Afghanistan for eighteen years. Particularly noteworthy in this episode are President Trump's comments on reducing US efforts to combat terrorism in Afghanistan, namely that it was 'time for someone else to do that work and it will be the Taliban and it could be the surrounding countries. … I really believe the Taliban wants to do something to show we're not all wasting our time' (BBC News 2020).

The singular declaration of a US president of the transformation of the Taliban from recognition as a terrorist organisation to a potential counter-insurgent highlights the powerful effect that acts of recognition, mis-recognition and non-recognition of armed non-state actors (ANSAs) can have in the course of civil conflict. This is only one speech by a US leader in a long-lasting conflict, and it may not in the long run have an impact, but it was an unusually visible marker of the underlying process that had to occur for the United States and the Taliban to reach a deal: that is, the United States had to change the way in which it labelled and recognised the Taliban in public, and the Taliban had to change the way in which it framed and recognised the United States to be able to negotiate an agreement. Moreover, to reach this deal the United States had to acquiesce to the Taliban's non-recognition of the Afghan government in Kabul, something that entity vigorously opposed.

These acts by the US president, Taliban leaders and the government in Kabul are just some examples of the important dynamic of civil conflict studied in this volume: what role do recognition, mis-recognition and non-recognition of ANSAs play in both civil conflict and international security? What explains the importance of recognition for both precipitating and resolving civil conflict? How can recognition be used to negotiate settlements and reach peace? Conversely, how can non-recognition create grievances among ANSAs and how do states use mis-recognition to apply labels to ANSAs that justify extreme measures? Does the timing of recognition help or hinder the cause of peace?

It is a truism to note that in the twenty-first century, the majority of political violence takes place in a setting of civil conflict and is perpetrated by or against ANSAs. This is highly consequential for a range of important institutions and processes that affect civilians, ranging from regime stability, to economic development, to exposure to violence, to internal displacement and international refugee flows. Moreover, as the post-Cold War unipolar moment fades and the liberal international order is increasingly under attack, great powers are now often competing, sometimes head to head, in civil wars ranging from Syria to Libya to South Sudan.

From a social science perspective, the role of recognition is little studied compared with other aspects of civil conflict (Clément et al. in this volume). The literature on the origins of, and solutions to, civil conflict is vast, and it has rarely examined recognition as a central dynamic, but rather as a tactical or political process, peripheral in its contribution to peacemaking. This volume provides an important argument for why we should reconsider the importance of recognition for civil conflict processes by focusing on the social-psychological reasons why recognition is important for armed non-state actors, and how mis-recognition and lack of recognition of ANSAs by state and international actors are an important source of grievance and conflict. While considerable work has been done on recognition and identity as an important aspect of individual psychology, the authors in this volume apply these theories to good effect to help us understand group dynamics among ANSAs. Moreover, the cases in this volume underscore that recognition is about more than gaining legitimacy as an ANSA; it is about identity and who defines it, and how those labels can create positive and negative boundaries for behaviour by both ANSAs and those with whom they are in conflict. Appropriate recognition can provide positive group self-esteem and a path to social reconciliation, while mis-recognition and non-recognition can fuel grievance and can be used by others to take extreme measures against ANSAs, particularly in the post-9/11 world where the label of 'terrorist' is used by states to justify almost any kind of action against targets (Clément et al. in this volume).

The bottom line is that this volume makes the case for why recognition matters for explaining ANSA and state behaviour during civil conflict and how a serious consideration of the process of recognition may suggest ways to reduce or end civil conflicts. Across a range of regions and ANSA types, the authors in this book demonstrate that recognition is highly relevant both psychologically and politically in civil conflicts. This book addresses an undertheorised process that, as the chapters in this volume show, makes an important contribution to peacemaking.

In the rest of this chapter, I will discuss some of the merits and contributions of this volume for the literature on civil conflict, as well as draw out commonalities among the cases considered and highlight some important differences. I will then suggest some areas for further research, as well as highlight some recommendations for policy-makers.

Contributions to understanding the role of recognition in civil conflict

One of the most important contributions of this book is to explore the links between recognition, grievance and grievance resolution. Cognitive psychology suggests that individuals require recognition from others for purposes of self-esteem and identity-building and maintenance. Recognition is thus a positive act, and, by contrast, non-recognition or mis-recognition is an affront to dignity, a wound to esteem and a cause for grievance (Clément et al. in this volume). This volume explores in depth the links between recognition, group identity and group esteem, which are important since individual identity and self-esteem often are connected to group identity.

The editors and authors of this volume argue that acts of recognition of armed non-state actors can have a similar effect of introducing positive dynamics into conflicts, opening space for negotiations. 'Thin' recognition is recognising an adversary as a legitimate interlocutor, someone with whom it is appropriate to negotiate or engage. 'Thick' recognition is the recognition of an adversary as a legitimate part of a society, someone whose interests should be taken into account during a process of reconciliation and peacemaking. By contrast, mis-recognition, such as labelling an armed non-state actor a 'terrorist' in the post-9/11 period, can not only psychologically wound ANSA members and contribute to group grievances, but can also place the target beyond the pale of negotiation, not only for states but for publics in general (Clément et al. in this volume).

It is clear, as many of the authors note, that there is a difference between recognition and legitimacy. Legitimacy is the acceptance of a particular set of rules, institutions or regimes as a correct and right way of governing under certain circumstances. Armed non-state actors can accrue legitimacy, as Pfeifer suggests about Hezbollah, and Boesten and Idler about the FARC, even as they are not recognised by important international and even domestic actors (Pfeifer; Boesten and Idler in this volume). But recognition can be an important part of bolstering legitimacy before other actors. The case of the FARC suggests that an important part of the peace process in Colombia that allowed for the demobilisation of the FARC and its (partial) transformation into a political actor was its recognition by the Colombian state and society as a legitimate actor in domestic politics (Felbab-Brown et al. 2017).

Yet, armed non-state actors can seek recognition for a variety of reasons, some of which include access to material support but for others to bolster their legitimacy. As Sienknecht documents in this volume for the case of the Kurdish PKK, armed non-state actors engage in what would appear to be a form of 'rebel' diplomacy to seek access to arms, supplies, training and other inputs to enable them to fight, first addressing the Soviet Union during the Cold War, and then the European Union. But the evolution of the PKK illustrates that ANSAs are aware of the interaction between the politics of recognition and legitimacy, first adopting a Marxist orientation during the Cold War to bolster the legitimacy of its claims to gain support from the Soviet bloc, then switching to a language of democracy and human rights during the 1990s as it sought support from the European Union at a time when the PKK's main adversary, the Turkish state, was engaged in accession talks and had to accommodate EU interests.

Recognition is an action performed for others to witness. Recognition does not just affect the actor and the target of action, but a range of external audiences, as each case studied in the volume demonstrates. The audiences for recognition include not only international organisations and states, but also governments, civil society and other armed non-state actors. Armed non-state actors differentiate among these audiences as they seek to justify recognition on different grounds, for example Hezbollah projecting one identity within domestic Lebanese politics and a somewhat different identity focused on the Israeli–Palestinian conflict in regional politics (Pfeifer in this volume). Recognition has both a horizontal dimension, by those with which the ANSA is in conflict, such as states, and a vertical dimension, by civil society and the general population, as both the cases of the FARC in Colombia and PIRA in Northern Ireland suggest (Boesten and Idler; Görzig in this volume). Armed non-state actors manage recognition and identity on multiple levels, and these identities are fluid and evolve in response to other actors and contextual pressures, as Görzig examines in the case of Northern Ireland.

Finally, it is important to stress that it is not only mis-recognition that can cause damage and grievances, but also acts of recognition. In the case of South Sudan, for example, efforts by regional negotiators to recognise the SPLM as the sole representative of resistance to the Sudanese state laid the seeds of a future civil war, as Pring (in this volume) suggests. Although this act of recognition sprung from the good intentions of mediators who sought to simplify and manage the original process that led to the 2005 Comprehensive Peace Agreement, ANSAs competing with the SPLM long resented this act of mis-recognition. Similarly, recognition of certain actors during the Cold War, for example by the United States, as 'freedom fighters', foreclosed the possibility of recognition by ideologically opposed actors, and vice versa, which may have contributed to prolonging conflicts in Central America and Southern Africa, to give but two examples. Although not applying to ANSAs, the non-aligned movement was, among other things, an attempt by developing states to recognise each other as following a different path during the Cold War, rejecting the politically motivated labels applied by the two superpowers.

Commonalities and differences in recognition processes and politics

Across the cases in this book, it is clear that states and international organisations use recognition strategically and politically, performing for their own audiences and not just the target of recognition. As Nwankpa demonstrates, the Nigerian state recognises and mis-recognises ANSAs such as Boko Haram to justify certain kinds of violence by state forces. But it also deliberately does not recognise other ANSAs who are also engaged in violence, such as the Fulani militia, to avoid the ethno-political implications of targeting groups who are ethnically aligned with important Nigerian elites.

There is not only a logic of consequences – material and ideational – but also a logic of appropriateness at work in these processes. By labelling, states can make certain policies seem appropriate to their audiences: their citizens, other states or international organisations. Applying the label of 'freedom fighter' to an ANSA justifies material assistance and renders it 'appropriate' by providing ideational cover for the state doing so, as the Reagan administration did with the Contra rebels in Nicaragua during the 1980s. On the other hand, certain labels foreclose some policy options. By labelling Uyghur dissent as rooted in economic dissatisfaction, for example, the Communist Party of China has made it 'inappropriate' to negotiate a political settlement (Chung in this volume). Similarly, after the 9/11 terrorist attacks in Washington DC and New York, applying the label 'terrorist' was convenient for states seeking to align themselves with the United States and make it 'appropriate' to receive material assistance. For example, during the 1990s the Colombian government was swift to label the FARC rebel group as a 'narco-guerrilla' organisation, clearly to appeal for US support as part of the global war on narcotics. Even so, it failed to gain US support to combat these rebels due to suspected ties between then Colombian president Samper and international drug trafficking. The US would only provide counter-narcotics assistance, not counterinsurgency aid, during this period. Yet, subsequent presidents in Colombia, Eduardo Pastrana and Alvaro Uribe, had more success by labelling the FARC 'narco-terrorists' after 9/11, securing billions in support via Plan Colombia. While some sectors of the FARC trafficked drugs and others used terrorist tactics, the audience for the Colombian government's labelling efforts was not the ANSA, but external audiences, particularly in the US Congress (Felbab-Brown et al. 2017).

One area where there are differences among the cases examined in this volume is in ANSAs' pursuit of recognition. While almost all ANSAs seek recognition appropriate to their identity and their cause, they do not seek recognition from all actors, and in fact some forms of recognition by outside actors can actually be damaging. As Kaden and Günther argue in the case of the so-called Islamic State, recognition by states was not something that IS leaders sought, in part because the concept of statehood was antithetical to their belief system. One of the fundamental problems IS leaders saw in the Islamic world was its division into states. They viewed states as diverting even the most faithful away from the tenets of their belief system, so they sought a universal Caliphate instead. In other cases, recognition by certain actors can actually harm an ANSA. The recognition of the PLO by Israel as part of the peace processes of the 1990s undermined the PLO's standing with some of its traditional supporters, who viewed this as a betrayal, a sign that the PLO had 'sold out'. This helped to bolster support for the more militant Hamas movement that now controls Gaza. We see a similar dynamic in Somalia, where the government legally recognised by other states and the international community is perceived as inauthentic by many Somali citizens, while al-Shabaab, a violent ANSA labelled a terrorist organisation by important external actors, is seen as an autochthonous and genuine expression of discontent, and hence a more legitimate organisation than the government by some within Somalia (Toros and Sugal in this volume).

Another area for differences is in the timing of recognition within a conflict. In line with the political nature of peace negotiations, appropriate recognition at the right time can be a key component of successfully concluding a settlement. Not only does the correct form of recognition provide the social-psychological reward identified by the organisers of this volume, but it also helps to cement the transition to a new identity focused on peace and reconciliation. As Görzig explains in the case of the PIRA, recognition as peacemakers by the British state and their opponents at the right point in time during the negotiation of the Good Friday accords was important to the leadership of this ANSA. This recognition was reinforced subsequently as others around the world seeking to negotiate peace settlements of their own sought out PIRA leaders for their expertise as peacemakers. It also helped cement this new identity with their followers at a critical time (Görzig in this volume). On the other hand, as the case of Southern Sudan suggests, forcing a certain kind of recognition on ANSAs during a peace settlement early on in the process, in this case grouping all such organisations in the South under the SPLM label, can prove to be disastrous to long-term prospects for peace (Pring in this volume).

Finally, Hensell and Schlichte make a strong case for the importance of world historical time for ANSA recognition processes. Simply put, it is easier to justify and support the activities of certain types of ANSA during certain historical periods than others. Although most of the cases discussed in this volume date from the post-Cold War period, there is enough evidence from previous historical periods to suggest that some ANSAs have been perceived as more legitimate than others depending on the international context at the time. Immediately post-Second World War, there was support for nationalist movements, particularly anti-colonial ones, as many new states entered the international system with the end of European empires (Hensell and Schlichte in this volume). The Cold War legitimised actions by Marxist ANSAs with audiences sympathetic to the Soviet cause, as the case of the Kurdish PKK suggests, whereas anti-communist organisations such as the National Union for the Total Independence of Angola received important support from the United States and apartheid South Africa during the Angolan civil war. Post-Cold War, we see a move towards espousing values supportive of democracy and human rights, while post-9/11 the use of violence by any ANSA risks the label of terrorism and drawing the ire of the great powers.

To the extent that there is a pattern across the cases in this volume, it is that recognition (and mis- or non-recognition) are part of a larger two-level game involving actors in conflict. ANSAs and the state interact with each other, yet each is also performing for its audiences (which will overlap but are not the same). The participants weigh the costs and benefits, material, ideational and psychological, of various forms of recognition. This process may in turn become part of how the state and ANSAs justify certain kinds of action, particularly violence in the case of non-recognition or mis-recognition, or mobilise particular audience members to commit more deeply to a cause. It is difficult to systematically predict when participants in a conflict between state and non-state actors will engage in recognition. It is a highly contingent process: recognition frequently emerges organically, although at times members of the audience may intervene strategically to facilitate the end of conflict. In addition, exogenous shocks, such as we see in several cases in this volume with the fall of the Soviet Union, can fundamentally alter the politics of recognition, essentially by changing the audience and their role in the conflict. Finally, because leaders are also human, they may misjudge, as occurred in Sudan, and add fuel to the fire rather than bring a conflict to a peaceful end.

Areas for further study

Given that recognition of ANSAs seems to offer many benefits for conflict settlement, and that a growing number of conflicts involve ANSAs, why have we not seen greater use of recognition as a tool for peacemaking? While the social-psychological rationale for recognition is clear from the work collected in this volume, there is a need for further research on the political and legal constraints on this process. In her chapter, Dudouet outlines some such important obstacles from a practitioner perspective. First, recognition risks legitimising criminal activity by violent groups, and practitioners worry what example this sets for non-violent groups with similar goals. Other ANSAs are constituted or motivated such that recognition may seem not to do much to advance the cause of peace, either because some groups (particularly religiously motivated ones) are seen as irrational by practitioners, not interested in state recognition, or so decentralised that their leadership is unable to 'deliver' their membership in return for recognition. Finally, once a negative label has been applied to a group, it becomes 'sticky', tying the hands of subsequent practitioners in dealing with ANSAs. As Dudouet points out, in such cases policies of engagement, which have more tactical objectives such as improving humanitarian conditions or exchanges of prisoners, may have greater value than full recognition.

There are further obstacles to more widespread use of recognition in conflict resolution. With rare exceptions, such as the creation of East Timor and South Sudan, international law places some challenging limits around the recognition of separatist ANSAs. For example, in South America and in Africa the international legal concept of *uti possidetis juris*, widely accepted by states in each region, fixes national boundaries on the basis of pre-independence colonial boundaries (Kacowicz 1998). This allows little room for meaningful recognition of separatist groups. Even for ANSAs that seek to operate within given national boundaries, so-called 'centre-seeking groups', the politics of recognition are such that states find it difficult to navigate the demands of the many audiences they face. These include not only civil society and national elites, but also the demands of other states and international organisations. In some cases, the decision about recognition is not available to states, since decisions of the United Nations Security Council, for example, may supersede national authority, as is the case with UNSC resolution 1267 declaring al-Qaeda a terrorist organisation and mandating a global sanctions regime against it (Trinkunas 2019). We need an improved understanding of the political and legal limits of recognition as a solution to conflicts.

Although Hensell and Schlichte (in this volume) offer an intriguing overview of the impact of world historical time on the ability to recognise ANSAs, almost all the cases in this volume date to the post-Cold War period. It would be useful to extend this analysis in time to deliberately focus on the post-Second World War and Cold War period to better understand the dynamics that made the recognition of certain kinds of ANSA more feasible in particular historical moments. In particular, we need to study the mechanisms that connect the politics and process of recognition with global trends.

In addition, we should acknowledge that the dynamics and ANSAs under study in this book have, with a few exceptions such as Hezbollah and the PKK whose origins date to the Cold War, emerged and evolved at the height of a global rules-based liberal international order that formed after the Second World War. This is a system that banned aggressive war and made 'state death' nearly impossible, which may have contributed to ANSAs operating within civil wars becoming one of the dominant forms of contentious politics. The near inviolability of recognised state boundaries following the founding of the United Nations in 1945 (Fazal 2011), coupled with state weakness in parts of the globe, have brought ANSAs into more prominent roles as providers of governance, even if they were not recognised as such by the state, or other states in the system (Clunan and Trinkunas 2010). This may help to explain why the politics of recognition seems to become particularly salient after 1945 rather than before.

Not only does the liberal international order place some limits on state behaviour (the liberal or rules-based dimension of the order), but it is also underpinned by the material and normative resources of the United States and its preferences with regards to ANSAs. As this book highlights, US preferences for decolonisation post-Second World War are part of what contributed to an era in which the recognition of national liberation movements was more possible, even if they resorted to violence. The ideological dimension of recognition during the Cold War is at least partially attributable to the United States. While ANSAs also pursued Soviet support, clearly the number of audiences that mattered in the Soviet sphere were more limited (due to the authoritarian nature of the system and the limited impact of public preferences) than they were in the West.

We should also look to the future, now that it is becoming clear that the liberal international order is fraying and great power competition has returned. We may be facing a new world historical period in which the politics of ANSA recognition once again becomes competitive, as was the case during the Cold War. The post-9/11 consensus among great powers on opposing terrorism, hence labelling many ANSAs as irredeemable due to their use of violence, may break down as the United States, Russia and China each back some ANSAs and oppose others. Already in Syria's civil war, we see this playing out, with the United States having backed some ANSAs, such as the Kurdish Peshmerga and the Syrian Democratic Forces, to fight the Islamic

State while targeting others, thought to be al-Qaeda affiliates, on the very same battlefield. In fact, US military doctrine is increasingly explicit about relying on ANSAs to conduct battlefield operations, with a light footprint of US forces in support, under an approach labelled 'by, through and with'. The object of reference is either ANSAs or local state forces, depending on whom the United States is supporting (Kaplan 2019). Similarly, Russian approaches to hybrid or grey zone warfare also increasingly rely on ANSAs, such as the pro-Russian militias fighting in Eastern Ukraine, or mercenaries such as the Wagner Group in Syria. Managing relations with ANSAs in these cases entails complex politics of recognition (Rondeaux 2019). The initial US search for non-Islamist, non-Kurdish ANSAs in Syria to support its efforts to combat the Islamic State was a near failure due to the stringent recognition requirements that policy-makers adopted (Felbab-Brown et al. 2017). As great power rivalry accelerates in the future, we should expect to see more relations between great powers and ANSAs, and therefore more complex and competitive politics of recognition.

Another new phenomenon at which we need to look in greater depth is the impact of information operations on ANSA recognition or mis-recognition. Although the world has focused mostly on the impact of disinformation campaigns on elections around the world, and more recently on the COVID-19 pandemic, recognition is clearly a process that can be vulnerable to deliberate disinformation campaigns. It may be increasingly beyond the capacity of either states or international organisations to move deliberately to recognise or mis-recognise armed non-state actors. The fusion of social media and traditional media into a global information ecosystem on the internet has meant that propaganda campaigns can now be conducted at scale, at high speed, at unprecedented range and at lower cost than ever before. Digital tools have democratised information production, and even relatively unskilled persons can produce official-looking documents or social media that purport to recognise or mis-recognise ANSAs on behalf of states and international actors. One example of this, although not applied to an armed non-state actor, is the demonisation of the Syrian 'White Helmets', a civil defence organisation, by Russian and Assad regime-backed disinformation operations. There is also some evidence of similar dynamics involving the Kurdish question during the Syrian civil war, particularly as pro- and anti-Kurdish information operations attempt to influence online narratives about the Kurdish role in the conflict (Starbird 2020; Starbird et al. 2018).

Moreover, it is increasingly apparent that we have entered a 'post-truth' moment where information is processed by most individuals not always rationally, but rather based on whether it is emotionally easy to process or appeals to faith (McDermott 2020). Social media make it possible for disinformation campaigns to take advantage of heuristic biases, such as those that lead persons to believe information they see frequently, or to find information carried on multiple channels more credible, to promote misinformation and disinformation. And all of this does not have to be done by malicious actors, because attractively packaged and persuasive falsehoods will be taken up by like-minded individuals on social media who will cause these messages to go viral within their informational echo chambers (McDermott 2020; Trinkunas et al. 2020). This is likely to create new challenges to the possibility of increasing the use of ANSA recognition as a tool for peacemaking.

Policy recommendations

One of the major conclusions that can be drawn from the work in this edited volume is that policy-makers need to think strategically about recognition as a positive element in the policy tool kit, not something to be given grudgingly. As Dudouet suggests in this volume, axiomatic approaches, such as 'no negotiations with terrorists', are not very useful, and policy-makers should consider carefully how groups are labelled. Labels frame groups with identities that may limit the policies a state can pursue to achieve peace. A label such as 'violent extremist' may make it impossible for states to pursue peacemaking. But, on the other hand, labels can be deployed to make negotiations and eventual recognition possible at the right moment in time, as occurred in Northern Ireland.

It is also important for policy-makers to recognise the politics of identity formation and the way in which labels are deployed by others to limit their scope of action. Other actors opposed to given ANSAs will clearly seek to apply labels that can in turn be used to appeal for action (or inaction) by policy-makers, particularly in states that are important sources of aid or military assistance, as we saw earlier in this chapter in the case of Colombia, the FARC rebels and the US Congress, or by China's fierce criticism of states and organisations concerned about the treatment of Uyghurs. More widely, the declaration by the Bush administration of a 'global war on terror' after the 9/11 attacks created incentives for regimes around the world to label troublesome ANSAs on their territories as terrorists, both to seek assistance from the United States, and to make it more difficult for these ANSAs to work with other states or international organisations and to seek recognition domestically. But as Dudouet points out, peacemakers also have opportunities to 'relabel' ANSAs in ways that are constructive for peace.

Policy-makers also need to consider carefully the timing of recognition and its impact on a given conflict. Is it opening doors to peace or prolonging conflict? As we saw in South Sudan, the wrong kind of recognition, even if well intentioned in the pursuit of peace, can sow the seeds for another civil conflict. Or else the timing of counter-ANSA measures, such as military operations or judicial sanctions, perhaps carried out because of lack of coordination within states, may interfere with peacemaking opportunities, making recognition less valuable to ANSAs or decreasing trust in peacemakers.

Finally, the cases presented in this volume make it clear that policy-makers need to be concerned with second- and third-order effects of recognition. When, how and how much recognition should be granted, whom it impacts and what negative effects it might cause should be questions that policy-makers ask themselves during peace processes. Recognition is a process performed for audiences, and those audiences are frequently global and have ready access to information and disinformation about ANSAs. How these audiences might react and interact is likely beyond the analytical capacity of most policy-makers or state bureaucracies, which will in turn place a premium on the ability of states to adapt and react quickly to the effects of recognition on peace processes.

Note

* The research reported here was funded in part by the Minerva Research Initiative (OUSD(R&E)) and the Army Research Office/Army Research Laboratory via grant #W911-NF-17-1-0569 to George Mason University. Any errors and opinions are not those of the US Department of Defense and are attributable solely to the author.

References

BBC News (2020), 'US and Taliban sign deal to end 18-year Afghan war', available online: www.bbc.com/news/world-asia-51689443 (29 February); last retrieved 14 May 2020.

Clunan, A. L. and H. A. Trinkunas (eds) (2010), *Ungoverned Spaces: Alternatives to State Authority in an Era of Softened Sovereignty* (Stanford, CA: Stanford University Press).

Fazal, T. M. (2011), *State Death: The Politics and Geography of Conquest, Occupation, and Annexation* (Princeton, NJ: Princeton University Press).

Felbab-Brown, V., H. A. Trinkunas and S. Hamid (2017), *Militants, Criminals, and Warlords: The Challenge of Local Governance in an Age of Disorder* (Washington, DC: Brookings Institution Press).

Kacowicz, A. M. (1998), *Zones of Peace in the Third World: South America and West Africa in Comparative Perspective* (Albany, NY: SUNY Press).

Kaplan, M. (2019), 'Thinking critically about "by, with, through" in Syria, Iraq, and beyond', *Lawfare*, available online: www.lawfareblog.com/thinking-critically-about-through-syria-iraq-and-beyond (20 January); last retrieved 14 May 2020.

McDermott, R. (2020), 'Psychological underpinnings of post-truth in political beliefs', in H. A. Trinkunas, H. S. Lin and B. Loehrke (eds), *Three Tweets to Midnight: Effects of the Global Information Ecosystem on the Risk of Nuclear Conflict* (Stanford, CA: Hoover Institution Press), pp. 17–38.

Rondeaux, C. (2019), *Decoding the Wagner Group: Analyzing the Role of Private Military Security Contractors in Russian Proxy Warfare* (Washington, DC: New America Foundation).

Starbird, K. (2020), 'Information operations and online activism within "NATO" discourse', in H. A. Trinkunas, H. S. Lin and B. Loehrke (eds), *Three Tweets to Midnight: Effects of the Global Information Ecosystem on the Risk of Nuclear Conflict* (Stanford, CA: Hoover Institution Press), pp. 79–111.

Starbird, K., A. Arif, T. Wilson, K. Van Koevering, K. Yefimova and D. Scarnecchia (2018), 'Ecosystem or echo-system? Exploring content sharing across alternative media domains', in *Twelfth International AAAI Conference on Web and Social Media*, Palo Alto, California, USA, 25–28 June.

Trinkunas, H. (2019), 'Financing terrorism', in E. Chenoweth, R. English, A. Gofas and S. N. Kalyvas (eds), *The Oxford Handbook of Terrorism* (Oxford: Oxford University Press), pp. 477–493. https://doi.org/10.1093/oxfordhb/9780198732914.013.29.

Trinkunas, H. A., H. S. Lin and B. Loehrke (eds) (2020), *Three Tweets to Midnight: Effects of the Global Information Ecosystem on the Risk of Nuclear Conflict* (Stanford, CA: Hoover Institution Press).

Index

Note: 'n.' after a page reference indicates the number of a note on that page

EU authorised representative for GPSR:
Easy Access System Europe, Mustamäe tee 50,
10621 Tallinn, Estonia
gpsr.requests@easproject.com

www.ingramcontent.com/pod-product-compliance
Ingram Content Group UK Ltd.
Pitfield, Milton Keynes, MK11 3LW, UK
UKHW021840100926
8556IPUK00004B/460
* 9 7 8 1 5 2 6 1 5 2 7 5 6 *